For Je[illegible]

with much admiration
and gratitude.

[illegible]

Cities, Agglomeration and Spatial Equilibrium

The Lindahl Lectures

The Lindahl Lectures are sponsored by Uppsala University and given every two years in honour of Erik Lindahl, a distinguished Swedish economist (1891–1960), Professor of Economics at Uppsala University (1942–58). In 1986 Uppsala University established the lectures in honour of Lindahl's contributions to monetary theory and public finance. Previous lecturers include:

1987 Professor Dale W. Jorgenson: *Tax Policy and US Economic Growth*

1989 Professor Anthony B. Atkinson: *The Design of Taxation and Social Security*

1991 Professor Joseph E. Stiglitz: *The New Welfare Economics: Public Policy in the Presence of Asymmetric Information*

1993 Professor Mervyn King: *Financial Markets and Economic Policy*

1996 Professor Agnar Sandmo: *The Public Economics of the Environment*

1999 Professor Peter A. Diamond: *Social Security Reform*

2002 Professor Timothy Besley: *Principled Agents? Motivation and Incentives in Government*

2004 Professor Edward L. Glaeser: *The Economics of Cities*

2006 Professor Richard Blundell: *Evaluating Welfare Reforms*

Cities, Agglomeration and Spatial Equilibrium

by

Edward L. Glaeser

OXFORD
UNIVERSITY PRESS

OXFORD
UNIVERSITY PRESS

Great Clarendon Street, Oxford OX2 6DP

Oxford University Press is a department of the University of Oxford.
It furthers the University's objective of excellence in research, scholarship, and education by publishing worldwide in

Oxford New York

Auckland Cape Town Dar es Salaam Hong Kong Karachi
Kuala Lumpur Madrid Melbourne Mexico City Nairobi
New Delhi Shanghai Taipei Toronto

With offices in

Argentina Austria Brazil Chile Czech Republic France Greece
Guatemala Hungary Italy Japan Poland Portugal Singapore
South Korea Switzerland Thailand Turkey Ukraine Vietnam

Oxford is a registered trade mark of Oxford University Press in the UK and in certain other countries

Published in the United States
by Oxford University Press Inc., New York

First published 2008

British Library Cataloguing in Publication Data

Data available

Library of Congress Cataloging in Publication Data

Data available

Typeset by SPI Publisher Services, Pondicherry, India
Printed in Great Britain
on acid-free paper by
CPI Antony Rowe, Chippenham, Wiltshire

ISBN 978–0–19–929044–4

1 3 5 7 9 10 8 6 4 2

Contents

1

Introduction

220 million Americans crowd together in the four percent of our country that is urban. 35 million people live in the vast metropolitan area of Tokyo, the most productive urban area in the world. Greater Mumbai has 16 million people, and Shanghai has 13 million. We choose to live cheek by jowl, in a planet with vast amounts of space. If the entire world lived in four person households in Texas, each household could have more than a tenth of an acre.[1] Yet despite all that land, we choose the proximity of cities.

The job of the urban economist is to make sense of all this concentration. The foremost question of urban economics is why cities exist. Almost everything else that urban economists do can be seen as part of answering this question. After all, we can't understand the demand for cities unless we understand how cities change people's lives. We can't understand the costs of cities without understanding housing markets. By studying ghettos and segregation, we understand why African-Americans chose urban life in the middle decades of the twentieth century, despite the fact that they were overwhelmingly choosing to live in ghettos.

The intellectual quest to understand cities is an exciting undertaking. Since so much of our species inhabits cities, there is a vast array of topics which can be linked to urban living. Urban economists can study the connection between cities and international trade or industrial organization or creativity in the arts. Cities are, after all, often ports, so there is a natural connection with trade. The degree of monopoly or oligopoly is often determined at the local level, which means that industrial organization is often linked to the size and nature of a metropolitan area. Artistic movements are often highly localized; they usually thrive because of the speedy exchange of new ideas along city streets.

[1] Texas has 261,797 square miles or 167,550,080 acres. The world has 6.6 billion people or 1.65 billion households of four which means more than one-tenth of acre for each household. Data for this calculation and the first paragraph are from the U.S. Census Bureau and the United Nations.

Understanding cities also requires the urban economist to draw on a wide variety of information sources. Economists tend to have a comparative advantage in working with data that has been collected by someone else. There is an abundance of well-collected data on cities in most developed countries that can be used by researchers.

But understanding cities requires more than current statistics. Many urban areas are extraordinarily ancient and their structures reflect events far in the past. We also need to know history if we are to understand our cities. I am also a big believer in the value of ethnography, which can give us a richer picture of urban life. Economists rarely perform their own ethnographies, and while I believe that specialization is a good thing, there is every reason to make use of the excellent work of our fellow social scientists who work in anthropology or sociology. Our approach to cities may differ from theirs, but there are still plenty of gains from trade.

The economic approach to cities starts with the assumption that locations are chosen and that those choices are not entirely irrational. Adults are not randomly sprinkled across space. They select one place over another, and in particular they choose cities. This statement does not mean to deny that many people just choose to stay put to keep their ties to friends and family. Still, even that is a choice and even in Europe, where mobility is much less than in the US, there are millions of people each year that move from place to place, choosing new locations.

To understand location choices requires us to understand the advantages and disadvantages of different locations. A big city may offer high wages and a fun nightlife, but may suffer from high prices and congestion. A town in Provence may offer good food and charming neighbors, but less access to good jobs. To understand why current concentrations of population exist, and to understand why cities rise and fall, it is necessary to dig deeper and try to understand what forces drive the choices that people make.

I believe that one of the defining characteristics of modern economics is that economic models begin with decision-making agents. In the context of urban economics, this means that our models must feature individuals who are making decisions across space. The usual assumption is that those individuals care about wages and prices and a bundle of other location-specific amenities, which can include the weather, commuting distance or local tax rates. In some of our models, everyone is assumed to be identical. Other models make an attempt to capture the great heterogeneity that exists within a population.

Since wages and prices are usually major ingredients in the decision-making process, the economic approach to cities generally requires other decision-making agents besides the individuals who choose locations.

Wages are formed through the interaction of labor demand and labor supply. Labor supply, at the local level, is formed by individual choices about location and work. Labor demand reflects the decisions of firms. As a result, a fully specified urban model, where wages are part of the people's decisions, must also include firms.

As in many areas of economics, urban economics tends to treat firms as unified decision-making agents rather than as collections of people who often have disparate objectives. Also as in many other fields, the norm is to assume that firms maximize profits. These assumptions are surely approximations, but more realistic approaches can become computationally difficult very quickly. The optimization decisions of firms then give us a labor demand function that generally depends on the productivity advantages of certain urban areas. In the economic geography models that followed Krugman (1991a,b), firms also produce goods for the local market. Their decisions, therefore, also impact the prices that people pay in given cities.

Since housing prices are so important to location choices, construction firms occupy a particularly special place within the field. The number of people that live in an area is almost perfectly correlated with the amount of housing in that area. It is difficult to make sense of much of the past 30 years of urban change without knowing something about housing supply. Understanding cities means understanding the housing market, and understanding the housing market requires us to consider the role of developers. I will assume that these developers are also profit maximizing agents. Unlike Henderson (1985), I will not be assuming that developers are entrepreneurial community-builders (although surely many are), but I will be assuming that they build to the point where the price of selling a home equals the marginal cost of building a home (including land costs, regulatory costs and so forth). While many of the developers that I have met care as much about the thrill of building a great structure as the bottom line, it still makes sense to stick with the most straightforward assumption about builder motivation.

As such, the three types of actors that are needed in any comprehensive urban model are employers, builders and ordinary people choosing between different locations. Their three optimization decisions essentially lead to three equations that are then solved for three unknowns: the price of housing, the wage and the number of people who live and work in a given locale. There are certainly other types of actors who could be included in an urban model, like political leaders, but while government is certainly an important part of how cities operate, including political actors seems less critical than including individuals, employers and builders.

If you wanted to eliminate one set of actors, it would be possible to say something about two of those variables but not all three. For example, the intra-urban Alonso–Muth–Mills model takes wages as given and then crafts a model built of only private individuals and builders. The interaction between these two types of agents can tell us about housing prices and density within a city, but not wages. The inter-urban Rosen–Roback model includes firms and individuals but not builders. This model can tell us about wages and prices, but it has trouble explaining the density of development in different locales.

Individual choice over locations produces the single most important concept in urban or regional economics: the spatial equilibrium. This core insight comes from the idea that if identical people are choosing to live in two different places then those two different places must be offering an equivalent bundle of advantages, like wages, prices and amenities. Essentially, there must be no potential for arbitrage across space. The connection between the spatial equilibrium concept and urban economics is analogous to the connection between the no-arbitrage equilibrium and financial economics. It is the bedrock on which everything else in the field stands.

That being said, it is worthwhile asking whether this assumption accurately depicts reality. There are many reasons why the spatial equilibrium concept might not hold perfectly. There might be imperfect information about the amenities, wages or housing costs in a particular area. People might have such heterogeneous preferences that there is literally no one on the margin between any two places. Moving costs might be so high that its spatial arbitrage becomes quite difficult. No one thinks that this assumption is a literal depiction of reality.

Still, models based on the concept of a spatial equilibrium do a generally good job of actually explaining the real world. Housing price patterns within a metropolitan area do show that higher amenities are offset by higher prices. Across metropolitan areas, higher wages are offset by higher prices. Great weather also comes with higher housing costs. If anything, there have been far fewer examples of breakdowns in the spatial arbitrage assumption in urban economics than in the no-arbitrage assumption in finance.

Why is it that the spatial arbitrage assumption seems to do so well with the data? The best explanation for this fact is that urban data is much more forgiving than data in finance. In finance, any time there are predictable real returns, this presents a challenge for the standard model. In urban economics, so many amenities are unobservable that it would be hard to imagine that you could convincingly claim that prices were so high or low in one place that we could reject the spatial arbitrage assumption. Another way to think about this is that while the spatial arbitrage assumption is only an approximation, our data is sufficiently rough that this approximation generally does a reasonable job of fitting reality.

The spatial equilibrium assumption provides some counter-intuitive implications. For example, while high real wages are often thought to be a good thing in cross-country work, high real wages in a city suggest that there is something else that is wrong about the place. The spatial equilibrium assumption implies that high real wages are being offset by something else that is bad about a place, like Anchorage's cold weather or other disamenities. If high real wages weren't offset by something bad then the market would adjust. This adjustment could take the form of migration, but even more easily, housing prices could just rise, which would cause real wages to fall back in line.

This type of logic also explains why urban economists have often been more interested in using population levels than income levels as a measure of urban success. Since high wages might just reflect the compensating differential that a firm needs to pay to locate in an unattractive environment, wages are a dangerous measure of urban success. High levels of population, however, tell us that people are voting with their feet to move to a particular place. As I will discuss in Chapter 3, I believe that good empirical work on cities generally looks at population, income and housing prices together in a framework that is derived from the spatial equilibrium assumption.

If urban economics has a second concept that comes close in importance to the spatial equilibrium assumption, it is agglomeration economies. Technically agglomeration economies exist whenever people become more productive through proximity to others. They can represent the gains that come from reducing transport costs for goods, as in Krugman (1991a,b), or the advantages associated with the free flow of ideas in dense, urban environments. Agglomeration economies are the catchall explanation for why cities can be so productive and why so many people flock to urban areas.

If the spatial equilibrium concept comes from the individual's location choice, agglomeration economies are inferred from the labor demand decisions of firms. High wages are a pervasive feature of cities (Glaeser and Maré, 2001). The spatial equilibrium concept maintains that these high wages must be offset by something else and indeed they are offset by high urban housing prices. In recent years, there is a strong connection between city size and nominal wages but no connection between real wages in a city and city population. The spatial equilibrium does not, however, explain the other puzzle that is created by high urban wages: why are firms willing to locate in places where workers are so expensive.

Firms' optimization decisions suggest that they are willing to pay more for workers only if workers are more productive. Higher wages mean that some force must be pushing up the marginal product of labor. This force could, in principle, reflect a greater abundance of capital, if labor and capital are complements, or it could reflect higher prices for finished goods or better technology. If firms get to choose their own capital and the price of capital is relatively constant over space, then higher prices or better technology seem to be the likely explanations for higher wages. High prices and especially productivity in urban areas can be called agglomeration economies.

Another way to understand agglomeration economies is to go back to a fundamental definition of cities: the absence of physical space between people and firms. Cities are density, proximity, closeness. The advantage of all that closeness is the absence of transportation costs. After all, in principle, firms in Dubuque can readily interact with firms in New York City, but they have to pay much higher costs. This fact has led urban economists to focus on the transportation cost advantages of locating in an urban area.

Cities eliminate transport costs for goods, people and ideas. The urban models in the new economic geography tradition tend to emphasize the costs savings associated with low shipping costs for goods (Fujita, Krugman and Venables, 2001). This is surely appropriate when looking at the nineteenth century when the costs of moving goods really were quite expensive. It is impossible to make sense of Chicago in 1900 without understanding the advantages in moving goods that came from clustering around the city's port and rail yards.

There are two ways in which transportation costs for goods created advantages to firms that located in a large city. Their first advantage can be termed the home market effect, meaning that when firms are close to one another and close to their eventual consumers, they save transport costs. This is the mechanism that lies at the heart of Krugman (1991a,b). That early paper emphasized proximity to customers, but it is only a slight variant to assume that the core urban edge comes from firms that have to pay less for intermediate goods. This mechanism drove firms to come to large cities in the 1900s and it still matters today. The abundant supply of business services is one factor that continues to make New York City and Chicago attractive places to locate a company headquarters.

In 1900, New York City and Chicago had a second transport cost related advantage that had nothing to do with the home market effect. They were both major transportation hubs. At the start of the nineteenth century, when ships grew larger, transatlantic shipping moved to a hub-and-spoke model, where large ships crossed the Atlantic and then transferred their cargo to smaller ships for coastal cruising. New York had the best combination of harbor, central location and river-based access to the hinterland, and unsurprisingly it became the great hub of the Atlantic trade. When the Illinois and Michigan Canal connected the Mississippi river system to the Great Lakes through the Chicago River, Chicago became the linchpin of a watery arc that went from New Orleans to New York. Initial water-based transport advantages were then augmented by the development of rail.

In the nineteenth century, when moving goods over land was expensive, access to the transport advantages in Chicago and New York made firms much more productive. The cities really grew up around transport nodes and many of the early industries in both places arose because of goods that were being shipped through. For example, sugar refining was one of New York's most important nineteenth century industries. Sugar refining located in New York because raw sugar was naturally being shipped through America's busiest port on its way from the Caribbean to American plates. Sugar refining in the tropics was impractical because sugar crystals coalesce on a hot sea voyage. Sugar refining in every town meant reproducing expensive refineries. Locating sugar refining in New York City saved on transport costs and made it possible to exploit economics of scale.

The impact that ports had on productivity made firms more profitable and wages higher in urban areas, but it is not technically an agglomeration economy. Ports are instead a natural advantage that makes one spot more productive than another, regardless of whether more people show up. Natural advantages that differ across space create a great challenge for measuring agglomeration economies since the existence of these advantages both raises wages and attracts people. If natural advantage isn't fully controlled for, then there will appear to be a correlation between the number of people and productivity that reflects heterogeneous natural advantage but that might be incorrectly interpreted as agglomeration economies. Distinguishing between agglomeration economies and natural advantage is one of the great challenges of empirical work on urban productivity (Ellison and Glaeser, 1997).

Agglomeration economies today are much less likely to do with the costs of moving goods. Over the twentieth century the real cost of moving a ton a mile by rail declined by more than 90 percent (Glaeser and Kohlhase, 2004) and that is just one transport technology. Trucks, cars, and airplanes all made it easy to ship goods over space. As a result, cities that once had an advantage based on moving goods over space lost that advantage and often lost their economic *raison d'être*. The Great Lakes region was once the heart of the American industrial economy, partially because of the advantages of easy access to raw materials, like iron and coal, and customers. Today, making cars in Tennessee or Korea does not create prohibitive transport costs, and thus manufacturers have moved.

While the agglomeration costs that were based on reducing transport costs for goods have disappeared, the agglomeration costs that are based on reducing transport costs for people and ideas remain. These agglomeration economies are the bedrock on which the successful twenty-first century cities from San Francisco to Tokyo rely. Transportation technology has made it easier to move people, but the main cost of moving people is their time and that has just gotten more and more valuable. As a result, cities are increasingly oriented around services, particularly business services, where interpersonal proximity still matters. The dense urban markets for these services then create gains from specialization and the division of labor.

The most successful cities of today seem to be particularly concentrated in idea-producing industries, like finance, new technology and the media. The idea that urban proximity helps the spread of knowledge and innovation is not new. Alfred Marshall famously wrote more than a century ago that in dense clusters "the mysteries of the trade become no mystery, but are, as it were, in the air" (Marshall, 1890). Jane Jacobs (1969) wrote extensively about cities as centers of innovation. Her view was that new ideas are formed by combining old ideas and in dense agglomerations, old ideas abound. It is hard to look at the agglomeration of Wall Street or Silicon Valley or Bangalore and not think that these cities specialize in speeding the flow of knowledge and that access to the knowledge in the cluster is today's most important agglomeration economy.

Beyond the spatial equilibrium concept and agglomeration economies, there are two other major elements in modern urban economics. First, cities are made of bricks and mortar and they are built around transportation technology. As a result, there are real gains from understanding the nature of the basic urban technologies and good urban economics draws on engineering. I think of John Meyer as the pioneer in transportation economics, who saw the need to combine economic insight with a detailed knowledge of what different transport modes cost and how they are operated. Meyer's observation is right not only for transportation policy, but also for understanding cities.

For example, the traditional monocentric city is really a function of the pre-twentieth century transportation technologies. In a world where moving goods by water and then by rail was pretty cheap, but moving goods on roads was extremely expensive, it made good sense to cluster activity around the great transport nodes. New York's downtown was built around its port; the city's midtown cluster was built around its rail terminal. As cars and trucks replaced rail and water, cities naturally dispersed since these newer technologies did not need big fixed station facilities. I will also argue that knowing the costs and speed of driving and taking public transportation is critical for understanding why poor people tend to live closer to city centers (and take public transit) while richer people tend to live further out (and drive).

Transportation technology isn't the only thing that impacts urban shape: building technologies are also important. New York's two business centers, midtown and downtown, also owe something to the fact that these are the two areas that have solid bedrock underneath them. Urban densities are determined by building heights, which are themselves a function of construction techniques, elevators and regulation. The differences between European cities built pre-elevator and American cities built post-elevator can be quite striking. There is actually a pretty fair amount of information about construction costs and technologies, and it pays to use that information when trying to understand cities.

The final major element of urban economics is government policy. For as long as there have been cities, governments have played a major role in shaping their form. Many of the oldest cities were essentially political capitals that formed around a powerful leader. Jerusalem, Rome, Paris, Beijing and Tokyo are all essentially imperial cities that grew great because powerful leaders built and often used the wealth of the hinterland to build up the urban area (Ades and Glaeser, 1995). In the late twentieth century, developing countries were particularly prone to policies, like pro-industrialization tariffs, that essentially taxed rural areas and subsidized urban growth.

On a more mundane level, government regulation throughout the developing world influences urban growth. Some of the most important urban amenities, like schools and crime, are strongly influenced by government activity. No city can survive long without clean water, which Ed Mills has described as the most important task of urban government. Roads are also publicly provided and they certainly shape the development of metropolitan areas (Baum-Snow, 2007).

Land use policy is a particularly significant way in which government regulation can impact growth. It may have been possible for social scientists to ignore the role of zoning and other policies when looking at American cities prior to 1970. Many cities were relatively unregulated and the regulations that did bind were probably not critical. However, over the last 30 years there has been an increasing tendency in many areas to place tight barriers that shut down new construction and stymie population growth. This is not obviously good or bad, but it certainly does matter for understanding urban development. Indeed, I think it is impossible to understand why Houston is growing so much more quickly than coastal California without understanding Houston's strong pro-development regulatory environment and California's post-1970 barriers to building. In a sense, the rise of American land use regulation is only bringing us in line with European norms (which doesn't make it right). European cities, like Paris, have long thought it appropriate to tightly control new construction and this helps us to understand why they look the way that they do.

Of course, it is important to bring policy into urban economics not only to understand cities, but to make the discipline useful. Urban economists have long had a strong view that a regular application of economics can improve local policy-making. I certainly share that bias. While I think that the first job of the economist is to understand the world, the aim of improving government policy comes only slightly behind.

What is this book?

This book is a development of lectures that I gave in 2004 at the University of Uppsala. Those lectures were essentially an overview of my research on cities. I decided to use the opportunity given to me with this volume to put together an overview of the economic theory that guides my thinking about cities. There are empirical discussions in this book, but it is essentially a collection of simple models which, I hope, illustrate the primary features of urban economics, especially the concepts of a spatial equilibrium and agglomeration economies.

The target readers for this book are graduate students in economics who are interested in cities. Some economists with PhDs or advanced undergraduates who have an interest in urban economics might also find it useful. More mathematically inclined sociologists and political scientists might also find sections of the book helpful, but they may also be annoyed by the volume's highly economics-centered nature. Lay readers should not be confused by the previous nine pages. This book is full of algebra and I have made little attempt to make it a fun read. I fully expect the readership of this volume to be, as Spinal Tap's manager once said, selective.

While my aim was to write something that would be useful for graduate students, this is no textbook. It is not a comprehensive survey of major work in urban economics. It is my own highly idiosyncratic take on the field. Moreover, it is oriented towards relatively simple models that should both be quite accessible to non-theorists and usable as the basis for empirical work. I view this as a supplemental volume for a course, not as a centerpiece.

Moreover, I tend to think that advanced PhD students don't really need textbooks and that they should be aggressively reading the literature on their own. Simple models rarely appear anymore in top journals, but they are still an essential part of any economist's tool kit. Those simple models give us the intuition about what our fields predict and they are usually the best starting place to run regressions. This book is a set of simple models that draw on older papers and that I have found useful.

While the specific form of most of the models in the text is generally my own formulation, many of them are based tightly on the work of others. For example, Chapter 2 goes through the permutations of the intra-urban spatial equilibrium model. This model is associated with William Alonso, Richard Muth and Edwin Mills. Jan Brueckner (1987) gave a particularly lucid presentation of the model in the *Handbook of Regional and Urban Economics*. I cannot imagine writing a book on urban economic theory that doesn't begin with this most central of models, but the ideas in that chapter are completely the work of others.

A quick overview of the influences on this book

Since this book is a distillation of what I have culled from the urban literature, it makes sense to give a thumbnail sketch of the post-war development of the field. Urban economics certainly has antecedents that go back more than a century. I have already quoted Alfred Marshall, who is particularly insightful on the sources of agglomeration economies. Adam Smith wrote a bit about cities. I tend to think that Smith's most important urban insight was actually not in the sections of the *Wealth of Nations* that explicitly address cities, but rather his observation that "the division of labor is limited by the extent of the market." I will discuss this at length in Chapter 4. Von Thunen's *Isolated State* is, of course, the teutonic grandfather of all urban theory.

But despite these early antecedents, urban economics as a field only took off in the post-war era. The field had a remarkable set of founding fathers and it was nurtured by very aggressive funding in the 1960s and early 1970s, when urban problems seemed important to everyone. If there is a seminal work in the modern field, it is William Alonso's *Location and Land Use*. This book really established the spatial equilibrium model and its power to understand intra-urban patterns of prices and land use. Alonso was not the only person working on this model at the time, but he certainly gets credit for having the first, elegant expression of the core ideas.

I tend to think that there are at least four other major figures in those early days who wrote papers or books that have since received hundreds of citations. Richard Muth published his masterwork *Cities and Housing* in 1969. Muth is more grounded in housing and construction than Alonso or Mills. His work is full of insights on housing supply that have been ignored for too long.

The third member of the AMM triumvirate is Edwin Mills, who is certainly among the field's most distinguished economists. He published his classic *American Economic Review* article on the location of economic activity within a city in 1967. Mills follows Alonso in using the spatial equilibrium model, but unlike Alonso, he has a much more complete model that includes production as well as living space. The ideas in this book were then extended in his masterful 1972 monograph *Studies in the Structure of the Urban Economy*. Mills has, of course, written a large number of other excellent papers, and has also contributed significantly to the field by training a number of superb students.

I may be showing a certain Harvard bias, but I also consider John Meyer and John Kain to be two other seminal figures in urban economics. Meyer wrote what may be the first serious piece of cliometrics (Conrad and Meyer, 1958), but his claim to urban fame comes from his book *The Urban Transportation Problem*, co-authored with Kain and Martin Wohl. The book is really the starting point for transportation economics, and understanding transportation is integral to understanding urban areas. Meyer deserves a fair amount of credit for pushing the need for economists to learn from engineers.

Kain is the seminal figure in the economic study of urban problems, especially those relating to race. His 1968 "Spatial Mismatch Hypothesis" paper in the *Quarterly Journal of Economics* really began the economic study of segregation and its consequences. There were many distinguished sociologists that had written great work on this topic long before Kain, from W.E.B. DuBois to Karl and Alma Taueber, but Kain brought this important issue into economics. He was also among the first economists to focus on America's growing decentralization of employment and its consequences for cities. His essay on "Gilding the Ghetto" in *The Public Interest* remains one of the most eloquent arguments for helping poor people, not poor places.

Two other, non-urban economists, enjoy a place in urban economics that is as central as these five early giants. Charles Tiebout is, of course, the father of modern local public finance. His ideas about the benefits of competition and diversity across city government remain at the center of most thinking about how to govern metropolitan areas. My discussion of urban government in Chapter 6 begins with Tiebout.

Thomas Schelling is a second outsider who had a deep impact on urban economics. His work on racial segregation and tipping is the theoretical counterpart to Kain's empirical work. My discussion of models of race in Chapter 5 is ultimately derived from Schelling.

I am giving short shrift to the regional scientists, Losch, Isard and Beckmann, who were making similarly impressive contributions to developing a social science of space. While there was a renewed connection between regional science and economics in the work of Masa Fujita and Paul Krugman, this older regional science literature was quite detached from much of the heart of urban economics. These major regional scientists had much less influence on the work of economists, although they were giants in their own field.

After this first wave of post-war urban economists, who made their first major contributions before 1971, there was a second wave of major urban economists in the 1970s: J. Vernon Henderson, John Quigley and Sherwin Rosen. J. Vernon Henderson's 1974 *American Economic Review* article on "The Sizes and Types of Cities" was the major breakthrough in thinking about overall city size, rather than about the internal structure of a city. Chapter 3 in this book can be seen as a lengthy extension of Henderson's pioneering work. Henderson has continued to make major contributions to the field in both theory and empirical work. Urban economics is a field that never really splintered off into theorists and empiricists, which is one of the reasons why I love it. Henderson is one of the leaders who made sure that theory and empirical work remained connected.

John Quigley's most important contributions have been in the area of housing economics. He wrote a series of papers that really forced economists to treat the heterogeneity in housing supply more seriously. His paper on racial difference in housing costs, with John Kain, is a masterpiece that shows that African-Americans pay more for housing in St. Louis, which suggests that they face external constraints in the housing markets.

Rosen is the bridge between Henderson and Quigley. His work on hedonic prices and the spatial equilibrium across space extended the spatial equilibrium model to inter-city comparisons. Rosen is more usually thought of as a labor economist than an urban economist, but he certainly bridged both fields and actually played a major role in training a number of urban economists.

In the 1980s, there were a host of terrific urban economists that built the field. Richard Arnott, Marcus Berliant, Jan Bruecker, "Chip" Case, David Ellwood, Joseph Gyourko, Robert Helsley, Yannis Ioannides, Peter Linneman, Ken Rosen, Ken Small, Robert Topel, Michelle White and Johnny Yinger and many others wrote terrific papers during this period. The major contributions of these authors, however, fit within the definitions of the field that were laid down in the 1960s and 1970s (as does my own).

The last major shift in the field occurred in the 1990s with the work of Paul Krugman and Masa Fujita. Krugman's 1991 *Journal of Political*

Economy paper is really the first entirely internally consistent spatial model where agglomeration economies are endogenously derived. The wave of theory papers that followed this innovation, sometimes called the "new economic geography," has been one of the most important enterprises in urban and regional economics. A particularly attractive outcome of this wave is that, because Krugman partnered with the great regional scientist, Masa Fujita, their work reunited urban economics and regional science. This is a very good thing.

While Krugman's work has certainly profoundly influenced my thinking, this book is relatively free of the new economic geography, except for two models in Chapter 4. The primary reason for this omission is that Krugman, Fujita and Venables have written their own superb book explaining the mechanics of these models. I cannot imagine a graduate student in urban economics surviving without that book. As such, I saw no reason to compete with them on their own ground.

My own work has often focused on the role of cities as centers for the transmission of ideas. That is an idea that has its roots in Marshall, but is associated most strongly with the work of Jane Jacobs (1969). Jane Jacobs, although not an urban economist, had a major influence on my work, but her ideas actually came to me, appropriately enough, through face-to-face interactions in the halls of the University of Chicago's Social Science Building.

In the mid-1980s, Paul Romer revolutionized the theory of economic growth with a model that generated increasing returns by recognizing the external effects of knowledge creation. Two of Romer's advisers were Robert Lucas and Jose Scheinkman. Lucas' own treatment of endogenous growth in "On the Mechanics of Economic Development" emphasizes the knowledge that is embedded within people and ties the transfer of knowledge to cities and the work of Jane Jacobs. Lucas taught me that paper in my first semester in graduate school, and that led me to Jane Jacobs and to the view that the idea transfers that happen in cities may be important, not just for urban economics, but for all of human development. My empirical exploration of Jacobs was a joint process with two inspiring mentors, Jose Scheinkman and Andrei Shleifer, and one also inspiring fellow graduate student: Hedi Kallal.

The plan of this book

The rest of this book rambles through five relatively long chapters. The next chapter is on various permutations of the Alonso–Muth–Mills model. The aim of that chapter was to introduce readers to the spatial equilibrium concept in its purest form. I believe that the

Alonso–Muth–Mills model is an intellectual starting point for any urban economist, and that every economist with an interest in cities should be not only familiar with AMM but able to apply it to a range of settings. The chapter shows how the model can be used to think about housing densities, the impact of different transport technologies, the centralization of the poor and job decentralization. I end the chapter by stressing the power of the model to make sense of urban history.

The third chapter focuses on the spatial equilibrium concept applied between urban areas. As mentioned above, this exercise has its roots in Henderson (1974) and Rosen (1979). I start with the basic model which can be used to make sense of differences in prices and wages across metropolitan areas and a dynamic version which is the basis for urban growth regressions. The spatial equilibrium model emphasizes that population level and housing prices are at least as important as income levels as measures of urban growth. Ideally, all three measures should be used at once. By looking at changes in housing prices, population and income there is some chance of assessing whether urban growth reflects rising productivity, rising amenities or a pro-development housing policy.

The spatial equilibrium model is the underpinning for all of my work on urban growth and the chapter discusses how the model is used to suggest that places with high levels of consumer amenities have been growing quickly since 1980. The model also suggests that the rise of the Sunbelt has much more to do with rising productivity and increasing housing supply then with an increasing willingness to pay for the sun as an amenity. One of the most striking facts about urban growth is the strong correlation between growth and initial skill levels (Glaeser and Saiz, 2004). The chapter shows the challenges that face a spatial equilibrium model with multiple skill levels. After deriving such a model, I show how it can be used to help understand the skills-growth connection.

I end the third chapter by turning to the use of the spatial equilibrium model in my work on housing supply with Joseph Gyourko. I first present a model that recognizes the durable nature of housing. Glaeser and Gyourko (2005) argue that a model with durable housing helps us to understand a number of important features of urban change. I end the chapter by sketching a higher frequency housing model that aims to make sense of changes in housing prices and construction levels over one, three and five year time intervals.

Chapter 4 turns to agglomeration economies. I begin with a discussion of the urban wage premium and the general connection between density and productivity. I then discuss the spillovers model of Ellison and Glaeser (1997) that emphasizes that geographic concentration can reflect either agglomeration economies or heterogeneity in natural advantage. I believe that the bulk of the evidence suggests that natural advantages are probably not all that important today, although they surely were in nineteenth century Chicago.

With this introduction, I then turn to a series of models of endogenous agglomeration economies. I start with a stripped down version of Krugman (1991) that emphasizes the transportation costs advantages of locating close to one another. I then present a variant of this model that is meant to refer to business services. This variant embeds the Becker and Murphy (1992) model of gains from specialization and the Smithian observation that the division of labor is limited by the extent of the market.

I then present a model of worker matching in cities that is close to Krugman (1991a,b). Krugman himself emphasizes the role that cities can play in allocating workers across firms in the event of a shock. I borrow Krugman's model and show that this same logic suggests that cities will enable workers to better match with employers. I also present a simple model of idea transmission in cities. I end the chapter by discussing models on the evolution of cities from goods-producing to idea-producing centers. This transmission is closely related to the transformation from sectoral to functional specialization emphasized by Duranton and Puga (2005).

Chapter 5 focuses on urban distress. I begin by discussing the concentration of the poor in cities. I start with a Schelling-type model and then discuss the role of housing and transportation technology. My view is that the desire of the rich to avoid the poor because of crime or the desire for segregated schooling may explain the segregation of rich and poor, but it does not explain the centralization of the poor and the suburbanization of the rich. I believe that multiple transportation technologies are more likely to explain the centralization of poverty.

I then turn to racial segregation in American cities. There are at least three significant questions about segregation which are still unsettled. How do you measure segregation? Why are segregation levels so high? What is the impact of segregation? Chapter 5 discusses these three core questions and tries to give some sense of the state of the literature. I then end the chapter by turning to crime and social interactions. In principle, social interactions need have nothing to do with social pathologies. Social interactions occur any time that one individual's action increases the probability that a neighbor will undertake that action. Some agglomeration economies can even be seen as social interactions. However, much of the research on social interactions has specifically focused on the spillovers in more harmful behaviors like crime or dropping out of school.

Chapter 5 discusses the theory and evidence on these social interactions. I also discuss the reasons for the long standing connection between crime and cities. I end the chapter by discussing riots, which are a particularly extreme example of the social interactions that can occur in violent behavior.

The final chapter is on cities and the government. The chapter is split into a section that tries to explain government policy and a section that discusses the implications of urban economics for good urban policy. The first section contains three models. The first follows from Tiebout (1956) and Bewley (1981) and looks at the impact of decentralization on the behavior of government. The second model examines local redistribution and how mobility interacts with redistribution. The third model looks at national redistribution and tries to explain why non-democratic governments are so generous to their capital cities.

The second half of this chapter is a collection of different results on urban policy. The first model follows from Tolley (1974) and looks at the implications of agglomeration economies for subsidizing particular locales. The second model provides the economic rationale for helping poor people rather than focusing on subsidizing poor places. The third model examines whether transfer payments should be indexed to local prices and the fourth model addresses optimal local tax policy and the fifth model looks at optimal land use regulations. This last model can be used to suggest that these regulations are too stringent in some areas (Glaeser and Ward, 2006).

I believe that cities are among the most fascinating social phenomena. I have been lucky to have had the chance to spend my life studying them. I also believe that economics gives us an extraordinary set of tools that can help us make sense of the world around us. I hope that this book is of some help to students who are thinking about spending their valuable time on the problems of the world's urban areas.

2

The spatial equilibrium within the city

To grasp any understanding of spatial equilibrium, it makes sense to start with the most successful model in urban economics: the Alonso–Muth–Mills (or AMM) model of location within a metropolitan area. This model was developed over a decade by Alonso (1964), Mills (1967) and Muth (1969). Brueckner (1987) gives a particularly beautiful exposition of the model.

This model has predictions for housing prices (or rents), density levels and the location of rich or poor within the city. It can help us to understand the impact that changes in transportation technology will have on urban prices and urban form. It guides our thinking about where the rich and poor locate within urban areas. It serves both as the workhorse for understanding the economics of cities and as a fitting introduction to the concept of a spatial equilibrium.

Spatial equilibrium in the Alonso–Muth–Mills model

The key theoretical element in urban economics is the idea of a spatial equilibrium: there are no rents to be gained by changing locations. This is a powerful concept that has been the cornerstone for thinking about such key urban topics as housing demand, the impact of transportation on density, and urban growth.

The starting point for urban equilibrium models is the Alonso–Muth–Mills model of residential location in a monocentric city. The core equations of this model and the notation are given in Table 2.1. There will be similar tables for almost all of the models that follow. My hope is that these tables will make the models somewhat easier to follow.

In this model, there is a city population level N which can be endogenously determined through a national labor market or which is

Table 2.1. Simplest version of the Alonso–Muth–Mills model

Actors	Working city inhabitants
They maximize	$\max_{C} U(C, L) = \max_{d} U(W - t(d) - r(d)L, L)$
They choose	Agents choose the distance from their house to the city center (d) that will maximize utility; hence, they are indifferent between residing in different locations—a result embodied in the spatial equilibrium concept.
First order condition	$r'(d) = -t'(d)/L$
Key equilibrium condition	For all $0 \leq d \leq \bar{d}$, $U(W - t(d) - r(d)L, L) = \underline{U}$ for some $\underline{U}$ (the spatial equilibrium concept)
Notation	$U(C, L)$:= an individual's utility function C := consumption = $W - t(d) - r(d)L$ L := units of land N := population W := wage d := distance from city center $\bar{d}$:= furthest possible distance between a home and city center $t(d)$:= commuting costs $r(d)$:= rental cost; also known as the rent gradient $\underline{r}$:= rent level at the city's edge (i.e. $r(\bar{d})$) NL := total units of available land (i.e. size of city) = $\pi\bar{d}^2$

exogenously given. When N is fixed, the model is described as a "closed city" model because the city's population is not formed through a spatial equilibrium with the outside world (Brueckner, 1987). When N is endogenously determined, the model is described as an "open city" model because the city's population is formed so that individuals are indifferent between living in the city and living somewhere else.

These N workers all must commute to a point in the center of the city, and all receive a wage of W. The commuting costs are a function of distance, denoted $t(d)$, where d is the distance from the city center. The primary element in these transport costs is likely to be time—at least for commutes involving public transportation and walking. Car commutes also involve significant time costs, but in this case, the non-time costs will end up being higher. All costs should be thought of as a flow of cost per time period.

The city can be treated as a featureless plane so that the distance minimizing structure will always be a circle. In the simplest version of the model, everyone uses exactly L units of land, and utility is $U(C, L)$, where C is consumption which is equal to income minus transport costs minus housing costs or $W - t(d) - r(d)L$, where $r(d)$ refers to the endogenously determined rental cost per unit of land at distance d from the city center. Also, for simplicity, we first ignore building structure. This model does have the capacity to determine the physical size of the city: N residents who each use L units of land must use NL units of land. NL must therefore equal $\pi\bar{d}^2$, where $\bar{d}$ reflects the furthest distance between home and city center. The value of $\bar{d}$ is $\sqrt{NL/\pi}$, but this result is of course an accounting identity, not a prediction with much economic content.

The only economic prediction of the model in this stripped down form comes from the spatial equilibrium concept: residents must be indifferent between residing at distance d and distance d' from the city center as long as d and d' are both less than $\bar{d}$. This indifference then implies that $\frac{d}{dd}U(W - t(d) - r(d)L, L) = 0$, or $r'(d) = -t'(d)/L$. The rents must decline with distance to exactly offset the increase in transportation costs. In the case where $t(d) = td$, the rent gradient will be linear: $r(d) = r(0) - td/L$.

This is the key prediction of the model and an illustration of the power of the spatial equilibrium concept. Land rents will fall with distance to the city center, and the magnitude of this fall will be determined by the costs of transportation. In Figures 2.1 and 2.2, I show housing price gradients from two cities: Boston and Chicago. These two cities were chosen because Boston is notorious for the difficulty of driving within the city, whereas Chicago is a much easier city to drive in. These graphs plot the logarithm of median housing values in a census tract against miles from the Central Business District. Both graphs show a decline, as predicted by the model. But in Boston, the graph is much steeper than in Chicago. As the model also predicts, the city with higher transportation costs has a steeper housing cost gradient.

To close the model, we must solve for $r(0)$, the rent at the city center. This is usually done by assuming that there is some alternative use of land which generates rents of $\underline{r}$, and this will naturally be the rent level at the city edge. Therefore

$$\underline{r} = r(\bar{d}) = r(0) - t\bar{d}/L = r(0) - \frac{t}{L}\sqrt{\frac{NL}{\pi}} \text{ or } r(0) = \underline{r} + \frac{t}{L}\sqrt{\frac{NL}{\pi}},$$

so rents equal

$$r(d) = \underline{r} + \frac{t}{L}\left(\sqrt{\frac{NL}{\pi}} - d\right)$$

and utility everywhere equals

$$U\left(W - \underline{r} - t\sqrt{NL/\pi}, L\right),$$

which is obviously increasing in W and decreasing in $\underline{r}$, t, and N.

To move from a closed to an open city model, we use spatial indifference across metropolitan areas to pin down the total city population. In

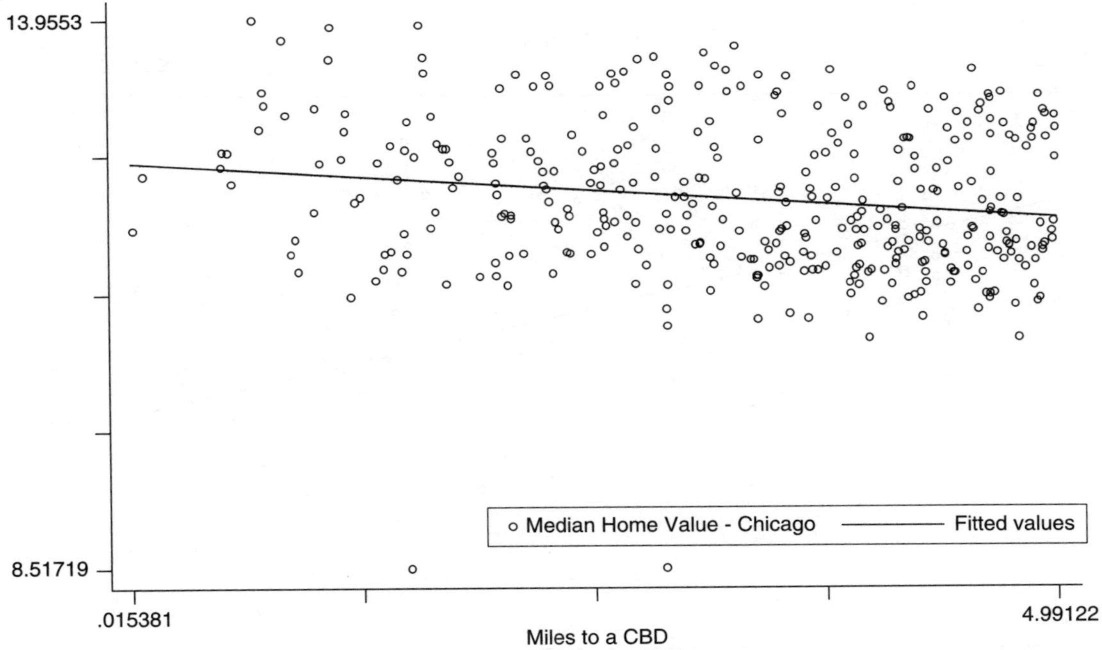

Figure 2.1. House price gradient for Chicago in 2000

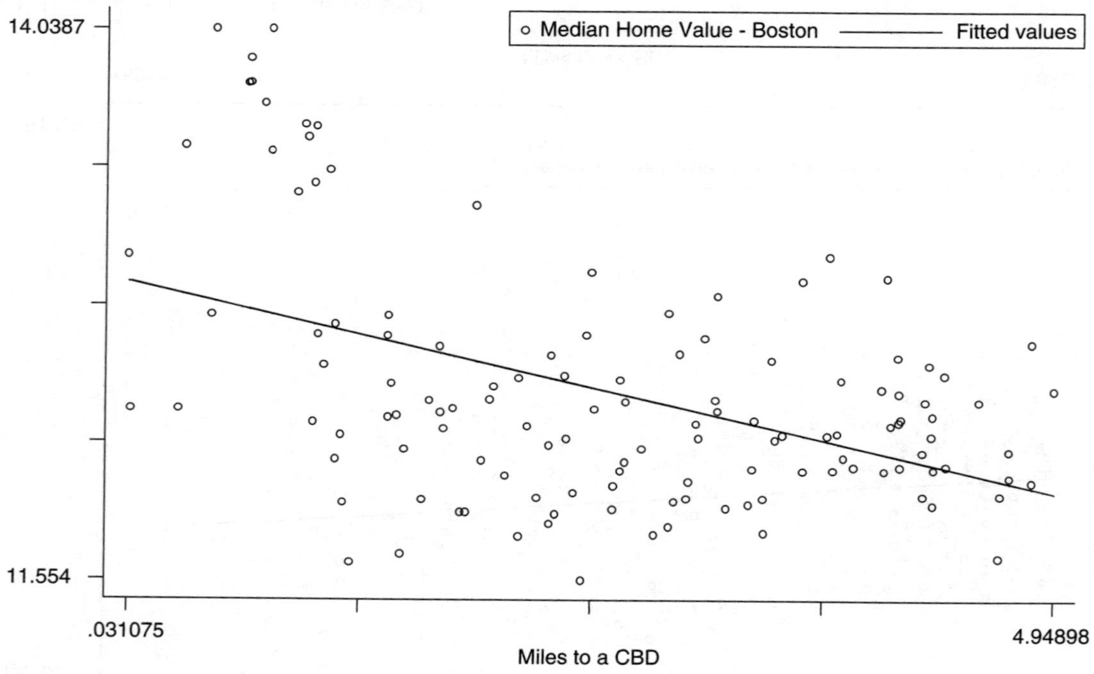

Figure 2.2. Housing price gradient for Boston in 2000

this model we continue to treat wages as exogenous. If the reservation utility in some other location or locations is $\underline{U}$, then the spatial equilibrium concept implies that $U\left(W-\underline{r}-t\sqrt{NL/\pi}, L\right)=\underline{U}$, and this equation then endogenously determines city size (population), namely the value of N. I am treating wages as fixed and exogenous, while surely it would be more desirable to have wages change with city size. I will address that possibility in the next chapter, which focuses on the inter-city spatial equilibrium.

Differentiating the spatial equilibrium equation tells us that N will rise with W and fall with $\underline{r}$ and t. Thus, we have the reassuring results that cities will grow when wages rise, and fall when transport costs rise or when the alternative value of land increases. If I went further and assumed that everyone consumed L units of land in the reservation locale as well, and if I assumed that consumption (net of commuting and housing costs) in the reservation local was equal to $\underline{C}$, then the spatial equilibrium assumption could be written $W-\underline{r}-t\sqrt{NL/\pi}=\underline{C}$, or

$$N=\frac{\pi}{L}\left(\frac{W-\underline{r}-\underline{C}}{t}\right)^2.$$

Assuming a two-dimensional city is quite natural, but there are even times when it is easier to assume that people live in one dimension along a line, as in Solow and Vickrey (1971). In this case, people spread out in either direction around the city center. In this case, the value of $\bar{d}$ is $NL/2$. Rents equal $r(d)=\underline{r}+\frac{t}{L}(.5NL-d)$ and utility everywhere equals $U(W-\underline{r}-.5tNL, L)$, which is obviously increasing in W and decreasing in $\underline{r}$, t, and N. If I assume that consumption (net of commuting and housing costs) in the reservation local was equal to $\underline{C}$, then city population will satisfy $N=2(W-\underline{r}-\underline{C})/tL$. In this case, the formula is pleasantly linear and population goes up more slowly with wages.

Transport technologies

One very simple extension to the model, used by Leroy and Sonstelie (1983) and many others, is to allow for multiple transportation models. The core equations of this model and the notation are given in Table 2.2. At its most general, allowing for multiple transportation modes just means thinking about $t(d)$ as a transport cost function where the optimal transport technology is chosen for each distance (as in Wheaton, 1977). In this case, it continues to be true that $r'(d)=-t'(d)/L$.

Table 2.2. Multiple transport technologies model

Actors	Working city inhabitants
They maximize	$\min_d t(d)$
They choose	Agents choose transport technologies to minimize transportation costs for each distance.
Key equilibrium condition	$r'(d) = -t'(d)/L$ (as before)
Notation	$d :=$ distance from city center $t(d) :=$ commuting costs $= td$ Variables for the non-fixed cost travel technology: $\bar{t} :=$ cost of travel per unit of distance Variables for the fixed cost travel technology: K := fixed cost $\underline{t} :=$ cost of travel per unit distance for the fixed cost technology *Note:* $\bar{t} > \underline{t}$

One particularly natural assumption is that there are two transport technologies: one of which involves no fixed cost, but has a cost of travel per unit distance of $\bar{t}$ and the other which has a fixed cost of K and a cost of travel per unit distance of $\underline{t}$, where $\bar{t} > \underline{t}$. The fixed cost is again supposed to be a flow cost paid for each unit of time. The fixed cost technology is meant to represent the automobile which requires significant expenditures even if it isn't used. The technology without fixed costs can be thought of as representing either public transportation or walking.

As people will want to minimize travel costs, they will choose the fixed cost technology if and only if $\bar{t}d > \underline{t}d + K$, or if they live more than $K/(\bar{t} - \underline{t})$ units from the city center. People who live close to their jobs will walk or take public transportation and will avoid the fixed costs associated with maintaining an automobile. People who live far will be willing to pay the fixed costs to reduce the variable costs of commuting.

The general result that $r'(d) = -t'(d)/L$ then implies that the rent gradient will decline in absolute value with distance from the center. For houses that are less than $K/(\bar{t} - \underline{t})$ units from the city center, the slope of the rent gradient will be $-\bar{t}/L$ since by moving one unit of distance closer, residents will save $\bar{t}$ worth of travel costs. For houses that are further than $K/(\bar{t} - \underline{t})$ units distance from the city center, the slope of the rent gradient will be $-\underline{t}/L$ since moving one unit of distance further out will increase travel costs by $\underline{t}$.

If $\sqrt{NL/\pi}$ is greater than $K/(\bar{t} - \underline{t})$, so at least some people in the city use the fixed cost technology (i.e. cars), then the rent gradient will equal

$$r(d) = \underline{r} + \frac{\bar{t}}{L}\left(\sqrt{\frac{NL}{\pi}} - d\right)$$

for distances that are within $K/(\bar{t} - \underline{t})$ units of the city center and

$$r(d) = \underline{r} + \frac{K}{L} + \frac{\underline{t}}{L}\left(\sqrt{\frac{NL}{\pi}} - d\right)$$

for distances farther than $K/(\bar{t} - \underline{t})$ units from the city center. This rent gradient will be convex, and this is a general feature of rent gradients with multiple transportation technologies. Whenever there are multiple transportation technologies, people will always use the technologies with lower per unit commuting costs when they are further from the city center. This optimization then in turn predicts that rent gradients will be steeper closer to the city center.

This result can readily be generalized to a discrete number of different transportation technologies each with a different fixed cost, denoted K_j, and each with a different transport cost per unit of distance, which is denoted t_j. I can assume that transport technologies with lower fixed costs always have higher transport costs. Who would ever use a transport technology that was worse along both dimensions? If I order the transport technologies on the basis of increasing fixed cost, then individuals will switch from low fixed cost, high travel cost technologies to higher fixed cost, lower travel cost technologies as they get further out from the city. The result will be that the cost of commuting becomes concave in distance from the city. As transport costs are concave, the rent gradient will be flatter away from the city center.

Congestion can produce a similar result (Solow and Vickrey, 1971). If transport costs increase with the number of people using the roads, then as more people use the roads closer to the city, then transport costs will be higher. For example, assume that cost per unit of distance is $t(q)$ where q represents the number of commuters using the road. The number of commuters using the road as distance d is the set of people who live beyond that point. As such, in a linear city, where N people live and consume one unit of land each, then the number of commuters at point d is $.5N - d$, so commuting costs equal $t(.5N - d)$ at that point, which means that transport costs are lower, further away from the center, and the rent gradient will again flatten out.

Endogenizing land areas

The previous section had three separate optimization margins: (1) where to live within the city; (2) whether to live in the city at all; and (3) what transportation technology to use. As such, the model generates predictions about the price of land at different distances from the city

Table 2.3. Model that endogenizes land areas

Actors	Working city inhabitants
They maximize	$\max_{C,L} U(C, L) = \max_{d,L} U(W - td - r(d)L, L)$ Example functional forms: $U(C, L) = C + \alpha \ln L$ $U(C, L) = C + \alpha L^{\beta}$
They choose	Agents choose distance from the city center (d) and size of land area (L) to maximize their utility.
First order conditions	$r'(d)L = -t/L$ and $-r(d)U_1(W - td - r(d)L, L) + U_2(W - td - r(d)L, L) = 0$
Notation	$U(C, L)$:= an individual's utility function C := consumption = $W - td - r(d)L$ L := units of land W := wage d := distance from city center $t(d)$:= commuting costs = td $r(d)$:= rental cost; also known as the rent gradient U_1 := the derivative of the utility function with respect to its first argument (income after transport costs and after housing costs) U_2 := the derivative of the utility function with respect to its second argument (land area) U_{ij} := derivative of U with respect to its ith and jth arguments

center, the overall size of the city and what type of transportation will be used at what distance from the city center. However, that section told us nothing about densities within the city. To address that we must endogenize the choice of land area. To handle this endogenization, we will now assume that the costs of transit are again linear, i.e. $t(d) = td$, and that there is only one transportation technology. The core equations of this model and the notation are given in Table 2.3.

If second order conditions hold (which I assume), optimal choice of land area then implies that

$$\frac{d}{dL}U(W - td - r(d)L, L) = -r(d)U_1(W - td - r(d)L, L) + U_2(W - td - r(d)L, L) = 0, \qquad (2.1)$$

where U_1 is the derivative of the utility function with respect to its first argument (income after transport costs and after housing costs) and U_2 is the derivative of the utility function with respect to its second argument (land area). We can use this equation to define a function $L(d)$ which is the land area chosen at distance d.

The spatial equilibrium concept continues to imply that $\frac{d}{dd}U(W - td - r(d)L, L) = 0$ or $r'(d) = -t/L$. In this case, however, L is not a constant but rather the optimal amount of land chosen at each distance from the city center. Differentiating the first order condition totally with respect to d, using the condition $r'(d) = -t'/L$, and using the notation U_{ij} to denote the derivative of U with respect to its ith and jth arguments produces

$$\frac{dL}{dd} = -\frac{tU_1(C, L)}{L\left(r(d)^2 U_{11}(C, L) - 2r(d)U_{12}(C, L) + U_{22}(C, L)\right)}. \tag{2.2}$$

The denominator of this expression is negative because we have assumed that second order conditions for optimal land use hold. The numerator is obviously positive. Therefore land usage always rises with distance from the city center. This equation provides us with the core result that we expect to see: people living in city centers live at higher densities than people living on the edges of cities.

While this proves that densities should decline with distance to the city center, this gives us little information about the functional form that densities should take. Where the rent gradient depends entirely on transport costs when land consumption is fixed (which are perhaps somewhat measurable directly) and when land consumption is endogenous, the actual shape of the density gradient depends on the utility function chosen.

For example, a particularly simply function is $U(C, L) = C + \alpha \ln L$ which yields the first order condition: $r(d) = \alpha/L$. Using the spatial indifference condition across cities, which implies that utility at the city center is $\underline{U}$, we know that

$$\underline{U} = W - r(0)L(0) + \alpha \ln L(0) = W - \alpha + \alpha \ln \alpha - \alpha \ln r(0) \quad \text{or} \quad r(0) = \alpha e^{(W - \underline{U} - \alpha)/\alpha}. \tag{2.3}$$

The spatial indifference condition within the city is $r'(d) = -t/L$, and this then produces the differential equation: $r'(d)/r(d) = -t/\alpha$. Solving this differential equation implies that

$$r(d) = r(0)e^{-(t/\alpha)d} \quad \text{or} \quad r(d) = \alpha e^{(W - \underline{U} - \alpha - td)/\alpha}$$

and the density gradient is

$$\ln\left(\frac{1}{L}\right) = \frac{W - \underline{U} - \alpha}{\alpha} - \frac{t}{\alpha}d. \tag{2.4}$$

The logarithm of land per person rises linearly with distance and the logarithm of density declines linearly with distance. Figure 2.3 shows this log-linear relationship for the case of Chicago. The regression fit is certainly imperfect, but the basic relationship seems strong and the functional forms don't appear to do grave injustice to the data. The exponential density gradient has been a workhorse of the empirical literature which has been based on that equation.

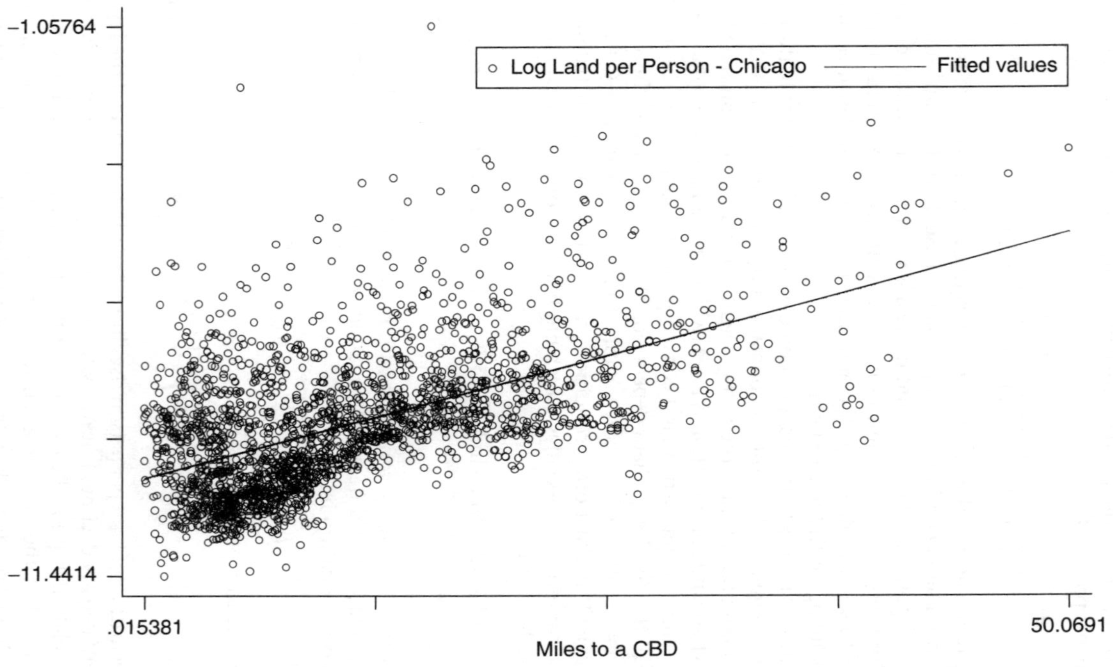

Figure 2.3. Density gradient for Chicago in 2000

The value of city size using the equations:

$$\underline{r} = \alpha e^{(W-\underline{U}-\alpha-t\bar{d})/\alpha}$$

(rents at the boundary equal the opportunity cost of land); or

$$\bar{d} = \frac{W-\underline{U}-\alpha}{t} - \frac{\alpha}{t}\ln\left(\frac{\underline{r}}{\alpha}\right)$$

(utility in the city equals the reservation utility). To solve for city size, we must use the equality

$$N = \int_{d=0}^{\bar{d}} 2\pi d e^{(W-\underline{U}-\alpha-td)/\alpha} d\,d.$$

A few other functional forms provide easy-to-use predictions about density gradients. For example, if $U(C, L) = C + \alpha L^{\beta}$, then the first order condition for land consumption implies that $r(d) = \alpha\beta L^{\beta-1}$. Rent at the city center again serves to keep people indifferent between this city and the reservation locale. This ensures that

$$\underline{U} = W - r(0)L(0) + \alpha L(0)^{\beta} = W + \alpha^{1/(1-\beta)}\beta^{\beta/(1-\beta)}(1-\beta)r(0)^{-\beta/(1-\beta)} \quad \text{or}$$

$$r(0) = \alpha^{1/\beta}\beta\left(\frac{1-\beta}{\underline{U}-W}\right)^{(1-\beta)/\beta}.$$

Using the spatial indifference equation, $r'(d) = -t/L$, and indifference across space (it is convenient particularly to use this for the person living exactly one unit from the city center) this equation implies that $r(d) = \alpha^{1/\beta}\beta(1-\beta)^{(1-\beta)/\beta}(\underline{U} - W + td)^{(\beta-1)/\beta}$ and the density gradient is

$$\ln\left(\frac{1}{L}\right) = \ln\left(\alpha^{1/\beta}(1-\beta)^{1/\beta}\right) - \frac{1}{\beta}\ln(\underline{U} - W + td). \tag{2.4'}$$

This specification suggests more of a log-log empirical specification, but it also requires an independent estimation of $\underline{U} - W$ which obviously makes things somewhat less attractive. The size of the city is again found by using the fact that the city is inhabited only to the point where $r(d) = \alpha^{1/\beta}\beta(1-\beta)^{(1-\beta)/\beta}(\underline{U} - W + td)^{(\beta-1)/\beta} = \underline{r}$, and then finding the total population living closer to the city than that distance.

Building housing

One of the classic permutations of this model assumes that housing space, rather than land, enters directly into the utility function. This approach is used by Muth (1969) and masterfully presented by Brueckner (1987). The core equations of this model and the notation are given in

Table 2.4. Model that endogenizes housing space: Firm's problem

Actors	Housing developers
They maximize	$\max_{K,L}\{p(d)F(K,L) - p_k K - r(d)L\}$
They choose	Developers choose the capital and land mix to produce the amount of housing that will maximize profit. Since there is free entry, this implies the zero profit condition.
First order condition	$\frac{p(d)F_K(K,L)}{p_k} = \frac{p(d)F_L(K,L)}{r(d)} = 1$ or $p(d)\,f'(k) = p_k$
Key equilibrium conditions	$p(d)F(K,L) = p_k K + r(d)L$ or $p(d)\,f(k) = p_k k + r(d)$ (the zero profit condition)
Notation	d := distance from city center $r(d)$:= rental cost; also known as the rent gradient $p(d)$:= price of housing L := units of land K := capital used in the production of housing p_k := price of capital $F(K,L)$:= housing technology/production function, which we assume exhibits constant returns to scale. $f(k) := F(K/L, \ell)$

Table 2.4. In this view, utility is defined over consumption and housing or $U(C, H)$, and housing is a function of capital (K) and land (L). If we let $p(d)$ be the price of housing, then again there are two key conditions. The first order condition for housing is that

$$-\,p(d)U_1(W - td - p(d)H, H) = U_2(W - td - p(d)H, H)\,. \qquad (2.5)$$

The spatial indifference equation is now $t = -p'(d)H$. The change from the previous models is housing that can be supplied with a technology $F(K, L)$, where the price of capital, K, is exogenous and fixed at p_k and the price of land, L, is endogenously determined and still denoted $r(d)$. The following two first order conditions will hold:

$$\frac{p(d)F_K(K,L)}{p_k} = \frac{p(d)F_L(K,L)}{r(d)} = 1.$$

If there is free entry among developers, then there will also be a zero profit condition: $p(d)F(K,L) = p_k K + r(d)L$.

Following Brueckner (1987), if $F(.,.)$ exhibits constant returns to scale, then let k denote K/L and define $f(k)$ to equal $F(K/L, \ell)$. In this case, the two conditions for development can be written: $p(d)\,f'(k) = p_k$ and $p(d)\,f(k) = p_k k + r(d)$. These two equations together connect changes in d with changes in capital intensity and changes in land rents. Totally

Table 2.5. Model that endogenizes housing space (modification of previous model): Firm's problem

Actors	Housing developers
They maximize	$\max_h\{p(d)hL - c(h)L - r(d)L\} = \max_h\{p(d)h - c(h) - r(d)\}$
They choose	Developers choose height of housing to maximize profits. Again, there is free entry, which implies the zero profit condition.
First order condition	$p(d) = c'(h)$
Equilibrium condition	$p(d)h = c(h) + r(d)$ (the zero profit condition)
Notation	d := distance from city center $r(d)$:= rental cost; also known as the rent gradient $p(d)$:= price of housing L := units of land h := height of housing H := amount of housing/lot size = hL $c(h)$:= cost of height per unit of land

differentiating the two equations with respect to d gives:

$$\frac{dk}{dd} = -\frac{p'(d)}{p(d)}\frac{f'(k)}{f''(k)} < 0,$$

and $p'(d)f(k) = r'(d) < 0$. Taking a second derivative of this condition gives:

$$p''(d)f(k) - \frac{p'(d)^2}{p(d)}\frac{f'(k)^2}{f''(k)} = r''(d).$$

This second term is positive, which means that the ability of capital to respond to changes in distance and changes in price will imply that the land rent gradient is less steep than the housing price gradient. If a Cobb–Douglas production technology is assumed to be $F(K, L) = K^{\gamma}L^{1-\gamma}$, then $r(d) = (1-\gamma)p(d)^{1/(1-\gamma)}p_k^{-\gamma/(1-\gamma)}\gamma^{\gamma/(1-\gamma)}$ and housing density at each distance equals $p(d)^{\gamma/(1-\gamma)}p_k^{-\gamma/(1-\gamma)}\gamma^{\gamma/(1-\gamma)}$.

An alternative formulation which I slightly prefer is to assume that H equals height, denoted h, times land area, where the cost of height is $c(h)$ per unit of land where $c'(h) > 0$ and $c''(h) > 0$. The core equations of this model and the notation are given in Table 2.5. In this case, the firm's problem is to maximize $p(d)hL - c(h)L - r(d)L$. This equation can be comfortably divided by L, and the two relevant conditions are the first order condition for height which is $p(d) = c'(h)$ and the zero profit condition $p(d)h = c(h) + r(d)$. Differentiating the first condition gives:

$$\frac{dh}{dd} = \frac{p'(d)}{c''(h)} < 0$$

so building height falls with distance from the city center. If $c(h) = c_0 h^\delta$ where $\delta > 1$, then $h = \delta^{1/(1-\delta)} c_0^{1/(1-\delta)} p(d)^{1/(\delta-1)}$ and $r(d) = (\delta - 1)\delta^{\delta/(1-\delta)} c_0^{1/(1-\delta)} p(d)^{\delta/(\delta-1)}$. If $\delta = 1/\gamma$ and $c_0 = p_k$ then the two formulations are identical.

The technology of creating space is actually quite well understood. Organizations like R.S. Means actually publish cost estimates for creating space. Interestingly, these costs don't suggest such pleasant continuous solutions. Single-family detached dwellings do show increasing costs per foot with the height of the building. Thus, for these buildings there is a clear tradeoff between the usage of land area (to get a bigger footprint) and the cost of construction. In taller, multi-family dwellings, it is less clear that there are increasing costs per square foot, at least in the range between seven and 40 storeys. Within this range, Means suggests that there are actually scale economies. As such, this would suggest that there is a range of single family households that perhaps rise to three stories, followed by a discrete break at some point where there is a jump to tall building.

To close the model, I assume that $U(C, H) = C + \alpha \ln H$, which yields the pricing equation $p(d) = \alpha e^{(W - \underline{U} - \alpha - td)/\alpha}$, which then yields: $r(d) = (\delta - 1)\delta^{\delta/(1-\delta)} c_0^{1/(1-\delta)} \alpha^{\delta/(\delta-1)} e^{\delta(W - \underline{U} - \alpha - td)/\alpha(\delta-1)}$. The derivative gives:

$$\frac{\partial \ln(r(d))}{\partial d} = -\frac{\delta t}{\alpha(\delta - 1)} < 0,$$

so as the cost of building high increases, the land rent gradient with city distance becomes flatter. As the cost of building up becomes flat (i.e. $c(h) = c_0 h$), the rent gradient approaches infinity.

People per unit of housing satisfies the equation $1/H = e^{(W - \underline{U} - \alpha - td)/\alpha}$ and housing per unit of land satisfies the equation $h = \delta^{1/(1-\delta)} c_0^{1/(1-\delta)} \alpha^{1/(\delta-1)} e^{(W - \underline{U} - \alpha - td)/\alpha(\delta-1)}$, so people per unit of land equals $\delta^{1/(1-\delta)} c_0^{1/(1-\delta)} \alpha^{1/(\delta-1)} e^{\delta(W - \underline{U} - \alpha - td)/\alpha(\delta-1)}$, and the population density gradient equals

$$\ln\left(\frac{\text{People}}{\text{Acre}}\right) = \frac{\delta(W - \underline{U} - \alpha)}{\alpha(\delta - 1)} - \frac{\delta t}{\alpha(\delta - 1)} d + \frac{1}{\delta - 1} \ln\left(\frac{\alpha}{\delta c_0}\right). \quad (2.6)$$

The impact of capital in the production is to steepen the density gradient. Close to the city center, people build tall buildings: land rents are quite high, and travel costs are low. As distance increases, housing density falls and people consume both more housing and more land.

One of the key lessons of urban economics is that cities are physical entities and housing supply is a critical determinant of urban form. Nowhere is this clearer than in the role that tall buildings played in creating the modern city at the turn of the last century. In that case, there were a number of building related innovations—the elevator may have been most important—than can be seen as reducing the cost of building up. In this model this is seen as a reduction in the value of δ, which will have the effect of steepening the density gradient as taller buildings are put in the urban core. The rise of high density dwellings, and the shape of what we think of as cities, was to a large extent the result of changes in building technology that made it possible to go up.

Improvements in building technology will make the city taller, but they won't necessarily make the city more compact. The spread of the city is determined again by the point where the value of land for residential purposes equals the value of land in its alternative (presumably agricultural) function. This equation is $\underline{r} = (\delta - 1)\delta^{\delta/(1-\delta)} c_0^{1/(1-\delta)} \alpha^{\delta/(\delta-1)} e^{\delta(W-\underline{U}-\alpha-t\bar{d})/\alpha(\delta-1)}$, and as long as reservation utility is fixed, the city will get bigger at least as long as δ is constrained to be greater than one. In reality, the reservation utility might not be fixed, but it remains true that while in a model with fixed city population a taller city invariably means a city with less footprint, and in a city with variable population, improvements in building technology will make the city both taller and more spread out.

Income heterogeneity

The previous versions of the model dealt with predictions about prices and density levels. They did not address the issue of where the rich and poor live within the city. Yet the locational patterns of rich and poor are among the most interesting features of cities. In most modern cities, the poor tend to live closer to urban areas and the rich tend to live somewhat further out. In some older cities, the rich live at the extreme center, surrounded by a ring of poverty and then another ring of wealth (Glaeser, Kahn and Rappaport, 2008). One job of an urban model is to explain these location patterns.

Any observers of wealth and poverty will naturally argue that many factors explain the tendency of the rich to suburbanize, which include better schools, lower crime and a host of factors mostly associated with avoiding the proximity of the poor (Miezkowski and Mills, 1993). These forces explain why rich should want to live with rich, but not why clusters of wealth should be located away from the urban center. The goal of an urban model of wealth and poverty is to explain the tendency of the poor to live close to the city center.

I now turn to a variant of the model with heterogeneous individuals, indexed by income or y. The core equations of this model and the notation are given in Table 2.6. I assume that there is a fixed supply of individuals within the city of each type that is denoted $g(y)$. To

Table 2.6. Model for income heterogeneity

Actors	Working city inhabitants
They maximize	$\max_{C} U(C, H(y)) = \max_{d} U(y - p(d)H(y) - t(y)d, H(y))$ Example functional form: $U(C, H) = aC^{\alpha} + H^{\beta}$
They choose	Agents choose the distance from their house to the city center (d) that will maximize utility; hence, they are indifferent between residing in different locations.
First order condition	$p'(d)H(y) = -t(y)$
Notation	$U(C, H)$:= an individual's utility function C := consumption = $y - p(d)H(y) - t(y)d$ d := distance from city center $p(d)$:= price of housing $t(y)$:= commuting costs (now as a function of income) y := income, which serves as an index for or type of each individual within the city y is distributed uniformly on $[y_{\min}, y_{\max}]$ $g(y)$:= fixed supply of individuals of type y $H(y)$:= fixed housing consumption for each individual of type y $t(y)$:= fixed transportation costs for each individual of type y

consider a particularly simple version of the model, assume that housing consumption is fixed at $H(y)$ for each type and transport costs $t(y)$ are also fixed. At any point where an individual of income y lives, it must continue to be true that $p'(d)H(y) = -t(y)$ so that there is no incentive to move either closer or further from the city center.

The key implication of the model is that rich people live further from the city center if and only if $(t(y)/H(y))$ is decreasing with y or $H'(y)/H(y) > t'(y)/t(y)$. If this is true, then the willingness to pay for housing for the rich actually declines more slowly with distance from the city center than the willingness to pay for housing amongst the poorer. The basic intuition is that the rich consume a lot of housing and therefore want to live where housing is cheap. Even if transportation costs are lower for the rich, the incentive remains for the rich to avoid the city center and flee to leafy suburbs where land can be gotten on the cheap.

To see this condition in action, I now turn to a few specific examples of the model. If we make the assumption y is distributed uniformly on the interval $[y_{\min}, y_{\max}]$, and that $H = L$, so that only land is used in the production of housing, then the spatial indifference equation $p'(d)H(y(d)) = -t(y(d))$ can be thought of as defining a relationship mapping d into y so that there is a level of distance chosen by each income level. This first order condition is accompanied by a second order condition $p''(d) > 0$. For all levels of d , land supplied equals land consumed or $\pi d^2 = \int_{x=0}^{d} H(y(x))\,dx$, and at the limit $\pi \bar{d}^2 = \int_{y=y_{\min}}^{y_{\max}} H(y)\,dy$.

The land cost at the edge of the city must again satisfy $p(\bar{d}) = \underline{r}$ where $\bar{d} = \sqrt{\frac{1}{\pi}\int_{y=y_{\min}}^{y_{\max}} H(y)\,dy}$.

A simpler version of the model assumes that housing consumption equals $H(y)$ and is a function of income but not price or distance. Commuting costs are $t(y)d$. The connection between transport costs and opportunity costs of time was emphasized by Becker (1965). I assume that y is distributed uniformly with density one on the interval [0, 1]. These assumptions fix the city's size with $\bar{d} = \sqrt{\frac{1}{\pi}\int_{y=0}^{1} H(y)\,dy}$. These assumptions are unattractive as housing quantities are independent of price and location, but they give us a very intuitive condition on the location of rich and poor.

Every person of all income levels will choose d to minimize $p(d)H(y) + t(y)d$, which means that $p'(d)H(y) = -t(y)$. Second order conditions require that $p''(d) > 0$—the price gradient must be convex. If I define $y(d)$ as the income level associated with distance d, then $p''(d) > 0$ implies that

$$\frac{t(y)H'(y) - H(y)t'(y)}{y'(d)} > 0. \tag{2.7}$$

This means that $y'(d) > 0$ if and only if $H'(y)/H(y) > t'(y)/t(y)$ or the elasticity of housing demand with respect to income is greater than the elasticity of transport costs relative to income. Rich people will live in the suburbs if and only if the elasticity of housing demand with respect to income is greater than the elasticity of travel costs per unit distance with respect to income. We will discuss the empirical implications of this in Chapter 5 and suggest that this condition does not seem to be met empirically (Glaeser, Kahn and Rappaport, 2008).

The overall connection between travel costs and income would combine the fact that the cost of time rises with income and the ability of people to chose different travel modes (as in Leroy and Sonstelie, 1983). A somewhat unrealistic continuous model of multiple modes might assume that transportation costs equal $yz(k)d$, where y is income, $z(k)$ is the time to commute each unit of distance and k is the amount spent on better transportation technology per unit distance (which reflects cars rather than public transportation). The core equations of this model and the notation are given in Table 2.7. If spending on this technology is proportional to distance, then k is chosen to minimize total transportation costs, which are $yz(k) + k$. Hence, $-yz'(k) = 1$ (where $z'(k) < 0$ and $z''(k) > 0$) which implies $\partial k/\partial y = 1/z''(k)y^2 > 0$. The total value of $t'(y)$ therefore equals $z(k) + z'(k)/z''(k)y$, and $yt'(y)/t(y)$ equals $1 + z'(k)/z(k)z''(k)$, which is less than one. The impact of adding technology is to reduce the relationship between travel costs and income that naturally occurs because income raises the value of time.

Table 2.7. Model for income heterogeneity and income-dependent travel costs (modification of previous model)

Actors	Working city inhabitants
Minimize	$\min_k \{yz(k) + k\}$
They choose	Agents choose k to minimize transportation costs.
First order condition	$-yz'(k) = 1$
Notation	$y :=$ income $z(k) :=$ time to commute each unit of distance $k :=$ amount spent on better transportation on technology per unit of distance

Glaeser, Kahn and Rappaport (2008) look specifically at the case of two transport modes and find that public transportation is disproportionately used by the poor and this usage can explain the centralization of poverty. Since transport costs are so much higher for the poor when they use public transportation, it makes sense for the poor to live closer to the city center. We calibrate a two mode model and show that given reasonable parameter values, it is not surprising to see poor people using public transportation living closer to the city than rich people driving.

A more attractive, but far more complicated, version of the model endogenizes both transport costs and the amount of housing. The core equations of this model and the notation are given in Table 2.8. A natural

Table 2.8. Model for income heterogeneity, income-dependent travel costs, and amount of housing (modification of previous model)

Actors	Working city inhabitants
They maximize	$\max_{C,H} U(C, H) = \max_{d,H} U(y - (t_0 + t_1 y)d - p(d)H, H)$ Example functional form: $U(C, H) = aC^{\alpha} + H^{\beta}$
They choose	Agents choose where to live (i.e. d) and how much housing to consume (i.e. H) so they can maximize their utility. This leads to spatial equilibrium.
First order conditions	$p'(d)H = -t_0 - t_1 y$ and $-p(d)U_1 + U_2 = 0$ For the example functional form: $a\alpha p(d)(y(1 - t_1 d) - t_0 d - p(d)H)^{\alpha-1} = \beta H^{\beta-1}$
Notation	$U(C, H) :=$ an individual's utility function $C :=$ consumption $= y - (t_0 + t_1 y)d - p(d)H$ $H :=$ amount of housing/lot size $d :=$ distance from city center $y :=$ income $t_0 :=$ physical travel cost for commuting a unit of distance $t_1 y :=$ time cost for travel that is proportional to income

assumption might be that commuting a unit distance involves both physical costs of t_0 and time costs that are proportional to income or $t_1 y$. I assume a utility function of $U(C, H) = aC^{\alpha} + H^{\beta}$.

Including the budget constraint in the utility function yields: $a(y(1 - t_1 d) - t_0 d - p(d)H)^{\alpha} + H^{\beta}$, which provides us with two first order conditions: $a\alpha p(d)(y(1 - t_1 d) - t_0 d - p(d)H)^{\alpha-1} = \beta H^{\beta-1}$ and $p'(d)H = -t_0 - t_1 y$. Differentiation yields:

$$\frac{\partial H}{\partial y} = \frac{a\alpha p(d)(1 - t_1 d)}{a\alpha p(d)^2 + \frac{1-\beta}{1-\alpha} a^{(\alpha-2)/(\alpha-1)} \alpha^{(\alpha-2)/(\alpha-1)} p(d)^{(\alpha-2)/(\alpha-1)} \beta^{1/(\alpha-1)} H^{(\alpha-\beta)/(1-\alpha)}},$$

and income will rise with distance from the city if and only if $t_1 + p'(d)H'(y) < 0$, which is the condition that $H'(y)/H(y) > t'(y)/t(y)$.

If this condition is assumed to hold for all of the relevant values of d, then the equilibrium is determined by the two first order conditions and the condition that ensures that supply equals demand: $\pi d^2 = \int_{y=0}^{y(d)} H(y, p(d))\, dy$, and a final condition that rent at the city's edge will equal the agricultural costs of land. These equations lack closed form solutions. The lack of solutions for even these particularly simple equations makes it easy to see why equilibria with continuous income distributions are difficult to use.

Endogenous and exogenous amenities

At this point, we have assumed that all amenities are constant within the city. This might not be the case either because of exogenous or endogenous amenities. If people are homogeneous and there are exogenous amenities that deliver a flow of A units of utility from living in a particular area and if lot sizes are fixed, then prices will just rise to offset the higher level of utility in the area. If the cash value of the amenity flow in one area is A and zero otherwise, then rents will be exactly A units higher in that high amenity area. This basic approach guides most of the empirical work that uses land prices to determine the value that people place on amenities. For example, Black (1999) represents a particularly elegant use of real estate data to determine the value people place on sending their children to better schools. The core equations of this model and the notation are given in Table 2.9.

When lot sizes are endogenized, then amenities will be associated both with higher prices and with higher densities. I assume again that $U(C, H) = C + \alpha \ln H$ for people who are not living in the high amenity area and $U(C, H) = C + A + \alpha \ln H$ in that area. Comparing two areas that are equidistant from the town center, let $p(d)$ reflect the cost of land in the

Table 2.9. Model for exogenous amenities

Actors	Working city inhabitants
They maximize	$\max_{C,H} U(C, H)$ Example functional form: $U(C, H) = \begin{cases} C + \alpha \ln H \text{ in the low amenity area} \\ C + A + \alpha \ln H \text{ in the high amenity area} \end{cases}$
They choose	Agents choose where to live (i.e. d) to maximize their utility. This leads to spatial equilibrium.
Equilibrium condition	$p_A(d) = e^{A/\alpha} p(d)$ (spatial equilibrium)
Notation	$U(C, H)$:= an individual's utility function, which differs between residents of low and high amenity areas C := consumption = $\begin{cases} y - p(d)H - t(d) \text{ in the low amenity area} \\ y - p_A(d)H - t(d) \text{ in the high amenity area} \end{cases}$ H := amount of housing/lot size d := distance from city center $t(d)$:= commuting costs = td y := income A := flow of exogenous amenities delivered to one area of the city but not to the others $p(d)$:= cost of land in the low amenity area $p_A(d)$:= cost of land in the high amenity area

low amenity area and $p_A(d)$ reflect the cost of land in the high amenity area. In both cases, land choices will be optimal so $p = \alpha/H$ and total utility will equal $y - \alpha - td + A + \alpha \ln \alpha - \alpha \ln p_A(d)$ in the high amenity area and $y - \alpha - td + \alpha \ln \alpha - \alpha \ln p(d)$ in the low amenity area. Spatial equilibrium then requires that $A = \alpha \ln(p_A(d)/p(d))$ or $p_A(d) = e^{A/\alpha} p(d)$ and the ratio of densities in the two areas likewise equals $e^{A/\alpha}$.

Just comparing prices without controlling thoroughly for land area will lead to an underestimate of the value of the amenity. The functional form assumption implies that total housing spending will be equal in the high amenity area and the low amenity area. The difference will be that in the high amenity area people are consuming smaller lots and paying more for them.

Perhaps the most important amenities within urban areas are those produced by neighbors. People seem willing to pay an inordinate amount to live among wealthy or well educated people. The model can incorporate those effects by returning to the case of wealth heterogeneity. In this case, I restrict myself to the exogenous lot size $H(y)$ function which means that we can only discuss the impact of these effects on price, not density. I look only at an equilibrium where people from one income level live at exactly the same distance. Furthermore, I assume that the flow of amenities equals $A(\hat{y})$ where $\hat{y}$ is the income of an individual's

Table 2.10. Model for endogenous amenities with wealth heterogeneity and exogenous lot sizes

Actors	Working city inhabitants
They maximize	$\max_d C = \max_d \{y - p(d)H(y) - t(y)d + A(\hat{y}(d))\}$
They choose	Agents choose where to live (i.e. d) to maximize their utility.
First order condition	$-p'(d)H(y) - t(y) + A'(\hat{y}(d))\hat{y}'(d) = 0$
Notation	C := consumption = $y - p(d)H(y) - t(y)d + A(\hat{y}(d))$ d := distance from city center $t(y)$:= commuting costs (as a function of income) $H(y)$:= housing consumption/exogenous lot size for each individual of type y y := income $\hat{y}(d)$:= the income of an individual's closest neighbors at a given distance (in equilibrium) $A(\hat{y})$:= amenity flow *Note:* Everyone receives the same amenity flow, and all people of one income level live at the same distance.

closest neighbors. In this case, everyone receives the some amenity flow. The core equations of this model and the notation are given in Table 2.10.

In equilibrium, each individual optimizes over location taking the location decisions of everyone else as given. In this case, optimal location choice maximizes $y - p(d)H(y) - t(y)d + A(\hat{y}(d))$ where $\hat{y}(d)$ reflects the average income level at a given distance in equilibrium. The first order condition for people of each income level is $-p'(d)H(y) - t(y) + A'(\hat{y}(d))\hat{y}'(d) = 0$ or

$$p'(d) = \frac{-t(y) + A'(\hat{y}(d))\hat{y}'(d)}{H(y)}.$$

The impact of these amenity spillovers on the gradient of prices with respect to distance depends on whether the rich are centralized or suburbanized. When the rich live in the suburbs, then the existence of these amenities will mute the tendency of prices to decline with distance. Since the prevailing pattern in American cities is the suburbanization of the well-to-do, this suggests that bid-rent gradients often understate the true value placed on proximity to downtown. When the rich live in the central city, as in some European cities like Paris, then the bid-rent gradient will be enormously steep as distance from the central city means both distance from work and lack of prosperous neighbors.

The condition for rich people living further away from the city center is again that this bid-rent gradient declines with income, which now requires that

$$\frac{H'(y)}{H(y)} > \frac{t'(y)}{t(y) - A'(\hat{y}(d))\hat{y}'(d)}.$$

The spillovers make this condition easier to hold, because the existence of these spillovers increases the price of land in areas where rich people like to live. Since rich people like to consume a lot of land, this further pushes them to live away from the central city, where land is cheap. This model can be complicated by endogenizing land area, and in some cases multiple equilibria can exist. Still, the basic intuition that location patterns of rich and poor can cause the relationship between prices and distance from the city to shift remains correct.

Job decentralization within the metropolitan area

In the previous sections, I assumed that everyone lives and works at the city center. While this assumption is in line with the traditional Alonso–Muth–Mills framework, it is increasingly empirically inappropriate for a world in which jobs are dispersed throughout the metropolitan area. In the overwhelming majority of metropolitan areas, more than three-quarters of employment is more than three miles from the city center (Glaeser and Kahn, 2001). Giuliano and Small (1991) is the seminal paper documenting the decentralization of population; Kain (1968) deserves significant credit for drawing early attention to this issue. Given the facts about decentralized employment, the urban model of a single employment center becomes increasingly obsolete. What use is a model based on the view that everyone commutes to the city center, if the majority of workers actually never come anywhere close to that center?

A number of different approaches have been suggested to capture the decentralization of employment. Fujita and Ogawa (1982) and Henderson and Mitra (1996) are the two most important papers that present models with multiple transportation modes. Lucas and Rossi-Hansberg (2002) present a particularly elegant general equilibrium of locational choice within a metropolitan area that fully endogenizes the location decisions of firms and workers, and allows for multiple employment locations.

The earlier models assume the existence of alternative employment centers that attract workers. These models include the decisions of both firms, which choose which employment center to use, and workers, who choose where to commute. For example, in the edge city model of Henderson and Mitra (1996), firms must be indifferent between locating in the city center or the edge city. The formation of the edge city is itself

Table 2.11. Alonso–Muth–Mills model adapted to studying job decentralization within the metropolitan area

Actors	City inhabitants who, unlike before, may not necessarily work in the city center
They maximize	$\max_{C,L} U(C, L) = \max_{d,L} U(W - \theta t(d) - (1 - \theta)\underline{t} - r(d)L, L)$ Example functional forms: $U(C, L) = C + \alpha \ln L$ $t(d) = td$
They choose	Agents choose distance from the city center (d) and size of land area (L) to maximize their utility.
First order conditions	$-\theta t'(d) = r'(d)L$ and $-r(d)U_1 + U_2 = 0$ For the example functional form: $r(d)L = \alpha$
Notation	$U(C, L)$:= an individual's utility function C := consumption = $W - \theta t(d) - (1 - \theta)\underline{t} - r(d)L$ L := units of land W := wage d := distance from city center $\underline{t}$:= cost of travel per unit distance for the fixed cost travel technology θ := percentage of the cost that an individual bears of commuting to the city center $1 - \theta$:= probability an individual bears transportation cost $\underline{t}$ that is unrelated to location (i.e. the percentage of workers who do not work in the city center)

an equilibrium phenomenon as developers decide whether to spend on the infrastructure needed for this edge to come about.

These models are too complex to be discussed here, so I will limit myself to a very simple twist on the basic Alonso–Muth–Mills model. The core equations of this model and the notation are given in Table 2.11. I assume that people only bear a percentage θ of the costs of commuting to the center. With probability $1 - \theta$ they bear transportation costs of $\underline{t}$ that are unrelated to location, which are perhaps equal to zero. This assumption can be thought of as representing the possibility that some percentage of work days workers just don't go into the city center. Alternatively, workers can be thought of as making location decisions before they learn whether they are going to work at home or in the city or to some other random location. Income in this case reflects their expected income depending on location choice.

This modeling assumption is best justified by simplicity and convenience, but there are empirical facts that support the use of this type of model as opposed to a model with a few discrete employment centers. To my eyes, the data on employment decentralization does not seem to suggest that people are reproducing employment centers that look like centralized cities. Chicago or Los Angeles are not characterized by three or four employment centers where the overwhelming majority of people work. Instead, employment is spread out in many different places. Given this spread, it may be better to think of people as either working downtown or working is some random location in the city outskirts.

Given the assumption that transport costs are paid only with some probability, and assuming the most basic assumption of homogeneous workers, the spatial equilibrium is now characterized by the two first order conditions:

$$\frac{d}{dd}U\,(W - \theta t(d) - (1-\theta)\underline{t} - r(d)L, L) = 0 \quad \text{and}$$

$$\frac{d}{dL}U\,(W - \theta t(d) - (1-\theta)\underline{t} - r(d)L, L) = 0.$$

The first condition gives us the new gradient $-\theta t'(d) = r'(d)L$, so as θ goes to zero the rent gradient flattens out. In the case where L is fixed, this result follows immediately.

When L is endogenous, then it is helpful to return to the logarithmic functional form, which gives us that $r(d)L = \alpha$ for all distances; also, assume that $t(d) = td$. In this case, the rent gradient satisfies

$$\log(r(d)) = \log(r(0)) - \frac{\theta t}{\alpha}d,$$

and more decentralization of employment causes the relationship between rents and distance to flatten. The relationship between density and distance flattens as well. This model predicts that in cities with more decentralized employment, distance will do a worse job of predicting price and density levels.

Figures 2.4–2.6, taken from Glaeser and Kahn (2001), look across American metropolitan areas at the impact of employment decentralization on urban structure. Using zip code data, we classify employment decentralization using a regression where employment density is regressed on distance from the city center. Places with steeper negative slopes are considered to be more centralized. Figure 2.4 shows that employment decentralization creates a weaker link between commute times and distance from the metropolitan area. Using census tract data, we regressed average commute time on distance from the city center to create our measure of the relationship between central locations and commute times. As Figure 2.4 shows, in places with more decentralized employment, commute times fall less steeply with distance from the metropolitan area.

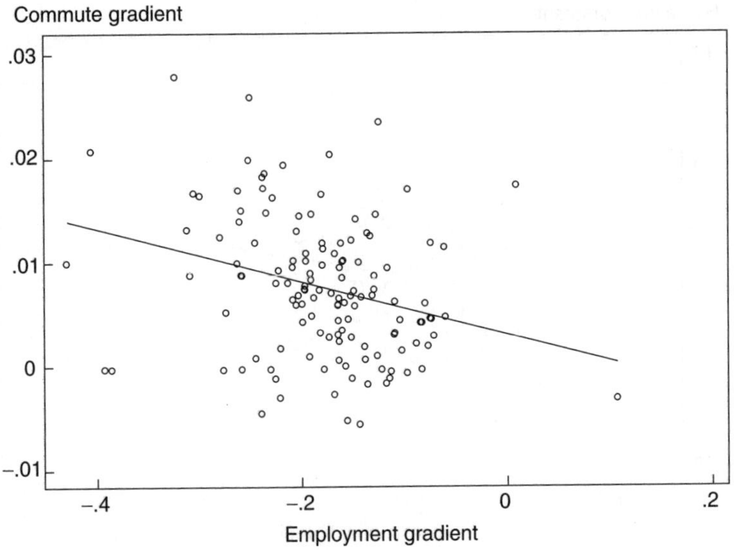

Figure 2.4. Cross-MSA employment and commute gradients

Since commute times fall less steeply with distance from the metropolitan area, the model predicts that prices should also fall less with distance from the metropolitan area. Figure 2.5 examines this relationship by comparing our employment decentralization measure with a measure of the relationship between home prices and distance to city center. This measure is formed by regressing the logarithm of home prices on distances to the city center. The figure shows that when employment is decentralized, prices decline less steadily with distance from the city center.

Figure 2.6 finally turns to population density. The model predicted that as employment gets more decentralized, population density will also be more weakly correlated with proximity to the city center. To capture the link between population density and proximity to the city center, we regressed the logarithm of population density on miles from the city center. The coefficient from this regression is then regressed across metropolitan areas on our employment decentralization measure. Just as the model predicts, places with decentralized employment also have decentralized population.

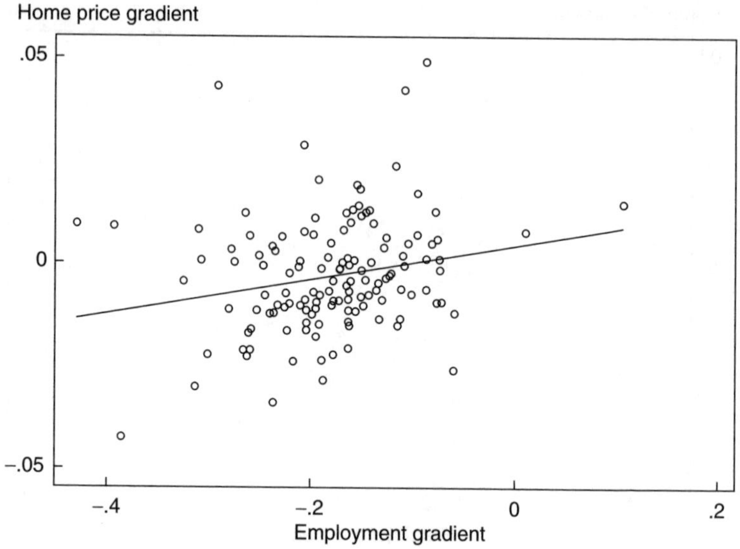

Figure 2.5. Cross-MSA employment and home price gradients

Using the model to understand urban history

The monocentric spatial equilibrium model seems beyond simple, but it is a powerful tool for making sense of urban structure and its changes over time. Anas, Arnott and Small (1998) provide a compelling overview of the history of urban form and use the monocentric model to make sense of it. The fundamental insight of the monocentric model is the important link between transportation technologies and urban prices and density. The earliest American cities were generally walking cities centered around a port. The port provided a natural city center and it made the city productive. People then clustered around the port, and prices fell rapidly with walking distance. When transport costs were particularly high, cities were small and dense.

In these early days, rich people appear to have lived close to the downtown. In Boston, the rich lived close to their wharves. In New York, the rich lived downtown even in the early Federalist period, and clustered particularly around the Bowling Green. When there was only one transport technology, the rich were willing to pay a premium to have a short commute. There were, of course, some wealthy urbanites

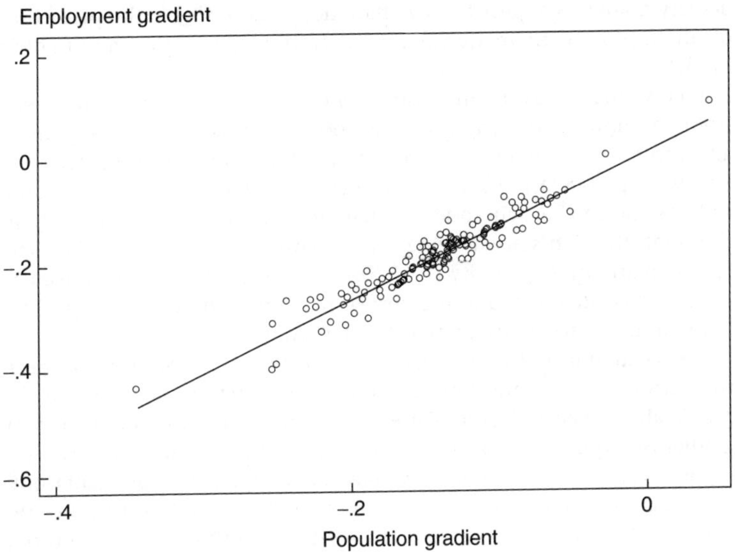

Figure 2.6. Cross-MSA employment and population gradients

with country residences, but if they worked regularly downtown, they also lived close to the downtown.

The century from 1820 to 1920 saw radical changes in commuting technology with the rise of the horse drawn omnibus, elevated trains, streetcars, subways and eventually buses with internal combustion engines. During this era, employment remained centralized, often around transportation infrastructure such as a port or a rail depot. The Chicago Stockyards, for example, were clustered next to the trains so that the slaughtered meat could be readily put into refrigerated rail yards. The city was still fundamentally monocentric, but now there were increasingly fast ways to get to the center.

All of the basic predictions of the model were vindicated over the nineteenth century. Cities expanded rapidly as better transportation technology made it easier to live further away and commute to the city center (Warner, 1962). While the data is limited, rent gradients appear to have flattened out. In some cases, the negative amenities associated with production (think of the stockyards), made living in downtown fairly cheap. Density levels increased everywhere, but the biggest increases in density were on the urban edge, not at the center, which implies that density gradients appear to have flattened. Again, this is the prediction of an improvement in transportation technology in the monocentric model.

Finally, there was an increasing tendency of the rich to live away from the downtown. The early transport technologies were expensive and represented the exchange of money for time. Unsurprisingly, the rich were particularly likely to use these early mechanisms of avoiding walking. Since the rich ended up having lower commuting costs than the poor, the rich started living further away from the city center. The paradigmatic American city of 1900 had poor laborers, who walked to work and clustered around the port or rail yards, and wealthier citizens, living in more luxurious quarters further away.

The great transportation change of the twentieth century has been the introduction of the internal combustion engine. The car had the predictable effects of further flattening the rent gradient and the density gradients. A quick comparison of Boston (a traditional city) and Las Vegas (a car city) shows how different car-based rent and density gradients look. Since cars were more affordable to the wealthy, the introduction of the automobile tended to exacerbate the tendency of the rich to live outside the city center.

The internal combustion engine was more than just another, faster commuting technology. The car is a point-to-point transit method while all of the older technologies were essentially hub-and-spoke, where people walked to a stop and then took the bus or train. The car made it possible to live at lower densities since it was unnecessary to walk to any bus stop or to walk to get groceries or perform any other function.

The second impact of the internal combustion engine was to break down the traditional monocentric city. These cities were generally built around a port or a rail yard but that transportation infrastructure became increasingly irrelevant over the twentieth century. Trucks don't require central stops and as a result, factories could be decentralized. The decentralization of employment has led to much flatter cities that look and feel completely different from the monocentric cities of the past. I now turn to applying the spatial equilibrium model across metropolitan areas.

3

The spatial equilibrium across cities

The previous chapter discussed models based on a spatial equilibrium within cities. In this chapter, I discuss models of spatial equilibrium across cities, or more properly, metropolitan areas. The spatial equilibrium approach to urban and regional economies hinges upon three distinct equilibrium conditions for residents, employers and builders. Together, these three equilibrium conditions form the basis for thinking about heterogeneity in prices, income levels and population densities across cities at a point in time and for thinking about how to interpret changes in prices, income levels and population densities.

The first equilibrium condition is the spatial equilibrium condition that occupies such a central place in urban and regional economics: individuals must be optimally choosing their location. When there are some people who are identical and when those people live in more than one area, this means that utility levels must be equal across space. Typically, I assume a single type of individual, and this then implies that utility levels must everywhere be equal across space. In the subsection on multiple skill levels, I examine a spatial equilibrium with two types of individuals. Even such a modest extension makes the algebra considerably more painful.

A primary difference between the within-city model and the across-city models is that while wages are generally thought to be constant within cities, wages certainly differ across metropolitan areas. The desire to endogenously determine wages means that the behavior of firms must also be modeled. While I am drawing a distinction between this cross-city equilibrium and the AMM model, Mills (1967) certainly models the endogenous determination of labor demand. I will even follow closely his choice of Cobb–Douglas production function.

The firm's optimization decision will be to choose the amounts of labor and capital to employ and to choose where to locate across space. Differences in productivity across space will play a major role in determining labor demand, but in this chapter I treat those differences as exogenous. Chapter 4 endogenizes those productivity differences and specifically focuses on why big cities may be more productive. If firms are identical and there is free entry within each city, then the optimizing behavior of firms can either be thought of as an employers' spatial equilibrium condition for firms, or perhaps more naturally, a non-spatial zero profit condition that must hold within each city.

The third equilibrium condition concerns behavior in the construction market: housing costs must be less than or equal to the price of new construction. If a city is growing, then prices must equal the cost of delivering new homes. If a city is in decline, then the price may be less than these costs. Again, this can be interpreted as a spatial equilibrium condition for developers, but it can also be seen as zero profit condition.

In this chapter, I will begin with a discussion of the static framework and its use in the work of Rosen (1979), Roback (1982) and Gyourko and Tracey (1991). While Mills (1967) and Henderson (1974) deserve major credit for developing the inter-city spatial equilibrium model, my own understanding of this topic was shaped primarily by the work of Sherwin Rosen. Indeed, Roback, Gyourko, Tracey and I are all his students, and all of our work on cities bears his unmistakable imprint. While Rosen is today remembered primarily for his striking contributions as a labor economist, his contributions to urban economics are just as significant.

After discussing the static spatial equilibrium model, I will then turn to a dynamic model and its use guiding urban growth papers such as Glaeser *et al.* (1992, 1995) and Glaeser and Shapiro (2002). The key empirical lesson of this model is that it is rarely enough to look at changes in area incomes. Researchers who come at sub-national data with instincts formed from nation-level empirical work often jump directly into running income growth regressions.

This tendency to focus overwhelmingly on local income levels is surely a mistake since migration within a country is so much freer than migration across national borders. When we are comparing two nations, and cross-national immigration is limited, then it is reasonable to interpret rising wages as reflecting increases in marginal productivity and labor demand. When we are comparing two cities or states, where intra-national migration is perfectly free, then we cannot so easily interpret those rising wages. In a reasonable model, rising local wages can reflect rising productivity, but it can just as easily reflect declining local amenities. This book takes the view that all empirical work by economists should ultimately be grounded in a somewhat plausible model, and for within-country empirical work, I consider the spatial equilibrium assumption to be a necessary ingredient in any plausible model that deals with cities.

In this dynamic section, I present a simple empirical framework that suggests that urban growth can come from rising productivity, rising amenities or rising housing supply. The application of this model to the rise of the Sunbelt suggests that warm places have generally grown because of rising productivity, especially in the immediate post-war decades, and rising housing supply, in the most recent decades. Rising amenities had little to do with the growth of places like Houston, Atlanta and Phoenix.

The third subsection of this chapter drops the assumption of one group of homogeneous people and considers the introduction of high and low skilled workers. Rauch (1993) documented that, holding individual skill levels constant, wages are higher in cities with more skilled workers. There has been a cottage industry following him estimating such human capital spillovers (e.g. Moretti, 2004). I tend to think that before we regress wages on the share of the city that is skilled, it makes sense to at least think about a spatial equilibrium model that can explain the distribution of skilled workers across space. Such a model is also needed to make sense of the correlation between city growth rates and the initial share of skilled people in the city (Glaeser and Saiz, 2004).

The fourth subsection of the model allows for durable housing. The developer's problem becomes considerably more complicated in this case, because the construction decisions essentially become a real option problem. The approach in this book follows Glaeser and Gyourko (2005), which is a paper about durable housing and urban decline. Our model creates predictions about how prices and quantities can respond differentially to shocks in those cities that have been in decline. There are many earlier models of durable housing that tended to focus on durability in growing cities, which are reviewed ably by Brueckner (2000). Muth (1969) himself has an excellent discussion of the durability of the housing stock.

The final subsection sketches the model from Glaeser and Gyourko (2006) which illustrates how an expanded Rosen–Roback approach can be used to think about high frequency changes in housing prices and new construction.

The static model and the Rosen–Roback framework

In the previous chapter, the spatial equilibrium required consumers to be indifferent between living close to the city center and far away. In the cross-city context, the spatial equilibrium assumption requires consumers to be indifferent between living in a city and living anywhere else. Generally, urban economists assume that there exists a reservation locale that delivers a fixed level of utility to all consumers.

To make things simple, inter-urban models tend to ignore intra-urban considerations like distance to the central business district. Instead, it is fairly standard to assume that all housing is equivalent within a

Table 3.1. Basic Rosen–Roback framework

Actors	Consumers of housing
They maximize	max{U(Wage − Housing Costs, Amenities)}
They choose	Consumers choose location to maximize utility
First order condition	$\frac{\partial(\text{Wages} - \text{Housing Costs})}{\partial \text{ Amenity}} = \frac{U_{Amenity}}{U_{Cash}}$
Notation	None

metropolitan area and to ignore commuting costs altogether. Indeed, to illustrate the basic principles of the model, I will go further and initially assume that people consume a fixed amount of housing in all metropolitan areas. The core equations of this model and the notation are given in Table 3.1.

If utility depends only on net income and amenities, where net income is Wage − Housing Costs, then U(Wage − Housing Costs, Amenities) must be constant across space. Even more simply, if amenities are monetized, so that they can just be thought of as a dollar valued income flow, then the condition is just that Wages − Housing Costs + Amenity Flows are constant. These amenity flows presumably also include commute times.

Even this simple assumption has empirical bite. It is quite common in discussions of housing affordability to focus on the share of income being spent on housing, as if this is a natural measure of the degree to which housing affordability is a problem within an area. The spatial equilibrium assumption suggests that this measure is not particularly meaningful or helpful. Consider two metropolitan areas, both of which have identical amenities, and one of which has annual wages of $40,000 per year. The other area has annual wages of $60,000 per year. If annual housing costs in the first area are $10,000, then the spatial equilibrium assumption requires housing costs in the second area to be $30,000. A spatial equilibrium can only be maintained if high housing costs offset high incomes, so that people are taking home $30,000 (after paying for housing) in both areas.

In the first low income area, housing costs are 25 percent of income. Generally, this would be seen as a reasonable number suggesting no problem with affordability. In the second, high income area, housing costs are 50 percent of income, which would generally be taken to suggest a huge affordability problem. Yet income after housing costs is the same in both areas, and the high housing costs in the second area are just offsetting higher income levels. The standard affordability measure is quite misleading and will tend to suggest affordability problems in all high income areas, even if high prices in those areas are the only way to maintain a spatial equilibrium. A more sensible approach would be to consider income net of housing costs, not housing costs as a share of income.

This framework with no other adjustments is used by Rosen (1979) and Roback (1982) to create a framework for assessing the extent to which consumers value or dislike certain amenities. Differentiating the utility function with respect to an amenity yields:

$$\frac{\partial(\text{Wages} - \text{Housing Costs})}{\partial \text{Amenity}} = -\frac{U_{\text{Amenity}}}{U_{\text{Cash}}}$$

(note that Cash = Wages – Housing Costs). The extent to which wages minus housing costs rises with an amenity is a measure of the extent to which that amenity decreases utility, divided by the marginal utility of income. If an amenity is associated with less income, after paying for housing, then that amenity seems to be providing some form of positive utility flow that compensates for this lower level of income.

A slightly more general formulation, shown in Roback (1982), postulates an indirect utility function V(Income, Housing Price, Amenity). Differentiating this equation then yields:

$$\frac{\partial V}{\partial \text{Income}} \frac{\partial \text{Income}}{\partial \text{Amenity}} + \frac{\partial V}{\partial \text{Housing Price}} \frac{\partial \text{Housing Price}}{\partial \text{Amenity}} + \frac{\partial V}{\partial \text{Amenity}} = 0.$$

Roy's lemma then yields:

$$\text{Housing Consumption} \times \frac{\partial \text{Housing Price}}{\partial \text{Amenity}} - \frac{\partial \text{Income}}{\partial \text{Amenity}} = \frac{\partial V / \partial \text{Amenity}}{\partial V / \partial \text{Income}}. \tag{3.1}$$

This equation again yields the implication that the value of an amenity equals the impact on housing prices minus the impact on income.

This equation was an advance over earlier housing price hedonics like Ridker and Henning (1967), because it recognized that income as well as housing prices change across metropolitan areas. While within-metropolitan area housing price hedonics can, perhaps, ignore different access to labor markets, across-metropolitan area work cannot make that assumption. Roback (1982) used this framework to figure out people's willingness to pay to avoid a variety of disamenities such as crime, particulates and snow. Gyourko and Tracy (1991) expanded this list of amenities to include a wide range of government-related local characteristics.

While the intuition of the Rosen–Roback model does not require specific functional forms, empirical work almost always turns to particular utility functions. I will now present a fairly standard set of assumptions

Table 3.2. General formulation of the Rosen–Roback model: Housing consumption

Actors	Consumers of housing
They maximize	$\max_{C,H} U(C,H) = \max_{C,H}\{\theta C^{1-\alpha}H^{\alpha}\} = \max_{H}\{\theta(W - r_H H)^{1-\alpha}H^{\alpha}\}$
They choose	Consumers choose housing to maximize utility
First order condition	$\frac{-r_H(1-\alpha)}{W - r_H H} + \frac{\alpha}{H} = 0$
Notation	C := tradable goods (priced at 1) consumed by consumer H := nontradable housing θ := index capturing amenities r_H := rental cost of housing W := income

which then produce a set of estimable equations. Consumers have Cobb–Douglas utility functions defined over tradable goods, denoted C and sold at a fixed price of one, and a non-traded housing, denoted H, and amenities, captured with an index θ. The index, θ, is meant to include the wide range of variables discussed by Roback (1982) and Gyourko and Tracy (1991). Today's utility is then $\theta C^{1-\alpha}H^{\alpha}$, where H is housing consumption and C is the consumption of all other goods. The core equations of this model and the notation are given in Table 3.2.

Optimizing behavior yields the indirect utility function $\alpha^{\alpha}(1-\alpha)^{1-\alpha}\theta W r_H^{-\alpha}$, where r_H is the rental cost of housing. This is also the indirect utility function associated with this utility function. For a spatial equilibrium to hold, this quantity must equal a reservation utility level denoted $\underline{U}$. Differentiating this equation with respect to A (where A is any exogenous variable) yields a variation on equation (3.1):

$$\frac{\partial \log(\theta)}{\partial \log(A)} = \alpha \frac{\partial \log(r_H)}{\partial \log(A)} - \frac{\partial \log(W)}{\partial \log(A)}. \qquad (3.1')$$

This suggests that multiplying the share of housing in consumption (about 30 percent) by the impact of an amenity of housing prices, and subtracting the impact of the amenity on wages will give the overall impact of the amenity on utility.

To close the model, I turn to the production and construction sectors. The core equations of the production sector model and the notation are given in Table 3.3, and the core equations of the construction sector model and the notation are given in Table 3.4. To include the production sector (or labor demand), I assume that every location in the US is characterized by a location-specific productivity level of A and firm output equals $AN^{\beta}K^{\gamma}Z^{1-\beta-\gamma}$, where A represents a city-specific productivity level, N represents the number of workers, K is traded capital, and Z is

Table 3.3. General formulation of the Rosen–Roback model (cont'd): The production sector

Actors	Firms in the production sector
They maximize	$\max_{N,K} \left\{ AN^{\beta} K^{\gamma} \bar{Z}^{1-\beta-\gamma} - WN - K \right\}$
They choose	Producers choose the number of workers and traded capital that would maximize profit
First order condition	FOC for labor: $\beta AN^{\beta-1} K^{\gamma} \bar{Z}^{1-\beta-\gamma} = W$ FOC for capital: $\gamma AN^{\beta} K^{\gamma-1} \bar{Z}^{(1-\beta-\gamma)/(1-\gamma)} = 1$
Notation	A := city specific production level N := number of workers in the city K := traded capital (priced at 1) Z := non-traded capital $\bar{Z}$:= fixed supply of non-traded capital

non-traded capital. Traded capital can be purchased anywhere for a price of one. The location has a fixed supply of non-traded capital equal to $\bar{Z}$. This formulation is a close descendant of Mills (1967).

This fixed capital allows there to be constant returns to scale at the level of each firm, but decreasing returns to scale at the level of city. This combination is necessary to create both a zero profit condition for firms and to ensure that the city will have a finite number of firms, even if housing supply was perfectly elastic. These decreasing returns are needed if the model is going to predict a city of finite size. In principle, I could drop the assumption of decreasing returns in production if I had either decreasing returns in the production of housing or congestion in

Table 3.4. General formulation of the Rosen–Roback model (cont'd): The construction sector

Actors	Firms in the construction sector
They maximize	$\max_{h,L}\{p_H hL - c_0 h^{\delta} L - p_L L\}$
They choose	Construction firms choose housing and land to maximize profits.
First order condition	FOC for height: $p_H = \delta c_0 h^{\delta-1}$
Key equilibrium condition	Zero profit condition: $p_H h = c_0 h^{\delta} + p_L$ (mathematically equivalent to the FOC for land)
Notation	h := height L := land hL := total housing supplied $\bar{L}$:= fixed quantity of land p_L := endogenous price for land p_H := endogenous price for height $c_0 h^{\delta} L$:= cost of producing hL units on top of L units of land

amenities. In this setting, the owners of the fixed capital are in a sense the residual claimants for the city, and the returns to this capital are one measure of the city's success. Firms behave competitively, so that their first order condition for capital delivers a labor demand curve: $\beta A^{1/(1-\gamma)}\gamma^{\gamma/(1-\gamma)} N^{(\beta+\gamma-1)/(1-\gamma)} \bar{Z}^{(1-\beta-\gamma)/(1-\gamma)} = W$.

Housing is produced competitively with height, denoted h, and land, denoted L. The total quantity of housing supplied equals hL. There is a fixed quantity of land in the location, which is denoted $\bar{L}$; this will in turn determine an endogenous price for land, denoted p_L, and housing, denoted p_H. The quantity of land can either be the actual measured quantity of land in an area, or the amount of land that is available to be developed, which is itself determined by land use regulations that I will discuss later.

The cost of producing hL units of structure on top of L units of land is $c_0 h^\delta L$. Given these assumptions, the profit to a developer of producing hL units of housing is $p_H hL - c_0 h^\delta L - p_L L$, where $\delta > 1$. The first order condition for height, $p_H = \delta c_0 h^{\delta-1}$, implies a total housing supply equation of $h\underline{L} = (p_H/\delta c_0)^{1/(\delta-1)}\, \underline{L}$. Free entry of developers implies that $p_H h = c_0 h^\delta + p_L$, which delivers housing prices as a function of population and income:

$$p_H = \delta^{1/\delta} c_0^{1/\delta} \left(\frac{\alpha N W}{\bar{L}}\right)^{(\delta-1)/\delta}.$$

What is the connection between this price of housing and the rental cost of housing paid by consumers? The usual approach is just to assume that r_H is a multiple of p_H. I denote this multiple μ. This multiplier reflects both the capital costs of borrowing money and the tax and maintenance costs associated with the housing. A reasonable value for μ might be .1.

Together the firms' labor demand equation, the equality between indirect utility in the town and reservation utility, and the housing price equation, are three equations with three unknowns (population, income and housing prices). Solving these equations for the unknowns gives us:

$$\log(N) = K_N + \frac{(\delta + \alpha - \alpha\delta)\log(A) + (1-\gamma)\left(\delta\log(\theta) + \alpha(\delta-1)\log(\bar{L})\right)}{\delta(1-\beta-\gamma) + \alpha\beta(\delta-1)} \tag{3.2}$$

$$\log(W) = K_W + \frac{(\delta-1)\,\alpha\log(A) - (1-\beta-\gamma)\left(\delta\log(\theta) + \alpha(\delta-1)\log(\bar{L})\right)}{\delta(1-\beta-\gamma) + \alpha\beta(\delta-1)} \tag{3.3}$$

and

$$\log(p_H) = K_P + \frac{(\delta-1)\left(\log(A) + \beta\log(\theta) - (1-\beta-\gamma)\log(\bar{L})\right)}{\delta(1-\beta-\gamma) + \alpha\beta(\delta-1)} \tag{3.4}$$

where K_N, K_W and K_P are constant terms that include parameters other than A, θ, and $\bar{L}$.

These equations then deliver the relationship between productivity, consumer amenities and housing supply and population, wages and housing prices. In many cases, density rather than overall population might be a more natural variable of interest. After all, counties and cities have amounts of land that are determined by forces outside of this model. In those cases, people per acre might be a more natural outcome to consider. If $L = \bar{L}$, then equation (3.2) can be rewritten as:

$$\log\left(\frac{N}{\bar{L}}\right) = K_N + \frac{(\alpha+\delta-\alpha\delta)(\log(A) - (1-\beta-\gamma)\log(\bar{L})) + (1-\gamma)\delta\log(\theta)}{\delta(1-\beta-\gamma)+\alpha\beta(\delta-1)}. \tag{3.2′}$$

Density is rising in amenities and productivity and declining in land area.

As an example of how this framework can be used, I now turn to the predictions of the model about the relationship between an exogenous variable, perhaps median January temperature, and prices, wages and density. I begin by assuming that for this variable, denoted X, $\log(A) = K_A + \lambda_A X + \mu_A$, $\log(\theta) = K_\theta + \lambda_\theta X + \mu_\theta$ and $\log(\bar{L}) = K_L + \lambda_L X + \mu_L$, where K_A, K_θ and K_L are constants, λ_A, λ_θ and λ_L are coefficients, μ_A, μ_θ and μ_L are error terms. In principle, the exogenous variable can increase productivity or amenities or the amount of land that is available for construction. Equations (3.2)–(3.4) then imply:

$$\log(N) = \kappa_N + \frac{(\alpha+\delta-\alpha\delta)\,\lambda_A + (1-\gamma)\,(\delta\lambda_\theta + \alpha(\delta-1)\lambda_L)}{\delta(1-\beta-\gamma)+\alpha\beta\,(\delta-1)} X + \mu_N, \tag{3.5}$$

$$\log(W) = \kappa_W + \frac{(\delta-1)\,\alpha\lambda_A - (1-\beta-\gamma)\,(\delta\lambda_\theta + \alpha(\delta-1)\lambda_L)}{\delta(1-\beta-\gamma)+\alpha\beta\,(\delta-1)} X + \mu_W, \tag{3.6}$$

and

$$\log(p_H) = \kappa_P + \frac{(\delta-1)\,(\lambda_A + \beta\lambda_\theta - (1-\beta-\gamma)\lambda_L)}{\delta(1-\beta-\gamma)+\alpha\beta\,(\delta-1)} X + \mu_p \tag{3.7}$$

where the κ_i terms are essentially constant terms that are independent of X and the μ_i terms are essentially error terms that are independent of X.

By estimating regressions where some X variable is connected with prices, density and income, we can provide estimates of λ_A, λ_θ and λ_L given values α, β, γ and δ. Specifically, if $\hat{B}_N$, $\hat{B}_W$ and $\hat{B}_P$ represented the estimated coefficients on an X variable for the population, wage and price change regressions, then

$$\lambda_A = ((1-\beta-\gamma)\hat{B}_N + (1-\gamma)\hat{B}_W), \qquad \lambda_\theta = \alpha\hat{B}_P - \hat{B}_W \quad \text{and}$$

$$\lambda_L = \hat{B}_N + \hat{B}_W - \frac{\delta\hat{B}_P}{\delta-1}.$$

To illustrate the approach, I can estimate the impact of January temperature on amenities, productivity and land availability using these equations and estimates of α, β, γ and δ. Using Census data, I estimate the relationship between January temperature and income, housing prices and population. Figure 3.1 shows the relationship between the logarithm of income in the metropolitan area and January temperature. The estimated coefficient is $-.0048$ with a standard error of .0007. For the logarithm of self-reported housing values, the estimated coefficient is $-.0008$ with a standard error of .0016. In the case of population, the estimated coefficient is .012 with a standard error of .004.

Using an estimate of .3 for α, which roughly corresponds to the share spent on housing in the consumer expenditure survey, these estimates suggest that λ_θ equals .0045, or a 10 degree increase in January temperature is worth the same as a .045 log point increase in income. People do seem to be paying for warmer winters, but they are paying in the form of lower wages rather than higher prices.

If I take .6 as an estimate of β (labor's share of inputs) and .3 as an estimate of γ (the share of inputs do to mobile capital), then the estimate value of λ_A is $-.0021$. Warm Januarys actually appear to be depressing productivity. Surely, this result does not reflect the causal impact of warm Januarys, which are unlikely to depress productivity. A more natural explanation is that omitted correlates of productivity are negatively correlated with warmth, quite possibly because it only makes sense to have a city in a cold place if that city has something else going for it.

The estimate of λ_L depends on δ, which is a parameter that reflects the elasticity of housing supply. The literature has not delivered tight estimates of δ, but if the parameter is greater than 1.5 (which seems like a reasonably low bound), the predicted value of λ_L lies between .0084 and .0096. Warmer Januarys are associated with more housing supply. One explanation for this is that places with warmer Januarys have a more permissive attitude towards new construction.

I will return to the impact of warmth later in this chapter after I have adapted the framework to look at urban dynamics. At this point, I do not mean these estimates to be taken particularly seriously, but rather as an illustration of how these equations can help us to think about the links between exogenous variables and the causes of urban wages, housing prices and population. The key is to recognize that there are a set of markets all of which interact and it is impossible to look at wages or prices or population alone.

One fact that seems to support the relevance of the spatial equilibrium approach is the tight correlation between area prices and area incomes. Figure 3.2 shows the correlation between median income and median housing values across the hundred largest metropolitan areas in the US

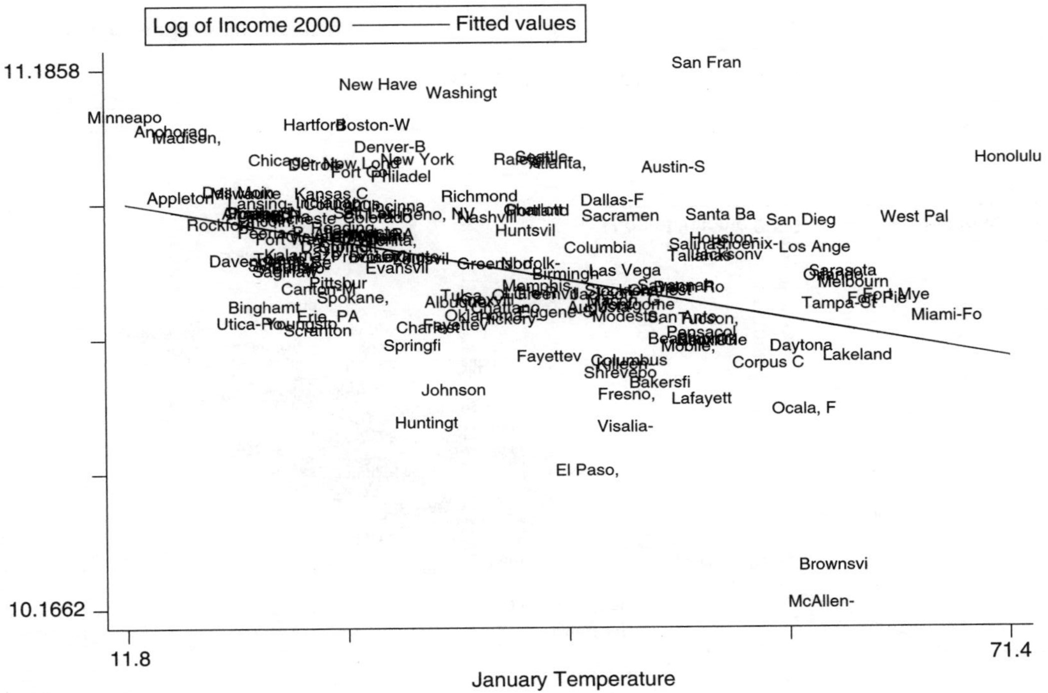

Figure 3.1. Income and January temperature by MSA

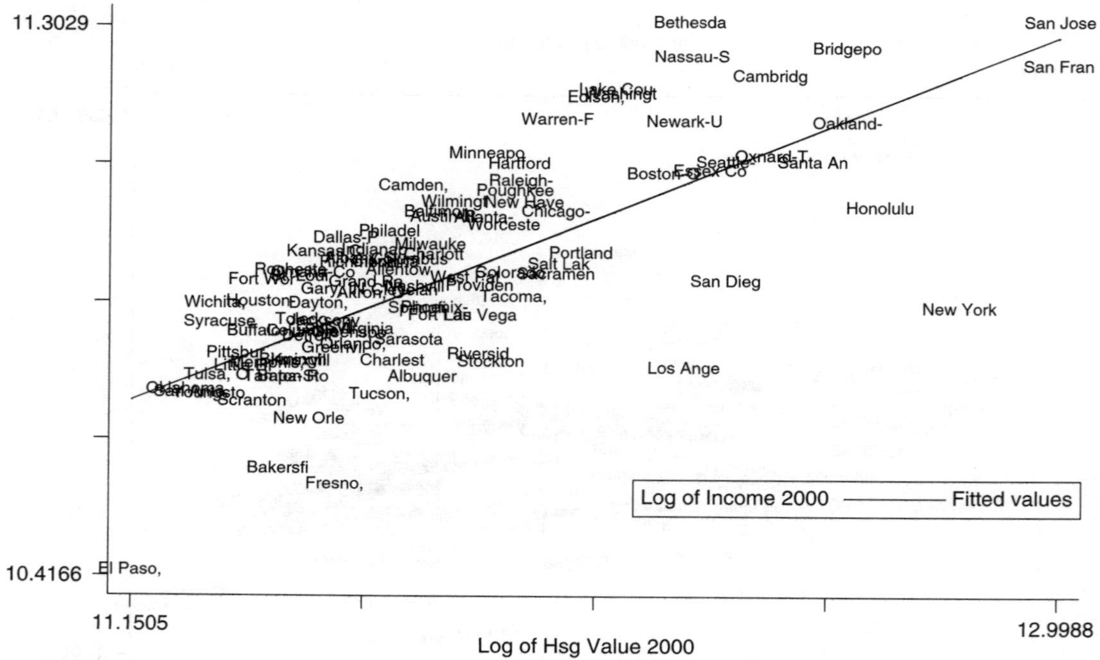

Figure 3.2. Income and housing value by MSA

in 2000. There is no sense in which one of these variables is causing the other. The model treats both as endogenous. Still, the link is interesting. The relationship shown in the graph is

$$\log(\text{Income}) = 7.2 + .32 \times \log(\text{Median Housing Value}). \quad (3.8)$$

The r-squared is 54 percent and the standard error on the housing price coefficient is .029. The tight relationship appears to support the spatial equilibrium assumption that high prices are offsetting high wages. The indirect utility function $\alpha^{\alpha}(1-\alpha)^{1-\alpha}\theta W p_H^{-\alpha}$ predicts if utilities are equalized across space, the derivative of log prices with respect to log income should be α, the share of income spent on housing. The current expenditure survey tells us that the average family spends 30 percent of its income on housing, suggesting that the coefficient in the regression should be about .3 which is about right. As such, the Cobb–Douglas formulation of this model looks reasonably good.

In a linear model where Income–Housing Costs + Amenities needs to be constant across space, we might expect a linear relationship of income on housing costs to yield a coefficient of one. If we thought that user costs were about 10 percent of housing prices, then the coefficient in an income price relationship should be about .1. Using the same 100 metropolitan areas, I estimate a coefficient of .092, which seems quite compatible with the view that income and housing values go together in the way suggested by the model.

If we invert the regressions, however, the results are far less impressive. When price is regressed on income for the same metropolitan areas, the coefficient is 5.2 rather than 10, which is far lower than the prediction of the model. The inverse coefficient from the logarithmic regression is 1.7, not three. Incomes seem to rise enough when prices rise, but prices don't rise enough when incomes rise. One explanation for this discrepancy is that there is more noise in the income variable than in the price variable. This noise might come from the fact that we are not controlling for human capital, or it might come from the fact that income at a point in time may be a noisy measure of the long term income prospects associated with a particular locale. This could explain the low coefficient when prices are regressed on incomes, because people don't expect high or low incomes in a place to last.

A second test of the model is that high amenities should be associated with lower real incomes since high real incomes are needed to offset low amenities in unattractive places. To test this hypothesis, we use the American Chamber of Commerce local price indices, which are supposed to correct for differences in purchasing power across cities. Most of the differences across areas in these price indices are the result of housing prices. We then divide incomes by these local prices indices and regress this real income number on one natural measure of amenities, median January temperature.

Figure 3.3 shows the relationship between real income and median January temperature across metropolitan areas. The relationship is negative, as the model suggests, and the regression fit in the line has a 22 percent r-squared and a slope of $-.0055$. This slope implies that as January temperature increases by 10 degrees, real incomes fall by approximately 1000 dollars. This can be interpreted as meaning that people are willing to pay 100 dollars for each extra degree of temperature during January.

Of course, it doesn't pay to take these results too literally. Obviously, there is heterogeneity across individuals and some people like cold weather. These real income differences can only tell us the willingness of the person on the margin of living in different cities to pay for added warmth. A second caveat is that since we are not controlling for human capital, we might expect the relationship to be understated if high human capital people tend to live in high amenity places.

The spatial equilibrium model can tell us about agglomeration economies: the extent that productivity rises with city size. Figure 3.4 shows the relationship between city size and income (not corrected for local prices) in 2000. This relationship is enormously positive, which, according to the spatial equilibrium framework, must mean that bigger cities are more productive. This positive relationship is also true when changes in income are regressed on changes in population as shown in Figure 3.5. This figure looks at 30 year changes in log of population and log of income and shows a positive effect. This city size–productivity relationship could in principle reflect reverse causality where more productive places get bigger, but most writers (e.g. Ciccone and Hall, 1996) interpret this relationship to be evidence that big cities become more productive. I will return to these issues in the next chapter.

However, the fact that nominal incomes increase with city size does not mean that real incomes do. Figure 3.6 looks at the relationship between real income, again calculated using the ACCRA price indices, and city size in 2000. The relationship is weak and slightly negative. Higher prices have more than offset higher wages. Figure 3.7 shows the same relationship in 1970, which was positive. The natural spatial equilibrium interpretation of this is that amenities were lower in big cities in 1970 than in smaller places. The comparison of Figures 3.6 and 3.7 can be interpreted to mean that 30 years ago cities were relatively unattractive places to live but today, big cities have positive amenities (Glaeser and Gottlieb, 2006).

The declining connection between real wages and city size is one example of the "Consumer City" phenomenon discussed by Glaeser, Kolko and Saiz (2001). That paper really has two themes. The main theme is that an increasingly footloose population, untied to older production amenities

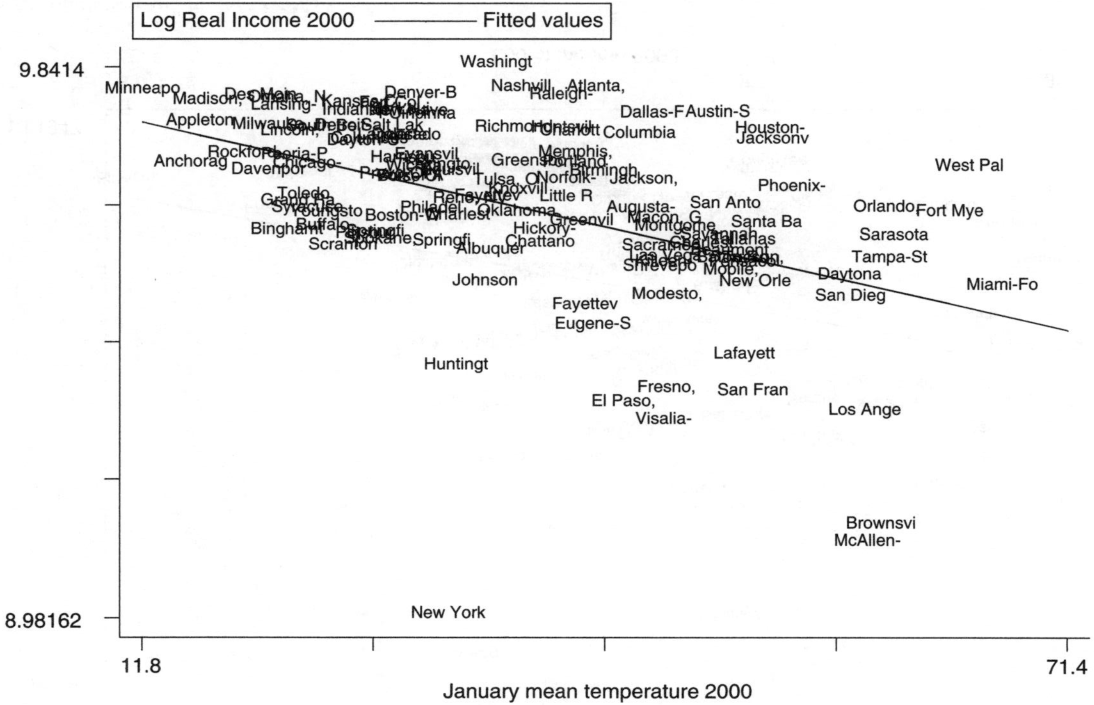

Figure 3.3. Real income and January temperature by MSA

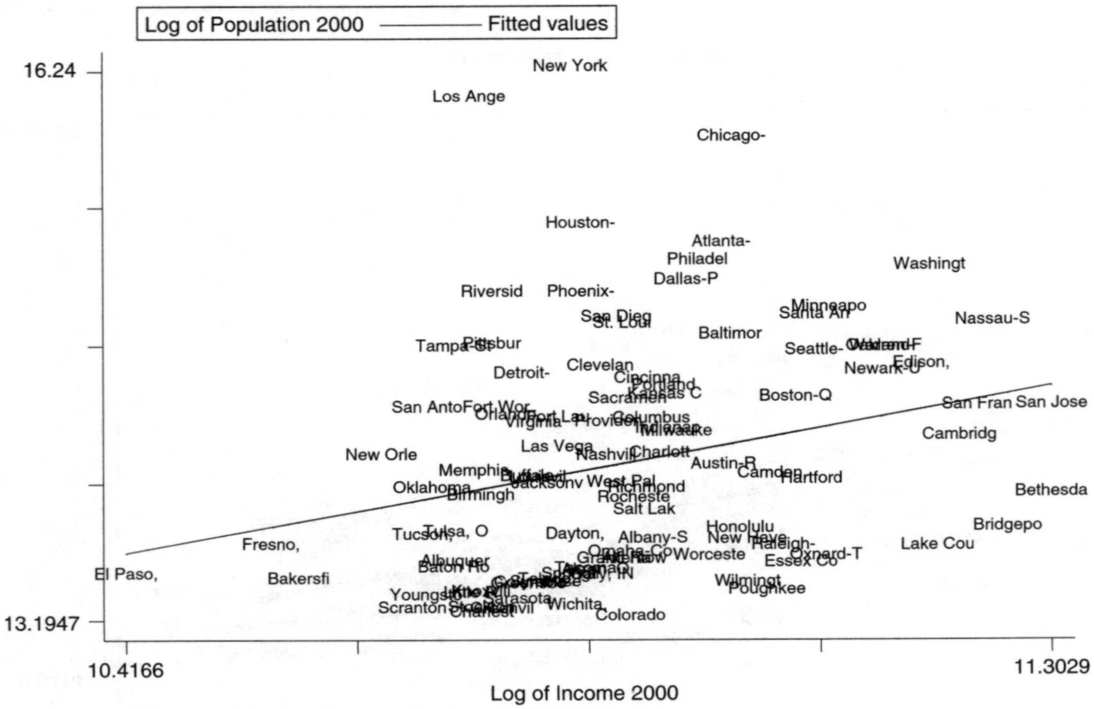

Figure 3.4. Population and income by MSA

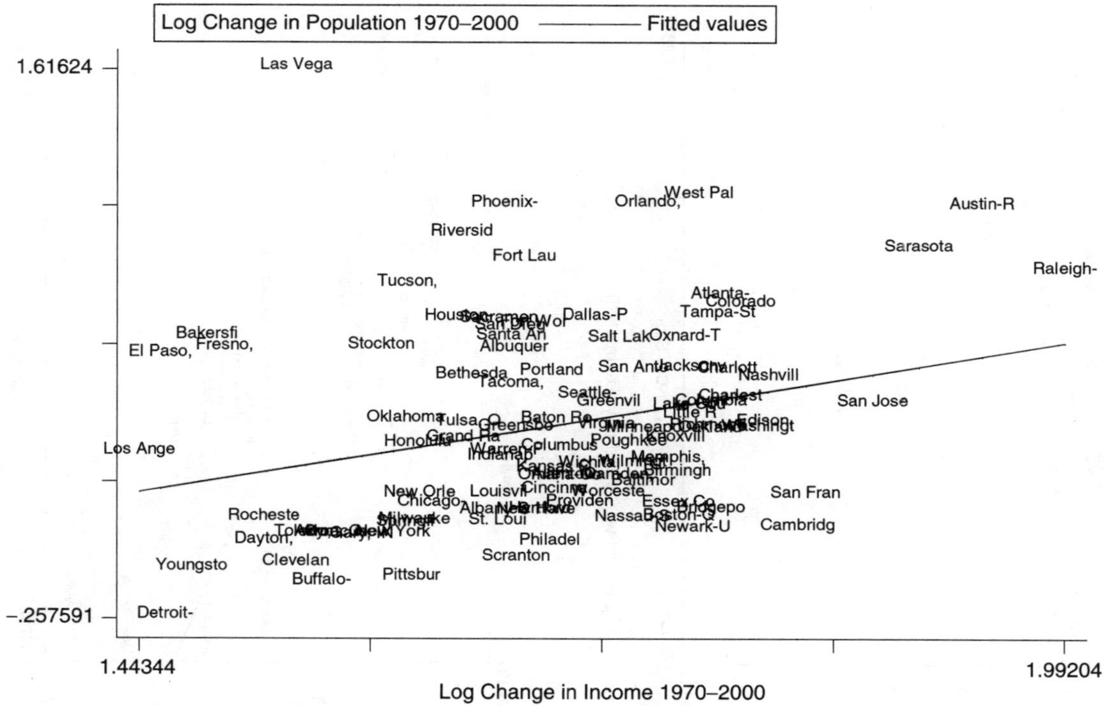

Figure 3.5. Change in population and income from 1970–2000 by MSA

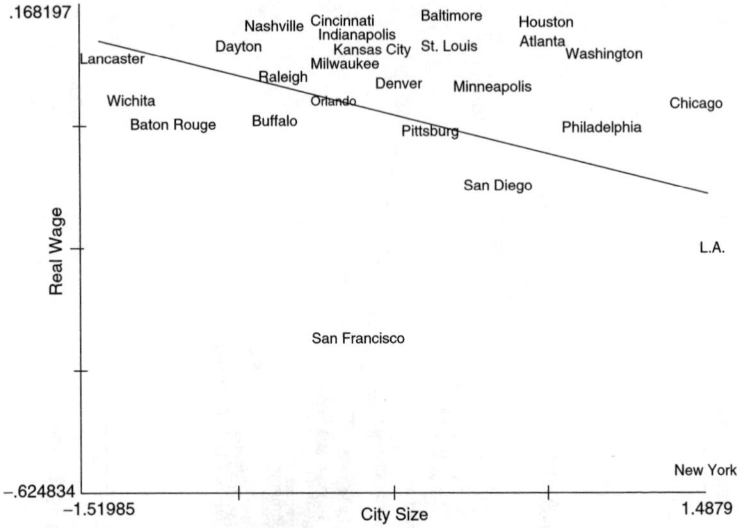

Figure 3.6. Log of real wages and city size in 1970

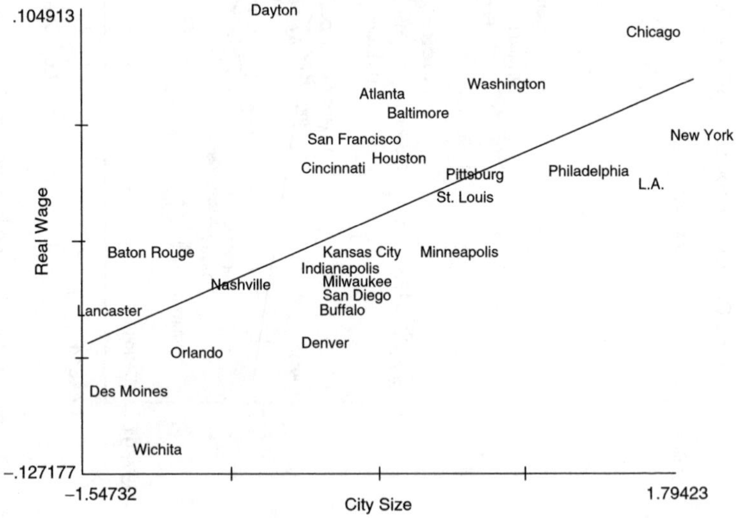

Figure 3.7. Log of real wages and city size in 2000

like rivers and coal mines, has moved towards high amenity areas. A secondary theme is that some older cities have managed to succeed in recent decades as centers of consumption, as well as centers of production.

The secondary theme is illustrated by the changes between 1970 and 2000 shown in Figures 3.6 and 3.7. That change suggests that bigger cities have had increases in amenity levels relative to smaller metropolitan areas. The perverse logic of the spatial equilibrium means that declining relative real wages are interpreted not as declines in productivity or well-being, but rather as rises in consumer amenities. This interpretation is buttressed by the fact that these cities have had very large increases in nominal wages, uncorrected for local prices of living, but that housing costs have gone up even more.

A second piece of evidence supporting the view that many older cities have become more attractive as places to live is the rise in reverse commuting. Thirty years ago, few people would have found downtown areas so attractive that they would live there and then commute to the suburbs. Today, such traffic patterns are common.

The more central theme of the paper is that declining transportation costs and rising incomes have made people increasingly willing and able to move towards high amenity places. The primary piece of evidence supporting this view is a regression where population change is regressed on housing prices that have been corrected for wages. The spatial equilibrium approach underpins this regression.

If housing supply differences are not important (which is a doozy of an assumption) and if the univariate regression of log prices on log income essentially correctly estimates the parameter $1/\alpha$, then the residual when log price is regressed on log incomes will equal a constant term plus $\log(\theta)/u$. This residual can then be used as a measure of consumer amenities. The reason for using this approach instead of using wages corrected for local prices is that the ACCRA figures are only available for a small number of areas historically.

If the change in the logarithm of population between 1980 and 2000 is regressed on this housing price residual, based on 1980 data, then there is a strong positive relationship, as shown in Figure 3.8. Places that had unusually high prices, relative to income, presumably because of high amenities, have been much more likely to grow. Much of this connection just reflects the strong correlation between climate and growth. Figure 3.9 shows the similar connection between median January temperature and growth with the same set of metropolitan areas over the same time period.

I do believe that this basic story is correct and that high amenity places have done well. Glaeser, Kolko and Saiz (2001) document similar correlations outside the US using different measures of amenities, such

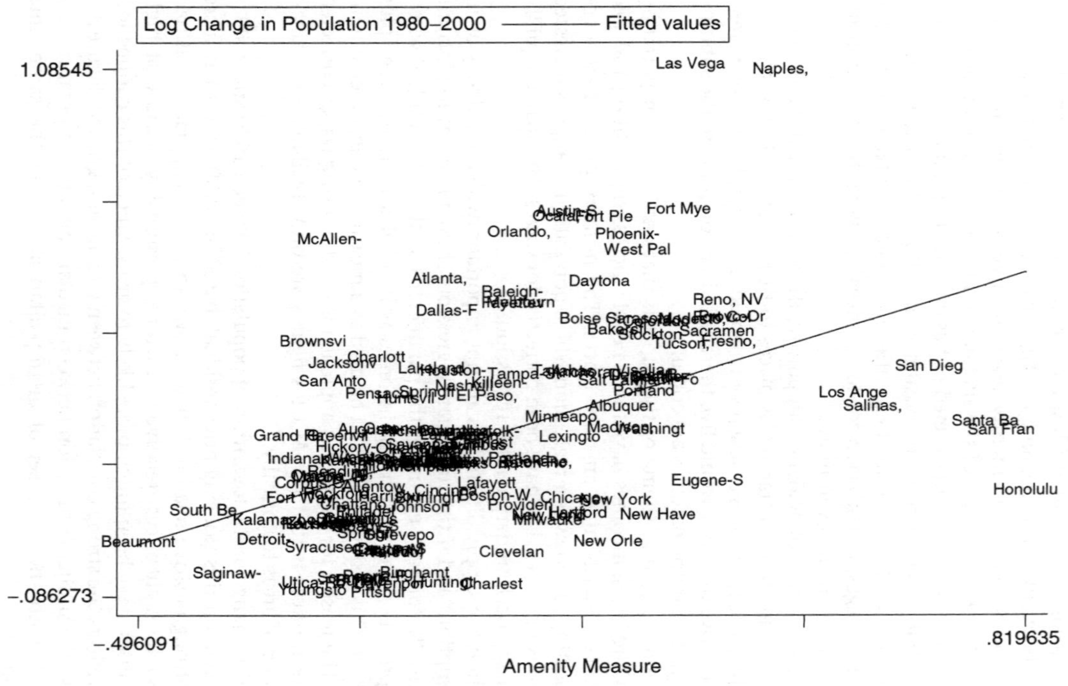

Figure 3.8. Change in population and initial amenities from 1980–2000 by MSA

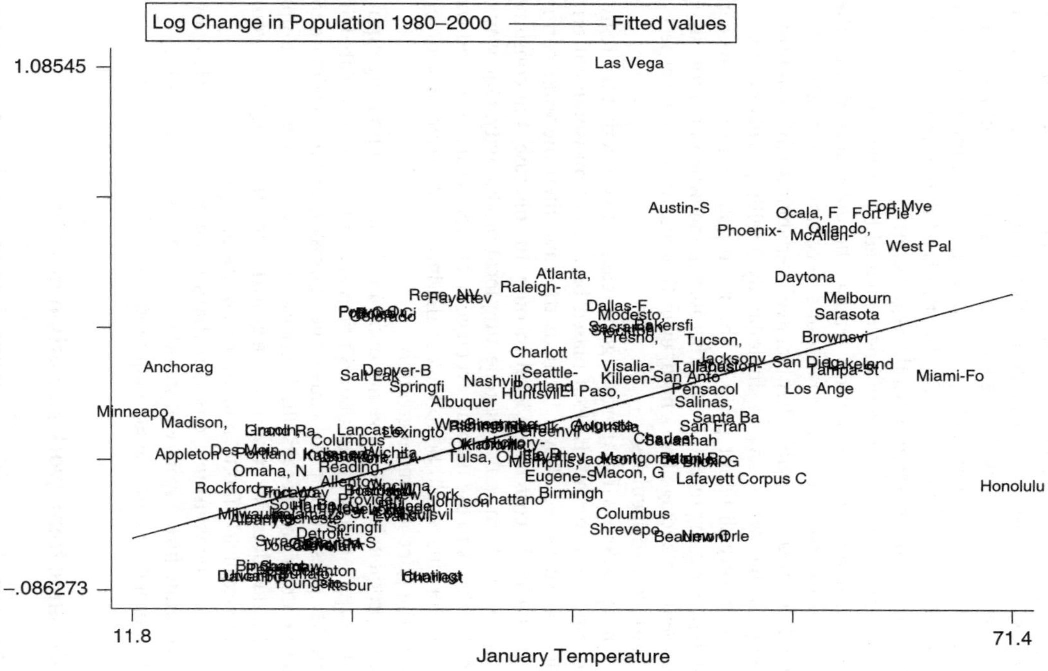

Figure 3.9. Change in population and January temperature from 1980–2000 by MSA

as restaurant availability. However, there are also reasons to be skeptical of the regression shown in Figure 3.8. One reason, which I think is less important, is that prices are themselves forward looking and high prices in 1980 might reflect the expectations of future growth. As a result, we should expect to see a positive correlation between this variable and future growth that works through expectations, not amenities. In fact, prices in 1980 did an extremely poor job projecting future price growth between 1980 and 1990, so I doubt that this is all that important. Still, it remains one of the problems with the regression.

In principle, this problem could be remedied by using rents. The big problem with rents is that renters tend to be quite special and they live in housing stock that is often quite very unrepresentative of the metropolitan area as a whole. Renters live overwhelmingly in multi-unit dwellings, while owners live in single-family dwellings. This means that they live in very different parts of the metropolitan area on average. I tend to prefer using prices to rents, because homeowners are more likely to represent the average household, even though the dynamic aspect of prices can create difficulties.

A second problem is that there are good reasons to think that the regression of prices on income is itself biased because of measurement error in prices, as suggested above. If this is the case, then the wage control may insufficiently correct for local income. In this case, the consumer amenities variable may also be reflecting local productivity. One way to correct for this is to use income averaged over more years. A second way to correct for this would be to look at the impact of assuming different slopes in the price-income regression.

A third problem is that I have not done anything about housing supply. Housing supply certainly influences prices and it will also correlate with growth. My guess is that this causes the regression to underestimate the impact of amenities, because high prices are correlated with low supply which should adversely impact future growth. Still, the right thing would be to more explicitly model and address housing supply.

The rise of the consumer city is perhaps more of a hypothesis than a fact. Hopefully future work will spend more time on this question. I now turn to a proper dynamic spatial equilibrium model.

The dynamic framework and urban growth

In some ways the spatial equilibrium framework is better adapted for urban change than examining the levels of urban development. When we look at changes in population, prices and income, omitted area level characteristics can be first differenced away. This fact means that issues like

Table 3.5. The dynamic framework: The production sector

Actors	Firms in the production sector
They maximize	$\max_{N_t, K_t} \left\{ A_t N_t^{\beta} K_t^{\gamma} \bar{Z}^{1-\beta-\gamma} - W_t N_t - K_t \right\}$
They choose	Producers choose the number of workers and traded capital that would maximize profit in each period t.
First order condition	FOC for labor: $\beta A N_t^{\beta-1} K_t^{\gamma} \bar{Z}^{1-\beta-\gamma} = W_t$ FOC for capital: $\gamma A N_t^{\beta} K_t^{\gamma-1} \bar{Z}^{\frac{(1-\beta-\gamma)}{(1-\gamma)}} = 1$
Notation	A := city specific production level N_t := number of workers in the city K_t := traded capital (priced at 1) Z := non-traded capital $\bar{Z}$:= fixed supply of non-traded capital

considering population or population density become largely irrelevant. However, the move from levels to changes requires a more serious treatment of housing prices and expectations of future housing price change.

In the static model, the price that people pay to live in an area and the price that developers receive for building are the same. In a dynamic model, the price that people pay to live in an area is best thought of as the cost of living in each period, which can either be thought of as a rental cost or the per period cost of owner-occupied housing. As such, the prices received by developers must be forward looking assessments of the willingness to pay to live in area over time. The bulk of the "dynamic" spatial equilibrium model is essentially just the static model repeated period after period. Housing prices are the one truly dynamic aspect of the model.

To use the spatial equilibrium model as a tool for work on urban growth, I leave the decision problems of consumers and firms essentially unchanged by assuming that these equilibrium conditions must hold perfectly at every time period. The core equations of this model and the notation are given in Table 3.5. The firm's problem is literally identical if I assume that capital is constantly being rented. Firms then continue to maximize $A_t N_t^{\beta} K_t^{\gamma} Z_t^{1-\beta-\gamma}$ at every period t. In that case, the dynamic labor demand curve implied by the firms first order condition is $A_t^{1/(t-\gamma)} \gamma^{\gamma/(1-\gamma)} Z^{(1-\beta-\gamma)/(1-\gamma)} N_t^{(\beta+\gamma-1)/(1-\gamma)} = W_t$. This simple formulation is most problematic if we are interested in high frequency dynamics. It does take time to install capital. A richer model, following in the tradition of Kydland and Prescott (1982), could in principle make firm behavior more dynamic. But over frequencies of a decade or more, it is not unreasonable to assume that capital is flexible and that the zero profit condition roughly holds.

Table 3.6. The dynamic framework: The consumer's problem

Actors	Consumers of housing
They maximize	Linear formulation: $$\max_{H_t} U(H_t) = \max_{H_t}\{W_t - R_t + \theta_t\}$$ Cobb–Douglas formulation: $$\max_{H_t} U(H_t) - \max_{H_t}\{\theta_t(W_t - R_t H_t)^{1-\alpha} H_t^{\alpha}\}$$
They choose	Consumers choose housing at every period t to maximize utility. However, now consumers make a discrete decision whether or to consume 1 unit of housing or not at all. As a result of utility maximization, they are indifferent across space, i.e. they have no incentives to move.
Key equilibrium condition	*Spatial equilibrium* Linear formulation: $$W_t - R_t + \theta_t = \underline{U_t}$$ Cobb–Douglas formulation: $$W_t = (\alpha(1+r))^{-\alpha}(1-\alpha)^{\alpha-1}(r-g)^{\alpha}\theta_t^{-1} P_t^{\alpha} U_t$$
First order condition	Cobb–Douglas formulation: $$\frac{-R_t(1-\alpha)}{W_t - R_t H_t} + \frac{\alpha}{H_t} = 0$$
Notation	H_t := nontradable housing (now set to 1 if the consumer decides to consume housing) in period t θ_t := index capturing amenities in period t $\underline{U_t}$:= reservation utility in period t R_t := rental cost of housing in period t W_t := income in period t r := interest rate g := endogenous growth rate of rental payments P_t := price of a house at time t $= \sum_{j=0}^{\infty}(1+r)^{-j} R_{t+j} = \frac{1+r}{r\ g} R_t$ $C(t)$:= construction costs of producing one unit of housing

Since the forward looking nature of housing prices creates some complications in the dynamic model, it is worthwhile to consider two different ways of modeling housing consumption. The core equations of this model and the notation are given in Table 3.6. The simpler option reduces housing consumption from a continuous choice down to a discrete decision of whether to consume exactly one unit or not. In this case, I revert to an additive model where the flow of utility in an area equals $W_t - R_t + \theta_t$ (where R_t is equal to the rental cost of one unit of housing at period t and θ_t is equal to an index capturing amenities at time t), and this must equal the reservation utility. Alternatively, the Cobb–Douglas utility function can be kept and this implies that $\alpha^{\alpha}(1-\alpha)^{1-\alpha}\theta_t W_t R_t^{-\alpha}$ equals the reservation utility in each time period. The Cobb–Douglas formulation allows some adjustment of housing consumption; the linear model does not. I will first use the Cobb–Douglas formulation and then revert to the linear formulation in the more complex dynamic models.

The price of a unit of housing at time t is equal to the discounted sum of future rents or $\sum_{j=0}^{\infty}(1+r)^{-j}R_{t+j}$ where r is the interest rate. The easiest assumption is that there will be a steady state growth in rental payments driven by steady state growth in underlying parameters. I start with this assumption and then move to richer dynamics at the end of the chapter. If rental payments are assumed to grow at a fixed rate g (which will be determined endogenously), so that $R_{t+j} = (1+g)^j R_t$, then housing prices at time t, denoted P_t, equal $\frac{1+r}{r-g}R_t$.

I can then include the supply sector in two ways. The simplest way is to assume fixed construction costs of C_t for producing each unit. If these costs are constant, so $g = 0$, then $R_t = \frac{rC_t}{1+r}$ for all time periods and the construction sector has essentially been eliminated from the model. Housing costs have essentially been pinned down by construction costs. There are areas of the United States, like Houston, where this assumption may not be so far-fetched.

If construction costs grow at a rate of g during each time period then housing costs will also rise at that rate, and $R_t = \frac{(r-g)(1+g)^t C_0}{1+r}$ if C_0 is the initial construction cost. In this scenario, the construction sector has completely determined housing costs and there is no role for either amenities or productivity to drive housing prices. This scenario is compatible both with the assumption that people consume a fixed quantity of housing and with the assumption that housing consumption is flexible.

These assumptions are attractively simple, but they have unattractive implications. First, since prices are pinned down by construction costs and since construction costs are essentially exogenous, the model will have little to say about the causes of price disparities across space. While construction costs may drive prices across great swaths of America (see Glaeser, Gyourko and Saks, 2005), they do not determine the costs of living in many of the most interesting metropolitan areas. This construction cost based model also predicts that productivity will have no impact on wages, since wages will remain low as long as prices remain low. While I do believe that there are many cases where high levels of urban productivity have had more of an effect on city size than on city incomes, I do think that a good model should at least allow the possibility that both city size and city incomes might rise with productivity. This requires a better set of assumptions about the construction industry.

A more complex assumption allows housing production just as before, but assumes that there is a fixed supply of lots that can be developed. The core equations of this model and the notation are given in Table 3.7.

Table 3.7. The dynamic framework: The developer's problem

Actors	Housing developers
They maximize	$\max_t \left\{ \frac{P_t - C_t}{(1+r)^t} \right\} = \max_t \left\{ \frac{\frac{1+r}{r-g}(1+g)^t R_0 - (1+g_c)^t C_0.}{(1+r)^t} \right\}$
	$- \max_t \left\{ e^{-rt}(e^{gt} P_0 - e^{g_c t} C_0) \right\}$ in the continuous time model
They choose	Developers choose a period t to develop and sell house with the goal of maximizing profit (i.e. the present value of the price at which they sell housing less the present value of the cost of constructing that housing).
Key equilibrium conditions	A developer ought to develop at time t and not wait when $P_t > \frac{r-g_c}{r-g} C_t$
	For the housing market to clear when the Cobb–Douglas utility function is used: $\frac{\alpha N_t W_t}{R_t} = H \left(\frac{(r-g)P_t}{(r-g_c)(1+g_c)^t} \right)^{\rho}$
Notation	g_c := growth rate of construction costs
	g_A := growth rate of productivity
	g_θ := growth rate of construction costs
	$C_0^*(t) := \frac{(r-g)P(t)}{(r-g_c)(1+g_c)^t}$
	$\bar{\omega} = \left(\frac{\alpha(r-g_c)^{\rho} \bar{Z}}{(1+r)H} \right)^{1-\beta-\gamma} \gamma^{\gamma}(\alpha(1+r))^{\alpha\beta}(1-\alpha)^{\beta(1-\alpha)}$

The cost of developing these lots is heterogeneous, and at time zero, there are HC_0^{ρ} that can be built for a price of C_0 or less. To capture changes in the supply environment, I assume that the costs of developing any one lot is rising over time so that $C(t) = (1+g_G)^t C_0$. As a result, at time t, there are $H\,(c/(1+g_C)^t)^{\rho}$ lots that can be developed at a cost of C. In a more complicated dynamic setting, which I will analyze later in this chapter, each lot is an option, and the building decision is more complicated.

Developers develop and sell their property for P_t or $\frac{1+r}{r-g} R_t$, and this price is growing at a rate g. The maximization decision can be thought of as choosing t, the time of development, to maximize

$$\frac{P_t - C_t}{(1+r)^t} = \frac{\frac{1+r}{r-g}(1+g)^t R_0 - (1+g_C)^t C_0}{(1+r)^t}.$$

Naturally, I assume that the growth rates are below the interest rate. In a continuous time model, this problem would be written $e^{-rt}(e^{gt}P_0 - e^{g_C t}C_0)$, which has the elegant and familiar stopping rule of building when $P_t = \frac{r-g_C}{r-g} C_t$. In our discrete world, that condition continues to have value, and it is profit maximizing to develop a lot at time t instead of waiting a period as long as $P_t > \frac{r-g_C}{r-g} C_t$. Of course, I am eliminating uncertainty, maintenance and many other interesting things that would add more notation.

The building condition implies that at any given point in time, there will be a marginal development, based on its time zero costs denoted C_0^*, where

$$C_0^*(t) = \frac{(r-g)P(t)}{(r-g_C)(1+g_c)^t},$$

and the total supply of housing will equal $H(\frac{(r-g)P(t)}{(r-g_C)(1+g_c)^t})^\rho$. In the case of Cobb–Douglas utility where individuals spend a fixed fraction of their income on housing, then the equilibrium condition for demand and supply of housing to equal is

$$\frac{\alpha N_t W_t}{R_t} = H\left(\frac{(r-g)P_t}{(r-g_C)(1+g_c)^t}\right)^\rho.$$

The model has now developed three primary equations: the spatial indifference condition for individuals:

$$W_t = (\alpha(1+r))^{-\alpha}(1-\alpha)^{\alpha-1}(r-g)^\alpha \theta_t^{-1} P_t^\alpha \underline{U}_t,$$

the labor demand equation from firm maximization:

$$A_t^{1/(1-\beta-\gamma)} \gamma^{\gamma/(1-\beta-\gamma)} \bar{Z} W_t^{(\gamma-1)/(1-\beta-\gamma)} = N_t,$$

and the equilibrium in the housing market:

$$\alpha(1+r)N_t W_t = (r-g)P_t H\left(\frac{(r-g)P_t}{(r-g_C)(1+g_c)^t}\right)^\rho.$$

Rearranging these equations produces

$$\bar{\omega}\theta_t^\beta \underline{U}_t^{-\beta} A_t (1+g_c)^{(1-\beta-\gamma)\rho t} = (r-g)^{(\rho-1)(1-\beta-\gamma)+\alpha\beta} P_t^{(\rho+1)(1-\beta-\gamma)+\alpha\beta} \qquad (3.9)$$

where

$$\bar{\omega} = \left(\frac{\alpha(r-g_C)^\rho \bar{Z}}{(1+r)H}\right)^{1-\beta-\gamma} \gamma^\gamma (\alpha(1+r))^{\alpha\beta}(1-\alpha)^{\beta(1-\alpha)}.$$

Equation (3.9) then allows us to solve for the growth rate of prices, wages and population, as a function of the growth rate of productivity, amenities and construction costs:

$$\log\left(\frac{P_{t+1}}{P_t}\right) = \frac{\log(1+g_A) + \beta\log\left(\frac{1+g_\theta}{1+g_U}\right) + \rho(1-\beta-\gamma)\log(1+g_c)}{(1-\beta-\gamma)(\rho+1)+\alpha\beta} \tag{3.10}$$

$$\log\left(\frac{W_{t+1}}{W_t}\right) = \frac{\alpha\log(1+g_A) + (1-\beta-\gamma)\left(\alpha\rho\log(1+g_C) - (\rho+1)\log\left(\frac{1+g_\theta}{1+g_U}\right)\right)}{(1-\beta-\gamma)(\rho+1)+\alpha\beta} \tag{3.11}$$

$$\log\left(\frac{N_{t+1}}{N_t}\right) = \frac{(1+\rho-\alpha)\log(1+g_A) + (1-\gamma)\left((\rho+1)\log\left(\frac{1+g_\theta}{1+g_U}\right) - \alpha\rho\log(1+g_C)\right)}{(1-\beta-\gamma)(\rho+1)+\alpha\beta}. \tag{3.12}$$

Returning now to the relationship between an exogenous variable, X, and these different forces, I assume that

$$\log(1+g_A) = K_A + \lambda_A X + \mu_A,$$

$$\log\left(\frac{1+g_\theta}{1+g_U}\right) = K_\theta + \lambda_\theta X + \mu_\theta$$

and

$$\log(1+g_C) = K_C + \lambda_C X + \mu_C,$$

where K_A, K_θ and K_C are constants, λ_A, λ_θ and λ_C are coefficients, and μ_A, μ_θ and μ_C are error terms. Just as in the static case, I allow the exogenous variable to influence amenities, productivity and the construction sector, but I am now assuming that the variable influences growth in amenities, growth in productivity and growth in construction costs.

Equations (3.10)–(3.12) then imply that if $\hat{B}_N$, $\hat{B}_W$ and $\hat{B}_P$ represent the estimated coefficients on an X variable for the population density, wage and price change regressions, then $\lambda_A = \left((1-\beta-\gamma)\hat{B}_N + (1-\gamma)\hat{B}_W\right)$ and $\lambda_\theta = \alpha\hat{B}_P - \hat{B}_W$, just as before, and $\lambda_C = \hat{B}_P + \frac{1}{\rho}\left(\hat{B}_P - \hat{B}_N - \hat{B}_W\right)$. The only difference between the static and dynamic case comes in the treatment of construction costs.

These equations suggest an empirical approach to urban growth. If we are interested in knowing how a particular variable, such as sunshine, manufacturing or a state tax rate, impacts urban growth, it really makes sense to simultaneously examine growth in population, income and prices. Looking at all three variables helps us to know whether the variable really did have a positive impact. For example, a variable that pushed up prices without pushing up population might be working mainly by restricting housing supply, rather than providing amenities or productivity. Moreover, the system of equations gives us a shot at figuring out the channel through which the variable operated.

Equations like these provide a theoretical justification for running logarithmic growth regressions and they provide a means of interpreting those regressions. My earliest work on urban growth (Glaeser *et al.*, 1992) only used the firm's demand curve so that changes in employment could be interpreted as changes in productivity. A justification for the use of a single equation is that this paper looked at growth of city-industries, meaning industrial groups within a metropolitan area. In principle, if one was running a regression with city-industry employment change as the dependent variable and including city and industry fixed effects, then the labor demand curve might well be the only curve that really matters, at least if labor is sufficiently mobile across industries. Unfortunately, Glaeser *et al.* (1992) does not actually control for city-specific fixed effects, so this justification is a bit shaky.

A second justification for focusing exclusively on the labor demand equation is that we are running regressions that focused on variables that seemed far more likely to impact productivity growth than amenity growth, such as industrial diversity and the degree of competitiveness. There are a number of mistakes in that paper, most notably our failure to correct for correlated errors within a metropolitan area. There are, however, two findings that have held up reasonably well. First, city-industry employment does mean revert. Second, growth is faster when industries are divided into many small firms rather than concentrated in a few large firms. The paper's third finding—that industrial diversity predicts growth—has been less robust.

The mean reversion of city-industry employment is, perhaps unsurprising but it does rule out the view that scale feeds upon itself, creating a self-sustaining cycle of growth. This fact does appear to reduce the importance of what we called Marshall–Arrow–Romer, or MAR, externalities at the city level. Those externalities exist when the growth rate of new technology rises with the scale of the operation.

Figure 3.10 illustrates the second finding of our paper: the strong negative correlation between average firm size in 1977 and employment growth between 1977 and 2000 across metropolitan areas. We interpreted the positive role of small firms as support for the views of Jane Jacobs and Michael Porter that competition and diversity were good for producing new ideas. There are certainly other interpretations. The growth of city-industries with many small firms might just be telling us that firm sizes also mean revert, for example. From a policy perspective, the fact does

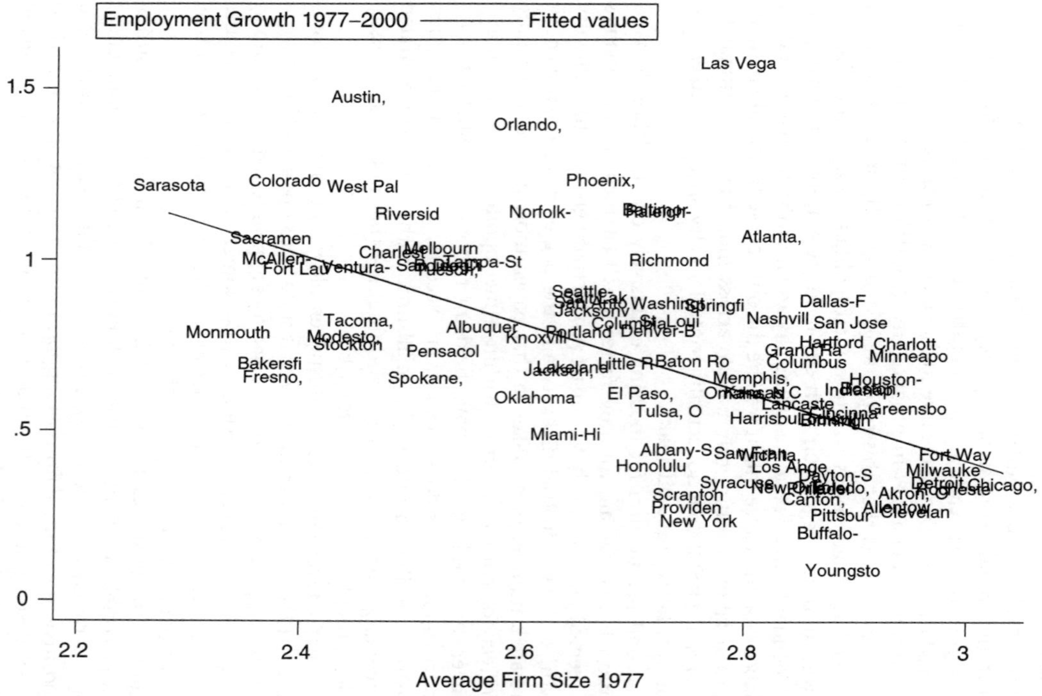

Figure 3.10. Employment growth and average firm size

seem to call into question the local government practice of chasing particularly large employers.

In Glaeser *et al.* (1995), I looked specifically at a wide set of correlates of city growth. That paper was among the first, along with Glaeser (1994) and Simon and Nardinelli (2002), that documents the connection between city level skills and growth that I will discuss in the next section. This fact is important for understanding the recent paths of different cities, although it may not be surprising—human capital predicts country level growth as well.

Glaeser *et al.* (1995) also documents the negative correlation between manufacturing and city growth and a general lack of correlation between urban growth and many other variables, like government spending, racial composition and segregation. We also found using our simple ordinary least squares framework that area growth rates were uncorrelated with initial area size. This finding is also associated with the work of Eaton and Eckstein (1997) which found a similar fact using Japanese and French data and considerably more statistical sophistication.

The Glaeser *et al.* (1995) model was housing free and looked only at income and population levels. The empirical model differs from the one above in that quality of life was allowed to change with both the level of population and the growth rate of population. Those assumptions could readily be incorporated in the model above, although since real wages appear to be constant with city size, it is less clear that we need to allow quality of life to change with city population.

Glaeser and Shapiro (2003) used the same basic model and essentially updated the regressions to include the 1990s. One modest innovation of that paper was to focus more on density and public transportation, in response to the view put forward that America was moving towards more traditional urbanism. We found little evidence for that view, but rather the evidence seemed to suggest that the move towards lower density, car-based living was as robust as ever. That paper also used population growth and made no effort to distinguish between variables that impact amenities or productivity.

Glaeser, Gyourko and Saks (2006) make the case that all of these attempts to look at urban growth without taking housing seriously are badly flawed. Figure 3.11 shows the correlation of growth in the housing stock and growth in the population between 1970 and 2000. The two variables are almost perfectly correlated, which doesn't mean that housing causes population growth, but it certainly suggests that variables that limit housing growth will surely limit population growth. At the very least, it suggests that I was pretty foolish in ignoring the housing sector when looking at urban growth.

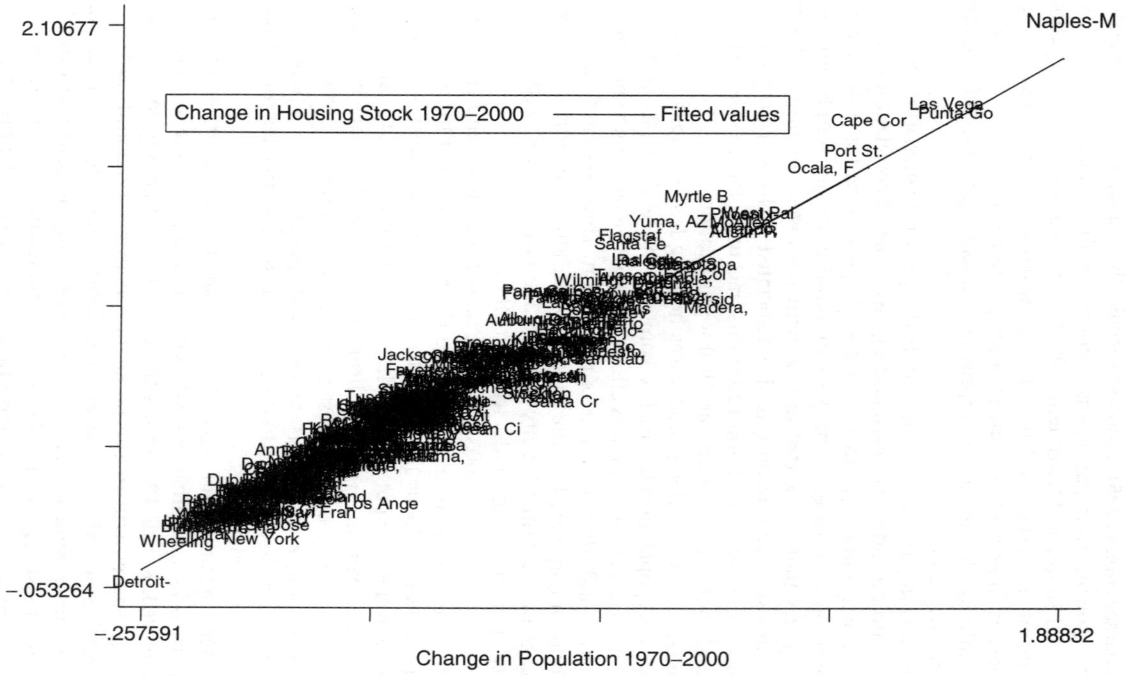

Figure 3.11. Change in housing stock and population from 1970–2000 by MSA

Glaeser and Tobio (2008) attempts to remedy that problem, although we do not deal with the dynamic, forward looking nature of housing prices. Whereas the model presented here incorporates housing supply heterogeneity by allowing for differential growth rates in the costs of housing construction, that model allows differential growth rates in the amount of land available for construction. The formulae for determining productivity and amenity growth from population, wage and price growth data are identical in the model described here and in the model used in that paper.

That paper starts with the correlation between measures of Sunbelt status and population growth and then tries to explain the sources of that correlation using the spatial equilibrium model. During the 20 years between 1950 and 1970, we find very significant productivity growth in the South, and that drives the population and income growth. Since 1970, we find that growth in housing supply is also extremely important. We find little evidence that amenities are growing in most of the Sunbelt or that these amenities are driving Sunbelt growth.

The negative result on amenities may be the most surprising result of the paper, because many observers have naturally connected the growth of the Sunbelt to an increasing desire to be around the sun. But if amenity growth was driving the growth of the Sunbelt then real wages should be declining in that region. That is a primary implication of the spatial equilibrium approach. But real wages have been rising steadily in the South and in many warmer areas. Moreover, much of the growth in the Sunbelt in recent decades has been in areas like Houston and Atlanta that have far from perfect climates. Coastal California is far more pleasant, and its growth is surely linked to increasing amenity growth or, equivalently, to an increasing willingness to pay for high amenities (as in Graves, 1980). In Coastal California, unlike in Houston, real wages have fallen substantially as housing price growth has far exceeded income growth.

Housing supply does matter and it is simply not credible to exclude housing from an examination of city or state growth. The growth of Houston or Atlanta has as much to do with their aggressive permitting policies as with anything else. The sluggish growth of Coastal California and high demand areas on the East Coast reflects the lack of housing supply growth in those areas, which is presumably related to limits on building. To exclude these factors from urban growth work is a big mistake. The power of local land use controls is even higher outside the United States. European cities have extremely strong controls that limit new construction; Mumbai is world famous for its draconian land use controls. If we are even going to understand these places, it will be necessary to follow an integrated approach that brings in housing supply.

Multiple skill levels and the rise of the skilled city

So far, this chapter has assumed that everyone is completely homogeneous. There are many ways to naturally relax that assumption. One approach is to allow heterogeneity in the tastes for living in a particular community. This would make the growth of a place less elastic with respect to local wages. Alternatively, I could assume that people differ by age or skill level. In this section, I will take the latter course and assume that there are people who are high skilled and people who are less skilled.

A focus on skills makes sense because of the robust interest in using American sub-national data to understand the changing impact of human capital. Across countries, there is a robust correlation between education and national growth (e.g. Barro, 1991). Within countries, there has been a remarkable increase in the returns to skill (e.g. Katz and Murphy, 1992). Some of the most influential work in the endogenous growth literature predicts that people will be more productive when they work around other skilled people (Lucas, 1988). Rauch (1993) pioneered the use of city-level data to test this hypothesis, and many others have followed him. Some agglomeration economies predict that skilled people may benefit more than others from certain types of agglomerations, which has also helped to generate an interest in skills and the city (Bacalod, Blum and Strange, 2007).

I have been particularly interested in the correlation between skills and urban growth that was discussed above. Figure 3.12 shows the connection between share of the population with college degrees in 1980 and population growth between 1980 and 2000. Skills also predict housing prices across metropolitan areas, as shown in Figure 3.13, and wages, as shown in Figure 3.14. Figure 3.13 just uses the median housing values from the 2000 Census. Figure 3.14 uses the residual from a wage regression where the logarithm of wage for men between the ages 25 and 55 has been regressed on a full range of individual level age and education dummies. The metropolitan area-specific wage premium is calculated by taking the metropolitan area average residuals from the equation.

The early presumption was that the correlation between skills and growth said something about the ability of skilled people to innovate and create new technologies and ideas. An alternative, productivity-based, explanation for the skills-growth fact is that human capital spillovers have increased in importance over time. Since both of these theories predict that initial skill levels are correlated with a growth in the productivity parameter, A, they are empirically indistinguishable.

However, it is also possible that skilled people are an amenity that has become more valuable over time or that skilled people do a better job of

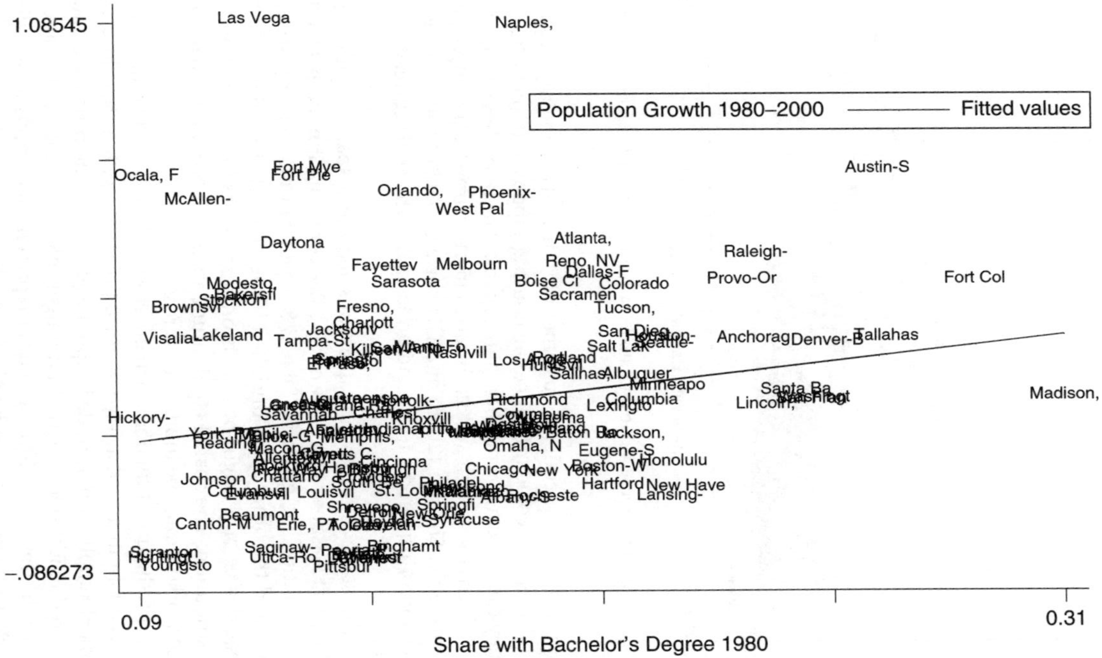

Figure 3.12. Change in population and initial share of population with a Bachelor's degree from 1980–2000 by MSA

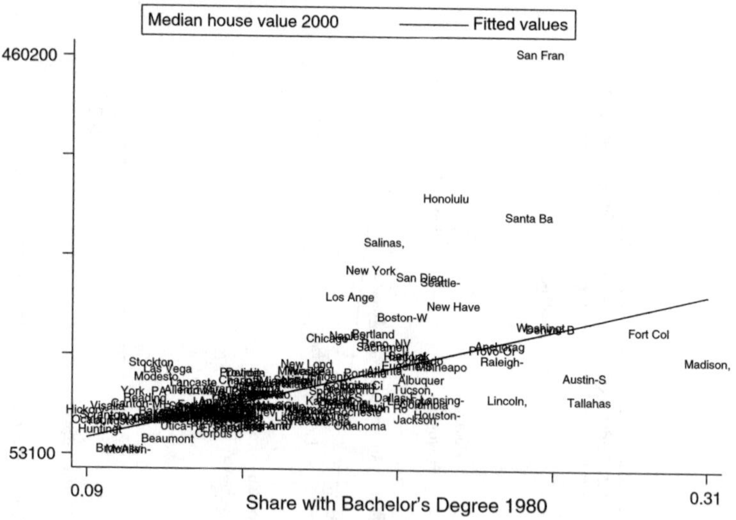

Figure 3.13. Median house value and share of population with Bachelor's degree by MSA

generating growth in endogenous amenities. It is also certainly possible that skilled people could influence the housing supply, although I suspect that they cause it contract rather than expand. The hypotheses that skills raise productivity growth and skills raise amenity growth are empirically distinguishable. Shapiro (2006) and Glaeser and Saiz (2004) both use a spatial equilibrium model to try and understand why skills correlate with growth.

Both the static and dynamic questions require a spatial equilibrium model with at least two types of workers. The core equations of this model and the notation are given in Table 3.8. I will call one type of workers "skilled" and the other type "unskilled." The name skilled might refer to a college degree or it might be a division that breaks lower down on the skill distribution. The spatial equilibrium assumption requires that both types of workers must be indifferent across space.

Firms' production functions remain $AN^{\beta}K^{\gamma}Z^{1-\beta-\gamma}$. As before, traded capital can be purchased anywhere for a price of one, but each location has a fixed supply of non-traded capital equal to $\bar{Z}$. The primary change on the production side is that N no longer refers to the overall quantity of workers in the city or firm but rather represents a composite of skilled and unskilled labor, specifically: $N = (\psi N_S^{\sigma} + N_U^{\sigma})^{1/\sigma}$, where N_S refers to the number of skilled workers, N_U refers to the number of unskilled workers, σ is a substitution parameter that varies from zero to one and ψ is a

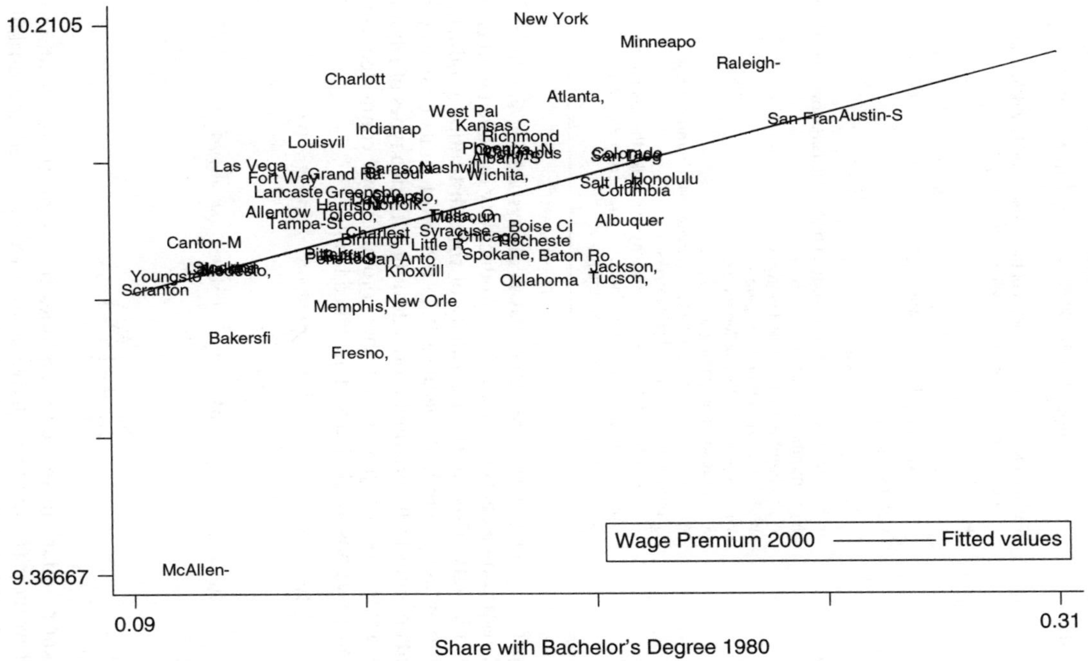

Figure 3.14. Wage premium and share of population with a Bachelor's degree by MSA

Table 3.8. Choosing high skilled and low skilled labor: The firm's problem

Actors	Firms
They maximize	$\max_{N_S, N_U, K} \{AN^{\beta}K^{\gamma}\bar{Z}^{1-\beta-\gamma} - W_S N_S - W_U N_U - K\}$
They choose	Firms choose the optimal level of high skilled and low skilled labor (N_S and N_U, respectively) that will maximize profits
First order conditions	FOCs for labor: $W_S = \psi N_S^{\sigma-1}\beta\gamma^{\gamma/(1-\gamma)}A^{1/(1-\gamma)}\bar{Z}^{(1-\beta-\gamma)/(1-\gamma)}N^{(\beta-\sigma+\sigma\gamma)/(1-\gamma)}$ $W_U = N_U^{\sigma-1}\beta\gamma^{\gamma/(1-\gamma)}A^{1/(1-\gamma)}\bar{Z}^{(1-\beta-\gamma)/(1-\gamma)}N^{(\beta-\sigma+\sigma\gamma)/(1-\gamma)}$ FOC for capital: $\gamma AN^{\beta}K_t^{\gamma-1}\bar{Z}^{(1-\beta-\gamma)/(1-\gamma)} = 1$
Notation	$N := (\psi N_S^{\sigma} + N_U^{\sigma})^{1/\sigma}$ = a composite of high skilled and low skilled labor N_S := number of high skilled workers N_U := number of low skilled workers W_S := number of high skilled workers W_U := number of low skilled workers σ := a substitution parameter $\in [0,1]$ ψ := a city-specific productivity parameter which impacts the productivity of the skilled workers ≥ 1 $\bar{H}$:= total housing available in the city (we make this assumption when consumption of housing is constrained) = $N_S + N_U$ $\Phi := \beta\gamma^{\gamma/(1-\gamma)}A^{1/(1-\gamma)}\bar{Z}^{(1-\beta-\gamma)/(1-\gamma)}N^{(\beta-\sigma+\sigma\gamma)/(1-\gamma)}$

city-specific productivity parameter that is always weakly greater than one. This parameter acts to increase the productivity of skilled workers in a particular city. This constant elasticity of the substitution production function is fairly standard, because it is the most functional way to ground an empirically oriented model dealing with two types of labor.

The firm's production function then produces two connected labor demand equations for skilled and unskilled labor:

$$W_S = \psi N_S^{\sigma-1}\beta\gamma^{\gamma/(1-\gamma)}A^{1/(1-\gamma)}\bar{Z}^{(1-\beta-\gamma)/(1-\gamma)}N^{(\beta-\sigma+\sigma\gamma)/(1-\gamma)}$$

and

$$W_U = N_U^{\sigma-1}\beta\gamma^{\gamma/(1-\gamma)}A^{1/(1-\gamma)}\bar{Z}^{(1-\beta-\gamma)/(1-\gamma)}N^{(\beta-\sigma+\sigma\gamma)/(1-\gamma)},$$

or

$$\frac{W_S}{W_U} = \psi\left(\frac{N_U}{N_S}\right)^{1-\sigma}.$$

The skill premium in this city combines the productivity premium of skilled workers (ψ) and the relative abundance of skilled and unskilled workers, which will be endogenously determined.

While we might like to infer something about ψ, the underlying skill bias of the region's technology, from the local skill premium, the equation makes it obvious that any such inference is not straightforward. The skill premium reflects both the bias of the technology, but also the supply of skilled and unskilled workers. A partial-equilibrium approach might be to measure the relative abundance of skilled and unskilled workers and then use a reasonable range of values for σ to correct for $(N_U/N_S)^{1-\sigma}$. This would require us to place a lot of faith in our estimates of σ. A more satisfying approach is to complete the system and model the labor supply decisions of skilled and unskilled individuals.

The problem with modeling these labor supply decisions is that in a world of perfect mobility, changes in productivity tend to show up exclusively in changes in quantities of skilled people, not in different returns to skilled people across space. This problem is particularly acute if skilled and unskilled people assume exactly the same type of housing and enjoy exactly the same amenities. In that case, different skilled premia across space are practically impossible. If one place offers particularly high wages for skilled people, then the housing prices that make skilled people indifferent between living in that place and living someplace else will surely be sufficiently high so that no unskilled people will be willing to live in that location.

I think that the most straightforward way of solving this modeling challenge is to assume that there are two different types of housing and that skilled and unskilled people have those different housing types. However, before getting to that solution, I will flounder a bit around alternative modeling strategies to show how they do not create a satisfying approach to skill heterogeneity across space.

One alternative is to modify the Cobb–Douglas utility function used above and assume that utility equals $\vartheta + \theta C^{1-\alpha}H^{\alpha}$, where θ represents the city-specific amenity index as before and ϑ represents a second city-specific amenity shifter. The core equations of this model and the notation are given in Table 3.9. The amenity index is a strong complement to wealth; the amenity shifter is not. When housing is homogeneous, total utility in the area then equals $\vartheta + \theta\xi W R^{-\alpha}$, where R continues to represent the rental cost of housing and $\xi - \alpha^{\alpha}(1-\alpha)^{1-\alpha}$. If I let $\underline{U}_S$ represent reservation utility for the skilled workers and $\underline{U}_U$ represent reservation utility for the unskilled workers, then the two labor supply equations are $\underline{U}_S = \vartheta + \theta\xi W_S R^{-\alpha}$ and $\underline{U}_U = \vartheta + \theta\xi W_U R^{-\alpha}$, or $W_S/W_U = (\underline{u}_S - \vartheta)/(\underline{u}_U - \vartheta)$. The skill premium is equal to the ratio of the reservation utilities when $\vartheta = 0$, which reminds us of why the most basic model fails to generate the observed heterogeneity in the skill premium over space.

The labor supply equation highlights the challenges that a spatial equilibrium creates for understanding local differences in the skill premium.

Table 3.9. Modeling strategies with homogeneous housing types: The consumer's problem with an amenity shifter

Actors	Consumers of housing
They maximize	$\max_{C,H}\{\vartheta+\theta C^{1-\alpha}H^{\alpha}\}=\max_{H}\{\vartheta+\theta(W-RH)^{1-\alpha}H^{\alpha}\}$ for $W\in\{W_S,W_U\}$
They choose	Both high skilled and low skilled consumers choose the level of housing that will maximize their utility.
First order condition	$\frac{-R(1-\alpha)}{W-RH}+\frac{\alpha}{H}=0$
Notation	C := tradable goods (priced at 1) consumed by consumer H := non-tradable housing R := rental cost of housing θ := city-specific amenity index ϑ := a second city-specific amenity shifter $\xi := \alpha^{\alpha}(1-\alpha)^{1-\alpha}$ $\underline{U}_S$:= reservation utility for high skilled workers $\underline{U}_U$:= reservation utility for low skilled workers

In the standard Cobb–Douglas case, when $\vartheta=0$, then there should be no heterogeneity in the skill premium across space. All of the differences in skill-based technology should show up in different quantities of skilled people, not in different returns to skill. This is obviously counterfactual, since there are differences in the skill premium across space, so the model has failed.

When $\vartheta\neq 0$ then there will be heterogeneity in the skill premium across metropolitan areas, but that heterogeneity will be driven by differences in ϑ, the amenity shifter, not differences in ψ, the variable that makes skilled people more productive. This model of consumer welfare suggests that places with higher skill premia are not places where skilled people are more productive but rather places where ϑ is high since $W_S/W_U=(\underline{U}_S-\vartheta)/(\underline{U}_U-\vartheta)$ is increasing with ϑ.

One implication of this variant of the model is that the skill premium should be lowest in places where the skill premium is lowest. Combining the spatial equilibrium condition, $W_S/W_U=(\underline{U}_S-\vartheta)/(\underline{U}_U-\vartheta)$, with the labor demand condition, $W_S/W_U=\psi(N_U/N_S)^{1-\sigma}$, yields:

$$\frac{N_U}{N_S}=\left(\frac{\underline{U}_S-\vartheta}{\psi(\underline{U}_U-\vartheta)}\right)^{1/(1-\sigma)}.$$

This ratio is also increasing with ϑ, so the amenity shift that causes the skill premium to rise causes the ratio of skilled to unskilled labor to fall. After all, this shift is essentially a labor supply shift. Unless there was some reason to believe in a strange correlation between ϑ and ψ, we

Table 3.10. Modeling strategies with homogeneous housing types: The consumer's problem with constrained consumption of housing

Actors	Consumers of housing
They maximize	$\max_{C,H} U(C,H) = \max_{C,H} \{\theta C^{1-\alpha} H^{\alpha}\} = \max_{H} \{\theta (W - RH)^{1-\alpha} H^{\alpha}\}$ when quantities are not binding (for $W \in \{W_S, W_U\}$)
They choose	Both high skilled and low skilled consumers choose the level of housing that will maximize their utility. However, in this model, it is assumed one or both types of consumers are constrained to consuming at least one unit of housing. Maximization of utility implies that consumers will be indifferent across space.
Key equilibrium conditions	*Spatial equilibrium conditions* When both high skilled and low skilled consumers are constrained to consuming one unit of housing $\underline{U}_S = \theta(W_S - R)^{1\ \alpha}$ $\underline{U}_U - \theta(W_U - R)^{1-\alpha}$ When high skilled consumers are unconstrained and low skilled consumers are constrained to consuming one unit of housing $\underline{U}_U = \theta(W_U - R)^{1-\alpha}$ $\underline{U}_S = \theta\xi W_S R^{-\alpha}$
Notation	Same as the notation in the table above.

should expect to see that where the skill premium is highest, there are the fewest skilled people. This implied negative correlation between skill shares and the skill premium occurs because when ϑ is high, the amenity returns to the unskilled are particularly high, which causes unskilled people to crowd into the area and push up the wage gap between skilled and unskilled workers.

A second way to change the model so that skill premia are not uniform across metropolitan areas, and are determined by the reservation utility, is to assume that everyone is constrained to consume at least one unit of housing. This quantity could reflect some sort of bare minimum required for survival, or alternatively, it might reflect a legally imposed minimum house size. The core equations of this model and the notation are given in Table 3.10. If this quantity is non-binding for both groups, then the model is unchanged, and I will not consider that case.

If this minimum quantity is binding for both groups then the spatial equilibrium conditions are $\underline{U}_S = \theta(W_S - R)^{1-\alpha}$ and $\underline{U}_U = \theta(W_U - R)^{1-\alpha}$ or

$$R = W_S - \left(\frac{\underline{U}_S}{\theta}\right)^{1/(1-\alpha)} = W_U - \left(\frac{\underline{U}_U}{\theta}\right)^{1/(1-\alpha)}.$$

This model also gives us that the skill premium in levels, although not in logs, is determined entirely by amenities and reservation values because

$$W_S - W_U = \left(\frac{\underline{U}_S}{\theta}\right)^{1/(1-\alpha)} - \left(\frac{\underline{U}_U}{\theta}\right)^{1/(1-\alpha)}.$$

Again, this gives us the uncomfortable fact that wage differences may not actually tell us much about productivity differences.

To close this model, I assume that the total housing available in the city is $\bar{H}$. I am not taking this model seriously enough yet to go through the work of endogenizing housing supply. Then combining the two spatial equilibrium conditions with the labor demand conditions yields $W_S = \psi \Phi N_S^{\sigma-1}$ and $W_U = \Phi N_U^{\sigma-1}$, where

$$\Phi = \beta \gamma^{\gamma/(1-\gamma)} A^{1/(1-\gamma)} \bar{Z}^{(1-\beta-\gamma)/(1-\gamma)} \bar{H}^{(\beta-\sigma+\sigma\gamma)/(1-\gamma)}.$$

The adding up constraint $N_S + N_U = \bar{H}$ then completes the urban system. The skilled population of the city will satisfy

$$\psi N_S^{\sigma-1} - (\bar{\mathrm{H}} - \mathrm{N_S})^{\sigma-1} = \frac{\underline{\mathrm{U}}_{\mathrm{S}}^{1/(1-\alpha)} - \underline{\mathrm{U}}_{\mathrm{U}}^{1/(1-\alpha)}}{\Phi \theta^{1/(1-\alpha)}}.$$

This equation then implies that the number of skilled workers is rising with the skill premium and declining in the reservation value of the skilled.

The parameter Φ includes all of the exogenous factors that increase overall city productivity and amenity levels and housing supply. As this parameter increases, the share of skilled workers will also rise. Since these factors tend to multiply productivity, more productive people get more and are more willing to pay high housing prices. This fact should give us some pause when we look at correlations between measures of productivity and the skill level in a city. That correlation could well reflect the propensity of the skilled to come to more productive places, not the ability of skilled people to generate more spillovers. The important work of Enrico Moretti (2004) that uses historical educational institutions as an instrument for local skill levels provides one approach to this problem. I will discuss this work more thoroughly when I put forward a model that I trust more.

Now I will turn to the case where unskilled workers are constrained in their housing choices and the skilled workers are not, which is roughly equivalent to a minimum housing requirement (either technological or regulatory) that binds for the poor but not for the rich. The core equations of this model and the notation are also given in Table 3.10. In this case, the two spatial equilibrium conditions are $\underline{U}_U = \theta(W_U - R)^{1-\alpha}$ and

$\underline{U}_S = \theta\xi W_S R^{\alpha}$, or

$$R = \left(\frac{\theta\xi W_S}{\underline{U}_S}\right)^{1/\alpha} = W_U - \left(\frac{\underline{U}_U}{0}\right)^{1/(1-\alpha)}$$

where as before, $\xi = \alpha(1-\alpha)^{1-\alpha}$. The wage premium must equal

$$\frac{W_S}{W_U} = \frac{W_S}{\left(\theta\xi W_S/\underline{U}_S\right)^{1/\alpha} + \left(\underline{U}_U/\vartheta\right)^{1/(1-\alpha)}}.$$

Any parameter, other than those explicitly in that equation (i.e. the reservation utilities, the amenity level) will cause the skill wage premium to rise if it causes the skilled wage level to fall in absolute terms, as long as

$$\left(\frac{\underline{U}_U}{\theta}\right)^{1/(1-\alpha)} < \frac{1-\alpha}{\alpha}\left(\frac{\theta\xi W_S}{\underline{U}_S}\right)^{1/\alpha}$$

which must always hold since $\alpha W_U < R$.

Factors that make skilled wages rise will have an offsetting impact on price. Since skilled people adjust their housing consumption and unskilled people do not, an impact on price that keeps skilled people whole will make unskilled people strictly worse off. To keep them indifferent, their wages must rise by more than the wages of the skilled do and this means that the wage premium will fall. In a model like this, a higher observed skill premium could readily reflect a lower technological return to skill (ψ), which may be an interesting theoretical curiosity, but it is unlikely to reflect reality.

The most straightforward way to ensure that productivity factors influence the skill premium is to assume that skilled and unskilled people consume different types of housing. This can be done by modelers' fiat (i.e. just assume that they live in two different neighborhoods), or it can be produced endogenously with a few simple assumptions. For example, we continue to assume that utility equals $\theta C^{1\alpha} H^{\alpha}$, but now assume that there are two different areas in the city with different housing supplies and different amenity flows.

The core equations of this model and the notation are given in Table 3.11. I assume that housing has different development costs, denoted c. For any given construction cost c, there is a supply of $\bar{H}_H c^{\rho}$ potential units of high amenity housing that yield an amenity flow of θ_H. This supply is increasing with c to capture the fact that the supply curve slopes up so that there are more units that can be developed at higher costs. There is a supply of $\bar{H}_L c^{\rho}$ units of low amenity housing that yields an amenity flow of θ_1 and that has a development cost of c. Higher amenity levels might reflect natural amenities, such as a water

Table 3.11. Modeling strategies with heterogeneous housing types: The developer's problem

Actors	Housing developers
They maximize	$\max\left\{\sum_{t=0}^{\infty}\frac{R}{(1+r)^t}-c\right\}$ where $R\in\{R_H, R_L\}, c\in\{c_H, c_L\}$
They choose	Developers choose the different levels of rent for both types of housing (R_H, R_L) that will maximize the net present value of rents minus construction costs. Because of free-entry, we derive the zero-profit condition.
Key equilibrium condition	*Zero-profit condition* $\sum_{t=0}^{\infty}\frac{R}{(1+r)^t}-c=0$ where $R\in\{R_H, R_L\}, c\in\{c_H, c_L\}$
Notation	$\bar{H}_H c^\rho$:= units of high amenity housing θ_H := high amenity flow $\bar{H}_L c^\rho$:= units of low amenity housing θ_L := low amenity flow c_H := development cost of high amenity housing c_L := development cost of low amenity housing ρ := supply coefficient R_H := rental cost of high amenity housing R_L := rental cost of low amenity housing $\zeta := \left(\frac{1+r}{r}\right)^\rho$ $\chi := \frac{R_H}{\alpha W_U}$

view, or amenities such as shorter commutes or access to the better schools.

I have assumed that the supply coefficient, the parameter ρ, is the same for both low and high amenity housing. This simplification is surely unrealistic in many settings where supply is far more elastic in low amenity areas than in high amenity areas. It would be a useful exercise to extend the model to consider two different elasticities of supply.

Developers maximize the net present value of rents minus construction costs. Unlike the previous section, I am now assuming that construction costs are fixed, but I will assume that rents are continuously growing at a rate that will be endogenously determined later. This means that development will occur to the point where $R = rc/(1+r)$ where r is the interest rate. If R_H denotes the cost of high amenity's housing, then the total supply of that housing will equal $H_H\zeta R_H^\rho$, where ζ denotes $\left(\frac{1+r}{r}\right)^\rho$. The supply of low amenity housing will equal $\bar{H}_L\zeta R_L^\rho$.

If $\theta_H/\theta_L = (R_H/R_L)^\alpha$, then both poor and rich people will be indifferent between the two areas. As such, the model doesn't predict sorting. One way to get the needed sorting across areas is again to fix a minimum amount of housing consumption of one. Such a condition can ensure

Table 3.12. Modeling strategies with heterogeneous housing types: The consumer's problem

Actors	Consumers of housing
They maximize	$\max_{C,H} U(C,H) = \max_{C,H} \{\theta_i C^{1-\alpha} H^{\alpha}\}$ for $i \in \{S, U\}$
Notation	$g_H :=$ growth rate for high amenity housing $g_L :=$ growth rate for low amenity housing $\bar{\omega} := (1+\rho)(1-\sigma) + \sigma\alpha$ $v_\psi := \frac{1}{\bar{\omega}} \log(\psi)$ $v_\theta := \frac{1+\rho}{\bar{\omega}} \log\left(\frac{\underline{U}_U \theta_H}{\underline{U}_S \theta_L}\right) + \frac{\alpha}{\bar{\omega}} \log\left(\frac{\bar{H}_H}{\bar{H}_L}\right)$ $X :=$ exogenous variable $\log(\psi) := K_\psi + \lambda_\psi X + \mu_\psi$ $\log\left(\frac{\underline{U}_U \theta_H}{\underline{U}_S \theta_L}\right) := K_\theta + \lambda_\theta X + \mu_\theta$ $\log\left(\frac{\bar{H}_H}{\bar{H}_L}\right) := K_H + \lambda_H X + \mu_H$ $K_\psi, K_\theta, K_H :=$ constants $\lambda_\psi, \lambda_\theta, \lambda_H :=$ coefficients $\mu_\psi, \mu_\theta, \mu_H :=$ error terms $\hat{B}_N :=$ estimated coefficients on an X variable for the population (assuming constant expected growth rates for the two types of housing) $\hat{B}_W :=$ estimated coefficients on an X variable for wage (assuming constant expected growth rates for the two types of housing) $\hat{B}_P :=$ estimated coefficients on an X variable for price (assuming constant expected growth rates for the two types of housing) $\theta :=$ the geometric mean of the two amenity levels $A := A_0 \left(\frac{N_S}{N_U}\right)^{\varphi}$ $t :=$ time period (for the dynamic framework)

that the two groups sort, even when the condition never binds in equilibrium. Rich people consume more than the minimum in the high amenity area. Poor people consume more than the minimum in the low amenity area, yet because the poor would like to consume less than the minimum if they moved into the high amenity area, the minimum will ensure sorting. Obviously, this is not the only scenario that can result, so I will need to assume conditions so that this occurs. I will assume parameter values so that this condition binds when the low skilled people choose to locate in the high skilled area. The core equations of this model and the notation are given in Table 3.12.

To be precise, the condition for the high skilled individual to weakly prefer the high amenity housing is that $\theta_H/\theta_L > (R_H/R_L)^{\alpha}$. This condition would also ensure that unskilled workers would prefer the high amenity region if they were unconstrained in both regions. Both skilled and unskilled workers are willing to pay just as much to live in the high amenity area, but the unskilled would just consume less housing in the more attractive area. The minimum housing size requirement provides us with a wedge that can make the high amenity area less attractive to the unskilled. Alternatively, I could change the utility function to make amenities more of a luxury good. This would be a lot harder.

When less skilled people are constrained, the condition for the less skilled to prefer the low amenity housing is that

$$\frac{\xi W_U}{(W_U - R_H)^{1-\alpha} R_L^{\alpha}} = \frac{(1-\alpha)^{1-\alpha}}{\chi^{\alpha}(1-\alpha\chi)^{1-\alpha}} \left(\frac{R_H}{R_L}\right)^{\alpha} \geq \frac{\theta_H}{\theta_L},$$

where $\chi = R_H/\alpha W_U$. The parameter χ is the ratio of actual consumption of less skilled people when they are buying high amenity housing to the desired consumption of less skilled when they are buying high amenity housing. The term $(1-\alpha)^{1-\alpha}/\chi^{\alpha}(1-\alpha\chi)^{1-\alpha}$ equals one, when $\chi = 1$, reflecting the fact that if the unskilled are constrained, they would make exactly the same choice about where to live as the more skilled. That term is also strictly rising with χ when

$$\alpha > \frac{1}{2}\left(\frac{\alpha W_U}{R_H} + 1\right),$$

which means that the condition is most likely to be satisfied when the housing constraint binds tightly. I will assume that this condition holds.

If high skilled people consume only high amenity housing and unskilled people consume only low amenity housing, then the price of high amenity housing is $R_H = (\alpha N_S W_S / \bar{H}_H \zeta)^{1/(1+\rho)}$ and the price of low amenity housing is $R_L = (\alpha N_U W_U / \bar{H}_L \zeta)^{1/(1+\rho)}$. The spatial equilibrium condition for high skilled individuals becomes

$$U_S = \theta_H W_S^{(1+\rho-\alpha)/(1+\rho)} \xi \left(\frac{\bar{H}_H \zeta}{\alpha N_S}\right)^{u/(1+\rho)}.$$

The spatial equilibrium condition for low skilled people is

$$\underline{U}_U = \theta_L W_U^{(1+\rho-\alpha)/(1+\rho)} \xi \left(\frac{\bar{H}_L \zeta}{\alpha N_U}\right)^{\alpha/(1+\rho)}.$$

Thus, both spatial equilibrium conditions give us that

$$\frac{W_S}{W_U} = \left(\frac{\theta_L \underline{U}_S}{\theta_H \underline{U}_U}\right)^{(1+\rho)/(1+\rho-\alpha)} \left(\frac{\bar{H}_L N_S}{\bar{H}_H N_U}\right)^{\alpha/(1+\rho-\alpha)}.$$

Using this condition, and the labor demand condition, $W_S/W_U = \psi(N_U/N_S)^{1-\sigma}$, implies that

$$\frac{N_S}{N_U} = \psi^{(1+\rho-\alpha)/((1+\rho)(1-\sigma)+\sigma\alpha)}\left(\frac{\theta_H \underline{U}_U}{\theta_L \underline{U}_S}\right)^{(1+\rho)/((1+\rho)(1-\sigma)+\sigma\alpha)}\left(\frac{\bar{H}_H}{\bar{H}_L}\right)^{\alpha/((1+\rho)(1-\sigma)+\sigma\alpha)},$$

$$\frac{W_S}{W_U} = \psi^{\alpha/((1+\rho)(1-\sigma)+\sigma\alpha)}\left(\frac{\theta_L \underline{U}_S}{\theta_H \underline{U}_U}\right)^{((1+\rho)(1-\sigma))/((1+\rho)(1-\sigma)+\sigma\alpha)}\left(\frac{\bar{H}_L}{\bar{H}_H}\right)^{\alpha(1-\sigma)/((1+\rho)(1-\sigma)+\sigma\alpha)}$$

and

$$\frac{R_H}{R_L} = \left(\psi\left(\frac{\theta_H \underline{U}_U}{\theta_L \underline{U}_S}\right)^{\sigma}\left(\frac{\bar{H}_L}{\bar{H}_H}\right)^{1-\sigma}\right)^{1/((1-\rho)(1-\sigma)+\sigma\alpha)}.$$

If the growth rates of rents are constant over time and equal to g_H for the high amenity housing and g_L for low amenity housing, then the prices of housing will equal $P_H = \frac{1/r}{r-g_H} R_H$ and $P_L = \frac{1/r}{r-g_L} R_L$. These equations then imply that

$$\log\left(\frac{N_S}{N_U}\right) = \frac{1+\rho-\alpha}{\bar{\omega}}\log(\psi) + \frac{1+\rho}{\bar{\omega}}\log\left(\frac{\underline{U}_U \theta_H}{\underline{U}_S \theta_L}\right) + \frac{\alpha}{\bar{\omega}}\log\left(\frac{\bar{H}_H}{H_L}\right) \quad (3.13)$$

$$\log\left(\frac{W_S}{W_U}\right) = \frac{\alpha}{\bar{\omega}}\log(\psi) - \frac{(1-\sigma)(1+\rho)}{\bar{\omega}}\log\left(\frac{\underline{U}_U \theta_H}{\underline{U}_S \theta_L}\right) - \frac{\alpha(1-\sigma)}{\bar{\omega}}\log\left(\frac{\bar{H}_H}{\bar{H}_L}\right) \quad (3.14)$$

$$\log\left(\frac{R_H}{R_L}\right) = \frac{1}{\bar{\omega}}\log(\psi) + \frac{\sigma}{\bar{\omega}}\log\left(\frac{\underline{U}_U \theta_H}{\underline{U}_S \theta_L}\right) - \frac{1-\sigma}{\bar{\omega}}\log\left(\frac{\bar{H}_H}{\bar{H}_L}\right) \quad (3.15)$$

where $\bar{\omega} = (1+\rho)(1-\sigma) + \sigma\alpha$. The price equation will be the same as the rent equation if the growth rate of high and low amenity rents is the same. One use of these equations is to note that if I use the notation $v_\psi = \frac{1}{\bar{\omega}}\log(\psi)$ and

$$v_e = \frac{1+\rho}{\bar{\omega}}\log\left(\frac{\underline{U}_U \theta_H}{\underline{U}_S \theta_L}\right) + \frac{\alpha}{\bar{\omega}}\log\left(\frac{\bar{H}_H}{\bar{H}_L}\right),$$

then the covariance of $\log(\frac{N_S}{N_U})$ and $\log(\frac{W_S}{W_U})$ equals $\alpha(1+\rho-\alpha)\text{Var}(v_\psi) - (1-\sigma)\text{Var}(v_\theta) - (1+\rho-2\alpha-\sigma+\alpha\sigma-\rho\sigma)\text{Cov}(v_\psi, v_\theta)$.

If the covariance term is small either because $(1+\rho-2\alpha-\sigma+\alpha\sigma-\rho\sigma)$ is close to zero or because the actual covariance is small, then the covariance between the skill premium and the skill ratio gives us a sense about what is actually driving the heterogeneity across space. If the correlation is positive, then this leads us to think that correlation in productivity levels (labor demand) is more important. If the correlation is negative, then this leads us to think that correlation in the amenity and housing related variables is more important.

In Figure 3.15, I show the relationship between this wage premium and the skill proportion. In general, places that have higher wages for college graduates have a higher proportion of college graduates. This suggests that labor demand factors may be driving the distribution of this population across metropolitan areas.

In a static framework, these equations help us assess the differential causes of differences in the skill premium or skill distribution across space. I begin with the equations

$$\log(\psi) = K_{\psi} + \lambda_{\psi} X + \mu_{\psi},$$

$$\log\left(\frac{U_U \theta_H}{\underline{U}_S \theta_L}\right) = K_{\theta} + \lambda_{\theta} X + \mu_{\theta}$$

and

$$\log\left(\frac{\bar{H}_H}{\bar{H}_L}\right) = K_H + \lambda_H X + \mu_H,$$

where K_{ψ}, K_{θ} and K_H are constants, λ_{ψ}, λ_{θ} and λ_H are coefficients, X is an exogenous variable and μ_{ψ}, μ_{θ} and μ_H are error terms. If $\hat{B}_N$, $\hat{B}_W$ and $\hat{B}_P$ represent the estimated coefficients on an X variable for the population, wage and price regressions (I assume constant expected growth rates for the two types of housing), then $\lambda_{\psi} = (1 - \sigma)\hat{B}_N + \hat{B}_W$, $\lambda_0 = \alpha\hat{B}_P - \hat{B}_W$, and $\lambda_H = \hat{B}_N + \hat{B}_W - (1 + \rho)\hat{B}_P$. This framework could be helpful in understanding the connection between exogenous amenity factors, like January temperature, and the distribution of skills across space.

To close the model, I must solve for the overall level of wages and population. The overall effective labor quantity can be written

$$N = N_S \left(\psi + \psi^{-\sigma(1+\rho-\alpha)/\bar{\omega}} \left(\frac{\theta_L \underline{U}_S}{\theta_H \underline{U}_H}\right)^{\sigma(1+\rho)/\bar{\omega}} \left(\frac{\bar{H}_L}{\bar{H}_H}\right)^{\frac{\alpha\sigma}{\bar{\omega}}}\right)^{1/\alpha},$$

which implies a labor demand curve of

$$W_S = \psi N_S^{(1-\beta-\gamma)/(1-\gamma)} \beta\gamma^{\gamma/(1-\gamma)} A^{1/(1-\gamma)} \bar{Z}^{(1-\beta-\gamma)/(1-\gamma)}$$

$$\times \left(\psi + \psi^{\sigma(1|\rho\alpha)/\bar{\omega}} \left(\frac{\theta_L \underline{U}_S}{\theta_H \underline{U}_H}\right)^{\sigma(1+\rho)/\bar{\omega}} \left(\frac{\bar{H}_L}{\bar{H}_H}\right)^{\frac{\alpha\sigma}{\bar{\omega}}}\right)^{(\beta-\sigma+\sigma\gamma)/\sigma(1-\gamma)}.$$

The labor supply/spatial indifference curve is

$$W_S = \left(\frac{\underline{U}_S}{\xi \theta_H}\right)^{(1+\rho)/(1+\rho-\alpha)} \left(\frac{\alpha N_S}{\bar{H}_H \zeta}\right)^{\alpha/(1+\rho-\alpha)}.$$

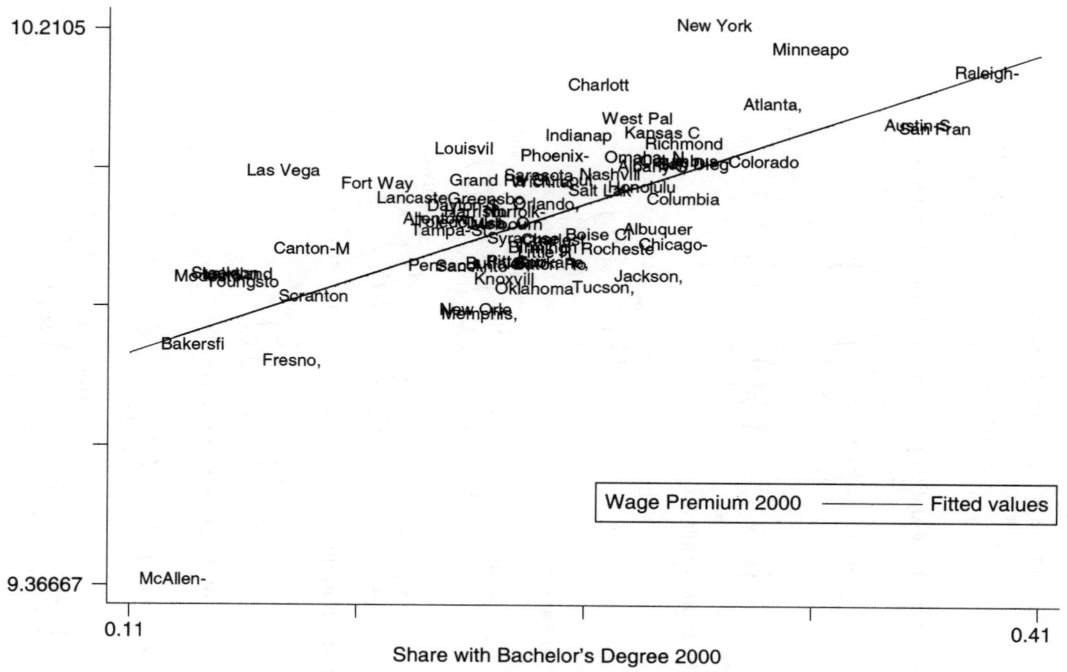

Figure 3.15. Wage premium and share of population with a Bachelor's degree by MSA

I use the notation θ to denote the geometric mean of the two amenity levels, so that $\theta_H = v^{.5}\theta$ and $\theta_L = \theta/v^{.5}$, where v is the ratio of the two amenity levels. If we set

$$\bar{\omega}_2 = (1-\beta-\gamma)(1+\rho)+\alpha\beta, \text{ and } \xi_2 = \left(\beta^{1-\gamma}\gamma^{\gamma}\bar{Z}^{1-\beta-\gamma}\right)^{(1+\rho-\alpha)/\bar{\omega}_2}(\xi)^{(1-\gamma)(1+\rho)/\bar{\omega}_2}\left(\frac{\zeta}{\alpha}\right)^{\alpha(1-\gamma)/\bar{\omega}_2},$$

then the size of the skilled population of the area equals

$$N_S = \xi_2 A^{(1+\rho-\alpha)/\bar{\omega}_2}\left(\psi^{1+\rho-\alpha}\left(\frac{v^{.5}\theta}{\underline{U}_S}\right)^{1+\rho}\bar{H}_H^{\alpha}\right)^{(1-\gamma)/\bar{\omega}_2}$$
$$\times\left(\psi+\psi^{\sigma(\alpha-\rho-1)/\bar{\omega}}\left(\frac{\underline{U}_S}{v\underline{U}_H}\right)^{\sigma(1+\rho)/\bar{\omega}}\left(\frac{\bar{H}_L}{\bar{H}_H}\right)^{\frac{\alpha\sigma}{\bar{\omega}}}\right)^{(\beta+\gamma\sigma-\sigma)(1+\rho)/\sigma\bar{\omega}_2}$$

and the total population equals

$$N_S+N_U = \xi_2 A^{(1+\rho-\alpha)/\bar{\omega}_2}\left(\left(\frac{v^{.5}\theta}{\underline{U}_S}\right)^{1+\rho}\bar{H}_H^{\alpha}\right)^{(1-\gamma)/\bar{\omega}_2}\Omega \quad (3.16)$$

where Ω equals

$$(\psi^{1+\rho-\alpha})^{(1-\gamma)/\bar{\omega}_2}\left(1+\psi^{(\alpha-\rho-1)/\bar{\omega}}\left(\frac{\underline{U}_S}{v\underline{U}_H}\right)^{(1+\rho)/\bar{\omega}}\left(\frac{\bar{H}_L}{\bar{H}_H}\right)^{\alpha/\bar{\omega}}\right)$$
$$\times\left(\psi+\psi^{\sigma(\alpha-\rho-1)/\bar{\omega}}\left(\frac{\underline{U}_S}{v\underline{U}_H}\right)^{\sigma(1+\rho)/\bar{\omega}}\left(\frac{\bar{H}_L}{\bar{H}_H}\right)^{\alpha\sigma/\bar{\omega}}\right)^{(\beta+\gamma\sigma-\sigma)(1+\rho)/\sigma\bar{\omega}_2}.$$

Using the notation $\bar{\omega}_3 = ((1-\beta-\gamma)(1+\rho)+\alpha\beta)(1+\rho-\alpha)/\alpha$, and

$$\xi_3 = \left(\frac{1}{\xi}\right)^{(1+\rho)/1+\rho-\alpha}\left(\frac{\alpha}{\zeta}\right)^{\alpha/(1+\rho-\alpha)}\xi_2^{\alpha/(1+\rho-\alpha)},$$

the income of the skilled people equals

$$W_S = A^{(1+\rho-\alpha)/\bar{\omega}_3}\bar{H}_H^{\alpha(1-\gamma)/\bar{\omega}_3}\left(\frac{\underline{U}_S}{v^{.5}\theta}\right)^{1-\alpha\beta/\bar{\omega}_2}\xi_3\psi^{\alpha(1-\gamma)/\bar{\omega}_2}$$
$$\times\left(\psi+\psi^{\sigma(\alpha-\rho-1)/\bar{\omega}}\left(\frac{\underline{U}_S}{v\underline{U}_H}\right)^{\sigma(1+\rho)/\bar{\omega}}\left(\frac{\bar{H}_L}{\bar{H}_H}\right)^{\alpha\sigma/\bar{\omega}}\right)^{(\beta+\gamma\sigma-\sigma)(1+\rho-\alpha)/\sigma\bar{\omega}_3}. \quad (3.17)$$

The average wage in the area equals

$$\widehat{W} = A^{\alpha/\bar{\omega}_2}\bar{H}_H^{\alpha(1-\gamma)/\bar{\omega}_3}\left(\frac{\underline{U}_S}{v^{.5}\theta}\right)^{(1+\rho)(1-\beta-\gamma)/\bar{\omega}_2}\xi_3\Omega_2 \quad (3.18)$$

where

$$\Omega_2 = \psi^{\alpha(1-\gamma)/\bar{\omega}_2}\left(1+\psi^{(\alpha-\rho-1)/\bar{\omega}}\left(\frac{\underline{U}_S}{\nu\underline{U}_H}\right)^{(1+\rho)/\bar{\omega}}\left(\frac{\bar{H}_L}{\bar{H}_H}\right)^{\alpha/\bar{\omega}}\right)^{-1}$$

$$\times\left(1+\psi^{(-1-\rho)/\bar{\omega}}\left(\frac{\underline{U}_S}{\nu\underline{U}_H}\right)^{(1+\rho)\sigma/\bar{\omega}}\left(\frac{\bar{H}_L}{\bar{H}_H}\right)^{\alpha\sigma/\bar{\omega}}\right)$$

$$\times\left(\psi+\psi^{\sigma(\alpha-\rho-1)/\bar{\omega}}\left(\frac{\underline{U}_S}{\nu\underline{U}_H}\right)^{\sigma(1+\rho)/\bar{\omega}}\left(\frac{\bar{H}_L}{\bar{H}_H}\right)^{\alpha\sigma/\bar{\omega}}\right)^{(\beta+\gamma\sigma-\sigma)(1+\rho-\alpha)/\sigma\bar{\omega}_3}.$$

These equations can then guide us on the human capital spillovers literature. This literature, which stems from Rauch (1993), asks whether there are general productivity spillovers associated with working around skilled people. I will model this assumption by allowing A to be a function of (N_S/N_U). Specifically, I assume that $A = A_0\,(N_S/N_U)^{\varphi}$. Since A does not influence the skill distribution, this equation then implies that

$$A - A_0\left(\psi^{1+\rho-\alpha/((1+\rho)(1-\sigma)+\sigma\alpha)}\left(\frac{\theta_H\underline{U}_U}{\theta_L\underline{U}_S}\right)^{1+\rho/((1+\rho)(1-\sigma)+\sigma\alpha)}\right.$$

$$\left.\times\left(\frac{\bar{H}_H}{\bar{H}_L}\right)^{\alpha/((1+\rho)(1-\sigma)+\sigma\alpha)}\right)^{\varphi}.$$

This can be readily inserted into equations (3.17) or (3.18) to give us a final formulation for the overall skills in the area.

I have already stressed that direct regressions where wages are regressed on area level skills are quite problematic because of the endogeneity of the skill distribution, but what about instrumental variables approaches, such as those of Moretti (2004) that use historical colleges as an instrument for schooling: How should we think about those instruments in a spatial equilibrium framework?

First, we cannot think of them as shifting N_S/N_U directly. Even if they drove some original distribution of skills, we cannot assume that migration ceased in 1940. The spatial equilibrium assumption requires us to assume that there has been a response. This doesn't mean that the instruments are useless. After all, they predict current skill levels, which would not be the case if they just determined some starting skill distribution which no longer matters.

Perhaps the most natural way to understand the instruments is through the increase in relative attractiveness of the city for skilled people. I have been interpreting the high amenity level as reflecting such things as views and schools, but perhaps it also reflects a historical connection of skilled people with an area, either because those people themselves now prefer living in the area or because they have built up amenities that apply specifically to skilled people. I find this interpretation reasonable, certainly it is among the best case scenarios for the instruments, but it still does create challenges for empirical estimation. As such, if we interpret the historical instruments as representing a shift in v, then we need to ask what impact that will have on wages.

An increase in v creates three effects on wages (of skilled workers), as shown in equation (3.17). First, it will increase A if the spillover is in operation. Second, the increase in the attractiveness of the area for skilled people will cause $\underline{U}_S/v_0^5$ to fall. This effect represents the fact that an increase in skilled people decreases the returns to unskilled people. Finally, there is a third effect that works on the overall amount of effective labor, because skilled workers are more productive, which has an ambiguous effect on the marginal product of effective labor, depending on whether $(\beta+\gamma\sigma-\sigma)(1+\rho-\alpha)$ is positive. If $(\beta+\gamma\sigma-\sigma)(1+\rho-\alpha)$ is close to zero, then we could also ignore this third effect.

My view is that the Moretti approach is certainly the best thing out there and strongly dominates the ordinary least squares approach that preceded it. As always, there is an issue about whether other variables that influence productivity are correlated with the instrument. Furthermore, his approach is entirely compatible with the spatial equilibrium model if we assume that his instruments are acting to increase the amenities of the city for high human capital people and if $(\beta+\gamma\sigma-\sigma)(1+\rho-\alpha)$ is small. If $(\beta+\gamma\sigma-\sigma)(1+\rho-\alpha)$ is not small, then at least we should recognize that these instrumental variable estimates combine a spillovers effect and the effect that works through the supply of effective labor. A decent estimate of that combined effect is better than the alternatives.

A second use of these equations is to form a theoretical basis for the empirical work on skills and city growth. If I assume that

$$\log\left(\frac{A_{t+1}}{A_t}\right) = K_A + \lambda_A\left(\frac{N_S}{N_S+N_U}\right) + \mu_A,$$

$$\log\left(\frac{\theta_{t+1}}{\theta_t}\right) = K_\theta + \lambda_\theta\left(\frac{N_S}{N_S+N_U}\right) + \mu_\theta,$$

and the skill distribution impacts no other variables, then

$$\log\left(\frac{(N_S+N_U)_{t+1}}{(N_S+N_U)_t}\right) = K_N + \left(\frac{1+\rho-\alpha}{\bar{\omega}_2}\lambda_A + \frac{(1+\rho)(1-\gamma)}{\bar{\omega}_2}\lambda_\theta\right) \times \left(\frac{N_S}{N_S+N_U}\right) + \varepsilon_A, \tag{3.19}$$

and

$$\log\left(\frac{\ddot{W}_{t+1}}{\widehat{W}_t}\right) = K_W + \left(\frac{\alpha}{\bar{\omega}_2}\lambda_A - \frac{(1+\rho)(1-\beta-\gamma)}{\bar{\omega}_2}\lambda_\theta\right)\left(\frac{N_S}{N_S+N_U}\right) + \varepsilon_A. \quad (3.20)$$

If $\hat{B}_N$ and $\hat{B}_W$ reflect the coefficients from the population growth and wage growth regressions respectively, then λ_A equals $(1-\beta-\gamma)$ $(\hat{B}_N + \frac{1-\gamma}{1-\beta-\gamma}\hat{B}_W)$ and λ_θ equals $\frac{\alpha}{1+\rho}(\hat{B}_N - \frac{1+\rho-\alpha}{\alpha}\hat{B}_W)$. As before, the underlying parameters are derived through a combination of the regression coefficients. The price regression can also give us a third degree of freedom.

This is the approach taken by Glaeser and Saiz (2004) and Shapiro (2006), who use these estimates to argue that the relationship between city growth and skills is driven by a connection between city skills and rising productivity, not rising amenities. These papers also find that wages, corrected for local price levels, are rising faster in areas that begin with more skills. This finding is also incompatible with the view that skills are driving up relative amenity levels.

Berry and Glaeser (2005) focus specifically on the connection between initial skills and growth in the skilled share of the population shown in Figure 3.16. There is a robust positive relationship since 1970 between the initial share of the population with college degrees and the growth in the share of the population with college degrees.

This investigation is essentially about changes in

$$\frac{N_S}{N_U} = \psi^{(1+\rho-\alpha)/((1+\rho)(1-\sigma)+\sigma\alpha)}\left(\frac{\theta_H \underline{U}_U}{\theta_L \underline{U}_S}\right)^{(1+\rho)/((1+\rho)(1-\sigma)+\sigma\alpha)}\left(\frac{\bar{H}_H}{\bar{H}_L}\right)^{\alpha/((1+\rho)(1-\sigma)+\sigma\alpha)},$$

the share of the population that is skilled. This regression could be used to investigate whether initial skills are correlated with changes in ψ or $(\frac{\theta_H \underline{U}_U}{\theta_L \underline{U}_S})$. In other words, whether there is a positive connection between skills and future skill growth because of growth in the skill-bias of technology, or the skill-bias of amenities. In principle, skills could also be correlated with changes in the housing supply, but this would require a slightly different set of assumptions about dynamic housing supply, more in line with differential growth rates for the different production costs.

Housing supply heterogeneity and urban decline

In the next two sections, I return to housing supply and draw on joint work with Joseph Gyourko, who deserves credit for anything good in this section and no blame for my excesses. First, I present material from Glaeser and Gyourko (2005) on durable housing and urban decline

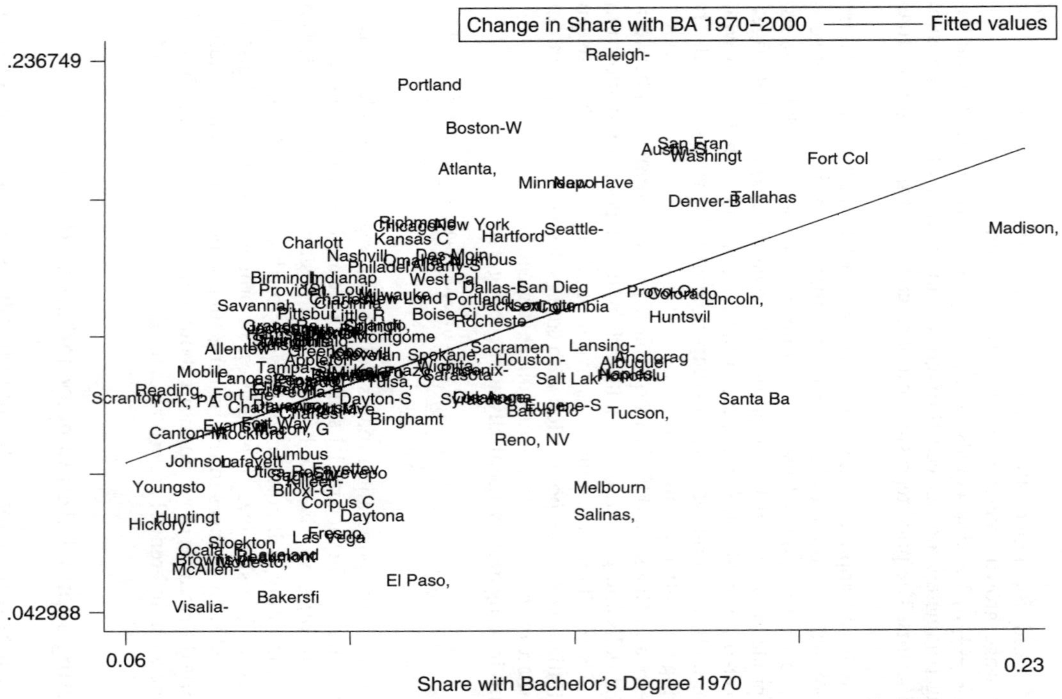

Figure 3.16. Change in the skilled share of the population and initial skilled share of the population from 1970–2000

and then I address the use of the spatial equilibrium approach to high frequency housing price dynamics, which is from Glaeser and Gyourko (2006).

Many cities in the US and throughout the world are in decline. Eight of the ten largest cities (and I mean cities not metropolitan areas) in the US in 1950 have a smaller population today. In the previous sections, I have dealt exclusively with cities with rising housing prices and new construction. This doesn't fit central city Detroit or Cleveland or Saint Louis. In those places, little new building occurs.

A related fact, shown in Glaeser and Gyourko (2005), is that low housing prices offset low income levels. The low prices in America's troubled areas are a natural implication of the spatial equilibrium. However, in many places, these prices are lower than the cost of new construction. As such, the prices, implied by wages and the spatial equilibrium assumption, violate the assumption that the construction industry is optimizing, or more correctly violate the assumption that the construction industry is optimizing and building. The most natural way to rationalize prices below construction costs is that housing was built during an earlier period when demand was more robust. Over time, that demand has fallen but the houses remain because they are durable.

To successfully model America's low income declining cities, we must recognize that housing is quite durable. It lasts for decades or even centuries and even if the demand for a place declines, its population may remain because of durable infrastructure. The durable nature of housing produces a kinked supply curve as shown in Figure 3.17. The kink occurs

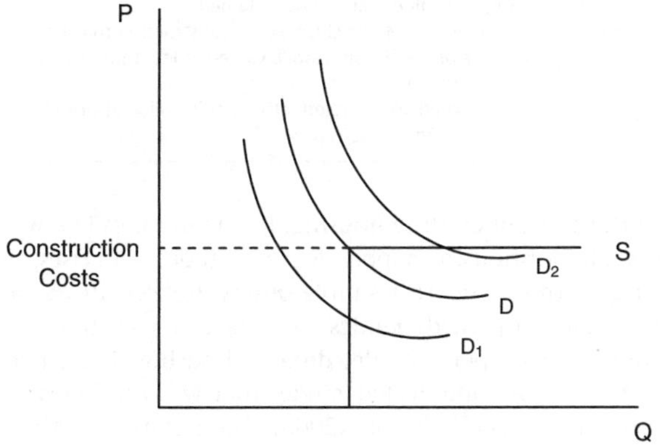

Figure 3.17.

Table 3.13. Modeling durable housing

Actors	Individuals, developers
They maximize	Individuals: Utility = Cash + City-specific amenities + Location-specific amenities Developers: Expected value of future net revenues, discounted continuously at rate ρ
They choose	Individuals: Location within the city Developers: Whether or not to build
Notation	w: city-specific wage level A: city-specific amenity level a: location-specific amenity level r: rent $\underline{U}$: reservation flow of utility θ: overall demand for the city, defined as $w + A - \underline{U}$ α, σ : parameters in the Brownian motion N: number of locations (lots) in the city $F(a)$, $f(a)$: CDF and PDF of a C: cost of building a house m: cost of using (maintaining) a house $\hat{a}(t) = m - \theta(t)$: the amenity level of the lowest quality occupied housing at time t ρ: continuous discount rate for developers θ^*: threshold value for a developer to build on a lot, equals $\lambda + m - a$ λ: parameter satisfying $\phi(\lambda - \rho C) + e^{-\phi\lambda} = 1$ ϕ: parameter, equals $\dfrac{2\rho}{\sqrt{\alpha^2 + 2\rho\sigma^2} - \alpha}$ $V(\theta)$: value of a house π : parameter defined as $\max(\theta + a - m, 0)$ k_j^i: constants of integration $Q(\theta)$: value of an empty lot a^*: least attractive lot-specific amenity level that will be developed $\underline{a}^*$: lowest amenity value lot that has been developed $\bar{\bar{\theta}}$: highest value that $\theta(t)$ has attained $f_{\min}$: Number of lots close to the construction margin S: share of the housing stock valued at less than the price of new construction $a_{\text{med}}(t)$: median occupied lot's amenity value at time t $a_{\text{mar}}(t)$: marginal lot in use

because of the stock of existing housing. If demand falls below this kink, then prices fall, but housing supply does not. If demand rises, then both prices and quantities rise. This simple observation creates a number of implications about urban dynamics that are generally born out in the data. However, to properly model durable housing, I need to present a considerably more complicated model that was originally an online appendix to Glaeser and Gyourko (2005). The notation of this model is given in Table 3.13.

I start with a standard spatial equilibrium. A person who chooses to live in a given house receives each period a city-specific wage level, w, a city-specific amenity level, A, a location-specific amenity level a, and pays rent r.[2] Free mobility implies that $w + A + a - r = \underline{U}$, where $\underline{U}$ refers to the reservation flow of utility. This equality implies that rent equals $w + A + a - \underline{U}$, or $r = \theta + a$, where $\theta \equiv w + A - \underline{U}$. In this case, I use θ to include wages, city-specific amenities, and reservation utility to form an overall demand for the city. The location-specific amenities might capture distance to the city center in a conventional monocentric model, but they can also reflect any exogenous characteristic that makes one place more desirable than another. As I have assumed throughout, the city is small and has no effect on the reservation utility.

I assume that θ follows a classic Brownian motion: $d\theta = \alpha dt + \sigma dz$. Location-specific amenities a are fixed over time. These amenities differ across the N lots that exist in the city and the distribution of a is characterized by a cumulative distribution $F(a)$ and a density $f(a)$. Each lot can only contain one house, and we assume that all houses are physically identical. Houses cost C to build and m to use (or maintain). If the resident pays m, then the house does not depreciate. If the owner does not pay m, then the house is not usable, but it becomes usable as soon as the resident pays m again. This can be understood as an endogenous depreciation model in which houses only leave the market when $r < m$, but even then, exit need not be permanent. Consequently, at any point in time, houses with values of a for which $m - \theta > a$ will not be in use. We let $\hat{a}(t) = m - \theta(t)$ denote the amenity level of the lowest quality occupied housing in the city in period t.

Developers make construction decisions to maximize the expected value of future net revenues, discounted continuously at a rate ρ.[3] Using the tools of Dixit and Pindyck (1994), we know that a developer, who owns a site with amenity level a, will build when θ equals a threshold value of $\theta^* = \lambda + m - a$, where λ satisfies the condition

$$\phi(\lambda - \rho C) + e^{-\phi\lambda} = 1$$

with

$$\phi = \frac{2\rho}{\sqrt{\alpha^2 + 2\rho\sigma^2} - \alpha}.$$

[2] It is easiest to think of everyone as a renter, but equivalently, every resident can be thought of as an owner-occupier where r represents the user cost of owner-occupied housing.

[3] Their maximand is $\int_{t=0}^{\infty} e^{-\rho t} n(t) dt$, where $n(t)$ refers to net revenues in each time period.

For values of θ above θ^*, building is strictly preferred, and for values of θ below θ^*, not building is strictly preferred.

Housing value is determined by the continuous time Bellman equation,

$$\rho V(\theta) = \pi + \frac{1}{dt}\mathrm{E}(dV(\theta)),$$

where E(.) represents the expectations operator, $V(\theta)$ represents the value of the house and $\pi = \max(\theta + a - m, 0)$. The value of the house itself only changes with θ, which follows the stochastic process $d\theta = \alpha dt + \sigma dz$. Therefore, Ito's lemma tells us that $E(dV) = \left(\alpha V'(\theta) + .5\sigma^2 V''(\theta)\right)dt$. The Bellman equation then can be rewritten as $\rho V(\theta) = \pi + \alpha V'(\theta) + .5\sigma^2 V''(\theta)$. Solving this differential equation tells us that $V(\theta)$ takes the form

$$V(\theta) = k + k_0\theta + k_1 e^{(-\alpha-\sqrt{\alpha^2+2\rho\sigma^2})\theta/\sigma^2} + k_2 e^{(-\alpha+\sqrt{\alpha^2+2\rho\sigma^2})\theta/\sigma^2},$$

where k, k_0, k_1 and k_2 are constants of integration.

In the region where $\theta + a > m$, the value function must take the form

$$V(\theta) = \frac{\theta + a - m}{\rho} + \frac{\alpha}{\rho^2} + k_1^a e^{(-\alpha-\sqrt{\alpha^2+2\rho\sigma^2})\theta/\sigma^2} + k_2^a e^{(-\alpha+\sqrt{\alpha^2+2\rho\sigma^2})\theta/\sigma^2},$$

and in the region where $\theta + a < m$, the value function takes the form

$$V(\theta) = k_1^b e^{(-\alpha-\sqrt{\alpha^2+2\rho\sigma^2})\theta/\sigma^2} + k_2^b e^{(-\alpha+\sqrt{\alpha^2+2\rho\sigma^2})\theta/\sigma^2},$$

where k_j^i are constants. As the value of $V(\theta)$ should go to zero as θ approaches $-\infty$, it must be that $k_1^b = 0$. The option value of leaving the house empty should go to zero as θ approaches $+\infty$, so $k_2^a = 0$. Thus, we have the solution that

$$V(\theta) = \frac{\theta + a - m}{\rho} + \frac{\alpha}{\rho^2} + k_1^a e^{(-\alpha-\sqrt{\alpha^2+2\rho\sigma^2})\theta/\sigma^2}$$

when $\theta + a > m$ and $V(\theta) = k_2^b e^{(-\alpha+\sqrt{\alpha^2+2\rho\sigma^2})\theta/\sigma^2}$ otherwise.

To solve for k_1^a and k_2^b, we use that fact that there can be no jumps in either $V(\theta)$ or $V'(\theta)$ at $\theta + a = m$ (the smooth pasting property). The first equality requires that

$$\frac{\alpha}{\rho^2} + k_1^a e^{(-\alpha-\sqrt{\alpha^2+2\rho\sigma^2})(m-a)/\sigma^2} = k_2^b e^{(-\alpha+\sqrt{\alpha^2+2\rho\sigma^2})(m-a)/\sigma^2}.$$

The second equality requires that

$$\frac{1}{\rho} - \frac{\alpha + \sqrt{\alpha^2 + 2\rho\sigma^2}}{\sigma^2} k_1^a e^{(-\alpha-\sqrt{\alpha^2+2\rho\sigma^2})(m-a)/\sigma^2}$$
$$= \frac{-\alpha + \sqrt{\alpha^2 + 2\rho\sigma^2}}{\sigma^2} k_2^b e^{(-\alpha+\sqrt{\alpha^2+2\rho\sigma^2})(m-a)/\sigma^2}$$

or

$$\frac{\left(\sqrt{\alpha^2+2\rho\sigma^2}-\alpha\right)^2}{4\rho^2\sqrt{\alpha^2+2\rho\sigma^2}}e^{(\alpha+\sqrt{\alpha^2+2\rho\sigma^2})(m-a)/\sigma^2}=k_1^a.$$

Solving these two equations yields:

$$\frac{\left(\sqrt{\alpha^2+2\rho\sigma^2}-\alpha\right)^2}{4\rho^2\sqrt{\alpha^2+2\rho\sigma^2}}e^{(\alpha+\sqrt{\alpha^2+2\rho\sigma^2})(m-a)/\sigma^2}=k_1^a$$

and

$$\frac{\left(\sqrt{\alpha^2+2\rho\sigma^2}+\alpha\right)^2}{4\rho^2\sqrt{\alpha^2+2\rho\sigma^2}}e^{(\alpha-\sqrt{\alpha^2+2\rho\sigma^2})(m-a)/\sigma^2}=k_2^b.$$

This implies that the value function is

$$\frac{\left(\sqrt{\alpha^2+2\rho\sigma^2}+\alpha\right)^2}{4\rho^2\sqrt{\alpha^2+2\rho\sigma^2}}e^{(-\alpha+\sqrt{\alpha^2+2\rho\sigma^2})(\theta+a-m)/\sigma^2}$$

when rents are negative and

$$\frac{\theta+a-m}{\rho}+\frac{\alpha}{\rho^2}+\frac{\left(\sqrt{\alpha^2+2\rho\sigma^2}-\alpha\right)^2}{4\rho^2\sqrt{\alpha^2+2\rho\sigma^2}}e^{(-\alpha-\sqrt{\alpha^2+2\rho\sigma^2})(\theta+a-m)/\sigma^2}$$

when rents are positive.

To calculate the point at which construction makes sense requires calculating the value of an empty lot. We use $Q(\theta)$ to capture this value and note that the differential equation $\rho Q(\theta)=\alpha Q'(\theta)+.5\sigma^2 Q''(\theta)$ again must hold. This tells us that $Q(\theta)=k_1^c e^{(-\alpha-\sqrt{\alpha^2+2\rho\sigma^2})\theta/\sigma^2}+k_2^c e^{(-\alpha+\sqrt{\alpha^2+2\rho\sigma^2})\theta/\sigma^2}$. As the option to build must approach 0 as θ approaches $-\infty$, it must be that $k_1^c=0$. We now use the notation that θ^* is the level of θ at which construction is optimal. As it would never make sense to build when $\theta+a<m$, we use the fact that $Q(\theta^*)=V(\theta^*)-C$ and $Q'(\theta^*)=V'(\theta^*)$ (i.e. the smooth pasting property) to solve for the constants. Together, these two conditions give us the equations:

$$\frac{\theta+a-m}{\rho}+\frac{\alpha}{\rho^2}+\frac{\left(\sqrt{\alpha^2+2\rho\sigma^2}-\alpha\right)^2}{4\rho^2\sqrt{\alpha^2+2\rho\sigma^2}}e^{(-\alpha-\sqrt{\alpha^2+2\rho\sigma^2})(\theta^*+a-m)/\sigma^2}-C$$

$$=k_2^c e^{(-\alpha+\sqrt{\alpha^2+2\rho\sigma^2})\theta^*/\sigma^2}$$

and

$$\frac{1}{\rho} - \frac{\left(\sqrt{\alpha^2 + 2\rho\sigma^2} - \alpha\right)}{2\rho\sqrt{\alpha^2 + 2\rho\sigma^2}} e^{(-\alpha - \sqrt{\alpha^2+2\rho\sigma^2})(\theta^* + a - m)/\sigma^2}$$

$$= \frac{\sqrt{\alpha^2 + 2\rho\sigma^2} - \alpha}{\sigma^2} k_2^c e^{(-\alpha+\sqrt{\alpha^2+2\rho\sigma^2})\theta^*/\sigma^2}.$$

Solving these equations yields:

$$\theta^* + a - m - \rho C = \frac{\left(\sqrt{\alpha^2 + 2\rho\sigma^2} - \alpha\right)}{2\rho}\left(1 - e^{-2\rho(\theta^* + a - m)/(\sqrt{\alpha^2+2\rho\sigma^2} - \alpha)}\right),$$

which if $\lambda = \theta^* + a - m$ and $\phi = 2\rho/(\sqrt{\alpha^2 + 2\rho\sigma^2} - \alpha)$ can be rewritten $\phi(\lambda - \rho C) + e^{-\phi\lambda} = 1$. Differentiating this equation yields:

$$\frac{\partial\lambda}{\partial C} = \frac{\rho}{1 - e^{-\phi\lambda}},$$

and for other variables denoted x (except for ρ):

$$\frac{\partial\lambda}{\partial x} = \frac{\partial\phi}{\partial x}\frac{e^{-\phi\lambda}}{\phi^2(1 - e^{-\phi\lambda})}\left(1 + \lambda\phi - e^{\phi\lambda}\right).$$

For any positive constant ϕ, $e^{\phi\lambda} > 1 + \lambda\phi$. Thus, the sign of $\partial\lambda/\partial x$ is the opposite of the sign of $\partial\phi/\partial x$, and simple differentiation gives us $\partial\phi/\partial\sigma < 0$ and $\partial\phi/\partial\alpha > 0$.

The equation $\theta^* = \lambda + m - a$ can be inverted, so we can say that for any given value of θ, there exists a value of a, denoted a^*, which represents the least attractive lot-specific amenity level that will be developed. As such, optimal development implies that the number of built-up lots in a growing city equals $N(1 - F(a^*))$. The value of λ, and, hence, θ^* (for a given a) or a^* (for a given θ) rises with C and σ and falls with α. As construction costs (C) rise or as the city's growth trend (α) falls, the threshold for construction increases and the level of development falls. As the degree of randomness (σ) rises, the option value of leaving a house empty rises and this also reduces the amount of development.

We then let $\underline{a}^* = \lambda + m - \bar{\theta}$ denote the lowest amenity value lot that has been developed in the city, where $\bar{\theta}$ is the highest value that $\theta(t)$ has reached. If $\theta(t)$ reaches a value greater than $\bar{\theta}$, new housing is built and the city grows, but if $\theta(t)$ falls below $\bar{\theta}$, the city does not necessarily shrink. All units remain occupied until $\bar{\theta} - \lambda > \theta(t)$ (or, equivalently, until $\hat{a}(t) > \underline{a}^*$). The size of λ determines the extent of the buffer zone in which demand can fall before the city loses population.

Because we can derive proofs in the case of the deterministic model, we proceed assuming that $\sigma^2 = 0$.[4] With simulations, we can further explore the impact of uncertainty. In deterministically growing cities, $\lambda = \rho C$ so $a^* + \theta - m = \rho C$, so that construction occurs to the point where the interest rate times construction costs equals net rents. In deterministically declining cities, λ satisfies $\rho(\lambda - \rho C) = -\alpha(1 - e^{\rho\lambda/\alpha})$, and $a^* = \lambda + m - \theta$. Net rents for new construction must exceed the interest rate times construction cost when rents are expected to decline.

We define time zero so that $\theta(0)$ is the historical maximum value that θ has reached (i.e. $\theta(0) = \bar{\theta}$). We also use the following linearizing approximation throughout the analysis:

Approximation 1: $\dfrac{F(a+x) - F(a)}{1 - F(a)} = f_{\min} x.$

Proposition 1 then follows (see Appendix for the proofs).

Proposition 1: *If $\theta(0) = \bar{\theta}$ then the growth rate of the city between period 0 and period t will equal $f_{\min}\alpha t$ if $\alpha \geq 0$, 0 if $0 > \alpha \geq -\rho^2 C/(\rho t + e^{-\rho t} - 1)$, and $f_{\min}(\alpha t + \lambda)$ if $-\rho^2 C/(\rho t + e^{-\rho t} - 1) \geq \alpha$.*

The proposition divides cities into three groups. Cities with positive growth trends grow at a rate equal to the trend rate times the time period times $f_{\min}$, where $f_{\min}$ reflects the number of lots close to the construction margin. Cities with negative values of α which are small in absolute value have no change in population. Rents and prices fall in these places, but there is no change in the number of occupied units because rents remain above maintenance costs. In cities with more substantial negative trends, the rents of some houses no longer cover maintenance costs, so they are left vacant. While these cities do have population losses, these losses are much smaller than the gains of growing cities whose trends are comparable in absolute value.

This sluggish response to negative shocks leads to Proposition 2:

Proposition 2: *If $\theta(0) = \bar{\theta}$, $f_{\min}$ is constant across cities, but α varies across cities then:*

(*a*) *If the distribution of α is symmetric and single peaked around $\hat{\alpha} > 0$, then the mean growth rate is greater than the median, but the difference between the mean and median growth rates falls with $\hat{\alpha}$.*

[4] Given that urban growth rates are remarkably correlated over time, treating them as being characterized primarily by different growth trends may not be a bad approximation in reality.

(*b*) *If* $\alpha = \alpha_0 + \beta z + \varepsilon$, *where z is an observable urban characteristic, and* ε *is symmetric, mean zero, and single peaked, then for any positive constant k, the derivative of growth with respect to z will be greater when* $z = (k - \alpha_0)/\beta$ *than when* $z = -(\alpha_0 + k)/\beta$.

The first part of the proposition states that if differences across cities are the result of different trends in demand, and if these trends are symmetrically distributed across cities, then population growth rates will be skewed to the left. Glaeser and Gyourko (2005) find that this is true empirically. There are some cities, like Las Vegas, that grow at extraordinary rates, but few cities decline by more than 10 percent a decade. The mean growth rate across cities is substantially higher than the median.

The second part of the proposition tells us that observable factors which impact city growth will have a greater impact on population growth when these observable characteristics predict a positive growth rate than they will when they predict negative growth. This result reflects the fact that durable housing restricts the tendency of cities to lose population, even if the level of demand for the city has fallen.

We now consider growth rates starting from time τ, so that for declining cities, $\theta(\tau)$ will not equal $\bar{\theta}$. Proposition 3 describes the persistence of growth rates:

Proposition 3: *The population growth rate between time* τ *and time* 2τ *equals the growth rate between time* 0 *and time* τ *if the city is growing. If the city lost population between time* 0 *and time* τ, *then the growth rate between time* τ *and time* 2τ *will equal* $1/(1 - (\lambda/ - \alpha\tau))$ *times the growth rate between time zero and time* τ.

Both growing and declining cities have persistent growth rates because we assumed that the urban dynamics are the result of deterministic trends. However, the relationship between past growth and future growth is stronger for declining cities. This strong persistence of decline occurs because the durability of housing delays the onset of population loss. As a result, past population loss understates the degree that demand for the city truly has fallen. Empirically, there is a remarkable tendency of decline to persist over decades, possibly because, as the model suggests, it takes a long time for housing to become unfit for use.

For declining cities, the value of $\bar{\theta} - \theta(\tau)$ can be measured using the share of the housing stock that is valued at less than the price of new construction (denoted S). If $\lambda > \bar{\theta} - \theta(\tau)$, no homes have yet fallen into disuse. Using Approximation 1, we know that the share of homes with prices less than the price of new construction (S) equals $f_{\min}(\bar{\theta} - \theta(\tau))$. If we then consider urban decline between time τ and time t (where

$t > \tau$), once homes start to decay, the share of housing priced less than construction costs rises to $f_{\min}\lambda$ and the rate of population decline equals $f_{\min}\alpha(t - \tau)$. Further calculations produce:

Proposition 4(a): *If there is variation in α across cities but $f_{\min}$ is constant, then the expected growth rate of a city between time τ and time t falls discontinuously as S rises from zero, is independent of S when S is greater than zero but less than $f_{\min}\tau\rho^2 C/(\rho t + e^{-\rho t} - 1)$, and then declines monotonically with S for higher values of S.*

The share of the initial stock of housing that is valued below construction costs reflects the size of the city's negative trend. When S is low, α is negative but small in absolute value, and the expected growth rate between time τ and time t is zero. For higher levels of S, the growth rate equals $f_{\min}(\lambda + \alpha(t - \tau)) - S$.

We can prove a result similar to Proposition 4(a) in the stochastic case, where we eliminate city-specific trends and assume that all cities have the same basic parameter values. At time τ, the city is again characterized by $\theta(\tau)$, the current value of θ, and $\bar{\theta}(\tau)$, the highest value that θ has reached by that time. The share of the housing stock that is priced below construction costs again equals $f_{\min} \max\left(\bar{\theta}(\tau) - \theta(\tau), \lambda\right)$ and Proposition 4(b) follows:[5]

Proposition 4(b): *Expected city population growth declines with S when S is less than λ, but then rises discontinuously at the point where S equals λ.*

This proposition reiterates the conclusion of Proposition 4(a) that increases in the share of housing with values below the cost of new construction lower the expected growth rate, but in this case there is a reversal of the comparative static at the point where S equals λ. This reversal occurs because once S equals λ, the large supply of cheap housing makes it easier to grow because these houses can be reoccupied more cheaply than houses can be built from scratch. Empirically, the share of housing that is priced below construction costs strongly predicts urban decline.

I now turn to the implications of the model for prices. Data availability forces us to focus on median prices and rents, and we let $a_{med}(t)$ refer to the median occupied lot's amenity value as of time t. As demand for a city changes, two things happen which cause the median rent to shift. First, the price of any given lot is directly determined by θ so demand directly moves prices. Second, the identity of the median lot will change as the size of housing stock changes. As cities build more homes, the median lot

[5] In this case, λ solves $(\lambda - \rho C)\sqrt{2\rho} = \sigma\left(1 - e^{-\lambda\sqrt{2\rho}/\sigma}\right)$.

will have a lower value of a because new construction has increased the number of fringe lots with low levels of site-specific amenities. This effect can help explain observations like Las Vegas (discussed above) where population soars and real rents actually fall. As the city grows, the median lot is becoming relatively less attractive.

We now treat $f(a^*)/2f(a_{\text{med}})$ as a constant and use the following approximation,

Approximation 2: $a_{\text{med}}(t) - a_{\text{med}}(\tau) = \frac{f(a^*)}{2f(a_{\text{med}})} \cdot (a_{\text{mar}}(t) - a_{\text{mar}}(\tau))$,

where $a_{\text{mar}}(t)$ denotes the marginal lot in use, which equals $a^*(t)$ in growing cities and $\hat{a}(t)$ in declining cities. We also now return to the deterministic model where home prices equal $(\theta + a - m)/\rho + \alpha/\rho^2$ in a growing city and $(\theta + a - m)/\rho + (1 - e^{\rho}(\theta + a - m)/\alpha)\,\alpha/\rho^2$ in a declining city. In a growing city, θ is rising and the value of a^* is falling over time because of new construction, so the overall change in the median housing price equals $(\alpha t/\rho)(1 - f(a^*)/2f(a_{\text{med}}))$. If a was distributed uniformly, then new supply would halve the positive impact of increasing demand on the median housing price. Following Proposition 1, in a declining city in which α is less than zero but greater than $-\rho^2 C/(\rho t + e^{-\rho t} - 1)$, there will be no supply response to urban decline. Hence, the change in demand will be fully reflected in price changes. For declining cities with values of α that are more negative, there will be a supply response that will mediate the price response and less attractive homes will leave the market.

These calculations and conclusions lead us to Proposition 5:

Proposition 5:

(A) *If $\alpha = \alpha_0 + \beta z + \varepsilon$, where z is an observable urban characteristic, and ε is symmetric, mean zero and single peaked, then for any positive constant k, the derivative of rent growth with respect to z will be less when $z = (k - \alpha_0)/\beta$ than when $z = -(\alpha_0 + k)/\beta$.*

(B) *If $\alpha = \alpha_0 + \beta z + \varepsilon$, where z is an observable urban characteristic, then the derivative of housing price growth with respect to z will jump from $\frac{\beta t}{\rho}(1 - \frac{f(a^*)}{2f(a_{\text{med}})})$ to $\frac{\beta t}{\rho}$ when $\alpha = 0$.*

(C) *For any growing city, housing price growth will equal $\frac{1}{\rho f_{\min}}(1 - \frac{f(a^*)}{2f(a_{med})})$ times the percentage growth in population. For any declining city, the ratio of housing price decline to population decline will be greater than this quantity.*

Part (A) of Proposition 5 tells us that the impact of exogenous characteristics on rent growth will be smaller for growing cities than for declining cities. This comes from the fact that durability means that the supply adjustment will be less for declining cities. Part (B) gives us a similar result for housing price changes. Part (C) suggests that the relationship between changes in prices and changes in population will be concave. The slope of price change on population change will be less for growing cities than for declining cities. This result stems from the smaller supply response for declining cities. These conclusions formalize Figure 3.17, which provides the essential intuition that urban growth should show up most in rising numbers of people, but urban decline should show up most in declining home prices.

The different implications for price and quantity changes may be the most distinct implication of the durable housing model. If housing was putty, not clay, then rising demand for a city would create more houses that have higher prices; declining demand would reduce the housing stock and cause housing prices to fall. Durability generates the asymmetry between housing prices and population growth. In growing cities, rising prices and rising population levels go together; but in declining cities, prices fall first and far more steeply than population declines.

Glaeser and Gyourko (2005) also look at this proposition empirically. We find that there is a kinked relationship between population growth and housing price growth. Positive population growth is only weakly associated with housing price growth, presumably because supply is expanding. Negative growth is very strongly associated with housing price declines. Exogenous variables, like the weather, also have a big positive effect on population but only a marginal effect on prices when they are positive, but they have a big negative effect on price and only a marginal effect on population when they are negative. These findings are exactly what the proposition predicts.

High frequency housing price dynamics

I end by sketching the ways in which Glaeser and Gyourko (2006) use a dynamic, spatial equilibrium model to make predictions about housing price and quantity dynamics.[6] The central point of that paper is that the spatial equilibrium model provides the right starting point for thinking about housing price changes. This paper has not been published, but I think that it fits so naturally into the major theme of this chapter that I will still discuss it briefly. The central point of that paper is that too much of the work on higher frequency housing price dynamics had come out of an asset-based approach to housing rather than a spatial

[6] Van Nieuwerburgh and Weill (2006) present a similar model in their exploration of long run changes in the distribution of income.

equilibrium approach to housing. Our goal was to see whether a spatial equilibrium approach could actually explain the patterns that we observe in the data.

As I have throughout this chapter, I assume that there is a "reservation locale" that delivers utility of $\underline{U}(t)$ in each period t and that user cost of housing in this locale always equals $rC/(1+r)$, where C is the cost of construction and r is the interest rate. I assume that this locale represents the many metropolitan areas in the American hinterland with steady growth and where prices stay close to the physical costs of construction (Glaeser, Gyourko and Saks, 2005).

As before, I focus on the dynamics in a single representative city (which is different from the reservation city). The utility flow for person i living in that city during period t is $W(i, t) + A(i, t)$, or wages plus amenities. I now take a short cut and assume that the differences between utility flow of the marginal resident in this city and the reservation utility level can be written as $\bar{D} + qt + x(t) - \alpha N(t)$. The exogenous components of city amenities and wages include a city-specific component (denoted $\bar{D}$), a city-specific time trend (denoted qt) and a mean zero stochastic component (denoted $x(t)$). The parameter α multiplies the city housing stock, $N(t)$ and captures the assumption that wages, amenities and the taste of the marginal resident for living in the locale can fall linearly with city size. A fixed supply of firms with quadratic production technologies and a uniform distribution of people's tastes for living in the city can give us this linearity. Alternatively, it is also possible for this welfare flow to be log-linear assuming different production technologies and tastes of preferences.

I further assume that $x(t)$ follows an auto regressive moving average (ARMA) (1, 1) process so that $x(t) = \delta x(t-1) + \varepsilon(t) + \theta\varepsilon(t-1)$, where $0 < \delta < 1$, and the $\varepsilon(t)$ shocks are independently and identically distributed with mean zero. The expected cost of housing in the representative locale equals $H(t)$ minus $\mathrm{E}_t(H(t+1))/(1+r)$, where $\mathrm{E}_t(.)$ denotes the time t expectations operator. The spatial equilibrium approach to housing implies that the difference between the cost of housing in the representative city and housing costs in the reservation locale, $rC/(1+r)$, should be understood as the cost of receiving the extra utility flow associated with locating in the city. If extra housing costs in the city equals extra utility delivered by the city, then

$$H(t) - \frac{\mathrm{E}_t(H(t+1))}{1+r} - \frac{rC}{1+r} = \bar{D} + qt + x(t) - \alpha N(t). \qquad (3.21)$$

This is a truly dynamic version of the Rosen–Roback spatial indifference equation, in which differences in housing costs equal differences in wages plus differences in amenities. We assume a transversality condition on housing prices so that

$$\lim_{j\to\infty}\left(\frac{H(t+j)}{(1+r)^j}\right)=0.$$

If housing supply were fixed, as it might be in a declining city, then the model is solved and prices satisfy

$$H(t)=C+\frac{(1+r)(\bar{D}-\alpha N+qt)}{r}+\frac{(1+r)q}{r^2}+\frac{(1+r)x(t)+\theta\varepsilon(t)}{1+r-\delta}. \quad (3.22)$$

Housing prices are a function of exogenous population and exogenous shocks to wages and amenities. The derivative of housing prices with respect to a one dollar permanent increase in wages will be $(1+r)/r$, just as discussed above. Some financial economists who have approached housing prices have suggested that predictability of those prices is a problem for a rational model, but in this model, everyone is rational and prices rise linearly with t.

We assume a construction section that supplies $I(t)$ units of new housing, and that $N(t)$ equals $N(t-1)+I(t)$. The costs of producing a house are $C+c_0t+c_1I(t)+c_2N(t-1)$, where $c_1>c_2$ because current housing production should have a bigger impact on current construction costs than past production. Investment decisions for time t are made based on time $t-1$ information, and there is free entry of risk neutral builders. If there is a positive amount of building (which we assume), then prices satisfy

$$\mathrm{E}_{t-1}(H(t))=C+c_0t+c_1I(t)+c_2N(t-1). \quad (3.23)$$

Equations (3.21) and (3.23) together describe housing supply and demand, and together generate the steady state values of housing prices, which equals a city-specific constant plus $(1+r)(\alpha c_0+qc_2)/(rc_2+\alpha(1+r))$ times time, investment and housing stock, which are denoted $\hat{H}(t)$, $\hat{I}$ and $\hat{N}(t)$ respectively. When $\hat{N}(t)\neq N(t)$, Glaeser and Gyourko (2006) prove that housing prices equal

$$H(t)=\hat{H}(t)+\frac{\bar{\phi}}{\bar{\phi}-\delta}x(t)+\frac{\theta}{\bar{\phi}-\delta}\varepsilon(t)-\frac{\alpha(1+r)}{1+r-\phi}\left(N(t)-\hat{N}(t)\right)$$

and new construction equals

$$I(t+1)=\hat{I}+\frac{(1+r)}{c_1(\bar{\phi}-\delta)}\left(\delta x(t)+\theta\varepsilon(t)\right)-(1-\phi)\left(N(t)-\hat{N}(t)\right),$$

where $\bar{\phi}$ and ϕ are the two roots of

$$c_1 y^2 - ((2+r)c_1 + (1+r)\alpha - c_2)y + (1+r)(c_1 - c_2) = 0 \quad \text{and}$$
$$\bar{\phi} \geq 1 + r \geq 1 > \phi \geq 0.$$

A temporary shock,ε, will increase housing prices by $(\bar{\phi}+\theta)/(\bar{\phi}-\delta)$ and increase construction by $(1+r)\,(\delta+\theta)\,/c_1(\bar{\phi}-\delta)$. As housing supply becomes more inelastic, the construction response to shocks falls and that causes the price increase to such shocks to increase. This housing price formula also delivers housing price predictability, which is not a problem for a rational expectations model. The predictability of prices comes in part from the convergence to steady state values and partially from the predictability of changes in labor demand.

The model can also make sense of the fact that prices mean revert, in the sense that price changes are negatively correlated over long enough horizons, while quantity changes strongly persist. This fact appears to be a little bit of a puzzle, at least if you just applied a static supply/demand view to understanding housing prices, but it turns out quite naturally. If there are large trends in demand for the city, these can create strong persistence of quantity changes. There is also a positive impact on price change persistence, but it will be weaker since these shocks are fully anticipated. If the unexpected shocks strongly mean revert, they can be too weak to overturn the persistence of population growth created by the city-specific trends, but still strong enough to overturn the persistence of price growth created by those same trends.

Glaeser and Gyourko (2006) use this model to simulate price changes and quantity changes and to see whether the moments simulated by the model match the moments of data in the real world. We look at the variance of price changes and construction changes and the positive serial correlation of price changes and investment in the housing stock. We do not look at the correlation between prices and quantities, because the paper shows that the models predictions about those correlations are enormously sensitive to the information structure of the model. If you know shocks a year ahead of time it generates a completely different predicted correlation than if you know shocks when they occur.

Overall, our results are mixed. The model can explain the moments of new construction, both its variability and its serial correlation. We can explain the five-year mean reversion of price changes, which comes from the fact that labor demand shocks also appear to mean revert. We can also explain the price variability of the average American city. We cannot, however, explain the price volatility of the more extreme metropolitan areas, such as those on the coasts, which is far too high to be explained by income variability in those regions. We also fail to explain the high frequency positive serial correlation of housing price changes.

I think that this exercise is useful, because I believe that the spatial equilibrium approach is really the only sensible approach to housing prices. A house is an asset, but its real value lies in the fact that it gives access to a particular locale. Only a spatial equilibrium approach embeds that basic insight.

4

Agglomeration economies

While the spatial equilibrium concept is the most important tool of urban economics, agglomeration economies are the topic that is most central to the discipline. Agglomeration economies are said to exist whenever an individual's productivity rises when he or she is near to other individuals. Agglomeration economies may be externalities, as in the case where productivity rises from being able to learn and imitate from a neighbor. Alternatively, the externalities may work entirely within the market. If a supplier and a customer get close together, they have become more productive by eliminating transport costs but there is no obvious externality.

Agglomeration economies are so central to urban economics because they provide an economic rationale for the existence of cities, but they are not the only possible explanation for urban concentration. For example, people might cluster together for social reasons or the protection of city walls. People might mass in a particular place because of a proximate natural resource like a port or a coal mine. Indeed, as I will stress later in this chapter, it is often hard to tell agglomeration economies from natural advantage.

Still, urban economists are drawn to the view that agglomeration economies are important both because of empirical observation and because of natural biases. People become urban economists, in part, because they think that cities are important, so we tend to like to think that cities actually cause productivity. Economists naturally think that people make choices based, at least in part, on financial concerns. This leads us to the view that cities form, in part, because of the financial gains from urbanizing, i.e. agglomeration economies. A third bias is the economist's taste for closed, parsimonious models. Agglomeration economies can explain urban density in a closed model that doesn't need to appeal to external factors, like ports or mines. Empirically, I think the evidence suggests that these external factors are no longer that important. The older cities were generally built around harbors, and those harbors were significant, but there is no natural advantage that can explain Las Vegas or Atlanta.

In an urban context, agglomeration economies can be understood as the beneficial consequence of reducing transport costs. After all, the literal consequence of density is proximity. The benefit from being in a city is closeness to the other people in that city. If an individual leaves a city, he or she can still interact with that city's residents; it will just be a little harder. The key advantage from proximity and therefore the key agglomeration economy is the reduction of transport costs for goods, for people and for ideas.

I start with a general discussion of the empirics of agglomeration economies that relies on a simple reduced form model to guide those empirics. I then turn to a series of models that capture the different potential causes for productivity to rise with concentration. The goal is to formalize the view that proximity reduces transport costs for goods, for people and for ideas. I start with a simple version of Krugman (1991a,b) that looks at transport costs for goods. I then turn to models about reducing transport costs for people, and end with models that emphasize the urban edge in transferring ideas.

Income and density

While people do live in cities for the lifestyle, most people throughout history have gone to cities for the money. Today and in the past, big cities have offered higher wages than small towns. Figure 4.1 shows the strong correlation between metropolitan area size and nominal wages across the 100 largest metropolitan areas in the US. Nominal wages are higher in big cities.

High wages in big cities are, of course, compensation for high urban prices and, at least in the past, disamenities. After all, before the twentieth century, moving to the city was associated with a significantly shortened lifespan. Today, these disamenities are far less common, and Figure 4.2 shows the flat relationship between city size and wages corrected for the American Chamber of Commerce Research Association (ACCRA) local cost of living index. High urban wages are being completely offset by high costs of living. As such, from the point of view of the individual decision-maker, there is no puzzle behind high urban wages: they are part of a spatial equilibrium where high prices offset high wages.

But as I have tried to emphasize throughout this book, understanding cities requires understanding at least three types of decision-making agents: individuals who are choosing where to live and work, firms that are choosing where to operate and how many people to employ and

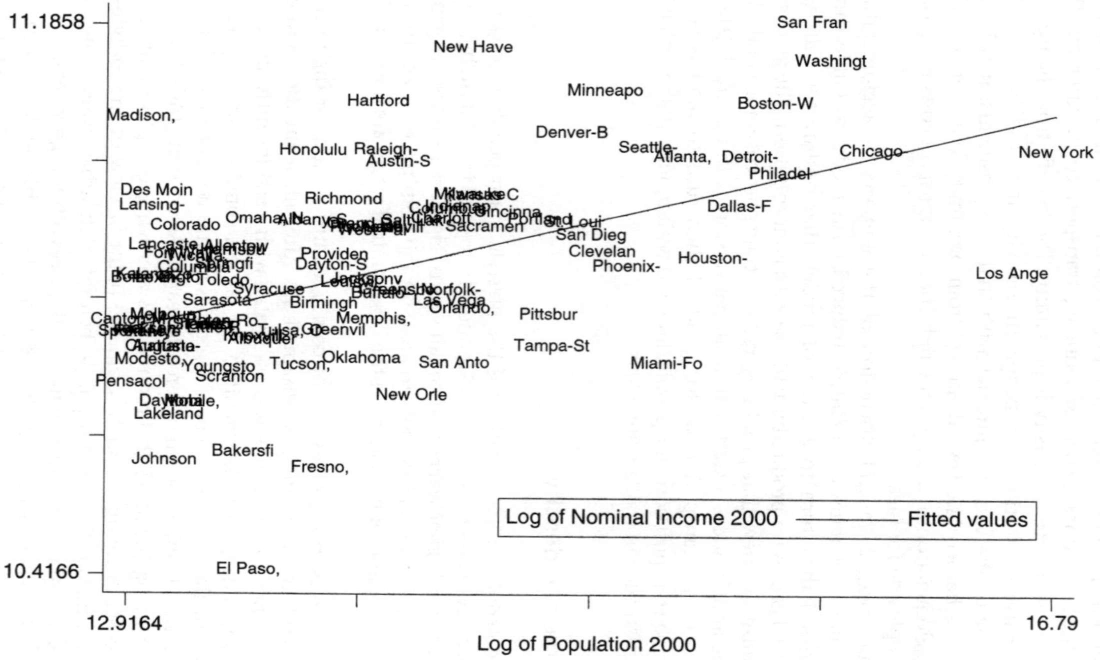

Figure 4.1. Nominal income and city size

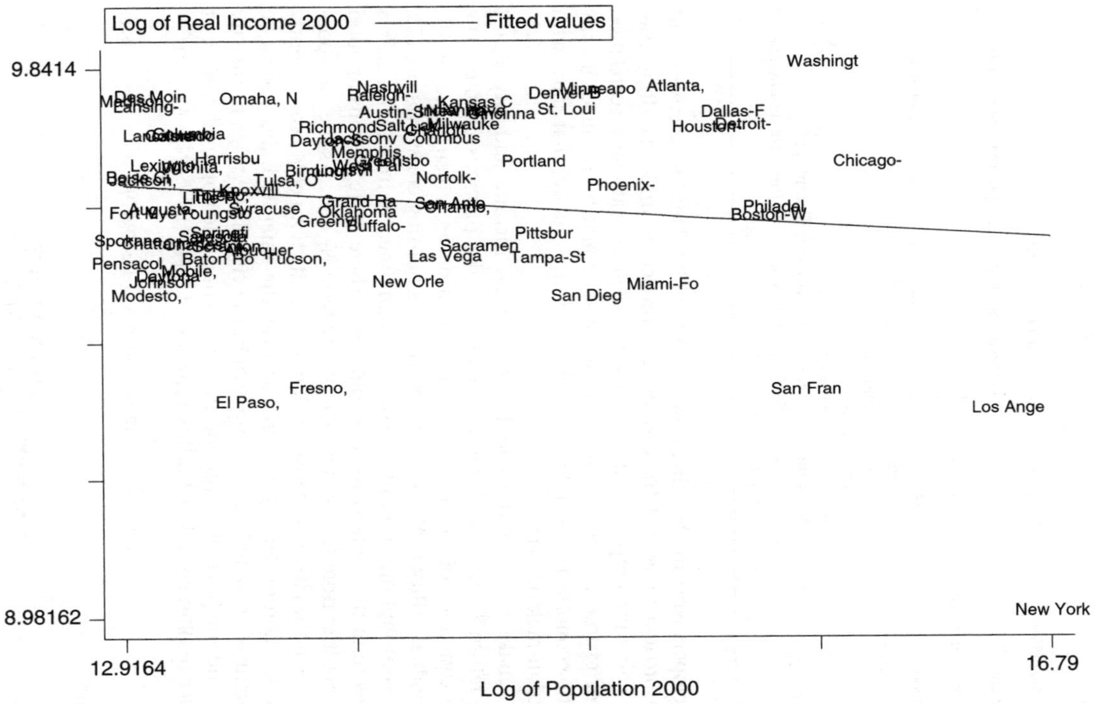

Figure 4.2. Real income and city size

Table 4.1. Housing consumption (akin to the Rosen–Roback framework in Chapter 3)

Actors	City inhabitants
They maximize	$\max_{C,H} \theta N_T^{-\eta} C^{1-\alpha} H^{\alpha} = \max_{H} (W - p_H H)^{1-\alpha} H^{\alpha}$
They choose	Individuals choose the amount of housing to maximize utility
First order condition	$\frac{-p_H(1-\alpha)}{W - p_H H} + \frac{\alpha}{H} = 0$
Notation	C := consumption of goods other than housing (priced at 1) H := nontradable housing θ := index capturing amenities p := price of housing W := income in the city N_T := total population in the city that is employed $N_T^{-\eta}$:= term reflecting the possibility that there are disamenities to living in larger cities

developers who are deciding how much to build. This perspective is part of a broader view that the economic approach to understanding cities can never use empirics without theory. I believe that every correlation or regression investigated by an economist should be justified, if only in the economists' head, by some kind of formal model that starts with decision-making agents.

To make sense of the correlation between income and city size, I will return to the basic framework used in the previous chapter. The core equations of this model and the notation are given in Table 4.1. Individual utility is $\theta N_T^{-\eta} C^{1-\alpha} H^{\alpha}$, where H is housing consumption, C is the consumption of all other goods, θ is an amenity index, and $N_T^{-\eta}$ is a new term that reflects the possibility that there more be consumption disamenities from living in a big city. The term N_T denotes the total population in the city. This consumption disamenity term could equivalently be a function of density, and in that case, the amenity index should be thought of as including the land area in the city. If the wage in the city is W and the price of consumption goods is one, then optimal consumer choice implies an indirect utility function of $\alpha^{\alpha}(1-\alpha)^{1-\alpha}\theta N_T^{-\eta} W p_H^{-\alpha}$, or

$$\log(W) = K_C - \log(\theta) + \eta log(N_T) + \alpha \log(p_H) \tag{4.1}$$

where

$$K_C = \log \frac{\text{Reservation Utility}}{\alpha^{\alpha}(1-\alpha)^{1-\alpha}},$$

which delivers the tradeoff between wages and housing prices. It also implies that real wages will be rising with city size if and only if $\eta > 0$.

As such, one interpretation of Figure 4.1 is that η is approximately zero. Glaeser and Mare (2001) use a figure like Figure 4.2 to make a second point about the connection between city size and wages. One possibility is that the correlation between nominal wages and city size is driven by higher ability people selecting to live in cities. In this case, the observed correlation would say more about omitted skill variables than agglomeration economies. However, if this correlation was driven mainly by omitted skills, then we should expect both nominal and real wages to rise significantly with city size. The fact that real wages do not rise with size can either mean that omitted ability variables are not important or that cities have profound consumption amenities that offset the rising ability levels.

I lean towards the interpretation that omitted skills, at least in the way that people normally think about them, are not that important in explaining the urban wage premium. There is no evidence that people select into cities on the basis of observable skill levels measured either with years of schooling or Armed Forces Qualification Tests (AFQT—a kind of IQ test). Controlling for observable skill measures like these does little to change the observed urban wage premium. I also think it is somewhat implausible that there are real big positive amenities that are serving to exactly offset higher urban ability levels and produce a flat relationship between city size and real wages.

The most important alteration from the previous model is that here I assume that firm productivity equals $AN_T^{\phi}N^{\beta}K^{\gamma}Z^{1-\beta-\gamma}$, where A represents a city specific productivity level, N represents the number of workers, K is traded capital, and Z is non-traded capital. The core equations of this model and the notation are given in Table 4.2. Traded capital can be

Table 4.2. The production sector (akin to the Rosen–Roback framework in Chapter 3)

Actors	Firms in the production sector
They maximize	$\max_{N,K} AN_T^{\phi}N^{\beta}K^{\gamma}Z^{1-\beta-\gamma} - WN - K$
They choose	Producers choose the number of workers and traded capital that would maximize profit. Each firm hires with the assumption that its actions will have no impact on the population level.
First order conditions	FOC for labor: $\beta AN_T^{\phi}N^{\beta-1}K^{\gamma}\bar{Z}^{1-\beta-\gamma} = W$ FOC for capital: $\gamma AN_T^{\phi}N^{\beta}K^{\gamma-1}\bar{Z}^{(1-\beta-\gamma)/(1-\gamma)} = 1$
Notation	A := city specific production level N := number of workers in the city (which is really equal to N_T) K := traded capital (priced at 1) Z := non-traded capital $\bar{Z}$:= fixed supply of non-traded capital $K_P := \log\left(\beta\gamma^{\gamma/(1-\gamma)}\bar{Z}^{(1-\beta-\gamma)/(1-\gamma)}\right)$

purchased anywhere for a price of one. The location has a fixed supply of non-traded capital equal to $\bar{Z}$. The change from the last chapter is the term N_T^{ϕ} which is meant to capture the possibility of agglomeration economies.

Later in this chapter, I will endogenize these agglomeration effects, but at this point, I simply use a reduced form. I assume that the agglomeration effects are external to the firm, and that each firm does not consider the impact that its hiring will have on the total city population. The agglomeration effects could be a function of total population or total density. If it is meant to capture a density effect, then we should think of A as including land area.

When firms behave competitively, their first order conditions deliver an aggregate labor demand curve $\beta A^{1/(1-\gamma)}\gamma^{\gamma/(1-\gamma)}N_T^{(\beta+\phi)/(1-\gamma)-1}\bar{Z}^{(1-\beta-\gamma)/(1-\gamma)} = W$ or

$$\log(W) = K_P + \frac{1}{1-\gamma}\log(A) + \left(\frac{\beta+\phi}{1-\gamma} - 1\right)\log(N_T), \tag{4.2}$$

where K_P is the logarithm of $\beta\gamma^{\gamma/(1-\gamma)}\bar{Z}^{(1-\beta-\gamma)/(1-\gamma)}$. This equation provides us with another take on the urban wage premium. Equation (4.2) implies that high wages in urban areas can be the result of agglomeration economies, if $(\beta+\phi)/(1-\gamma) > 1$, or a result of a correlation between high levels of productivity and population levels.

One attempt to assess the magnitude of agglomeration economies is to regress income on population or density and try to instrument for population using something like historical population. Ciccone and Hall (1996) is the classic example of this exercise. They find a robust connection between density and productivity that persists when they use nineteenth century variables, such as population density in 1880, railroads and distance to the Eastern seaboard, as instruments. Naturally, for this exercise to have any hope of validity, we would need to assume that historical variables, such as population, were uncorrelated with current levels of productivity.

Moreover, even if this orthogonality condition is satisfied, it is not straightforward to understand how this exercise makes sense in a spatial equilibrium. Did the migration not adjust to productivity in the twentieth century? One view is that local productivity (A) is a function of past population, in which case ϕ might equal zero but A might be a function of the lag of population. Alternatively, as I discussed in my interpretation of the Moretti (2004) evidence on human capital spillovers, historical population data might indicate that these cities had positive amenities for some people who had a long history living in those areas.

To close the model, I will assume the housing sector is literally unchanged from the baseline in the last chapter. The core equations of

Table 4.3. The construction sector (akin to the Rosen–Roback framework in Chapter 3)

Actors	Firms in the construction sector
They maximize	$\max_{h,L}\{p_H h - c_0 h^{\delta} - p_L\}$
They choose	Construction firms choose housing to maximize profits.
First order condition	FOC for height: $p_H = \delta c_0 h^{\delta-1}$
Key equilibrium condition	Housing market clearance: $\frac{\alpha N_T W}{p_H} = k_H\, p_H^{1/(1-\delta)} \underline{L}$
Notation	$k_H := (\delta c_0)^{1/(\delta-1)}$; that is, k_H is a constant defined so that housing supply is equal to $k_H\, p_H^{1/(1-\delta)} \underline{L}$ $h :=$ height $L :=$ land $hL :=$ total housing supplied $\bar{L} :=$ fixed quantity of land $p_L :=$ endogenous price for land $p_H :=$ endogenous price for height $c_0 h^{\delta} L :=$ cost of producing hL units on top of L units of land Used later on: $K_N := \frac{\left(1-\alpha+\frac{\alpha}{2-\delta}\right)K_P - K_C - \left(\alpha - \frac{\alpha}{2-\delta}\right)\log\left(\frac{\alpha}{k_H \underline{L}}\right)}{1+\eta-\left(1-\alpha+\frac{\alpha}{2-\delta}\right)\left(\frac{\beta+\phi}{1-\gamma}\right)}$ $K_W = \left(\frac{\beta+\phi}{1-\gamma}-1\right)K_N + K_P$

this model and the notation are given in Table 4.3. Total housing supply in the area equals $k_H p_H^{1/(1-\delta)}\underline{L}$ where k_H is a constant, p_H is the price of housing services and $\underline{L}$ is the land area in the city. Housing demand is $\alpha N_T W/p_H$, so that the equilibrium housing price will satisfy

$$\log(p_H) = \frac{1-\delta}{2-\delta}\log\left(\frac{\alpha N_T W}{k_H \underline{L}}\right).$$

Combining this with equations (4.1) and (4.2) yields:

$$\text{Log}(N_T) = K_N + \frac{\left(1-\alpha+\frac{\alpha}{2-\delta}\right)\text{Log}(A) + (1-\gamma)\text{Log}(\theta)}{(1+\eta)(1-\gamma) - \left(1-\alpha+\frac{\alpha}{2-\delta}\right)(\beta+\phi)} \tag{4.3}$$

and

$$\text{Log}(W) = K_W + \frac{\left(\eta+\alpha-\frac{\alpha}{2-\delta}\right)\text{Log}(A) + (\beta+\phi-(1-\gamma))\text{Log}(\theta)}{(1+\eta)(1-\gamma) - \left(1-\alpha+\frac{\alpha}{2-\delta}\right)(\beta+\phi)}, \tag{4.4}$$

where

$$K_N = \frac{\left(1 - \alpha + \frac{\alpha}{2-\delta}\right) K_P - K_C - \left(\alpha - \frac{\alpha}{2-\delta}\right) \mathrm{Log}\left(\frac{\alpha}{k_H \underline{L}}\right)}{1 + \eta - \left(1 - \alpha + \frac{\alpha}{2-\delta}\right)\left(\frac{\beta+\phi}{1-\gamma}\right)}$$

and

$$K_W = \left(\frac{\beta + \phi}{1 - \gamma} - 1\right) K_N + K_P.$$

These two equations imply that if the logarithm of wages is regressed on the logarithm of city size—assuming nothing else differs across cities and that amenities and productivity are independent—the coefficient will equal:

$$\frac{\left(1 - \alpha + \frac{\alpha}{1-\delta}\right)\left(\eta + \alpha - \frac{\alpha}{2-\delta}\right) \mathrm{Var}(\mathrm{Log}(A)) - (1-\gamma)^2 \left(1 - \frac{\beta+\phi}{1-\gamma}\right) \mathrm{Var}(\mathrm{Log}(\theta))}{\left(1 - \alpha + \frac{\alpha}{2-\delta}\right)^2 \mathrm{Var}(\mathrm{Log}(A)) + (1-\gamma)^2 \mathrm{Var}(\mathrm{Log}(\theta))}. \tag{4.5}$$

This term is negative if urban differences are driven primarily by amenities and positive if urban differences are driven primarily by productivity.

One important fact is that this regression coefficient gives us little hope of identifying the true agglomeration parameter: ϕ. Regressing income on population or density seems quite likely to confound a large number of variables.

The model suggests that ϕ might be inferred from examining the impact that an amenity had on both population and income. Amenity shocks provide us with a reason why population would rise in a way that isn't driven by productivity. The ratio of the derivative of income with respect to an amenity relative to the derivative of population with respect to an amenity is proportional to $-1 + (\beta + \phi)/(1 - \gamma)$. If the parameters β and γ are known, then this would be enough to inform us about the size of the agglomeration effect. Of course, this procedure would require us to have a lot of faith in the Cobb–Douglas formulation, and that faith may be misplaced.

The methodological difficulties inherent in estimating agglomeration economies does not mean that they don't exist. The correlation between city size, or density, and income is certainly extremely robust. From the labor supply side, this correlation surely reflects the need to pay people more to compensate them for high urban prices. From the labor demand side, this correlation surely reflects a higher marginal productivity of labor in dense areas. It isn't quite clear if this high marginal productivity of labor is the result of agglomeration, or if high productivity creates both the agglomeration and the high wages. Certainly, estimating the exact value of an agglomeration parameter is quite difficult. Nonetheless, I tend to think that the evidence does seem to suggest that people become more productive when they locate near one another.

Measuring concentration: Natural advantage vs. agglomeration

The inability to differentiate between unobserved productivity differences and agglomeration effects plagues the attempt to interpret the connection between income and density. It also confounds attempts to interpret the geographic concentration of industry. When we look at industries, rather than cities, it becomes quite hard to use income data to infer anything about agglomeration economies. After all, wages should be constant across industries within an urban area for comparably skilled workers. Of course, it is possible that workers are getting rents that reflect local productivity, but there has not been much of a tendency to use rent-sharing model of wages and assess the reasons why some firms are more productive in some places.

An alternative approach is to follow Henderson (2003) and use firm productivity measures to assess agglomeration effects. This is useful work, but it is hampered by two main problems. First, such firm level data is rarely readily accessible. Second, marginal productivity should tend to be equal to wages which should be equalized across industries. Of course, average productivity might still differ across industries within a given area, but this requires some strong theoretical assumptions.

The spatial equilibrium assumption makes spatial heterogeneity in productivity and incomes hard to interpret, but quantities of employment should still provide us with information about the extent of agglomeration economies. If an industry is tightly clustered in one location, then we would tend to infer that there must be strong agglomeration economies in that industry. If an industry is geographically dispersed, then we naturally think that agglomeration economies are weaker in that industry. Just as in the case of the income-density relationship, however, high levels of industrial concentration might reflect agglomeration or productive amenities that are quite concentrated over space.

I will formalize this intuition with the model of Ellison and Glaeser (1997). This model is unique among the models in this chapter in that it is really not a spatial equilibrium model, but rather a statistical model that was designed to provide the basis for an index of geographic concentration. In the paper, we do present the model as one of spatial choice, but firms are sufficiently idiosyncratic so that spatial choice does not

Table 4.4. Modeling an index of the geographic concentration of firms

Actors	Firms
They maximize	$\log(\text{profits}) = \log(\bar{\pi}_i) + \varepsilon_{ki}$
They choose	Location (i)
Key results	$E\left[\sum_i (s_i - x_i)^2\right] = \left(1 - \sum_i x_i^2\right)\left(\gamma + (1-\gamma)\sum_k z_k{}^2\right)$
	$\dfrac{\sum_i (s_i - x_i)^2] - \left(1 - \sum_i x_i{}^2\right)\sum_k z_k{}^2}{\left(1 - \sum_i x_i{}^2\right)\left(1 - \sum_k z_k{}^2\right)}$ is an unbiased estimate of γ
Notation	γ^S : probability that a firm locates in the same location as its immediate predecessor.
	$1 - \gamma^S$: probability that a firm chooses its location randomly (throws a dart at a map)
	π_{ki} : profits to firm k in location i
	ε_{ki} : Weibull random variable independent of $\bar{\pi}_i$
	$\bar{\pi}_i$: innate advantages of location i
	x_i : the total share of the country's manufacturing employment in location i
	γ^{na} : parameter capturing the degree of heterogeneity in the underlying natural advantage of different regions
	S_i : share of an industry's employment in location i
	γ : parameter defined as $\gamma = \gamma^{na} + \gamma^S - \gamma^{na}\gamma^S$
	z_k : the share of the industry's employment in firm k

imply indifference across space. The core equations of this model and the notation are given in Table 4.4.

There are really two lines of thought about developing indices. One view is that indices can be derived from axioms as in Sen (1976). When this approach works well, a sensible set of axioms implies a single index which can then be used to measure the concept in question (income inequality, geographic concentration, etc.). The alternative approach derives an index as a measure of a parameter in a reasonable model. This view makes no claim that the index is the unique measure of the concept in question, but rather that under a reasonable set of assumptions it is one measure of the concept.

The elegance of the axiomatic approach is undeniable, but it does hinge critically on there really only being one sensible measure of the concept. If there is only one sensible measure, then in principle the model-based approach should do as well, since it produces a sensible measure and by assumption, it must be unique and therefore also be the axiomatic measure. In the more likely scenario that there are many such measures, then the axiomatic approach won't really work, unless one of the axioms is sufficiently specific that it rules out lots of alternative sensible measures.

The model-based approach makes no claim to being unique, and has the added strength of being readily interpretable as a parameter of a model.

The Ellison and Glaeser (1997) index of geographic concentration starts with the assumption that firms choose locations by throwing darts at a map of the United States. This dartboard approach is not meant to suggest brain-free randomness, but rather that idiosyncratic features of individual firms make one area more or less attractive than another. Agglomeration economies are incorporated by assuming that the firms make decisions sequentially (perhaps one firm is opening after another) and with probability γ^S, the firm chooses its location based on the decision of its immediate predecessor. With probability $1 - \gamma^S$ the firm just throws a dart at the map.

The parameter γ^S is a measure of the agglomeration economies that lurk behind geographic concentration. When this measure is high, then firms greatly value locating near one another. When the parameter goes to zero, then firms are more or less indifferent to the location of their neighbors. Ideally, a measure of geographic concentration will deliver an estimate of γ^S. As we will see differentiating γ^S from the degree of heterogeneity in natural advantage is not straightforward.

In the absence of agglomeration effects, we assume that the profits associated with firm k locating in location i, denoted π_{ki}, satisfy $\log(\pi_{ki}) = \log(\bar{\pi}_i) + \epsilon_{ki}$. The variable ϵ_{ki} is a Weibull random variable that is independent of $\bar{\pi}_i$. The variable $\bar{\pi}_i$ reflect the location's innate advantages for this specific industry. Nature determines these advantages before any firm chooses its location.

The Weibull assumption implies that the probability that any firm will locate in location i, conditional on the values of $\bar{\pi}_i$, equals $\bar{\pi}_i/\Sigma_j\bar{\pi}_j$. In other words, the ratio of this parameter to the sum of this parameter across all regions determines the unconditional probability of locating in that area. We then make two assumptions about the expectation and variance of $\bar{\pi}_i/\Sigma_j\bar{\pi}_j$. First the expectation of $\bar{\pi}_i/\Sigma_j\bar{\pi}_j$ equals x_i, the total share of the country's manufacturing employment in that location. Second, the variance of $\bar{\pi}_i/\Sigma_j\bar{\pi}_j$ equals $\gamma^{na}x_i(1 - x_i)$.

The assumption about the expectation of $\bar{\pi}_i/\Sigma_j\bar{\pi}_j$ seems fairly reasonable. On average firm locations should be expected to equal the overall distribution of employment. This assumption means that our measure has nothing to say about the overall concentration of manufacturing employment, but only the degree to which one or another industry is more concentrated than manufacturing as a whole. For the purposes of this index, we assume that there is no information about the factors that might influence $\bar{\pi}_i$, other than the area's manufacturing employment. In Ellison and Glaeser (1999), we use available data to try to estimate these variables.

The parameter γ^{na} captures the degree of heterogeneity in the underlying natural advantage of different regions. When γ^{na} is high, then regions differ significantly from each other on the basis of unobserved natural advantages. As γ^{na} goes to zero, then the heterogeneity in natural advantage goes to zero.

One possible distribution for $\bar{\pi}_t$ that satisfies these criteria is that each of these variables are independent random variables that are scaled so that $2\left[\frac{1-\gamma^{na}}{\gamma^{na}}\right]\bar{\pi}_i$ follows a χ^2 distribution with $2\left[\frac{1-\gamma^{na}}{\gamma^{na}}\right]x_i$ degrees of freedom. In this case, the expectation of $\bar{\pi}_i/\Sigma_j\bar{\pi}_j$ equals x_i, and the variance of $\bar{\pi}_i$ is $\left[\frac{\gamma^{na}}{1-\gamma^{na}}\right]x_i$. The variance of the underlying shocks is obviously determined by the level of the parameter γ^{na}.

This model delivers predictions about a modified Herfindahl index of geographic concentration. If we let s_i denote the share of an industry's employment in location i, then the classic Herfindahl index of geographic concentration for that industry equals $\Sigma_i s_i^2$. If there are I total geographic areas, then this index runs from 1 to I, when employment is evenly distributed across all industries, to 1, if industry is completely concentrated in a single area. This index has the unfortunate property of not correcting for the different sizes or innate attractiveness of different areas. As such, Krugman (1991) and others use a modified Herfindahl index equal to $\Sigma_i(s_i - x_i)^2$. This index runs from zero, if all industries follow the exact same distribution as manufacturing as a whole, to $1 + \Sigma_i x_i^2 - 2x_j$, if the industry is entirely concentrated in location j. This term can approach 2, if all of the other manufacturing employment is located in another locale.

The critical proposition of Ellison and Glaeser (1997) states that our assumptions, particularly the assumption that each firm follows its predecessor with probability γ^S and otherwise chooses location i with probability $\bar{\pi}_i/\Sigma_j\bar{\pi}_j$, imply that the expectation of $\Sigma_i(s_i - x_i)^2$ equals $(1 - \Sigma_i x_i^2)(\gamma + (1-\gamma)\Sigma_k z_k^2)$, where $\gamma = \gamma^{na} + \gamma^S - \gamma^{na}\gamma^S$ and z_k reflects the share of the industry's employment that is in firm (or more properly plant) k. The measure $\Sigma_k z_k^2$ is a plant-based Herfindahl index of industry concentration.

This proposition has two notable features. First, the correction for the industry Herfindahl index corrects for the inherent lumpiness of plant location when plants are large. We should not be surprised that an industry with only two plants happens to locate in only two counties. By correcting for the firm size with the Herfindahl index, we address this lumpiness.

Second, the index makes it clear that spillovers and heterogeneous natural advantage are observationally equivalent if the only thing we know is the geographic concentration of employment. This concentration could just as readily be explained by spillovers or natural advantage.

This observational equivalence pushes us to suggest that an unbiased estimate of γ could be one measure of geographic concentration. Following the core proposition, $\Sigma_i(s_i - x_i)^2 - (1 - \Sigma_i x_i^2)\Sigma_k z_k^2/(1 - \Sigma_t x_i^2)(1 - \Sigma_k z_k^2)$ provides us with just such an unbiased estimate of γ. This concentration measure essentially starts with the modified Herfindahl index, $\Sigma_i(s_i - x_i)^2$, and then subtracts a term that is proportional to the Herfindahl index of plant sizes. This correction deals with the inherent geographic lumpiness of industries that are lumpily distributed in a few plants. This difference is then divided by $(1 - \Sigma_i x_i^2)(1 - \Sigma_k z_k^2)$ to produce a total estimate of $\gamma^{na} + \gamma^S - \gamma^{na}\gamma^S$.

Ellison and Glaeser (1997) then take this measure to the data and look at geographic concentration across American industries. We look at the concentration of four-digit industries using both counties and states as measures of geography. Employment data comes from County Business Patterns which frequently suppresses data for confidentiality reasons. We used an inference algorithm to deal with this problem in the paper. At a later date, we had access to unrestricted Census data and found that our results based on inferred data were almost identical to the results based on complete data.

One natural question is whether all the work to correct for the lumpiness of plant sizes makes a difference. It turns out that it does. In many cases, almost one-half of the observed raw geographic concentration can be attributed to the random variation due to lump plants. Moreover, the importance of the lumpiness differs significantly across industries so that some industries look far less concentrated once we control for the lumpiness of plants and others do not. For example, household vacuum cleaners and small arms ammunition are both industries that look reasonably concentrated if we use $\Sigma_i(s_i - x_i)^2$ as the measure of concentration. However, these industries are concentrated in very few plants and after correcting for this industry-level plant Herfindahl, their measured concentration levels, i.e. γ, are among the lowest of all industries.

Our core finding is that the median manufacturing industry isn't very concentrated. The median estimate of γ when we use county data is .005. When we use state level data, the median estimate of γ is .023. If we thought that all of the concentration was coming from spillovers, these estimates would suggest that a plant has a one-half of one percent chance of following its predecessor's county and a 2.3 percent chance of following its predecessor's state. These figures don't seem that large to me, and for many industries the measure of γ isn't obviously different from zero.

But while the median industry may not be very concentrated, there are many industries that do display remarkably large levels of concentration. For example, the state level estimate of γ is .63 for fur goods (our most concentrated industry), which has long been a famous example of industrial concentration (Fuchs, 1957). The state level estimate of γ is .38 for carpets and rugs and .32 for costume jewelry. As a general rule, the distributions are strongly skewed, with a long right tail made up of highly concentrated industries.

In some of these high γ industries, it is hard to imagine that there are innate natural advantages that drive the concentration. Fur goods, for example, are overwhelmingly located in New York, which has not been a big natural producer of furs for 300 years. Even John Jacob Astor, the city's legendary fur dealer, imported his wares. In other cases, like wines and brandy, the concentration does appear to be linked to the production of grapes in California. Certainly, the measures of concentration alone give us little sort out natural advantage and spillovers.

Ellison and Glaeser (1999) take a first stab at addressing the importance of natural advantage by estimating the values of $\bar{\pi}_i$ for different industries in a first stage regression where industry concentration is regressed on state characteristics, such as coal price, interacted with the industry characteristics, such as coal use. We use 16 such interactions as well as basic controls for state population and manufacturing employment. Somewhat remarkably, the interactions all have the right sign and are almost uniformly significant. We then use the predicted share, based on this regression, instead of the manufacturing share, in forming our estimate of γ. In other words, the new estimate is $\Sigma_i(s_i - \hat{s}_i)^2 - (1 - \Sigma_i \hat{s}_i^2)\Sigma_k z_k^2/(1 - \Sigma_i \hat{s}_i^2)(1 - \Sigma_k z_k^2)$ where $\hat{s}_i$ reflects the predicted share of employment based on the regression.

Our control variables reduce the mean level of γ from .051 to .041. The share of industries with values of γ greater than .1 falls from 12.8 percent to 9.6 percent. These changes can be viewed in two different ways. One view is that our controls are quite coarse, and yet we cause the measured value of γ to drop to 20 percent, which suggests that natural advantage is certainly important. An alternative interpretation is that even with a fairly large number of controls, there are still a significant number of industries with very high levels of concentration. Probably the right view is that natural advantage is quite important, but there are still plenty of cases where concentration is due to spillovers, not observed innate attributes of particular places. I now turn to models that can explain those spillovers.

Reducing transport costs

I now turn to a simplified version of a Krugman-style agglomeration model. The core equations of these models and their notation are given in Tables 4.5–4.7. My treatment of these models is briefer than they deserve,

Table 4.5. Consumption across cities in the presence of transport costs: The consumer's problem

Actors	Consumers living in two cities
They maximize	For consumers living in the first city: $\max\left\{\int_{j=0}^{J} C_j^{\sigma} + \lambda_1\left(1 - \int_{j=0}^{0_F J} p_j C_j - \frac{1}{\tau}\int_{j=\theta_F J}^{J} p_j c_j\right)\right\}$ For consumers living in the second city: $\max\left\{\int_{j-0}^{J} c_j^{\sigma} + \lambda_2\left(W_2 - \frac{1}{\tau}\int_{j-0}^{\theta_F J} p_j c_j - \int_{j-\theta_F J}^{J} p_j c_j\right)\right\}$ (the $\delta(N)$ is absorbed by the lambdas)
They choose	Consumers choose the bundle of goods produced in both cities that will maximize their utility
First order conditions	For consumers living in the first city: If $j \leq \theta_F J$, $\sigma c_j^{\sigma-1} = \lambda_1 p_j$ If $j > \theta_F J$, $\sigma c_j^{\sigma-1} = \lambda_1 p_j/\tau$ Budget constraint: $1 - \int_{j=0}^{\theta_F J} p_j c_j - \frac{1}{\tau}\int_{j=\theta_F J}^{J} p_j c_j = 0$ For consumers living in the second city: If $j \leq \theta_F J$, $\sigma c_j^{\sigma-1} = \lambda_2 p_j/\tau$ If $j > \theta_F J$, $\sigma c_j^{\sigma-1} = \lambda_2 p_j$ Budget constraint: $w_2 \frac{1}{\tau}\int_{j=0}^{\theta_F J} p_j c_j - \int_{j=\theta_F J}^{J} p_j c_j = 0$
Notation	$\delta(N)$:= fraction of utility that individuals receive due to congestion (can be thought of as a congestion cost) N := population of the city J := measure of products individuals consume Utility := $\delta(N)\int_{j=0}^{J} c_j^{\sigma}$ c_j := individual's consumption of good j p_j := price of good j β := marginal cost of producing the good in the first city, where the wage is the numeraire w_2 := wage in the second city τ := fraction that remains of 1 good after it is transported to a city (i.e. $1-\tau$ is lost in transport) θ_F := share of products made in the first city (endogenous) θ_W := share (and absolute number) of workers in the first city (endogenous) λ_1 := the Lagrangian multiplier in the first city λ_2 := the Lagrangian multiplier in the first city

Table 4.6. Consumption across cities in the presence of transport costs (cont'd): The producer's problem

Actors	Firms in both cities
They maximize	For firms producing good j in the first city: $\max\left\{(p_j-\beta)p_j^{-1/(1-\sigma)}\left(\theta_w\left(\frac{\sigma}{\lambda_1}\right)^{1/(1-\sigma)}+(1-\theta_w)\left(\frac{\sigma\tau}{\lambda_2}\right)^{1/(1-\sigma)}\right)-\alpha\right\}$ For firms in the second city: $\max\left\{(p_j-\beta w_2)p_j^{-1/(1-\sigma)}\left(\theta_w\left(\frac{\sigma\tau}{\lambda_1}\right)^{1/(1-\sigma)}+(1-\theta_w)\left(\frac{\sigma}{\lambda_2}\right)^{1/(1-\sigma)}\right)-\alpha w_2\right\}$
They choose	Firms in both cities choose prices p_j to maximize profits from selling goods in both cities.
First order conditions	For firms producing good j in the first city: $p_j=\beta/\sigma$ For firms producing good j in the second city: $p_j=\beta w_2/\sigma$
Notation	Same as the notation from the table above.

because I have little comparative advantage in writing about the new economic geography. Krugman himself and his many co-authors have already done a superb job of making these models accessible. Still, given the importance of these models to the literature, I must at least present a simple model that is a coarse version of Krugman (1991a,b).

Table 4.7. Consumption across cities in the presence of transport costs (cont'd): The labor market

Actors	Firms and workers
They maximize	None explicitly; see below for an explanation
They choose	Firms decide how many employees they ought to hire to maximize profits; workers choose firms that maximize their utility. This results in the clearance of the labor market.
Key equilibrium condition	*Clearance of the labor market* In the first city: $\theta_W=\theta_F\left(\alpha J+\sigma\left(\frac{\theta_w}{\theta_F+(1-\theta_F)\tau^{\sigma/(1-\sigma)}W_2^{-\sigma/(1-\sigma)}}+\frac{(1-\theta_w)\tau^{\sigma/(1-\sigma)}w_2}{\theta_F\tau^{\sigma/(1-\sigma)}+(1-\theta_F)w_2^{-\sigma/(1-\sigma)}}\right)\right)$ In the second city: $1-\theta_W=(1-\theta_F)$ $\times\left(\alpha J+\sigma W_2^{-\sigma/(1-\sigma)}\left(\frac{\theta_w\tau^{\sigma/(1-\sigma)}}{\theta_F+(1-\theta_F)\tau^{\sigma/(1-\sigma)}w_2^{-\sigma/(1-\sigma)}}+\frac{(1-\theta_w)w_2}{\theta_F\tau^{\sigma/(1-\sigma)}+(1-\theta_F)w_2^{-\sigma/(1-\sigma)}}\right)\right)$
Notation	Same as the notation from the table above.

Krugman-style models need both an agglomerative and a decentralizing force. In Krugman (1991a,b), the decentralizing force came from having a primary sector that was evenly distributed across space. When they agglomerate, individuals must pay more for access to this primary sector, which might represent the added costs of paying to ship agricultural products. In later variants of the model, commuting costs created the decentralizing costs.

Because the focus here is on agglomeration, I will treat congestion costs in a particularly simple fashion. I assume that there is a congestion cost paid by individuals that causes them to lose utility; specifically, their utility will be multiplied by $\delta(N)$, where N is the population of the city and $\delta(N)$ is decreasing in N. This cost might reflect an amenity index as discussed in the previous chapter or perhaps the costs of commuting. Individuals consume measure J of products and receive utility of $\int_{j=0}^{J} c_j^{\sigma}$ from these goods, so total utility is $\delta(N)\int_{j=0}^{J} c_j^{\sigma}$ where c_j denotes the individual's consumption of good j.

Each firm produces its own individual good. There is a linear production technology with fixed costs, so to produce x units of this good requires $\alpha + \beta x$ units of labor. I let the wage in the first city be the numeraire so that the marginal cost of the good in that place equals β. The wage in the second city is denoted w_2.

The key transport assumption is that these costs are "iceberg," which is to say that if one unit of the good is shipped, τ units of the good arrives or $1-\tau$ units of the good are lost in transport. I let θ_F denote the share of products being made in the first city and θ_W denote the share (and absolute number) of workers in the first city. These are both endogenous variables.

This model is solved by starting with deriving consumer demand for an individual conditional on living in a city. The core equations of this model and its notation are given in Table 4.5. I assume that products are indexed so that all goods for which j is less than $\theta_F J$ are made in the first city and the others are made in the second city. The prices are the prices paid before transport costs. Consumer demand is then found by maximizing the Lagrangian:

$$\int_{j=0}^{J} c_j^{\sigma} + \lambda\left(1 - \int_{j=0}^{\theta_F J} p_j c_j - \frac{1}{\tau}\int_{j=\theta_F J}^{J} p_j c_j\right),$$

where λ is the multiplier. The first order conditions for consumption then imply that $\sigma c_j^{\sigma-1} = \lambda p_j$ or $\left(\sigma/\lambda p_j\right)^{1/(1-\sigma)} = c_j$ for goods produced in the first city and $\sigma c_j^{\sigma-1} = \frac{\lambda}{\tau} p_j$ or $\left(\sigma\tau/\lambda p_j\right)^{1/(1-\sigma)} = c_j$, for goods produced in the second city. Using the budget constraint to solve for λ then gives us that

$$\lambda = \sigma\left(\int_{j=0}^{\theta_F J} p_j^{-\sigma/(1-\sigma)} + \int_{j=\theta_F J}^{J} \tau^{\sigma/(1-\sigma)} p_j^{-\sigma/(1-\sigma)}\right)^{1-\sigma}$$

in the first city.

For workers in the second city, demand for goods from the first city equals $(\sigma\tau/\lambda_2 p_j)^{1/(1-\sigma)} = C_j$ and demand for goods from the second city equals $(\sigma/\lambda_2 p_j)^{1/(1-\sigma)} = c_j$ where λ_2 refers to the Lagrangian multiplier for those consumers. This multiplier satisfies

$$\lambda_2 = \sigma W_2^{\sigma-1}\left(\int_{j=0}^{\theta_F J} \tau^{\sigma/(1-\sigma)} p_j^{-\sigma/(1-\sigma)} + \int_{j=\theta_F J}^{J} p_j^{-\sigma/(1-\sigma)}\right)^{1-\sigma}.$$

Putting these together, the total demand for a good being produced in the first city equals

$$\theta_W\left(\frac{\sigma}{\lambda p_j}\right)^{1/(1-\sigma)} + (1-\theta_W)\tau^{\sigma/(1-\sigma)}\left(\frac{\sigma}{\lambda_2 p_j}\right)^{1/(1-\sigma)}$$

and total firm profits are

$$(p_j - \beta)p_j^{-1/(1-\sigma)}\left(\theta_W\left(\frac{\sigma}{\lambda p_j}\right)^{1/(1-\sigma)} + (1-\theta_W)\tau^{\sigma/(1-\sigma)}\left(\frac{\sigma}{\lambda_2 p_j}\right)^{1/(1-\sigma)}\right) - \alpha.$$

The total demand for a good being produced in the second city equals

$$\theta_W \tau^{\frac{\sigma}{1-\sigma}}\left(\frac{\sigma}{\lambda p_j}\right)^{1/(1-\sigma)} + (1-\theta_W)\left(\frac{\sigma}{\lambda_2 p_j}\right)^{1/(1-\sigma)}$$

and firm profits are

$$(p_j - \beta W_2)p_j^{-1/(1-\sigma)}\left(\theta_W \tau^{\sigma/(1-\sigma)}\left(\frac{\sigma}{\lambda}\right)^{1/(1-\sigma)} + (1-\theta_W)\left(\frac{\sigma}{\lambda_2}\right)^{\frac{1}{1-\sigma}}\right) - \alpha W_2.$$

All firms are sufficiently small that their pricing decisions do not impact the two multipliers, so the familiar constant markup means that in the first city $p_j = \beta/\sigma$ and in the second city $p_j = \beta W_2/\sigma$. In the first region the zero profit condition is $(p_j - \beta)$ Output $= \alpha$. In the second region, the zero profit condition is $(p_j - \beta W_2)$ Output $= \alpha W_2$. Using the solution for price, output per firm in both regions is equal to $\sigma\alpha/(1-\sigma)\beta$. Constant output per firm across regions implies that that $\theta_W = \theta_F$ and I use the notation θ for both. The core equations of this model and its notation are given in Table 4.6.

Since total labor supply (one) must equal total labor demand, $J(\alpha + \beta\sigma\alpha/(1-\sigma)\beta) = 1$, which implies that $J = (1-\sigma)/\alpha$ so that the number of firms is pinned down exclusively by the elasticity of substitution and the fixed cost of setting up a firm. J would also scale up with the total population that is shared between the two cities, but I have fixed that at one. The very simple solution—that labor is always proportional to the number of firms—is one of the glories of this model. Of course, it should be recognized that these particular functional forms, so perfectly picked to yield elegant solutions, are in no sense general. The elegance comes at the cost of turning off different ways in which variables may impact the system.

These calculations then mean that two multipliers are

$$\lambda = \sigma^{1+\sigma}\beta^{-\sigma}\left(\frac{1-\sigma}{\alpha}\right)^{1-\sigma}\left(\theta + (1-\theta)\tau^{\sigma/(1-\sigma)}W_2^{-\sigma/(1-\sigma)}\right)^{1-\sigma}$$

and

$$\lambda_2 = \sigma^{1+\sigma}\beta^{-\sigma}\left(\frac{1-\sigma}{\alpha}\right)^{1-\sigma} W_2^{\sigma-1}\left(\theta\tau^{\sigma/(1-\sigma)} + (1-\theta)W_2^{-\sigma/(1-\sigma)}\right)^{1-\sigma}.$$

Firm output in the first region is

$$\frac{\alpha\sigma}{(1-\sigma)\beta}\left(\frac{\theta}{\theta + (1-\theta)\tau^{\sigma/(1-\sigma)}W_2^{-\sigma/(1-\sigma)}} + \frac{(1-\theta)\tau^{\sigma/(1-\sigma W_2)}}{\theta\tau^{\sigma/(1-\sigma)} + (1-\theta)W_2^{-\sigma/(1-\sigma)}}\right).$$

Since this must equal $\sigma\alpha/(1-\sigma)\beta$ this implies that

$$\theta = \frac{\tau^{\sigma/(1-\sigma)}W_2^{1/(1-\sigma)} - 1}{\tau^{\frac{\sigma}{1-\sigma}}\left(W_2^{\sigma/(1-\sigma)} + W_2^{1/(1-\sigma)}\right) - W_2^{(1+\sigma)/(1-\sigma)} - 1}, \qquad (4.6)$$

which can be thought of as a labor market clearance condition.

These solutions can then be used to find the crucial spatial equilibrium condition that requires total utility to be equal in both regions. Total utility for a worker in the first city equals

$$\delta(\theta)\left(\frac{1-\sigma}{\alpha}\right)^{1-\sigma}\sigma^{\sigma}\beta^{-\sigma}\left(\theta + (1-\theta)\tau^{\sigma/(1-\sigma)}W_2^{-\sigma/(1-\sigma)}\right)^{1+\sigma}.$$

The utility for a worker in the second city equals

$$\delta(1-\theta)\left(\frac{1-\sigma}{\alpha}\right)^{1-\sigma}\sigma^{\sigma}\beta^{-\sigma}W_2^{\sigma}\left(\theta\tau^{\frac{\sigma}{1-\sigma}} + (1-\theta)W_2^{-\sigma/(1-\sigma)}\right)^{1+\sigma}.$$

The spatial equilibrium requires that these two utility levels be equal:

$$\delta(\theta)\left(\theta + (1-\theta)\tau^{\sigma/(1-\sigma)}W_2^{-\sigma/(1-\sigma)}\right)^{1+\sigma} = \delta(1-\theta)W_2^{\sigma} \times \left(\theta\tau^{\sigma/(1-\sigma)} + (1-\theta)W_2^{-\sigma/(1-\sigma)}\right)^{1+\sigma}. \qquad (4.7)$$

Together (4.6) and (4.7) represent a system with two equations and two unknowns: the share of the population in the first region and the wage in the second region. The core equations of this model and its notation are given in Table 4.7.

There is an equilibrium that satisfies both (4.6) and (4.7) where exactly one half of the people and firms occupy each region. This equilibrium may not be stable, as I will discuss below, but at least it always exists. In this symmetric case, wages are the same between the two regions and both equal one and prices are the same. Individual utility equals $\delta(.5)\left(\frac{1-\sigma}{\alpha}\right)^{1-\sigma}\sigma^{\sigma}\beta^{-\sigma}\left(.5+.5\tau^{\sigma/(1-\sigma)}\right)^{1+\sigma}$, which is the relevant measure of social welfare since firm profits are always zero.

Is there also an equilibrium in which all of the firms and all of the workers are only in one city? I will assume that the first city is the city where everyone is located. If this equilibrium exists then consumer welfare is $\delta(1)\left(\frac{1-\sigma}{\alpha}\right)^{1-\sigma}\sigma^{\sigma}\beta^{-\sigma}$.

A complete equilibrium, even one where no one lives in the second city, should also specify a wage for workers that choose to move to the second city. For a one-city equilibrium to exist, there must be a hypothetical wage in the second city that is sufficiently high so that no firms would form there and sufficiently low so that no workers would receive a higher utility in the second city. Another way to think about this is that we are interested in equilibria that are robust to an epsilon perturbation where a tiny measure of firms and workers migrate to the second city.

The condition that new firms would not like to enter in the second city is that $w_2 > \tau$ so that the wage discount that comes from moving to the second city is not large enough to pay for the cost of moving all of the goods over space. The condition that workers prefer the first city is that $(\delta(1)/\delta(0))^{\frac{1}{\sigma}}\tau^{(-1-\sigma)/(1-\sigma)} > w_2$. Thus, for there to exist a wage in the second city which is too high to attract firms and too low to attract people, it must be true that $\delta(1)/\delta(0) > \tau^{2\sigma/(1-\sigma)}$. The one-city equilibrium exists if and only if the ratio of the utility losses due to congestion is higher than the transportation cost parameter to the power $2\sigma/(1-\sigma)$.

Three factors ultimately determine whether a one-city equilibrium exists. First, the one-city equilibrium is less likely to exist if utility declines sharply with population. Second, the one-city equilibrium is more likely to exist when transport costs are sufficiently high. In that case, there are more substantial transport costs advantages from locating in a single area. Finally, one city equilibrium is more likely to exist when σ is high. This parameter is generally interpreted to reflect the extent of scale economies, since higher values of σ mean larger markups. Following this interpretation used by Krugman (1991a,b), scale economies also support the one-city equilibrium.

On a positive level, this model can be seen as making sense of the pattern of urban decentralization in the US in the twentieth century. At the start of the century, transport costs were high and people clustered in cities. Over the course of the century, transport costs fell and people decentralized to take advantage of high consumer amenities in lower density places. This story misses much of the richness in urban change over the past 100 years, but there is a basic truth to it that is quite important.

One reasonable question is whether it is ever possible to get trapped in a Pareto inferior equilibrium. Since profits are always zero, it is enough to look at worker utility to determine whether welfare is higher. Comparing the two worker welfare expressions in the one-city and two-city models, welfare is higher if everyone lives in the single city if and only if $\frac{\delta(1)}{\delta(.5)} > \left(.5 + .5\tau^{\sigma/(1-\sigma)}\right)^{1+\sigma}$. Since the two-city equilibrium always exists, and this condition can certainly hold, it follows that it is possible to have too much decentralization relative to the Pareto optimum.

Is it possible that the one-city equilibrium exists, even if it is Pareto inferior to the two-city equilibrium? This requires that $\frac{\delta(1)}{\delta(0)} > \tau^{2\sigma/(1-\sigma)}$ and $\frac{\delta(1)}{\delta(.5)} < \left(.5 + .5\tau^{\sigma/(1-\sigma)}\right)^{1+\sigma}$. The best case for the two-city equilibrium is when $\delta(.5)$ is equal to $\delta(0)$ so that there is no amenity loss from living in a city with one half of the population relative to living in an empty city. In that case, it is possible both for the one-city equilibrium to exist and for it to be Pareto inferior whenever $\left(.5 + .5\tau^{\sigma/(1-\sigma)}\right)^{1+\sigma} > \frac{\delta(1)}{\delta(.5)} > \tau^{2\sigma/(1-\sigma)}$. This inequality certainly holds for some values of $\delta(1)/\delta(.5)$ whenever τ is sufficiently low. It is certainly quite possible that there will be an inefficient city that is too big. Obviously, as the congestion forces become sufficiently weak, so that $\delta(1)/\delta(.5)$ is close to one, then the agglomeration economies mean that population dispersal is inefficient.

Since the two-city equilibrium can be Pareto inferior and since it always exists, it is possible that the population is too dispersed. However, we might want to ask whether a highly Pareto inferior two-city equilibrium is a reasonable expectation. For this reason, it is interesting to consider whether the two-city equilibrium is "stable." Stability, in a static model like this one, is always a somewhat sloppy concept.

One way to think about stability is to treat the share of the population living in city one as an exogenous variable and then ask whether, at an equilibrium point, the net benefits of living in city one decreases as the share of the population living in city one increases. If the net benefits of living in city one increase as city one's population increases, then the situation can be said to be unstable.

I will consider an equilibrium unstable if the difference between utility in the two cities:

$$\delta(\theta)\left(\theta+(1-\theta)\tau^{\sigma/(1-\sigma)}w_2^{-\sigma/(1-\sigma)}\right)^{1+\sigma}$$
$$-\delta(1-\theta)w_2^{\sigma}\left(\theta\tau^{\sigma/(1-\sigma)}+(1-\theta)w_2^{-\sigma/(1-\sigma)}\right)^{1+\sigma},$$

rises with θ. Differentiating this utility difference around the symmetric equilibrium yields:

$$\left(.5+.5\tau^{\sigma/(1-\sigma)}\right)^{\sigma} \text{ times } \delta'(.5)\left(1+\tau^{\sigma/(1-\sigma)}\right)$$
$$+(1+\sigma)\left(1-\tau^{\sigma/(1-\sigma)}\right)\delta(.5)\left(2-\frac{\sigma}{2-2\sigma}\frac{\partial w_2}{\partial\theta}\right).$$

The equation is solved by plugging in the solution for $\partial w_2/\partial\theta$ found by differentiating equation (4.6). Evaluating this differential at the symmetric equilibrium yields:

$$\frac{\partial w_2}{\partial\theta}=\frac{-4(1-\tau^{\sigma/(1-\sigma)})(1-\sigma)}{1+\sigma+(1-\sigma)\tau^{\sigma/(1-\sigma)}}.$$

Putting this in the expression tells us that the equilibrium is unstable if and only if

$$2(1+\sigma)\frac{1-\tau^{\sigma/(1-\sigma)}}{1+\tau^{\sigma/(1-\sigma)}}\left(1+\frac{\sigma\left(1-\tau^{\sigma/(1-\sigma)}\right)}{1+\tau^{\frac{\sigma}{1-\sigma}}+\sigma\left(1-\tau^{\sigma/(1-\sigma)}\right)}\right)>-\frac{\delta'(.5)}{\delta(.5)}. \quad (4.8)$$

The right hand side of this inequality is the elasticity of congestion with respect to city size. When this is low, then the two-city equilibrium is less likely to be stable. The left hand side is uniformly falling with τ meaning that as transport costs fall, the two-city equilibrium is increasingly less likely to be stable. If τ is sufficiently small, then higher values of σ will also cause the equilibrium to become less stable, reflecting the impact the scale economies have on the gains from agglomeration.

The division of labor is limited by the extent of the market

A simple, elegant model of the division of labor is given by Becker and Murphy (1992). The core equations of this model and its notation are given in Table 4.8. In their paper, a continuum of tasks must all be accomplished to create a final output. They assume a Leontief technology so that final output, Y, equals the minimum of $Y(S)$ where S indexes the tasks and runs from zero to one. Output is produced by a team of size n, and each person specializes in $1/n$ tasks.

Table 4.8. Division of labor (Becker and Murphy 1992)

Actors	Employees on a production team
They maximize	Economic productivity
They choose	Individuals must choose how to split their time between time to spent specializing through education and time spent producing.
Output	Total output is given by $\frac{\gamma^{\gamma}hn^{1+\gamma}}{(1+\gamma)^{1+\gamma}}$.
Notation	Y := final output S := tasks (index runs from 0 to 1) n := total team size T_w := time spent producing T_s := time spent in schooling h := general schooling level $E(S)$:= skill level in skill $S = hT_s^{\gamma}$

Output is equal to time spent producing T_W times the skill level, denoted E(S). The skill level is itself equal to hT_s^{γ}, where h reflects the general schooling level and T_s equals the time spent in training. There is a total time budget $\frac{1}{n}(T_W + T_s) = 1$, where 1 reflects the total time of the person that must be allocated across the $1/n$ tasks. Output maximization sets $T_w = n/(1+\gamma)$ and $T_s = \gamma n/(1+\gamma)$. Total output in each task is therefore equal to $\gamma^{\gamma}hn^{1+\gamma}/(1+\gamma)^{1+\gamma}$ and that is also equal to the total output of the group. Per capital output in the group equals $\gamma^{\gamma}hn^{\gamma}/(1+\gamma)^{1+\gamma}$ which is obviously rising with group size.

This model delivers a type of agglomeration economy. Larger group sizes enable people to specialize in a finer set of tasks and that in turn enables them to become more skilled in those tasks. Since people don't need to learn about everything, they can become more skilled at a narrower set of things. This specialized knowledge then makes the team more productive. While this is a good model of a production unit, it doesn't actually work as a model of cities on its own.

We now return to the Dixit–Stiglitz technology used above where a final output is formed by assembling inputs from different suppliers. The core equations of this model and the notation are given in Table 4.9. Total output equals $\left(\int_{j=0}^{J} x_j^{\sigma}\right)^{1/\sigma}$. This can be thought of as a firm that buys business services and combines them to form a total output. This output is sold for a price of 1 and there is free entry at zero cost into the assembly side of the market. The demand curve for each good is the first order condition for a firm $p_j = x_j^{\sigma-1}\left(\int_{j=0}^{J} x_j^{\sigma}\right)^{(1-\sigma)/\sigma}$. The total range of inputs is fixed at J, but individuals can select the number of inputs in which they choose to produce.

As in the Becker–Murphy model, total output equals T_W times the skill level, denoted E(S) and E(S) equals hT_s^{γ}. Individuals will always choose

Table 4.9. Division of labor in cities

Actors	Employees on a production team in a city
They maximize	Economic productivity
They choose	Individuals must choose how to split their time between time to spent specializing through education and time spent producing.
Equilibrium state	Total output is given by $\frac{\gamma^{\gamma} hn^{1+\gamma}}{((1+\gamma)J)^{1+\gamma}}$. Therefore, the equilibrium price for each task equals $(1-\sigma)/\sigma$. This gives $c(\pi) = \frac{\gamma^{\gamma} hn^{\gamma} J^{(1-\sigma-\gamma\sigma)/\sigma}}{(1+\gamma)^{1+\gamma}}$. Consumer utility is equal to $\left(\frac{n(1-\sigma)}{\alpha}\right)^{1-\sigma}\left(\frac{\sigma}{\beta}\right)^{\sigma}$.
Notation	J := total number of inputs in which individuals may choose to produce x_j := production of inputs j $\left(\int_{j=0}^{J} x_j^{\sigma}\right)^{1/\sigma}$ = total output p_j := price of product j S := tasks (index runs from 0 to 1) n := total team size T_w := time spent producing T_s := time spent in schooling h := general schooling level $E(S)$:= skill level in skill $S = hT_s^{\gamma}$ $c(s)$:= housing cost curve c_j := total demand for j $\alpha + \beta x$:= production costs (measured in units of labor)

their time spent investing to maximize total revenues since there is no cost to producing more of the product. In this case, the fixed markup rule implies that there is always a positive benefit from producing more of the good and everyone makes as much as they can. Output per person in each task will equal $\gamma^{\gamma} nn^{\gamma}/((1+\gamma)J)^{1+\gamma}$, which means that the price for each task will equal $J^{(1-\sigma)/\sigma}$. Individual income in this sector will equal $\gamma^{\gamma} hn^{\gamma} J^{(1-\sigma-\gamma\sigma)/\sigma}/(1+\gamma)^{1+\gamma}$. This is obviously increasing in n.

To close this model, we use an open city model, where we assume that the supply of housing in the city is distinguished by a cost curve $c(n)$. This means that the city size satisfies $c(n) = \gamma^{\gamma} hn^{\gamma} J^{(1-\sigma-\gamma\sigma)/\sigma}/(1+\gamma)^{1+\gamma}$. For this to be a stable equilibrium, the elasticity of housing costs with respect to city population would have to be greater than γ. Just as in the Becker–Murphy model, having more people means more specialization and the ability to produce more of a given task.

This does capture one element of Smith's observation that the division of labor is limited by the extent of the market. As goods are strong complements, the ability to specialize hinges on the ability of other people to supply the other goods that come together in making the composite goods. Since big cities have a supply of these other goods, it is easier to specialize in a narrow range of products. This effect, however, is entirely about a deep market supplying complementary products, not about the downstream market.

It is, however, reasonably straightforward to have a model that connects the division of labor with downstream demand. In fact, the Krugman (1991a,b) model really already does this. Assume that products can only be sold within the city and that the city population has a fixed size of n. Assume further that utility is $\int_{j=0}^{J} c_j^{\sigma}$ and that production costs are again $\alpha + \beta x$ units of labor. The wage is again the numeraire. Total demand is $(n/J)\left(\beta^{\sigma}/\sigma^{\sigma} p_j\right)^{1/(1-\sigma)} = c_j$, so that firms set prices equal to β/σ and free entry then implies that $n(1-\sigma)/\alpha = J$. Consumer utility is equal to $(n(1-\sigma)/a)^{1-\sigma}(\sigma/\beta)^{\sigma}$, which is certainly increasing in city size. If we interpret J as the amount of specialization, then rising city size generates many more occupations and higher well being. Again, the mechanism is that fixed costs get spread over larger markets, which enables more products or more types of products to be produced.

Labor market pooling

In this section, I again start with Krugman's (1991a,b) simple model of labor pooling, and this model has its roots in Marshall (1890). The core equations of this model and the notation are given in Table 4.10. Assume that there are J firms, each of which sells a good for a price of one. Total output for firm j equals $A_j L - .5L^2$ and profits equal $A_j L - W_k L - .5L^2$, where W_k is the equilibrium wage in city K. The parameter A_j is stochastic with mean $\hat{A}$ and variance σ_A^2. The realization of A_j is observed after people have chosen their locations, but people are able to switch employers after that point. Labor demand for each firm will be $A_j - L = W_k$.

Assume that there are J firms and measure N of population that are allocated across K cities so that each city has J/K firms and N/K people. After the realization of shocks, labor demand in each city will satisfy

$$\frac{K}{J}\sum A_j - \frac{N}{J} = W_k,$$

so that the expectation of the wage is equal to the expectation of A minus N/J. If cities grow larger—so that K declines—but we hold the number of workers and firms constant, there is no increase in expected wages.

Profits, however, will equal $.5\left(A_j - \frac{K}{J}\sum A_j + \frac{N}{J}\right)^2$. If the individual firm shocks are distributed independently then the expected value of this quantity equals $.5\left(\frac{N}{J}\right)^2 + .5\left(1 - \frac{K}{J}\right)\left(\sigma_A^2 + \hat{A}^2\right)$. This profit is obviously decreasing in the number of cities, or increasing in city size. The impact of city size is higher when the variation in A_j is higher.

Table 4.10. Model for labor market pooling

Actors	Firms
They maximize	Firms maximize profit: $$\max\{A_jL - W_kL - .5L^2\}$$
They choose	Firms choose to enter cities where the level of labor will maximize their profit.
First order condition	Before realization of shocks: $$A_jL - W_kL - .5L^2$$ After realization of shocks: $$\frac{K}{J}\sum A_j - \frac{N}{J} = W_k$$
Notation	J := number of firms, each of whom sells a good at price 1, spread across the cities K := number of cities L := labor A_j := stochastic shocks whose realization is observed after people have chosen their locations. Note that people can still switch employers $A_jL - .5L^2$:= output of firm j $A_jL - W_kL - .5L^2$:= profits of firm j W_k := the equilibrium wage in city k $\hat{A} := E[A_j]$ σ_A^2 := var$[A_j]$ F := cost of entry to a city N_k := fixed population of city k J_k := the number of firms that chose to enter city k

This simple, elegant model gets the logic of labor market pooling across quite clearly. Big cities are more efficient because of something that could be called statistical returns to scale. Expected profits are generally increasing in the variability of key parameters, like productivity, because of LeChatelier's principle; but for this principle to work, firms must be able to adjust their inputs. The bigger the city, the easier it becomes to adjust labor supply. This means that in large cities, labor is able to move from less productive firms to more productive firms. This mobility in turn makes the cities more productive.

The logic of this becomes even plainer with an even more trivial example. Assume that firms use a constant returns to scale production technology with productivity of A_j and that A_j takes on the value of 0 with probability one-half and one with probability one-half. Assume further that there are two firms and measure one of workers. If the two firms operate in two different cities, then the expected productivity will equal .5 since one-half of the time the output will equal one and one-half of the time the output will equal zero. However, if the two firms operate in the same city then the expected output will equal .75, if the productivity shocks are independent, since at least one of the firms has productivity of one three-quarters of the time. The agglomeration of firms increases efficiency since people can move to the most productive firm in the area.

The only problem with this model, as it is written, is that none of the benefits directly accrue to workers, so it does not yet explain the urban wage premium. However, in a competitive market with different size cities, we would certainly expect to see higher wages and higher prices in a bigger city. To keep this simple, I assume that city sizes are fixed so that city j has population N_k. This fixed population may reflect a fixed housing stock, but it is really just a cheat so that I don't have to deal with the endogeneity of city size. I will assume that housing prices move to ensure a spatial equilibrium for workers across cities.

There is free entry among firms in the two cities for a cost F and they will enter to the point where expected profits are zero. If I let J_k denote the number of firms that chose to enter the city, then the expected wage in the large city will equal $\hat{A} - N_k/J_k$.

Post-entry, the expected value of firm profits in the big city will equal $.5\,(N_k/J_k)^2 + .5\,(1 - 1/j_k)\,(\sigma_A^2 + \hat{A}^2)$. Free entry implies that this must equal F, which then implies that

$$\frac{J_k}{N_k} = \frac{\sqrt{\frac{(\sigma_A^2+\hat{A}^2)^2}{N_k^2} + 4\left(2F - (\sigma_A^2 + \hat{A}^2)\right)} + \frac{(\sigma_A^2+\hat{A}^2)}{N_k}}{4F - 2\left(\sigma_A^2 + \hat{A}^2\right)}.$$

Differentiating this expression then gives us that the derivative of J_k/N_k with respect to N_k, city size, is

$$\frac{(\sigma_A^2 + \hat{A}^2)\left(\sigma_A^2 + \hat{A}^2 + \sqrt{(\sigma_A^2 + \hat{A}^2)^2 + 4N_k^2\left(2F - (\sigma_A^2 + \hat{A}^2)\right)}\right)}{2N_k^2\left(2F - (\sigma_A^2 + \hat{A}^2)\right)\left(\sigma_A^2 + \hat{A}^2 + \sqrt{(\sigma_A^2 + \hat{A}^2)^2 + 4N_k^2\left(2F - (\sigma_A^2 + \hat{A}^2)\right)}\right)}$$

which must always be positive. Greater opportunity for profit draws in more firms to the big city and there is a higher ratio of firms to workers.

The higher number of firms will increase expected wages, since expected wages equal $\hat{A} - N_k/J_k$, and higher urban wages will be offset by higher urban prices. This model predicts that large cities will have lots of little employers that pay a wage premium to workers. The labor market pooling effect does not directly enhance worker productivity, but as more firms are attracted to the bigger cities, this indirectly causes worker wages to rise and predicts the positive association between city size and wages that we see in the data.

There are many cities where this model does not seem to fit well. The large smokestack cities of America's industrial heartland were certainly not characterized by many small firms exchanging workers. More generally, big firms have tended to be located in big cities, which is the opposite of what this model predicts.

However, just because there are plenty of examples of cities where the model's fit is tenuous doesn't mean it doesn't have value. The dense clusters of Wall Street or Silicon Valley do have many moderate size firms that regularly increase or decrease their employment levels. Workers do rapidly shift across firms as their levels of productivity wax and wane. I think that the labor market pooling model does a good job of capturing the reality of worker mobility in these dense, modern clusters.

Matching in cities

Another agglomeration model that emphasizes statistical returns to scale is about matching in cities. The basic idea is that the quality of match between employer and employee is uncertain. With more employers to choose among, the expected match quality will rise. This model is quite close to the labor market pooling model, because the labor market pooling allows firm quality to be stochastic and then agglomeration economies ensue because workers are able to move from less productive to more productive firms. In a matching model, the match is stochastic, but the abundance of firms makes it easier to move to the firm with the best match. Helsley and Strange (1990) is the classic paper in this area. I present a somewhat simpler model that gets across the basic idea. The core equations of this model and the notation are given in Table 4.11.

I will assume that there are no constraints on the number of employees that a firm can hire. The total productivity of individual i at firm j is denoted A_i^j. I will assume that workers have all the bargaining power, so that their wage is equal to their productivity. Alternatively, the productivity parameter can also be thought of as including the non-pecuniary elements in the job. Certainly, these non-pecuniary elements play a big role in determining the rewards that people get from different occupations.

In the easiest version of this model, workers immediately observe their productivity at all of the firms in the city. The workers then select the firm with the highest productivity match and go to work at that firm. If A_i^j were distributed on the unit interval and if its values were independent across firms, then the expected value of the best match is $J/(J+1)$. This value starts at 1/2 and approaches 1 as the number of firms becomes sufficiently large. Notably, the benefits of city size are quite concave. Going from 1 to 2 employers increases the expected productivity by 33

Table 4.11. Matching in cities

Actors	Employees in cities
They maximize	Lifetime earnings
They choose	In each period, individuals choose between working at their current "best-fit" job or sampling another job
Expected welfare	$EW = \frac{1}{2r}\left(\frac{q}{1+r}\right)^{J}\left(\frac{-2q}{(j+1)} - \frac{(1+r-q)^2(1+q) - rq^2(2+r-q)}{(1+r-q)}\right) + \frac{(1+r)(1+r-q^2)}{2r(1+r-q)}.$
Notation	A_i^j := total productivity of individual i at firm j J := total number of firms in the city r := future discount rate A^* := indifference productivity value, at which an individual will be indifferent between sampling another job and staying put. $\hat{j}$:= number of firms remaining that the individual has not sampled $A^*_{\hat{j}}$:= the productivity which makes a person indifferent between accepting that productivity and sampling another job when there are $\hat{j}$ jobs remaining to be sampled $V_{\hat{j}}(A)$:= the expected lifetime earnings to an individual with $\hat{j}$ jobs left to sample $q := 1 + r - \sqrt{r(1+r)} = A^*$ EW := expected welfare

percent. Going from 10 employers to 20 employers increases the expected productivity by less than five percent.

I now turn to a more dynamic matching model. In this case, I assume that individuals hop between jobs, learning about the best match for them. This is framed in terms of workers and firms, but it could be easily recast as reflecting social matching in the city. Cities are good job markets, but they are marriage markets as well (Costa and Kahn, 2000).

I assume that individuals live forever and discount the future with a discount rate r. People are risk neutral. Once an individual i commits to a firm j, that individual's earnings equals $\frac{1+r}{r}A_i^j$. If an individual moves to a new firm, in the first year he receives the expected value of A_i^j. I again assume that A is uniformly distributed on the unit interval, so this equals .5. I assume that individuals can always return to a job that they have sampled in the past and that again there are J employers in the town.

Optimal strategy consists of cutoff rules at which people stop searching. Obviously, an individual who has a job with a productivity of one will stay there and an individual who has a job with a productivity of zero will not (we assume there are no moving costs). The costs of searching are the foregone expected earnings in the next period which are equal to the most productive job that the individual has sampled minus .5—the pay in a new job. If A' denotes the most productive job that an individual has sampled, then the costs of sampling again must rise with A' and the expected benefits of sampling must fall with A'. Since the net benefits of sampling are continuous with A' (everything is continuous), then there must be a value of A', denoted A^*, at which individuals are indifferent between sampling another job and staying put.

The critical thing that makes this model easy is that the value of A^* is independent of the number of jobs left to sample. In other words:

Claim 1: If an individual is indifferent between searching and accepting his best job, when that best job offers productivity A^* and when there are $\hat{J}$ firms remaining that the individual has not sampled, then that individual will also be indifferent between searching and accepting his best job when the job offers productivity A^* and when there are $\hat{J}+1$ firms remaining that the individual has not sampled.

To prove Claim 1, let $A^*_{\hat{J}}$ denote the productivity which makes the person indifferent between accepting that productivity and sampling another job when there are $\hat{J}$ jobs remaining to be sampled. Let $A^*_{\hat{J}+1}$ denote the productivity which makes the person indifferent between accepting that productivity and sampling another job when there are $\hat{J}+1$ jobs remaining to be sampled. Let $V_{\hat{J}}(A)$ denote the expected lifetime earnings to an individual with $\hat{J}$ jobs left to sample, and whose most productive job so far delivers a productivity of A. Since the worker can always ignore the last firm sampled, it must be the case that no one is made worse off by having more firms to sample so that $V_{\hat{J}+1}(A) \geq V_{\hat{J}}(A)$.

With that notation, I will prove the claim by contradiction. First, assume that $A^*_{\hat{J}+1} < A^*_{\hat{J}}$ so that individuals get pickier over time and accept jobs when there are $\hat{J}+1$ firms left to sample that they would not accept when there are $\hat{J}$ firms left to sample. If $A^*_{\hat{J}+1} < A^*_{\hat{J}}$, then there exists a value of A, denoted $\tilde{A}$, at which search is optimal when there are $\hat{J}$ firms left to sample but not when there are $\hat{J}+1$ periods left to sample, or that

$$\frac{r}{2(1+r)} + \frac{r}{(1+r)^2}\left(\tilde{A}V_{\hat{J}-1}(\tilde{A}) + \int_{\tilde{A}}^{1} V_{\hat{J}-1}(A)dA\right) > \tilde{A} >$$

$$\frac{r}{2(1+r)} + \frac{r}{(1+r)^2}\left(\tilde{A}V_{\hat{J}}(\tilde{A}) + \int_{\tilde{A}}^{A^*_{\hat{J}}} V_{\hat{J}}(A)dA + \frac{(1+r)(1A^{*2}_{\hat{J}})}{2r}\right).$$

This inequality implies that

$$\tilde{A}V_{\hat{J}-1}(\tilde{A}) + \int_{\tilde{A}}^{1} V_{\hat{J}-1}(A)dA > \tilde{A}V_{\hat{J}}(\tilde{A}) + \int_{\tilde{A}}^{1} V_{\hat{J}}(A)dA,$$

but that is impossible since $V_{\hat{J}-1}(\tilde{A}) \leq V_{\hat{J}}(\tilde{A})$.

Now assume that $A^*_{\hat{J}+1} > A^*_{\hat{J}}$ so that people get less picky as they sample more jobs. This case does seem intrinsically more plausible, but may also be rejected. First, note that A^*_1 solves

$$\frac{1+r}{r}A^*_1 = \frac{1}{2} + A^*_1\frac{\frac{1+r}{r}A^*_1}{(1+r)} + (1-A^*_1)\frac{\frac{1+r}{r}\left(\frac{1+A^*_1}{2}\right)}{(1+r)},$$

so that $A^*_1 = \frac{1+r+A^{*2}_1}{2(1+r)}$, i.e. $A^*_1 = 1+r-\sqrt{r(1+r)}$. Next note that if $A^*_{\hat{J}+1} > A^*_{\hat{J}}$ then $A^*_{\hat{J}+1}$ solves the same functional equation as $A^*_{\hat{J}}$ does. It then follows by induction on $\hat{J}$ that $A^\times_{\hat{J}+1} = 1+r-\sqrt{r(1+r)}$ for all $\hat{J}$, which is a contradiction to the assumption that $A^\times_{\hat{J}+1} > A^*_{\hat{J}}$, since it implies that $A^*_{\hat{J}+1} = A^*_{\hat{J}} = \cdots = A^*_1 = 1+r-\sqrt{r(1+r)}$.

I let q denote the quantity $1+r-\sqrt{r(1+r)}$. From the proof of Claim 1, it is clear that $A^\times_{\hat{J}} = q$ for all $\hat{J}$.

The fact that individuals use a fixed cutoff rule makes it relatively easy to compute expected welfare EW as a function of J, the total number of employers:

$$\begin{aligned}\text{EW} = {}& \frac{q^{J+1}}{2r}\left(1+r-(1+r)^{1-J}+\frac{2J}{(J+1)(1+r)^J}\right)\\ &+\frac{(1-q^2)(1+r)}{2r(1+r-q)}\left(1+r-q\left(\frac{q}{1+r}\right)^{J-1}\right)+\frac{(1+r)(q^2-q^{J+1})}{2r}\\ &-\frac{(1+r)(1-q)q^2}{2r(1+r-q)}+\frac{(1-q)q^3}{2r(1+r-q)}\left(\frac{q}{1+r}\right)^{J-1},\end{aligned}$$

or

$$\begin{aligned}\text{EW} = {}& \frac{1}{2r}\left(\frac{q}{1+r}\right)^J\left(\frac{-2q}{(J+1)}-\frac{(1+r-q)^2(1+q)-rq^2(2+r-q)}{(1+r-q)}\right)\\ &+\frac{(1+r)(1+r-q^2)}{2r(1+r-q)}.\end{aligned}$$

The term $(1+r-q)^2(1+q)-rq^2(2+r-q)$ can be rewritten as $r(1+r)(1+r+2r^2-2r\sqrt{r(1+r)})$, which is strictly positive. As a result, the terms in parentheses that are being multiplied by $\left(\frac{q}{1+r}\right)^J$ are also negative. Rising values of J then make this expression larger, which gives us the result that clustering firms together increases the expected lifetime productivity, by increasing the probability of a good match.

Learning in cities

The chapter has so far emphasized the benefits that urban proximity can create by reducing the costs of shipping goods or connecting people. I now turn to the role that cities play in facilitating the flow of ideas.

Why do we think that the cities have an edge in facilitating the flow of ideas? The first set of evidence was anecdotal and relied on observations of urban learning and innovation. Alfred Marshall (1890) famously observed that

> Great are the advantages which people following the same skilled trade get from near neighborhood to one another. The mysteries of the trade become no mystery, but are as it were, in the air . . .

Marshall certainly did not have statistics to back him up. Presumably, his comment was based on insight and observation. Jane Jacobs (1969) followed Marshall in stressing the theme of ideas in cities. She was a great observer, but also brought together a number of real world examples, such as the invention of the bra, in which urban proximity spurred the flow of ideas. My own personal favorite of these anecdotes is that Isaac Singer supposedly got the idea to improve the sewing machine when he saw one in a Boston shop window.

Localized chains of artistic creativity provide another example of the power of cities to spread ideas. There is a remarkable tendency of artistic greatness to cluster in particular places during particular epochs: Renaissance Florence, eighteenth century Vienna, Impressionist Paris. Just as clustering of industries within a country provides some evidence for spillovers, this clustering provides evidence for intellectual spillovers. Of course, it could just be natural advantage, but most of the stories of natural advantage (like Medici or Hapsburg patronage or access to the Roman sources) look weak under examination (e.g. there was plenty of patronage in other places).

Turning to the history of these periods, it is pretty clear that the artists knew each other well and learned regularly from one another. In some cases, it is possible to trace the path of an innovation, such as *linear perspective*, which is the ability to use geometry to produce the illusion of three dimensions in a two dimensional painting. Linear perspective seems to have been first understood by the polymathic architect Brunelleschi who passed it along to his friend and traveling companion Donatello, who first used it in a low relief sculpture. Masaccio, another Florentine, then made the leap to painting in the Brancacci chapel. Masaccio's chapel then provided a school for other painters to learn the technique; he himself taught it to his apprentice Fra Lippi who passed the knowledge along to his student Botticelli. Linear perspective then allowed painters to create more complex paintings with greater verisimilitude.

Statistics also support the contention that idea seem to spread more easily over short distances. Jaffe, Trajtenberg and Henderson (1993) provide a particularly vivid statistical account of a process similar to the diffusion of linear perspective. They examine patent citations which show the intellectual influences that lead to new patenting innovations and find that people are much more likely to cite others who are in the same geographic area. Even in areas of relatively advanced technology, where ideas are supposed to move freely, there is a strong tendency for patents to be geographically localized.

Patent and innovation data also show that these new innovations are generally concentrated in big urban areas. For example, Audretsch and Feldman (1996) look at a data sample of commercial innovations in the US in 1982. These innovations tend to be applied considerably more regularly than the patents discussed above. There is a strong tendency for these innovations to be clustered in the largest cities.

The connection between skills and city growth has also been interpreted as suggesting that cities succeed by spreading ideas (Glaeser *et al.*, 1995). There are certainly other interpretations of the skills-growth connection, but it is reasonable to think that one reason why skilled cities are succeeding is that those places have done well at harnessing the ability of cities to speed the flow of innovations between smart people. The tendency of skilled people to attract more skilled people (Berry and Glaeser, 2005) can also be seen as reflecting the urban ability to move ideas across people. The tendency of highly skilled industries to locate in city centers (Glaeser and Kahn, 2001) is yet another piece of evidence supporting the connection between urban density and ideas.

The evidence on human capital spillovers also can be seen as supporting the view that urban density helps knowledge spread. As discussed in the previous chapter, Rauch (1993) shows that workers in skilled cities are paid more, holding their own skills constant. Moretti (2004) repeats this exercise using historical colleges as an instrument for city skill levels.[7] Glaeser and Saiz (2004) and Shapiro (2006) show that the connection between individual wages and city-level skills has been rising over time. The evidence for human capital spillovers also supports the view that cities promote productivity by connecting people to smart people with good ideas.

[7] Acemoglu and Angrist (1999) do not find evidence for human capital spillovers when they look at the state level. However, their source of variation is state compulsory attendance laws which act primarily to reduce the minimum level of education. The workers impacted by these laws seem unlikely to be those who are actually producing new ideas.

Table 4.12. {0, 1} Model of idea transmission in cities

Actors	People in cities
They maximize	Lifetime wages
They choose	People choose where to live; they therefore implicitly choose only to interact with people in their community. (Whenever a person with skill level j interacts with someone who has skill level $j' > j$, then the person's skills increase to skill level $j+1$ with probability c.)
Transition equation	The transition equation for the share of people with skill level one is: $\pi\left(1, t+\frac{1}{D}\right) = \delta^{1/D}\pi(1, t) + \delta^{1/D}c\pi(1, t)(1-\pi(1, t))$.
Equilibrium condition	$\frac{\beta\delta(w(1)-w(0))\left(1+c-\delta^{-1/D}\right)}{1\beta\delta\left(\delta^{-1/D}c\right)} = \frac{kN}{2(1-\beta\delta)}$
Notation	c := probability of learning N := city population $D(N)$:= meetings per period δ := individual survival probability $\pi(j, t)$:= share of population with skill level j at time t $w(j)$:= wage of individual with skill level j d := distance of individual from center of the city k^*d := cost of commuting from distance d to center β := individual's future discount factor

A final piece of evidence on the connection between cities and idea flows is provided by Glaeser and Mare (2001) who look at the wage patterns of migrants who come to and leave cities. The paper shows that there is, on average, a dramatic urban wage premium, but that migrants who come to cities do not immediately receive that premium. Instead, over time their wage growth is more robust. When individuals leave cities, they do not lose their wage premium, but receive lower wage gains in the non-urban area. More generally, there is a strong interaction between urban status and experience, suggesting that the urban wage premium accumulates over time.

This evidence is not compatible with the view that cities make workers more productive through a simple urban productivity level effect. If that were the case, then migrants should receive a large wage gain when they come to cities and suffer a dramatic wage loss when they leave (at least in nominal terms). The steady wage gains in urban areas are more compatible with a dynamic process that could involve better matching between workers and firms, as described above, or could involve a learning process. According to this view, cities are forges of human capital where individuals acquire skills by being around other smart people. I now turn to a model that illustrates how that process might work that follows from Glaeser (1999).

Table 4.13. Continuous model of idea transmission in cities

Actors	People in cities
They maximize	Lifetime wages
They choose	People choose where to live; they therefore implicitly choose only to interact with people in their community. (Whenever a person with skill level j interacts with someone who has skill level $j' > j$, then the person's skills increase to skill level $j+1$ with probability c.)
Transition equation	The transition equation for the share of people with skill level one is: $\Pi\left(j, t+\frac{1}{D}\right) = \delta^{1/D}\Pi(j,t) + \delta^{1/D}c\Pi(j,t)\pi(j-1,t)$.
Equilibrium condition	$\dfrac{\alpha\delta\beta\left(1-\left(2-\delta^{-1/D}\right)^{D}\right)\left(\frac{c}{\delta^{-1/D}-1}-1\right)}{1-\delta\beta\left(2-\delta^{-1/D}\right)^{D}} = \dfrac{kN}{2}$
Notation	$c :=$ probability of learning $N :=$ city population $D(N) :=$ meetings per period $\delta :=$ individual survival probability $J :=$ maximal skill level of individuals in the city $\pi(j,t) :=$ share of population with skill level j at time t $\Pi(j,t) := \int_j^1 \pi(j,t)$ $w(j) :=$ wage of individual with skill level j $d :=$ distance of individual from center of the city $k^*d :=$ cost of commuting from distance d to center $\beta :=$ individual's future discount factor

To make things simple, I will assume that skill levels S are positive integers and that wages are a fixed function of skills $w(S)$. The essence of the learning model is that people become skilled by interacting with skilled people. The core equations of this model and the notation are given in Tables 4.12 and 4.13. Thus, I assume that whenever a person with skill level j interacts with someone who has skill level $j' > j$, then the person's skills increase to skill level $j+1$ with probability c. (The person with skill level j', who already knows more than the person with skill level j, receives nothing from the connection.) I assume that each interaction occurs with a randomly drawn member of the population. Wages equal a constant times the skill level, which would occur when there is a linear production technology mapping skill levels into output and all goods are traded globally.

The somewhat ad-hoc assumption that drives the agglomeration economy is that the frequency of meetings is a function of density, that is, that people clustering together leads to more regular connections.[8] In

[8] While this assumption does seem plausible, it should be understood that density should really be understood relative to the prevailing transportation technology. Wall Street is undoubtedly dense, but Silicon Valley is as well, because there are so many smart people in that area who are within easy driving distance of one another.

any case, I assume that each person has $D(N)$ meetings per period, where N is city population (perhaps relative to land area) and $D'(N) > 0$. I will assume that the environment is stationary and N is constant over time.

I assume that once people choose a location, they remain there for life, presumably because moving costs are high. I also assume that individuals, regardless of age or skill level, survive each period with probability δ. Every $1/D$th period, $\delta^{1/D}$ survive, so that $1 - \delta^{1/D}$ die during each of these meeting periods. When people die, they are replaced by new entrants having skill levels of zero. In equilibrium, the cost of living in the city will offset the expected lifetime earnings benefits from living in the city.

To solve the model, I begin with a situation in which there are only two skill levels: zero and one, with respective associated wages $w(0)$ and $w(1)$. I let $\pi(1, t)$ denote the share of the population with skill level one at time t. The share of the population with skill level zero at that time is, of course, $1 - \pi(1, t)$. The transition equation for the share of people with skill level one is

$$\pi\left(1, t + \frac{1}{D}\right) = \delta^{1/D}\pi(1, t) + \delta^{1/D}c\pi(1, t)(1 - \pi(1, t)). \tag{4.9}$$

The people who have skill level one at time $t + 1/D$ are those who had those skills at time t and survived, and those who moved from having skill level zero to skill level and also survived. The share of the population that increased their skill level is equal to the share of people with skill level zero initially that interacted with someone with skill level one, $\pi(1, t)(1 - \pi(1, t))$, times c, the probability that learning took place.

If the population is steady, I can let $\pi(1)$ refer to the share of the population with skill level one at any time period. The transition equation then implies that $1 - \pi(1) = (\delta^{-1/D} - 1)/c$, assuming that $1 + c > \delta^{-1/D}$, so that this quantity is less than one. The share of unskilled workers is therefore declining in c the imitation rate, and falling with N, since D rises as N rises. The faster rate of connection in bigger cities leads to a faster skill accumulation and a generally more skilled city. Of course, the skills that are being discussed here are best thought of as informal, post-school education.

To close the model, I assume that this is a monocentric linear city in which everyone consumes one unit of land and the cost of commuting is kd, where d is the distance from the center and the value of land on the edge of the city is zero. As such, the total land plus commuting costs for everyone must be $kN/2$. I assume further that, in the reservation locale, there is no learning, so that everyone earns $w(0)$ in perpetuity and pays neither land nor commuting costs.

If individuals are paid at the beginning of each period and discount the future with a discount factor β, then the lifetime spatial equilibrium condition is that

$$\sum_t \delta^{t-1}\beta^{t-1}\left(w(0)(1-c\pi(1))^{t-1}+w(1)\left(1-(1-c\pi(1))^{t-1}\right)-\frac{kN}{2}\right)$$
$$=\sum_t \delta^{t-1}\beta^{t-1}w(0). \qquad (4.10)$$

As $1-c\pi(1)=\delta^{-1/D}-c$, the spatial equilibrium (4.10) can also be written as

$$\frac{\beta\delta(w(1)-w(0))\left(1+c-\delta^{-1/D}\right)}{1-\beta\delta\left(\delta^{-1/D}-c\right)}=\frac{kN}{2(1-\beta\delta)}. \qquad (4.10')$$

As long as the spatial equilibrium is stable, which requires $D'(N)$ not to be too large, then city size will be increasing with $(w(1)-w(0))$, falling with k, rising with c and rising with both patience and the survival rate. These last comparative statistics reflect the fact that moving to a city is essentially an investment in which people earn real wage losses early in life, because they have to pay higher rents, in exchange for higher wages later on in life.

The model can easily accommodate a large range of skill values. The core equations of this model and the notation are given in Table 4.13. I let $\pi(j,t)$ denote the share of the population with skill level j at time t, and $\Pi(j,t)=\int_j^1 \pi(j,t)$ denote the share of people with skill level j or above at time t. I also let J denote the highest level of skills in the city. In this case, the transition equation is

$$\Pi\left(j,t+\frac{1}{D}\right)=\delta^{1/D}\Pi(j,t)+\delta^{1/D}c\Pi(j,t)\pi(j-1,t). \qquad (4.11)$$

The steady-state value of $\pi(j)$ for all values of j other than J will equal $(\delta^{-1/D}-1)/c$, assuming that this is less than one. The steady-state value of $\pi(J)$ equals $1-J^{(\delta^{-1/D}-1)/c}$. Holding J constant, the share of the population in the largest skill level is rising with city size. The highest value of J that can be supported in steady state is the largest integer that is less than $c/(\delta^{-1/D}-1)$, which is obviously rising with city size. As such, bigger cities can support a large range of skill levels.

The expected skill gain for a person with skill level $j<J$ between time t and time $t+1/D$ equals $j+c\left(1-(j+1)\frac{\delta^{-1/D}-1}{c}\right)$, assuming that he stays alive. If $\pi(j)$ equals $(\delta^{-1/D}-1)/c$, which I assume, then $(J+1)(\delta^{-1/D}-1)/c=1$ and so this equation holds at $j=J$ as well. In this case, the expected skill level at time $t+1/D$ for a person with skill level zero at time 0 is $\left(\frac{c}{\delta^{-1/D}-1}-1\right)\left(1-\left(2-\delta^{-1/D}\right)^{Dt}\right)$. To calculate expected earnings in this case, assume that $w(S)=w(0)+\alpha S$ for all skill levels S.

The lifetime expected earnings benefit from living in a city is therefore equal to

$$\frac{\alpha\delta\beta\left(1-\left(2-\delta^{-1/D}\right)^{D}\right)\left(\frac{c}{\delta^{-1/D-1}}-1\right)}{(1-\delta\beta)\left(1-\delta\beta\left(2-\delta^{-1/D}\right)^{D}\right)},$$

so the spatial equilibrium is now given by

$$\frac{\alpha\delta\beta\left(1-\left(2-\delta^{-1/D}\right)^{D}\right)\left(\frac{c}{\delta^{-1/D-1}}-1\right)}{1-\delta\beta\left(2-\delta^{-1/D}\right)}=\frac{kN}{2}.$$

The model captures a number of features of the data. People have steeper wage profiles in cities. There is a complementarity between skills and cities. Faster learning in cities has little value if everyone has a low skill level. As people are distributed across a greater range of skills, the returns to being in a city increase. A long time horizon helps to make living in cities more valuable, which is perhaps why more young people tend to locate in metropolitan areas.

Testing different theories: The coagglomeration evidence

The models that I have discussed in this chapter have shown different ways in which agglomeration might increase productivity. I have not discussed any evidence suggesting which of these mechanisms might be important. There are many different ways of assessing the significance of different types of evidence that are ably summarized by Rosenthal and Strange (2004).

One method is to follow Henderson (2003) and look directly at firm productivity and regress that productivity on agglomeration of different industries. As I discussed above, this approach is useful but also faces challenges, such as the problem of endogeneity. If we see that productivity is higher when some other firms are nearby, we do not know if that means that those firms are creating productivity or productivity is attracting those firms. Rosenthal and Strange (2006) have an elegant paper that uses the presence of bedrock to instrument for firm location, and this is surely the best effort to deal with this problem. Using measures like wages instead of productivity does not help the problem, and indeed raises a number of questions about labor market equilibria that only further confuse the issue.

A second method is to look at quantities. Do we see more firm entry in areas where there are already concentrations of other firms? Carlton

(1983) is a pioneer in this type of study. Rosenthal and Strange (2005) is an excellent contribution to this literature.

My own preference has been to use evidence from coagglomeration. Dumais, Ellison and Glaeser (1997) was a first effort in this direction; Ellison, Glaeser and Kerr (2007) is a more successful attempt. The basic idea is to look at cross-industry flows to assess the ways in which firms interact with each other. Input–output tables, for example, tell us whether firms buy and sell to one another. If agglomeration is driven by an attempt to minimize transport costs for goods, then we would expect that different industries that buy and sell to one another should locate near one another.

Employment patterns, for example, tell us what types of workers are employed by different pooling. If we think that labor market pooling, for example, was an important source of agglomeration then we should expect to see industries that use the same type of workers coagglomerate with each other. Intellectual spillovers are the hardest hypothesis to test. Luckily, Scherer (1984) provides an input–output matrix for citations across industries. This enables us to look at whether industries that use each others' patents also colocate near one another. While this does show up in the cross-industry patent citation patterns, it is perhaps a less than perfect measure of other forms of less formal intellectual spillovers.

The general problem with using input–output matrices, which is addressed by Ellison, Glaeser and Kerr (2007) but not Dumais, Ellison and Glaeser (1997) is that input–output matrices or employment patterns may also themselves be a function of location patterns. In other words, industry *i* may buy a lot from industry *j* because they have, for reasons of historical accident, tended to locate near one another. As such, moving to industry coagglomeration patterns doesn't intrinsically solve any of the endogeneity problems that plague the other methods of rooting out the sources of agglomeration economies.

Ellison, Glaeser and Kerr (2007) approach this endogeneity problem by using British data for input–output flows, employment patterns and patent citations, and using American data for coagglomeration patterns. If random patterns of historical accident are driving American input–output tables, then they certainly won't be driving the input–output tables in another country. I would also be surprised if American locations were driving the patterns of British employment. The UK data give us a picture of industrial interactions that are hopefully purged of the influence of American geography. Of course, the British data may be a noisy measure of the true technological relationships in the US, but this problem will generally cause a bias towards finding no effect.

When we look at state-level coagglomeration, we find roughly equal effects of input–output relationships and labor sharing. A one standard deviation increase in either variable increases the degree of coagglomeration by about .15 standard deviations, when we don't include the technology transfer variable. With that variable, the impact of a one standard deviation increase in any one of the three variables causes the coagglomeration measure to increase by one-tenth of a standard deviation.

At lower levels of geography, input–output relationships become somewhat more important than labor sharing. A one standard deviation increase in the input–output measure causes coagglomeration to increase by one-tenth of a standard deviation when we exclude the technology transfer measure. A one standard deviation increase in the labor sharing variable causes the coagglomeration measure to increase by about one-twentieth of a standard deviation. When we include the technology transfer measure, it has the strongest impact at the county level, at least using the British measures as instruments.

Overall, the results suggest that all of the different agglomerating forces have some degree of importance, at least within manufacturing. However, as manufacturing is becoming a smaller and smaller share of US employment, this may be less important for the country as a whole. In the next section, I explore the impact of changes in transportation and communication technology and agglomeration economies.

The evolution of agglomeration economies

In this final section of this chapter, I turn to changes in agglomeration economies over time. Over the twentieth century, the real costs of moving a ton a mile by rail declined by more than 90 percent (Glaeser and Kohlhase, 2004). The introduction of other technologies—like trucks and planes—has been even more dramatic. 100 years ago, it was quite expensive to move heavy goods long distances. Today, it is cheap. The impact of this has surely been to decrease the productivity benefits associated with clustering to reduce transport costs for goods. After all, in this globalized world, there are plenty of highly productive firms that produce manufactured goods and sell them halfway across the planet.

This claim does not actually contradict the Ellison, Glaeser and Kerr (2007) evidence discussed immediately above. It is entirely possible that manufacturing firms locate close to one another to save transport costs for goods and that those transport costs are still not all that important for the rest of the economy. If there isn't much heterogeneity in natural advantage across space, then tiny differences in transportation costs could still motivate location decisions. Moreover, manufacturing doesn't represent all that much of the economy and it is a sector that is particularly suburbanized. Manufacturing firms locate in middle density counties, away from big cities, but also away from the truly isolated areas. One reason why manufacturing fled urban areas is that as shipping moved from train to truck, it became increasingly sensible to move away from rail yards to areas with easy access to highways.

Services, and particularly high human capital sectors, are particularly likely to locate in the urban core (Glaeser and Kahn, 2001). These sectors don't actually produce goods too often, so what is driving their decision to agglomerate? The simplest theory—which surely has much truth in it—is that they are agglomerating to reduce the costs of moving people. Delivering services almost always involves face-to-face travel, and cities reduce the amount of that travel that is needed. While technology has made moving goods far less expensive, the costs of moving people is still in many cases quite high, because time is a critical ingredient in moving people and the value of time increases, roughly, with wages (Becker, 1965). As the costs of moving goods has plummeted, the costs of moving people—at least for moderate distances—may well have gone up substantially over the twentieth century. Over longer distances, our technological improvements have probably pushed travel times down fast enough to offset the increase in the value of time.

One reason that we see the business service oriented cities of today is that those agglomerations serve to reduce the travel times of people. While the Krugman model was designed around shipping goods, it wouldn't be all that hard to reinterpret it as a model of services, so the basic framework could be kept. Naturally, all of the other agglomeration economies that hinge on saving transport costs for people, like labor market pooling or matching, still continue to operate and make agglomerations attractive.

There is also a sense in which many of today's most productive urban areas thrive by being in the idea business. Wall Street and the City of London are financial districts where money is made by understanding risk and pricing better than anywhere else. Technological cities like Bangalore or Silicon Valley thrive by producing new innovations. Certainly, the wage premium associated with being around smart people has risen steadily over the last 30 years (Glaeser and Saiz, 2004). It is reasonable to suspect that knowledge-based agglomeration economies are increasingly important in the world's most successful cities.

In a paper that is close in spirit to Duranton and Puga (2005), Glaeser and Ponzetto (2007) suggest that a reduction in transportation costs could be responsible both for the decline of cities that specialize in making goods and for the rebirth of cities that have focused on producing ideas. The basic idea of this model is that a reduction in the transport costs for goods may increase the returns for innovation by increasing the size of the market and reducing delivery costs. If urban density helps the innovation process by connecting smart people, then a decline in the cost of moving goods over space may well have increased the returns to innovating and increased the returns for locating in cities that help generate ideas. The "death of distance" may have been bad news for Detroit, but it is just fine for New York's hedge funds that specialize in the Yen carry trade.

There is some evidence that supports this view. High human capital industries have become more important in successful cities. Those cities that specialized in those industries initially have become much more successful, while manufacturing cities have fared poorly. At the least, the model helps to rationalize the fact that in a world where declining transport costs have supposedly made the world flat, the wage premium and real estate costs associated with living in New York or London are higher than they ever have been in the past.

Of course, this view begs the question of whether further improvements in information technology will make the urban edge in facilitating face-to-face communications obsolete. The claim that information technology will kill cities has been around since the nineteenth century when some pundits claimed that the telephone would make cities unnecessary. That didn't happen. Gaspar and Glaeser (1998) suggest that it isn't even obvious that improvements in electronic interactions make face-to-face interactions less valuable. It is at least theoretically possible that electronic interactions and face-to-face interactions are complements, not substitutes. If they are complements, then we should expect further improvement in electronic interactions to make cities more, not less, attractive.

The model of Gaspar and Glaeser (1998) has three stages. First, individuals decide whether or not to locate in a city. Second, individuals decide whether or not to work independently or to pursue a partnership with someone else. Third, individuals who decide to pursue a partnership learn the productivity of that partnership and decide how intensively to develop that partnership. The core equations of this model and the notation are given in Table 4.14. Developing the partnership requires interactions which can either be electronic or face-to-face. I will start with the second stage and return to the urbanization decision once the main details of the model have been worked out.

In the second stage, individuals know their return from engaging in independent production and that is denoted R. In equilibrium, there will be an individual who is on the margin between producing independently and producing interactively and that person can be described by his value of R, denoted R^*. The number of people who produce interactively can be denoted $H(R^*)$ where $H(x)$ is a function that denotes the share of the

Table 4.14. Modeling interactions

Actors	Individuals
They maximize	Expected returns
They choose	First, whether to locate in the city or the hinterland Second, whether to engage in a collaborative project or an individual one Third, if they collaborate, whether to communicate face-to-face or by telephone
Key equations	$\alpha^* f(i_F^*(\alpha^*)) - ct_F - \frac{ci_F^*(\alpha^*)}{\beta_F} = \alpha^* f(i_P^*(\alpha^*)) - \frac{ci_P^*(\alpha^*)}{\beta_P}$ $R^* = \int_{\alpha=\alpha_{min}}^{\alpha^*} \left(\alpha f(i_P^*(\alpha)) - \frac{ci_P^*(\alpha)}{\beta_P}\right) g(\alpha) + \int_{\alpha=\alpha^*}^{\alpha_{max}} \left(\alpha f(i_F^*(\alpha)) - ct_F - \frac{ci_F^*(\alpha)}{\beta_F}\right) g(\alpha)$
Notation	R: return from independent production R^*: value of R for which a person is on the margin of independent and collaborative production $H(R^*)$: number of people who choose to produce interactively. $H(x)$ denotes the share of the population with values of R below x $\alpha f(i)$: returns to interactive production α: productivity of a match between collaborators i: intensity with which a match is pursued $G(.)$ and $g(.)$: the CDF and pdf of α t: time expended on a match c: cost of time $\beta_P t$: intensity from use of a phone β_F max $[0, t - t_F]$: Intensity from face-to-face time t_F: fixed cost of face-to-face communication $i_P^*(\alpha)$: optimal intensity for a person using the phone $i_F^*(\alpha)$: optimal intensity for a person communicating face-to-face $t_P^*(\alpha)$: optimal amount of time invested for a person using the phone $t_F^*(\alpha)$: optimal amount of time invested for a person communicating facet-to-face α^*: value of α for which the returns to meeting face-to-face are the same as the returns to using the phone λt_F: fixed cost of face-to-face interactions in the city N: number of people in the city $kN/2$: cost of living in the city α_C^*: cutoff for using electronic technology in the city α_H^*: cutoff for using electronic technology in the hinterland R_C^*: cutoff for producing interactively in the city R_H^*: cutoff for producing interactively in the hinterland

population with values of R below x. If an individual decides to produce independently then he receives R and nothing else happens.

If the person decides to produce interactively, then his returns can be written $\alpha f(i)$, where α denotes the productivity of the match, i describes the intensity with which the match is pursued and $f(.)$ is a concave function. Match quality is randomly distributed with density $g(.)$ and cumulative distribution function $G(.)$.

Intensity is produced with time and with interactions that can either be electronic or face-to-face. Time has a cost of c times t—the amount of time expended. If an individual uses the electronic technology, like a telephone, then the intensity equals $\beta_P t$. If an individual uses the face-to-face technology, then the intensity equals $\beta_F \max[0, t - t_F]$.

The parameter t_F is meant to reflect the fixed costs involved in face-to-face interactions, like the time of getting to meet each other. I assume that $\beta_F > \beta_P$, so that face-to-face interactions are more productive than electronic interactions once the fixed cost is paid. Improvements in electronic interactions may have narrowed the gap between meeting face-to-face and electronic meetings, but electronic interactions are still an imperfect substitute for meeting in person.

Given these two technologies, the optimal technology given that a person is using a phone will maximize $\alpha f(\beta_P t) - ct$, which implies that $\alpha\beta_P f'(\beta_P t) - c$. I use this condition to define $i_P^*(\alpha)$ as the optimal level of interactions condition on the match quality and condition on the phone being used. The value of $i_P^*(\alpha)$ equals $f'^{-1}\left(\frac{c}{\alpha\beta_P}\right)$ which is rising with α. Likewise, I can define the value of $i_F^*(\alpha)$ which equals the optimum level of intensity conditional on α and conditional on using face-to-face interactions. The value of $i_F^*(\alpha)$ equals $f'^{-1}\left(\frac{c}{\alpha\beta_F}\right)$ which is also rising with α. I also define $t_P^*(\alpha) = i_P^*(\alpha)/\beta_P$ as the optimal amount of time used when using the phone and $t_F^*(\alpha) = t_F + i_F^*(\alpha)/\beta_F$ as the optimal amount of time spent when meeting face-to-face.

The net return from meeting face-to-face equals $\alpha f(i_F^*(\alpha)) - ct_F - ci_F^*(\alpha)/\beta_F$. The net return from using electronic interactions equals $\alpha f(i_P^*(\alpha)) - ci_P^*(\alpha)/\beta_P$. I assume that the returns from interacting using the telephone are positive for all match qualities.

Since $i_F^*(\alpha) > i_P^*(\alpha)$, the derivative of the returns to face-to-face interactions with respect to α is always greater than the derivative of the returns to electronic interactions with respect to the same variable. I assume that there are some matches where the quality is sufficiently low that it only makes sense to use electronic interactions and that there are some interactions where it makes sense to use face-to-face interactions. As such, continuity ensures that there must exist a value of α, denoted α^* where returns from meeting face to face are the same as the returns from connection electronically. More formally, α^* satisfies

$$\alpha^* f(i_F^*(\alpha^*)) - ct_F - \frac{ci_F^*(\alpha^*)}{\beta_F} = \alpha^* f(i_P^*(\alpha^*)) - \frac{ci_P^*(\alpha^*)}{\beta_P}.$$

The model says that for the most valuable partnerships we meet face-to-face, but for less valuable relationship we don't, and just use electronic interactions.

The model is meant to address the question of what will happen when electronic interactions become more efficient or when β_P rises. The first effect of improvements in electronic technology is that some interactions will switch from using the face-to-face technology to using the electronic technology. The derivative of α^* with respect to β_P equals

$$\frac{\alpha^* T_P^*(\alpha^*)}{\beta_P (T_F^*(\alpha^*) T_P^*(\alpha^*))} > 0.$$

This is the direct effect of improving information technology—people do indeed switch from meeting face-to-face to using electronic media.

But the model includes a second margin—the decision of whether or not to interact at all. This margin is defined by equating the returns from acting independently (R^*) with the expected returns from operating with someone else. The key equation is

$$\begin{aligned} R^* = & \int_{\alpha-\alpha_{\min}}^{\alpha^*} \left(\alpha f(i_P^*(\alpha)) - \frac{c i_P^*(\alpha)}{\beta_P} \right) dG(\alpha) \\ & + \int_{\alpha-\alpha^*}^{\alpha_{\max}} \left(\alpha f(i_P^*(\alpha)) - c t_F - \frac{c i_F^*(\alpha)}{\beta_F} \right) dG(\alpha). \end{aligned} \quad (4.12)$$

Differentiating this equation gives us that the derivative of R^* with respect to β_P is $\int_{\alpha=\alpha_{min}}^{\alpha^*} \frac{c i_P^*(\alpha)}{\beta_P^2} dG(\alpha)$, which is positive. The improvements in electronic communications make it more likely that people will be interactive since better technology raises the expected returns from interactions.

Can an improvement in electronic technology increase the total number of face-to-face interactions? The number of face-to-face interactions equals $H(R^*)(1 - G(\alpha^*))$ and the derivative of this with respect to β_P equals

$$H'(R^*)(1 - G(\alpha^*)) \int_{\alpha=\alpha_{\min}}^{\alpha^*} \frac{c i_P^*(\alpha)}{\beta_P^2} dG(\alpha) - H(R^*) g(\alpha^*) \frac{\alpha^* T_P^*(\alpha^*)}{\beta_P \left(T_F^*(\alpha^*) - T_P^*(\alpha^*) \right)}. \quad (4.13)$$

This expression is positive if and only if

$$\frac{H'(R^*)}{H(R^*)} \int_{\alpha=\alpha_{\min}}^{\alpha^*} c T_P^*(\alpha) dG(\alpha) > \frac{g(\alpha^*)}{1 - G(\alpha^*)} \frac{\alpha^* T_P^*(\alpha^*)}{\left(T_F^*(\alpha^*) - T_P^*(\alpha^*) \right)}. \quad (4.14)$$

If there are a lot of people on the margin of being interactive, then this inequality may hold. If there are a lot of people on the margin between using electronic interactions or face-to-face interactions then it may not. It is certainly possible that the improvement in electronic technology can increase the number of face-to-face interactions, as long as the elasticity of the number of relationships with respect to the returns to those relationships is sufficiently high. As electronic interactions become more efficient, the entire economy becomes more interactive and that causes the number of face-to-face interactions to rise as well. The key modeling trick that gets this to work is the introduction of two margins: an intensive margin of using electronic or face-to-face communications and an extensive margin of choosing whether or not to be interactive at all.

To embed this in an urban model, I assume that in period one, people choose whether to live in the city or in the hinterland. As before, I assume that the cost of living in the city is $kN/2$ which is meant to capture the combination of commuting and housing costs in a linear city where everyone consumes exactly one unit of land. I assume that the city's only benefit is to reduce the costs of face-to-face interactions, so that these costs equal λt_F in the urban area, where $\lambda < 1$. I let α_C^* and α_H^* denote the cutoff points for using electronic technology in the city and hinterland respectively. I let R_C^* and R_H^* denote the cutoff point for interacting in the city and the hinterland respectively. I also let $h(.)$ and $H(.)$ denote the density and cumulative distribution of R.

With this notation, the spatial equilibrium that equates utility in the city and the hinterland will determine city size:

$$\int_{R=R_C^*}^{R_{\text{Max}}} R\,dH(R) + H(R_C^*)\begin{bmatrix} \int_{\alpha=\alpha_{\min}}^{\alpha_C^*}\left(\alpha f\left(i_P^*(\alpha)\right) - \frac{ci_P^*(\alpha)}{\beta_P}\right)dG(\alpha) + \\ \int_{\alpha=\alpha_C^*}^{\alpha_{\max}}\left(\alpha f\left(i_F^*(\alpha)\right) - \lambda c t_F - \frac{ci_F^*(\alpha)}{\beta_F}\right)dG(\alpha) \end{bmatrix} - .5\,\text{kN}$$

$$= \int_{R-R_H^*}^{R_{Max}} R\,dH(R) + H(R_H^*)\begin{bmatrix} \int_{\alpha=\alpha_{\min}}^{\alpha_H^*}\left(\alpha f\left(i_P^*(\alpha)\right) - \frac{ci_P^*(\alpha)}{\beta_P}\right)dG(\alpha) + \\ \int_{\alpha=\alpha_H^*}^{\alpha_{\max}}\left(\alpha f\left(i_F^*(\alpha)\right) - c t_F - \frac{ci_F^*(\alpha)}{\beta_F}\right)dG(\alpha) \end{bmatrix}. \tag{4.15}$$

The derivative of N with respect to β_P equals $2/k$ times

$$H\left(R_C^*\right)\int_{\alpha=\alpha_{\min}}^{\alpha_C^*}\frac{ci_P^*(\alpha)}{\beta_P^2}dG(\alpha) - H(R_H^*)\int_{\alpha=\alpha_{\min}}^{\alpha_H^*}\frac{ci_P^*(\alpha)}{\beta_P^2}dG(\alpha).$$

This term is positive if and only if city dwellers use telephones more often than the residents of the hinterland. City dwellers will use telephones more often the residents of the hinterland if

$$\frac{H'(R^*)}{H(R^*)}\int_{a=a_{\min}}^{a^*} cT_P^*(a)dG(a) > \frac{g(a^*)}{1-G(a^*)}\frac{a^*T_P^*(a^*)}{\left(T_F^*(a^*)-T_P^*(a^*)\right)}.$$

This is the same condition that ensures that face-to-face and electronic communications are complements. As such, the question of whether face-to-face and electronic interactions are complements or substitutes is equivalent to the question of whether improvements in electronic communications will make cities more populous.

The model illustrates one way in which electronic interactions can be a complement to face-to-face interactions and cities, but there are certainly many other stories. Electronic interactions might be useful in arranging face-to-face meetings. In lengthy relationships, both types of meetings might be used. In no sense did I mean to rule out other ways in which the two types of interactions were complements, but instead just illustrated how a model would work with one particular source of complementarity.

The model has only made the case that it is possible that improvement in electronic technology will make cities more attractive. It is also certainly possible that electronic interactions may make cities less appealing. As such, it is an empirical question whether electronic interactions and face-to-face interactions are complements or substitutes. Gaspar and Glaeser (1998) put forth a number of suggestive pieces of evidence about the complementarity between these two forms of interactions. Subsequent papers have added to the literature.

As a first piece of evidence, we cite data from Japan showing that there is a strong positive link between telephone usage and urban city size. There is also a positive correlation between urbanization and telephone usage across countries, controlling for other measures of the level of development, such as GDP. There is also a tendency for people who call each other to live close to one another, which also supports the complementarity hypothesis if we think that people who live close to one another are more likely to meet face-to-face.

Subsequent papers that look at internet usage and city size have found more mixed results. Sinai and Waldfogel (2004) provide mixed evidence. Local internet providers are more common in cities, but isolated people are less likely to connect to the internet. Forman, Goldfarb and Greenstein (2003) also find that the connection is less common in cities, but they find that the cutting edge technologies are more common in big cities. I take these two papers to suggest that there is no clear answer from Internet usage.

Another piece of evidence comes from the adoption of the telephone over the twentieth century. While experts a century ago argued that telephones were likely to reduce urbanization, there is no time series connection within the US between telephone usage and reduced urbanization. Many of the first telephone systems were installed in urban areas.

Business travel gives us a direct measure of the demand for face-to-face contact. If electronic interactions reduced the demand for personal meetings, then we should see a decline in business travel as electronic communications increase. Certainly, there have been spectacular improvements in electronic technology over the last 20 years. Business travel has, however, risen spectacularly just as electronic interactions have become more efficient. This increase in business travel survives controlling for the decrease in air travel costs following deregulation. At least with this one measure, new technologies appear to be encouraging face-to-face contact.

A final piece of evidence comes from Silicon Valley itself. It is a remarkable fact that the most famous modern example of an industrial agglomeration is in an industry that has the best access to new technologies. If an industry should have been able to disperse with access to electronic technologies, it should have been computing. Yet computers are exactly the area where agglomeration economies appear to be most robust. Personally, I take this as meaning that we should expect to see agglomeration economies for many decades to come.

5

Urban distress

Cities are centers of great poverty and great wealth. Within the US, the poverty rate is typically far higher in central cities than it is in outlying areas. As is so often the case, poverty is accompanied by crime, single-parent families and lower quality public services, like schooling. In this chapter, I turn to the economics of urban distress. The first section of the chapter focuses on the causes of urban poverty. The second section looks at the measurement, causes, and consequences of segregation. The third section looks at crime, riots, and social interactions.

As I have argued throughout this volume, the hallmark of urban and regional economics is the spatial equilibrium concept—the idea that people are indifferent across space. Nowhere is the power of this concept more obvious than in the examination of urban poverty. Many people see urban poverty as evidence of the weakness of cities. The spatial equilibrium concept turns this intuition on its head, and suggests that urban poverty is evidence of urban strength. The economic approach to cities argues that cities are poor because poor people choose cities, not because cities make people poor.

There is much evidence to support this view. In the US, at least, the poor are fairly geographically mobile. About 38 percent of Americans who are over 15 and were earning less than $25,000 in 2004 changed houses between 2000 and 2005. More than 18 percent of that population changed counties over the same time period. Even some of the poorest centers of despair in the county attract significant migrant flows. 13.8 percent of the residents of central city Detroit, one of America's poorest areas, came into the city from a different county between 1995 and 2000.[9] Moreover, longer term urban residents are no poorer than recent migrants. If anything, recent migrants are particularly likely to lack

[9] All data is from the US Census at www. Census.org. Mobility by income is available at http://www.census.gov/population/www/socdemo/migrate/cps2005-5yr.html

financial resources. The attraction of immigrants to urban areas further supports the idea that cities have a special attraction for the poor.

None of this is meant to suggest that there aren't also adverse consequences associated with living in urban centers of poverty. In the second and third sections of this chapter, I discuss the evidence that concentrations of poverty lead to adverse outcomes, especially for young people. While I believe that there is certainly evidence that these so-called neighborhood effects can be important, I also believe that the starting point for economists must be to apply the spatial equilibrium model and look for the reasons why poor people sort into metropolitan areas.

The causes of urban poverty: Housing, spillovers and transportation

I begin with a simple model that draws heavily from the work of Thomas Schelling (1971, 1978). The core equations of this model and the notation are given in Table 5.1. The starting point is to look at segregation of rich and poor and then try to understand why the poor might be particularly segregated into cities. I consider a two-group model which could represent rich and poor, black and white, or immigrant and native; I will use the example of rich and poor people. We normalize the overall size of

Table 5.1. Model for the segregation of the rich and the poor

Actors	Rich people, poor people
They maximize	Utility = Cash – Housing cost – Transportation costs + Spillovers
They choose	Location: central city or suburb. People must be indifferent across space, trading off the cost of housing, social spillovers, and transportation costs of the two regions.
Key conditions	We have three potential equilibria: Cost of city housing = $K + \Delta$ Cost of city housing = $K + \Delta + a_R v(P/C)$ Cost of city housing = $K + \Delta - \left(a_P v(1) - a_P v\left(1 - \frac{1-P}{C}\right)\right)$
Notation	P: total share of population that is poor C: homes in the central city K: construction cost of home in suburbs τ : transportation cost in city $\tau + \Delta$: transportation cost in suburbs p^i : share of population in location i that is poor $a_P v(P^i)$: neighborhood spillover for a poor resident of location i $a_R v(P^i)$: neighborhood spillover for a rich resident of location i D: premium for city housing θ : adjustment for spillover effect of the poor in a suburb

the population to equal one. A share of the population, P, is in the poor group. We start off by assuming two locations, which might represent central cities and suburbs. There are C homes in the central city and this number is fixed.

Homes in the suburbs are built at a construction cost of K and there is free entry in this construction. Equilibrium in the housing market then implies that the cost of a suburban home will equal K and the number of suburban homes will equal $1 - C$. This set up is meant to capture some of the realities of the US post-war housing market which had abundant new construction in the outlying areas of its metropolitan regions.

We assume that utility is "Cash – Housing Costs – Transportation Costs + Neighborhood Spillovers." Housing costs will be determined endogenously, and at first we will assume that transportation costs are τ in the city and $\tau + \Delta$ in the suburbs. If the share of the poor in community i is P^i , then the contribution of neighborhood spillovers to utility is $a_P v(P^i)$ for the poor and $a_R v(P^i)$ for the rich. We will assume that $v(P^i)$ is positive and increasing, and $v(0) = 0$.

The $a_P v(P^i)$ and $a_R v(P^i)$ functions can capture a wide number of reasons why people's utilities might depend on their neighborhoods. One possible scenario is that the rich receive negative utility from being around the poor and the poor don't care about the identity of their neighbors. The rich might be uncomfortable with the real correlates of poorer neighbors (like crime), they might just want to impress people by living in a rich neighborhood or they might just dislike the poor. This setting would be the class-based equivalent of many standard views of racial discrimination. In this scenario, $a_R = -1$ and $a_P = 0$.

Alternatively, both rich and poor might dislike the consequences of poverty equally, which would mean that $a_R = a_P = -1$. Perhaps the poor actually like living around other poor people, while the rich like being around other rich people. In this case, we would have that $a_R = -1$ and $a_P = 1$. In all these different scenarios we can make the simplifying assumption that $v(P^i) = vP^i$, where v is a constant.

Let us further assume that all poor people and all rich people are identical so that there are just two types of people. Furthermore, I assume that $C > P$ and $C > 1 - P$, so that the poor people cannot fill up either the central city or the suburbs. There are now three potential equilibria. In one equilibrium, the rich and poor are equally split between the two areas, so that the proportion of poor people in both areas is P. In this case, the cost of housing in the central city is $K + \Delta$. Just as in the monocentric model, higher housing prices are needed to offset the lower costs of commuting. This is obviously an equilibrium since neighborhood spillovers for both groups are identical in both areas (although not identical for both groups), and since housing prices have been chosen to keep housing plus transport costs the same between the two areas, no one has an incentive to move.

In a second potential equilibrium, all of the poor people live in the central city and the rich are split between the central city and the suburb. In this case, the price of housing in the central city is $K + \Delta + a_R v(P/C)$. This price is set so that it compensates the rich city resident who is on the margin of living in the suburbs for the lower commuting costs and to avoid proximity to the poor. In principle, when $a_R < 0$ city prices can either be higher or lower than suburban prices, depending on whether commuting advantages are more or less important than the disadvantages associated with living near the poor.

For this to be an equilibrium, it must be that poor people do not want to leave the city at the prevailing prices; for this to be the case it must be that $a_P > a_R$, which means that poor people must enjoy the company of other poor people more than rich people do. Notice that this segregated equilibrium can exist when both rich and poor like the poor or both rich and poor dislike the poor. The only critical ingredient is that the rich like being around the poor less than the poor like the being around the poor. I have assumed a linear utility function, but if the utility from cash net housing and transport costs was concave, then the condition $a_P > a_R$ could come from diminishing marginal returns to cash if being around poor people was generally unattractive.

A third equilibrium has all of the rich people in the central city and some poor people in the suburbs. In this case, the housing price in the central city is

$$K + \Delta - \left(a_P v(1) - a_P v \left(1 - \frac{1-P}{C} \right) \right).$$

If $v(P^i) = vP^i$ then this price equals

$$K + \Delta - a_P v \left(\frac{1-P}{C} \right) \quad \text{if} \quad v(P^i) = vP^i.$$

If $0 > a_P$, then city properties would go for a premium both because of fast commute times and because city dwellers don't have poor neighbors. For this to be an equilibrium, it must be that $a_P > a_R$, so that the rich are willing to pay more than the poor to escape poorer neighbors.

So far, we have identified three equilibria: two that hold when $a_P > a_R$ and a single symmetric one that holds generally. When $a_R > a_P$, the model gives a clear prediction that we should expect to see mixing. Is there any way to use this model to give us a sense of which of these three equilibria are more likely when $a_P > a_R$?

One trick is to assume that we are considering a single period of an infinite horizon dynamic game where people rent housing and adjust their neighborhood choice in every period. We then assume that people's utility is based on the share of the neighborhood that was poor in the last period, P^i_{t-1}, and ask which equilibria are stable. In which equilibria will a small deviation in one period cause a larger deviation in the next period and thus be unstable? Moreover, in which equilibria will a small deviation correct itself over time? I will assume that the sizes of the city and suburbs are fixed. Since construction costs no longer pin down the price of suburban housing, I lose the ability to talk about price levels. The model will, however, still deliver the price difference for housing in the suburbs and the central city, letting D denote the premium for city housing.

If both groups are going to live in both locations at time t then the equilibrium condition must be

$$\alpha_R\left(v\left(P^{\text{City}}_{t-1}\right) - v\left(P^{\text{Suburb}}_{t-1}\right)\right) = D - \Delta = \alpha_P\left(v\left(P^{\text{City}}_{t-1}\right) - v\left(P^{\text{Suburb}}_{t-1}\right)\right), \quad (5.1)$$

which, if $\alpha_R \neq \alpha_P$, can be true if and only if $P^{\text{City}}_{t-1} = P^{\text{Suburb}}_{t-1} = P$. For any other allocation at time $t-1$, all the poor people will inhabit a single location at time t and so segregation will occur. If $P^{\text{City}}_{t-1} > P^{\text{Suburb}}_{t-1}$ and $\alpha_P > \alpha_R$, then the poor will be willing to pay more to live in the city and $P^{\text{City}}_t = P/C = P^{\text{City}}_{t+j}$ for all positive j.

If $P^{\text{City}}_{t-1} < P^{\text{Suburb}}_{t-1}$ then $P^{\text{Suburb}}_t = P/(1-C) = P^{\text{Suburb}}_{t+j}$ for all positive j. An initial tendency of the poor to cluster either in the city or suburb will cause complete segregation of rich and poor in either place when $\alpha_P > \alpha_R$. The model therefore really suggests that except for the knife edge of starting at the point where $P^{\text{City}}_{t-1} = P^{\text{Suburb}}_{t-1} = P$, we should expect complete segregation.

When people try to explain why poor people live in cities or, equivalently, why the middle classes suburbanize, they often turn to forces that we would capture with the functions $\alpha_P v(P^i)$ and $\alpha_R v(P^i)$. Urban crime, bad urban schools, and racial discrimination may all be forces that drive middle class suburbanization (Miezkowski and Mills, 1993), but they do not actually *explain* suburbanization because these things are themselves a function of the distribution of rich and poor over space.

I would capture these arguments by assuming that crime or poor school quality are a function of the amount of poverty in the area and then assume that the rich care more about crime or schools, but this would just be the model that I have sketched. That model can certainly deliver segregation of rich and poor, but it does nothing to explain why the poor are so much more likely to be urbanized. If you thought that the initial distribution of poverty was completely random (in the sense that

$P_{t-1}^{\text{City}} > P_{t-1}^{\text{Suburb}}$ was as likely as the reverse), then the expected proportion of cities that are poor would be fifty percent.

One easy way to tweak the model would be to assume that the impact of the poor is worse in urban areas, so that the spillover functions $a_P v(P^i)$ and $a_R v(P^i)$ become $\theta a_P v(P^{\text{Suburb}})$ and $\theta a_R v(P^{\text{Suburb}})$ where $\theta < 1$. In this case, there still exists a mixing equilibrium which satisfies $v\left(P_{t-1}^{\text{City}}\right) = \theta v\left(P_{t-1}^{\text{Suburb}}\right)$ when $a_P \neq a_R$. In this case, urban poverty must be lower than suburban poverty for the symmetric equilibrium to last, which seems to suggest that this adjustment does little to help us understand why the poor live in cities.

However, this equilibrium condition would also determine the initial conditions under which the city or the suburbs attract the poor. In this case, the rich will be the group that suburbanize as long as $v\left(P_{t-1}^{\text{City}}\right) > \theta v\left(P_{t-1}^{\text{Suburb}}\right)$ and $a_P > a_R$. This condition becomes more and more likely as θ falls, which can be interpreted as meaning that the poverty of cities becomes more likely if urban density increases the costs of living around poor people relative to the suburbs.

In words, this alteration of the model tells us that if (1) rich people dislike poor neighbors more than poor people do (which is the necessary ingredient for segregation), and if (2) suburbs mitigate the consequences of living around the poor (for rich and poor alike), then we should expect to see poverty disproportionately in central cities. There is surely some truth to this view; lower densities should reduce the impact of one's neighbors. In the final section of this chapter, I will discuss the evidence suggesting that there is a connection between cities and crime that goes beyond the fact that cities attract the poor. However, this version of the model still suggests that there should be some metropolitan areas where poor people live disproportionately in the suburbs—something that is not true for any one of America's metropolitan areas.

A second reason to be skeptical about this explanation of urban poverty is that it seems to imply a coordination failure, at least if $0 > a_P > a_R$ so that the poor do inflict social costs on all their neighbors and $v(P^i) = vP^i$ so that the effects are linear. In this case, the total social loss (combining additively across all people) from living around the poor equals $-v\left(a_R P + (a_P - a_R)\, P^2/C\right)$ if the poor live in the city and $-\theta v\left(a_R P + (a_P - a_R) P^2/(1 - C)\right)$ if the poor live in a suburb. As long as C is not too much greater than one-half, the social losses will always be lower if the poor are suburbanized, where they impose less damage. Since there are less social gains from the suburbanization of the poor, we might expect a market economy or developers (as in Henderson, 1985) to manage the achievement of this outcome. For these reasons, I now turn to alternative explanations of the concentration of poverty in urban centers, and assume hereafter that $\theta = 1$.

Table 5.2. Model for the segregation of the rich and the poor modified with transportation costs

Actors	Rich people, poor people
They maximize	Utility = −Transportation Costs
They choose	Location: city vs. suburb; mode of Transportation: public vs. car. People must trade off between the monetary cost and the time cost of transportation modes, as well as of location.
Key conditions	For moving to the suburbs to impact the commuting costs of the rich less than those of the poor: $(1-\lambda\gamma)\Delta > \max(S, 0)$
Notation	λ: cost of a unit of time to the rich τ: time cost of public transit in city $\tau+\Delta$: time cost of public transit in suburb P_{Car}: fixed cost of a car $\gamma\tau$: time cost of a car in city $\gamma\tau+\gamma\Delta$: time cost of a car in suburb S: consumer surplus to the poor of buying a car in the suburbs

One alternative hypothesis is that the rich are better able than the poor to pay the costs of commuting in from the suburbs, as discussed in Chapter 2. Central cities have public transportation; suburbs require cars. If the rich find it much easier to afford the one car per adult lifestyle of suburbia, then we shouldn't be surprised to see the rich living disproportionately away from central cities.

While I have already shown how this mechanism works in the monocentric model, for completeness, I will also show how it works in this simpler setting. The core equations of this model and the notation are given in Table 5.2. I just assume now that the commuting costs differ between rich and poor. A unit of time has cost 1 for the poor and $\lambda > 1$ for the rich. There are two forms of transportation: public and private. Public transport uses τ units of time in the city and $\tau + \Delta$ units of time in the suburbs. A car requires a fixed cost of P_{Car} but requires $\gamma\tau$ units of time in the city and $\gamma\tau + \gamma\Delta$ units of time in the suburbs. I want to focus on the particular set of parameter values where $(1-\gamma)\lambda\tau > P_{\text{Car}} > (1-\gamma)\tau$, which I believe roughly characterize the US. If those parameters hold, then the rich buy cars no matter where they live, but the poor don't buy cars if they live in the central city.

If $P_{\text{Car}} > (1-\gamma)(\tau+\Delta)$ then the poor never buy cars. In that case, the increase in transport costs for the rich if they suburbanize is $\gamma\lambda\Delta$ while the increase in transport costs for the poor if they suburbanize is Δ. In this case, if $1 > \lambda\gamma$ it will be cheaper for the rich to commute than for the poor to commute. Even though the rich have a higher cost of time, cars move sufficiently fast that the rich don't mind the suburban commute as much. If $P_{\text{Car}} < (1-\gamma)(\tau+\Delta)$, then the poor will not own cars in the city but they will in the suburbs. If they suburbanize, the increase in transport costs to the poor is $\gamma\Delta + P_{Car} - (1-\gamma)\tau$. If $P_{Car} > (1-\gamma)\tau + (\lambda - 1)\gamma\Delta$, then the increase in commuting costs for the poor is higher than the increase in commuting costs for the rich.

For transportation costs to explain the suburbanization of the rich, it must be that their commuting costs are lower. This requires either that $P_{Car} > (1-\gamma)(\tau + \Delta)$ and $1 > \lambda\gamma$ or $P_{Car} < (1-\gamma)(\tau + \Delta)$ and $P_{Car} > (1-\gamma)\tau + (\lambda - 1)\gamma\Delta$. To combine these two conditions, let $P_{Car} = (1-\gamma)(\tau + \Delta) - S$, where S is the consumer surplus for the poor from buying a car in the suburb. Then the condition for the suburbs to have a lower impact on the commuting costs of the rich is $(1 - \lambda\gamma)\Delta > \max(S, 0)$, which is more likely to hold when $\lambda\gamma$ is low.

If $a_P = a_R$ then this condition is enough to ensure that the rich will suburbanize. Glaeser, Kahn and Rappaport's (2007) empirical work essentially assumes away such social spillovers and looks at whether differential transport costs can on their own explain the puzzle of urban poverty. If $a_P > a_R$, then it remains possible for there to be equilibria where the poor completely suburbanize even if their commuting costs are higher. A completely decentralized outcome might then have the rich remain in the city even though they have lower commuting costs. In this case, however, the ability to coordinate would enable people to avoid this less than optimal outcome.

A third explanation is that suburban housing is better suited to the needs of the rich. One variant of this hypothesis is that urban housing is older and of lower quality, and that the rich are willing to pay more to avoid lower quality housing. This hypothesis is connected to "filtering:" the idea that housing is built for the rich but then dilapidates and is later used by the poor (Muth, 1969). Bond and Coulson (1989) is a particularly important and well-crafted paper in the filtering literature.

A second variant is that land is particularly abundant in the suburbs and that the rich want to consume more land. Multi-family units are, for example, much more common in urban areas, and rich people may not like living in apartments. One simple way of capturing this is to assume that the rich suffer a dollar-denominated utility loss of δ_R from living in urban housing, while the poor suffer a dollar-denominated utility loss of δ_P from living in urban housing. In this case, as long as $\delta_R > \delta_P$, we should see the poor benefitting from living in urban areas, which could also explain their urbanization.

To get to a more standard condition on the housing explanation for the urban centralization of the poor, I will modify the model. The core equations of this model and the notation are given in Table 5.3. First, I will drop all of the social spillovers. Next I will assume there is a total amount of land of L_{City} in the central city and that there is a total

Table 5.3. Model for the segregation of the rich and the poor modified with housing costs

Actors	Rich people, poor people
They maximize	Utility = Cash − Transportation Costs − Housing costs
They choose	Location: city vs. suburb. People must trade off the availability of land in the suburb with the commuting advantages of the city.
Key conditions	The poor will urbanize only if $\lambda_{Land} > \lambda$
Notation	P: proportion of population that is poor L_{City}: total land available in city L_{Suburb}: total land available in suburb λ_{Land}: land consumption of a rich person Δ: extra cost of commuting from suburb for the poor $\lambda\Delta$: extra cost of commuting from suburb for the rich

quantity of land L_{Suburb} in the suburbs. Poor people always consume one unit of land, while rich people consume λ_{Land} units of land. I continue assuming that L_{City} and L_{Suburb} are greater than P, so that even if all poor people live in either area there can still be some rich people in both areas. I return to the assumption of different commute times, and now assume that extra costs of commuting from the suburbs remains Δ for the poor and $\lambda\Delta$ for the rich.

If poor people all live in the city or the suburb, the rich will still be the marginal suburbanites. The premium paid per unit of urban land that offsets the extra commuting costs for the rich will thus equal $\lambda\Delta/\lambda_{Land}$. Given this price premium, the poor will choose to urbanize if and only if $\Delta > \lambda\Delta/\lambda_{Land}$ or $\lambda_{Land} > \lambda$. The key is that the increase in the land demand for the rich must more than offset the increase in the time cost of commuting for the rich. This is the analogous condition to those shown in Chapter 2 for the monocentric model. These changes are often applied to the data as elasticities, so this condition is interpreted as meaning that the elasticity of demand for land with respect to income must be higher than the elasticity of travel costs with respect to income (Becker, 1965).

If time were the only component to travel costs, then we might think that travel costs rise proportionately with the opportunity cost of time, or the wage. That would remain the right elasticity if people treated the cost of time spent commuting as a fixed multiple of the cost of time spent working. Alternatively, if people were able to use different technologies that involved fixed costs, then this would cause the elasticity of the cost of time spent commuting with respect to income to fall and possibly even reverse, as in the multiple mode example discussed above.

There is often confusion over whether the correct income elasticity for housing concerns land area or total housing spending. There are some models where the income elasticity of spending on housing and spending on land area are identical; those models obviously predict that one could use either elasticity. Empirically, however, the two elasticities are quite different. In models where the rich buy land and fancy buildings, and where the price of supplying the structure is unrelated to the price of the land, there is no sense in which the income demand for structure should have any impact whatsoever on the suburbanization of the rich. In this case, the rich will buy nicer buildings in all areas but this creates no added incentives for them to suburbanize, assuming that the supply condition holds. Rich people buy fancy appliances that are included in measured housing consumption. If those appliances cost the same in the city and suburbs, then they create no incentive to move away from the center. The desire to buy more land, not to buy fancy appliances, drives the rich to move to the outskirts of town where land is cheaper.

Evidence on poverty and centralization across cities

Glaeser, Kahn and Rappaport (2007) investigate the potential reasons for the centralization of poverty. The paper examines both housing and transportation reasons that the poor are disproportionately centralized. We first estimate the elasticity of housing consumption, measured in units of land, with respect to income. Traditional analyses of this elasticity have focused on the relationship between total spending on housing and income and found high elasticities. As discussed earlier, I think that this is a mistake, because it is demand for land, not for appliances, that pushes people to move to where land is cheap.

Our estimates of the elasticity of land demand with respect to income range from .1 to .4. If we consider only people who live in single-family detached houses, the estimated elasticities are low, generally below .2. When we include those who live in multi-family dwellings, the elasticities rise because poor people live disproportionately in high-rise dwellings that use much less land. As such, there is a significant relationship between land use and income, but this comes primarily from the tendency of rich people to live in single-family detached dwellings.

In the working paper version of the paper, we estimate how much the average housing bundle of the rich and of the poor changes between central cities and suburbs. If housing costs were driving the rich to suburbanize, we should find their typical housing consumption gets cheaper, relative to the bundle of housing consumed by the poor, when they suburbanize. We do not find that to be the case.

We find more evidence supporting the role of public transportation in explaining the centralization of the poor. We find a strong link between access to public transportation and the location of the poor. We find that when subway stops open, neighboring census tracts often get poorer. We then calibrate a simple model and find that given travel times and income level, we should expect to see the rich buying cars and suburbanizing.

Racial segregation

The two-group model described above was used to describe the urbanization of rich and poor, but the basics of the model are closer to the literature on residential segregation and the implications of the model are quite similar. I will perturb that model slightly. The core equations of this model and the notation are given in Table 5.4. First, I assume that the two areas—previously city and suburb—are now two equally sized neighborhoods. I continue to use P as notation, but it now denotes the share of the population that is in the racial minority, which for the purpose of this model will be the share of the population that is black. I now assume that whites pay costs of $a_W P^i$ from living in a community with a proportion P^i of blacks. Blacks receive a benefit of $a_B P^i$ from living in a community with a proportion P^i of blacks. This is analogous to the previous model in which the rich and poor received spillovers of $a_R v(P^i)$

Table 5.4. Model for residential racial segregation

Actors	White people, Black people
They maximize	Utility = Cash − Spillovers + Community-specific preference
They choose	Location: city vs. suburb. People must trade off the social spillover, their taste for the specific communities, and the price premium associated with the communities.
Key conditions	Price premium conditions: $Q + a_W P^1 - a_W^* = a_W P^2,\ Q + G - a_B P^1 - a_B^* = -a_B P^2$ Equilibrium condition: $Q = 2a_W(P - P^1) + F^{-1}\left(\frac{1 - 2P + P^1}{2(1 - P)}\right)$ $= 2a_B(P^1 - P) + F^{-1}\left(\frac{2P - P^1}{2P}\right) - G$
Notation	P: proportion of total population that is Black P^i: share of population in location i that is Black $a_W P^i$: spillover cost to White people from living in community i $a_B P^i$: spillover benefit to Black people from living in community i a: individual taste for community one, distributed symmetrically about zero with cdf $F(a)$ G: tax imposed on Blacks in community 1 Q: price premium for community 1

and $\alpha_P v(P^i)$ from living in a neighborhood where proportion P^i of the population belong to the poor group. However, here α_W, α_B are assumed positive.

My final perturbation from the previous model is to allow there to be heterogeneity in preferences for the two communities. I assume that both whites and blacks have an individual specific taste for community one, denoted a, that is distributed symmetrically around zero with a distribution $F(a)$ for both ethnic groups. Since everything is symmetric up to this point, I will always assume the first community has a (weak) majority of whites. I further assume that a tax of G is imposed on blacks who want to move into the first community. This tax is meant to include the wide range of barriers that whites put up to stop blacks from coming into their communities, including restrictive covenants and targeted anti-black violence.

There is again a potential for multiple equilibria in this model. If Q denotes the price premium associated with the first neighborhood, then Q must always satisfy $Q + \alpha_W P^1 - a^*_W = \alpha_W P^2$ because there will always be white people who are living in both communities. The term a^*_W captures the preference of the marginal white resident for the first neighborhood; everyone who likes that neighborhood more than the marginal resident will live in neighborhood one while everyone who likes that neighborhood less than the marginal resident will live in neighborhood two. If there are also blacks who live in both neighborhoods, then there is a parallel condition $Q + G - \alpha_B P^1 - a^*_B = -\alpha_B P^2$ that makes the black marginal resident indifferent between the two locales.

If $G = 0$, then there continues to exist a symmetric equilibrium where the proportion that is black is the same in both areas, and where housing prices are the same in both areas. In a non-symmetric equilibrium where only whites live in both areas, $P^1 = 0$ and $P^2 = 2P$. This also implies that the marginal white resident will have a value of a^*_W that solves $\frac{1}{2} = (1 - F(a^*_W))(1 - P)$ or

$$a^*_W = F^{-1}\left(\frac{1-2P}{2(1-P)}\right).$$

This then implies that

$$Q = 2\alpha_W P + F^{-1}\left(\frac{1-2P}{2(1-P)}\right),$$

which combines the price that the whites are willing to pay to avoid blacks and the fact that the marginal resident of the first neighborhood has a slight preference for living in the second neighborhood.

For this to be an equilibrium, it must be that

$$2(\alpha_W + \alpha_B)P + F^{-1}\left(\frac{1-2P}{2(1-P)}\right) + G > a_{\max},$$

where $a_{\max}$ is the highest value of a, so that none of the blacks in the second neighborhood want to live in the first neighborhood. If $a_{\max}$ is finite, then high enough values of G will ensure that this condition holds. Alternatively, if the distribution of a is unbounded then this condition will never hold and there will always be some blacks in both communities. In this case, there will not be perfect segregation: blacks and whites will live in both communities. The adding up of constraints give us that

$$P^2 = 2P - P^1 \quad \text{and that} \quad \frac{1-P^1}{2} = (1 - F(a_W^*))(1-P)$$

or

$$a_W^* = F^{-1}\left(\frac{1-2P+P^1}{2(1-P)}\right) \quad \text{and} \quad \frac{P^1}{2} = (1 - F(a_B^*))P$$

or

$$a_B^* = F^{-1}\left(\frac{2P-P^1}{2P}\right).$$

The equilibrium conditions are

$$\begin{aligned} Q &= 2\alpha_W(P - P^1) + F^{-1}\left(\frac{1-2P+P^1}{2(1-P)}\right) \\ &= 2\alpha_B(P^1 - P) + F^{-1}\left(\frac{2P-P^1}{2P}\right) - G. \end{aligned} \tag{5.2}$$

This can be rewritten as $2(\alpha_W + \alpha_B)(P - P^1) + G = H(P^1)$ where

$$H(P^1) = F^{-1}\left(\frac{2P-P^1}{2P}\right) - F^{-1}\left(\frac{1-2P+P^1}{2(1-P)}\right)$$

Therefore we also get that

$$H'(P^1) = \frac{-1}{2Pf\left(\frac{2P-P^1}{2P}\right)} - \frac{1}{2(1-P)f\left(\frac{1-2P+P^1}{2(1-P)}\right)} < 0.$$

Using the same, somewhat casual ideas about stability discussed above, an equilibrium can be thought of as stable if an initial perturbation in the share of blacks in the first neighborhood leads to a smaller perturbation the period after that. This requires that

$$\frac{\partial P_t^1}{\partial P_{t-1}^1} = \frac{-2(a_W + a_B)}{H'(P_t^1)} < 1$$

which requires the densities of tastes to be sufficiently low. Essentially, this stability condition is satisfied whenever demand curves for the two neighborhoods are downward sloping. We will go further and assume that in the stable equilibrium this condition holds for all t, i.e. that

$$\frac{-2(a_W + a_B)}{H'(P^1)} < 1.$$

If this condition holds, we can also sign the following comparative statics:

$$\frac{\partial P^1}{\partial a_W} = \frac{\partial P^1}{\partial a_B} < 0 \quad \text{and} \quad \frac{\partial P^1}{\partial G} < 0.$$

These unsurprising comparative statics tell us that the number of blacks in the primarily white neighborhood will decline as the whites' dislike of blacks increases, or as the black preference for blacks increases, or as the tax imposed on blacks moving into the white neighborhood increases.

These three comparative statics give us the core three theories that lie behind regulation: (1) white decentralized racism; (2) white centralized racism; and (3) black decentralized clannishness. The first theory suggests that whites are more likely to live with other whites because of a_W—the white preference for their own race. This term can be called racism, but it might refer to any reason why whites prefer people of their own skin color, including shared types of consumption or social habits, and does not mean to imply race-based tastes. This theory is particularly associated with Schelling (1971). The second theory emphasizes the ability of whites to make it difficult for blacks to enter into their neighborhoods. This hypothesis is particularly associated with Kain (1968) and Kain and Quigley (1972). The third theory emphasizes the preferences of blacks themselves, who might, like immigrants historically, have good reasons for preferring the company of people like themselves.

While the mere existence of segregation gives us no ability to distinguish between the three theories, the price differential between the two neighborhoods does help us distinguish between white decentralized racism and the other two hypotheses. If we assume that

$$\frac{1}{2(1-P)f\left(\dfrac{1-2P+P^1}{2(1-P)}\right)} > 2a_W,$$

so that the white demand curve for the first neighborhood slopes downward, then this is enough to ensure that $\partial Q/\partial a_B < 0$ and $\partial Q/\partial G < 0$. If we assume that

$$\frac{1}{2Pf\left(\frac{2P-P^1}{2P}\right)} > 2\alpha_B,$$

so that the black demand curve for the first neighborhood slopes downward, then this gives us that $\partial Q/\partial \alpha_W > 0$. Together these conditions imply that when segregation is caused by black preferences or centralized racism, we should expect to see a premium for living in a black neighborhood. When segregation is caused by white preferences, we should expect to see a premium for living in a white neighborhood.

These price implications are a natural continuation of the logic of Becker (1957). Unconstrained cost minimization leads to lower costs. When segregation is caused by an external constraint on black choices, the centralized racism tax, then we should expect to see blacks pay more. When segregation is caused by an internal constraint on black choices, black preferences, then we should also expect to see blacks pay more. When segregation is caused by an internal constraint on white choice, or white decentralized racism, then we should expect to see whites pay more.

Social scientists have struggled with the measurement of segregation for more than 50 years. Two of the most common measures are the dissimilarity index and the isolation index. The dissimilarity index is

$$\begin{aligned}\text{Dissimilarity} &= \frac{1}{2}\sum\nolimits_{\text{Areas}}\left|\frac{\text{Black}_{\text{Area}}}{\text{Black}_{\text{Total}}} - \frac{\text{Non-Black}_{\text{Area}}}{\text{Non-Black}_{\text{Total}}}\right| \\ &= \frac{1}{2(1-P)}\sum\nolimits_{\text{Areas}}\left|\frac{\text{Black}_{\text{Area}}}{\text{Black}_{\text{Total}}} - \frac{\text{Total}_{\text{Area}}}{\text{Total}_{\text{Total}}}\right|, \end{aligned} \tag{5.3}$$

where P remains the share of the overall population that is black. Verbally, this index can be described as the share of blacks (or non-blacks) that would need to move areas for the distribution of blacks to be constant over space. The index runs from zero to one, where zero suggests perfect integration and one implies complete segregation. Taeuber and Taeuber (1965) are particularly associated with the early use of this index.

The index has certain attractive features. If the number of blacks, or non-blacks, in the city increases and that increase acts to multiply the number of blacks (or non-blacks) in each area by the same constant, then the index does not change. If an area is split into two identical sub-components, then the index will also not change. Of course, if an area is split and the two sub-areas are not identical, then the index will rise. This means that dissimilarity will always (weakly) increase when it is measured using smaller geographic units. In practice the measure is often quite higher with smaller units. If segregation were measured at the person level the measure would be one, and if the city as a whole were the only geographic area then the measure would be zero.

In the two area model discussed above, the dissimilarity index equals $(P - P^1)/2P(1 - P)$ which runs from zero (in the case of perfect segregation) up to $1/2(1 - P)$, which can equal one only as P rises to one half (the measure needs to be recalculated if the blacks are in the majority). This emphasizes an added point about the dissimilarity index. If the minority is too small to fill up an entire neighborhood, then the index cannot equal one because even if the entire minority lived in one place, only a subset of the minority would have to move to achieve perfect integration.

The index can also be re-written:

$$\text{Dissimilarity} = \frac{1}{2(P - P^2)} \sum_{\text{Areas}} \frac{\text{Total}_{\text{Area}}}{\text{Total}_{\text{Total}}} \left| \frac{\text{Black}_{\text{Area}}}{\text{Total}_{\text{Area}}} - \frac{\text{Black}_{\text{Total}}}{\text{Total}_{\text{Total}}} \right|. \quad (5.4)$$

The most common alternative is the isolation index, measured as

$$\text{Isolation} = \sum_{\text{Areas}} \frac{\text{Black}_{\text{Area}}}{\text{Total}_{\text{Area}}} \times \frac{\text{Black}_{\text{Area}}}{\text{Black}_{\text{Total}}}. \quad (5.5)$$

This measure can be verbally interpreted as the percentage of blacks in the area where the average black lives. As it stands, the isolation index will increase as the share of minorities in the city increases. One natural normalization is to subtract the overall share of minorities in the community from the isolation index to form a modified isolation index, described as Isolation*. A little algebra shows the fundamental similarity between isolation and dissimilarity indices:

$$\begin{aligned}
\text{Isolation}^* &= \sum_{\text{Areas}} \left(\frac{\text{Black}_{\text{Area}}}{\text{Total}_{\text{Area}}} \times \frac{\text{Black}_{\text{Area}}}{\text{Black}_{\text{Total}}} \right) - \frac{\text{Black}_{\text{Total}}}{\text{Total}_{\text{Total}}} \\
&= \sum_{\text{Areas}} \left(\frac{\text{Black}_{\text{Area}}}{\text{Total}_{\text{Area}}} \times \frac{\text{Black}_{\text{Area}}}{\text{Black}_{\text{Total}}} \right) + \frac{\text{Black}_{\text{Total}}}{\text{Total}_{\text{Total}}} - 2\frac{\text{Black}_{\text{Total}}}{\text{Total}_{\text{Total}}} \\
&= \sum_{\text{Areas}} \left(\frac{\text{Black}_{\text{Area}}}{\text{Total}_{\text{Area}}} \times \frac{\text{Black}_{\text{Area}}}{\text{Black}_{\text{Total}}} \right) + \sum_{\text{Areas}} \text{Total}_{\text{Area}} \frac{\text{Black}_{\text{Total}}}{\text{Total}^2_{\text{Total}}} - 2\sum_{\text{Areas}} \frac{\text{Black}_{\text{Area}}}{\text{Total}_{\text{Total}}} \\
&= \frac{1}{\text{Black}_{\text{Total}}} \left(\begin{array}{l} \sum_{\text{Areas}} \text{Total}_{\text{Area}} \left(\frac{\text{Black}_{\text{Area}}}{\text{Total}_{\text{Area}}} \right)^2 + \sum_{\text{Areas}} \text{Total}_{\text{Area}} \left(\frac{\text{Black}_{\text{Total}}}{\text{Total}_{\text{Area}}} \right)^2 \\ -2\sum_{\text{Areas}} \text{Total}_{\text{Area}} \frac{\text{Black}_{\text{Area}}}{\text{Total}_{\text{Area}}} \times \frac{\text{Black}_{\text{Total}}}{\text{Total}_{\text{Total}}} \end{array} \right) \\
&= \frac{\text{Total}_{\text{Total}}}{\text{Black}_{\text{Total}}} \left(\begin{array}{l} \sum_{\text{Areas}} \frac{\text{Total}_{\text{Area}}}{\text{Total}_{\text{Total}}} \left(\frac{\text{Black}_{\text{Area}}}{\text{Total}_{\text{Area}}} \right)^2 + \sum_{\text{Areas}} \frac{\text{Total}_{\text{Area}}}{\text{Total}_{\text{Total}}} \left(\frac{\text{Black}_{\text{Total}}}{\text{Total}_{\text{Total}}} \right)^2 \\ -2\sum_{\text{Areas}} \frac{\text{Total}_{\text{Area}}}{\text{Total}_{\text{Total}}} \frac{\text{Black}_{\text{Total}}\text{Black}_{\text{Area}}}{\text{Total}_{\text{Total}}\text{Total}_{\text{Area}}} \end{array} \right) \\
&= \frac{1}{P} \sum_{\text{Areas}} \frac{\text{Total}_{\text{Area}}}{\text{Total}_{\text{Total}}} \left(\frac{\text{Black}_{\text{Area}}}{\text{Total}_{\text{Area}}} - \frac{\text{Black}_{\text{Total}}}{\text{Total}_{\text{Total}}} \right)^2. \quad (5.5')
\end{aligned}$$

Comparing the last line of (5.5′) with (5.4) shows that the dissimilarity index represents an absolute value measure of the share of blacks in an area and the average share of blacks in the community, weighted by the share of the population in each area, while the isolation index represents a Euclidean (ℓ^2) norm of the distance between those two measures. This delivers the intuition that Isolation weights extreme areas more than dissimilarity. An alternative way of writing the adjusted isolation index is

$$\text{Isolation}^* = P \sum\nolimits_{\text{Areas}} \frac{\text{Total}_{\text{Total}}}{\text{Total}_{\text{Area}}} \left(\frac{\text{Black}_{\text{Area}}}{\text{Black}_{\text{Total}}} - \frac{\text{Total}_{\text{Area}}}{\text{Total}_{\text{Total}}} \right)^2. \qquad (5.5'')$$

The dissimilarity index is an ℓ^1 norm of the distance between the share of blacks in an area and the share of non-blacks in an area. The isolation index is an ℓ^2 norm of the same distance.

There is essentially a deep mathematical relationship not just between the different measures of segregation, but also between these measures and the measures of industrial concentration and social interaction discussed earlier. When I discussed employment agglomeration in the previous chapter, I used the standard concentration index, which is

$$\sum\nolimits_{\text{Areas}} \left(\frac{\text{Employment}_{\text{Area}}}{\text{Employment}_{\text{Total}}} - \text{Weight}_{\text{Area}} \right)^2;$$

this is essentially identical to the ℓ^2 based isolation index when the weight in each area is the share of the total population in each area.

There were two adjustments to this raw measure discussed previously (both of which come from Ellison and Glaeser, 1997). This first is to adjust the measure by using the Herfindahl index of the industry, which corrects for the fact that industrial employment may be concentrated in a few large plants. The Herfindahl index for this group is $1/\text{Black}_{\text{Total}}$, which should be small enough that it will make little difference to the calculations. The second correction is to divide this measure by $1 - \sum_{\text{Areas}} \text{Weight}^2_{\text{Area}}$, which should be quite close to one given the large number of census groups or blocks used in calculating the usual dissimilarity or isolation index.

The isolation and dissimilarity indices do seem sensible, but they are not particularly grounded in any form of theory. As I have discussed previously, geographic concentration measures (of industry or race) can in principle be derived either from a model, as in Ellison and Glaeser (1997), or from axioms. In the modeling approach, the concentration index has an interpretation as a parameter of that model. In the axiomatic approach, the index is understood to satisfy certain desirable properties. Echnique and Fryer (2007) present an axiomatic approach to segregation that produces a spectral segregation index. Beyond their paper, little work has been done with this index to date, but it may in time come to supplant the previous indices. It has the enormous advantages of being grounded, although it suffers from being somewhat more complicated to explain.

Evidence on segregation

Most of the empirical literature on segregation falls into three distinct camps. One branch of the literature looks at the extent of segregation. While there were many city-level analyses of segregation that go back more than a century (most notably DuBois' *The Philadelphia Negro*), cross-city comparisons in segregation were generally a post-war phenomenon. Taueber and Taueber (1965) represents a particularly comprehensive and compelling look at segregation using the 1950 and 1960 censuses. They use block level data, which is somewhat finer than the more common tract level data. Their book contains a sensible discussion of different segregation measures, including others that I have not discussed, and a number of important facts about segregation.

The authors showed extremely high levels of segregation throughout the US, but they also documented interesting regional differences. For example, Northern ghettos are great expanses of single-race communities. Southern segregation is a much more patchwork affair, with blacks living in separate small areas that are not all that geographically distant from white areas. These two patterns also partially reflect the tendency of Northern blacks to work in large factories that were near large ghettos and the tendency of Southern blacks to work in domestic service, which created a need to be close to whites.

A large amount of research then followed the work of Taeuber and Taeuber (1965). Massey and Denton (1993) represents a particularly comprehensive overview documenting the extent of segregation in America. Farley and Frey (1994) provided an update of the segregation measures to the 1990 census. While these are both major contributions, in my view, these authors tended to understate the broad national changes in segregation that had occurred throughout the twentieth century.

Figure 5.1, which updates figure 1 from Cutler, Glaeser and Vigdor (1999), shows the pattern of segregation from 1890 to 2000. There are difficulties in creating such a long time series of segregation. Generally speaking, consistent tract-level data are not available prior to 1940, and political wards must be used. Since wards are larger geographic units than tracts, segregation levels are lower using ward-level data. The paper tries to correct for this problem using 1940 data, in which we have both ward- and tract-level segregation measures. Secondary issues concern changing

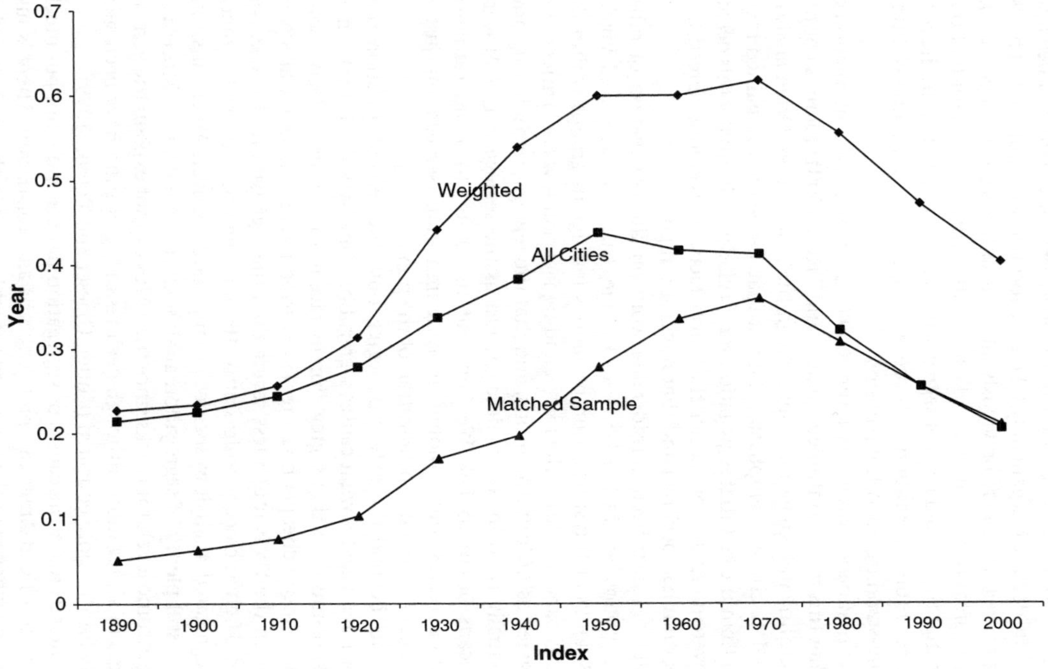

Figure 5.1. Index of dissimilarity from 1890–2000

metropolitan area boundaries and the changing sample of metropolitan areas.

The figure shows a broad pattern where segregation rose steadily from 1890 to 1950, stayed constant from 1950 to 1970 and then declined after 1970. The decline has generally taken the form of small numbers of blacks living in areas that were previously all white and has been steepest in the growing areas of the Sunbelt and the suburbs. One interpretation of that fact is that the desired level of segregation is lower today than in the past, so we see more integration in those areas that are newer and less driven by long-standing historical patterns.

After that paper was written, the 2000 Census offered a confirmation of whether this trend continued. Glaeser and Vigdor (2001) found a continuing decline in segregation, especially in the newer cities. Other analysts of the data chose to emphasize the fact that segregation remained high, rather than the fact that segregation was declining. Essentially this debate was over interpretation rather than over facts, as everyone agreed that segregation had declined and that it was still high.

There has also been considerable work on the segregation of other ethnic groups within the US. For example, Cutler, Glaeser and Vigdor (2008) looks at the segregation of various immigrant groups within the US. This paper confirms the long-standing fact that few ethnicities are as segregated as African-Americans, and that the segregation of immigrants has actually risen in recent decades, just as the segregation of African-Americans began to fall. We find that the desire to avoid car-based suburbs explains some amount of rising immigrant segregation, just as it explains the urban centralization of the poor.

Moving beyond the extent of segregation, the second question that people have asked is what causes segregation. One hypothesis that can be readily dismissed is that segregation by race in the US just reflects poorer people living in cheaper housing. The segregation of rich people and poor people in the US is much less severe than the segregation of blacks and whites. High socioeconomic status African-Americans are today much less segregated than low socioeconomic status African-Americans, but there is still plenty of segregation at all socioeconomic levels. Moreover, rising income levels for blacks since the 1970s cannot explain the general changes in segregation, although declines in segregation have been seen mostly for the more educated (Cutler, Glaeser and Vigdor, 1999).

The literature on the causes of segregation has generally not put much weight on African-American preferences as an explanation. There is just too much evidence in the statements of whites and in the track record of barriers to black mobility that points to the two other theories: centralized and decentralized white racism. None of this is meant to deny that many African-Americans have preferred the company of their own race, although even that fact surely owes something to costs imposed on them by the white community.

As suggested above, one way to test for the relative importance of centralized versus decentralized white racism is to look at housing prices. If barriers to mobility drive segregation, then prices should be higher in black neighborhoods. If the white preference for being around other whites is driving segregation, then living in white neighborhoods should come at a premium.

Kain and Quigley (1972) began the literature on tests of this kind. Using data from St. Louis, they found that African-Americans actually paid more for housing, quality adjusted, than whites. This evidence gave credence to the centralized racism view of segregation, but it has been challenged by a wide number of studies which have almost uniformly found that African-Americans were paying less for housing. The defense that John Kain gave against those studies was that they did not sufficiently control for the quality of housing.

While I find that defense not wholly convincing, I certainly do believe that there are often enormous unobserved quality differences between the housing occupied by whites and African-Americans that are impossible to fully control for. As such, Cutler, Glaeser and Vigdor (1999) took an alternative approach that looked not at the mean difference between black and white housing costs but rather the extent to which that difference increased or decreased with the level of segregation in the metropolitan area.

If segregation is driven by centralized racism, white housing should get less expensive relative to black housing in more segregated areas. If segregation is driven by decentralized racism, then white housing should get more expensive relative to black housing in more segregated areas. This procedure enables us to ignore any quality differences that are common throughout the US, but it will be problematic if the quality differences are correlated with the level of segregation.

In our work, we found that in 1940 blacks did indeed pay more for housing in more segregated cities. By 1970, this effect had essentially disappeared. By 1990, whites were paying more for housing in more segregated cities. This data suggests that segregation in 1940 primarily reflected barriers to black mobility, since African-Americans appear to be paying more for housing in more segregated cities. By 1990, segregation appears to primarily reflect the white taste for living with other whites, since whites pay more in more segregated areas. The results suggest that American cities followed a time path from centralized to decentralized racism.

While these results are more suggestive than definitive, they do match the institutional history of American segregation, where barriers to black mobility that were once ubiquitous became illegal. The declining numbers of purely lily-white census tracts and their replacement with slightly more segregated census tracts that include small numbers of generally more educated African-Americans are also compatible with the view that the barriers to black housing choices have declined.

A final literature on the causes of black segregation looks at the behavior of real estate agents who steer blacks to black neighborhoods. John Yinger is surely the dominant figure in this research area, and he has certainly documented a prevailing pattern where black buyers are targeted to black areas. It remains unclear whether this is actually an important driver of residential segregation or simply reflects a perfectly rational (and efficient) tendency of real estate agents to steer buyers to homes that are more likely to appeal to them.

While segregation is intrinsically interesting, it is far more interesting if it also impacts outcomes for African-Americans. Among economists, John Kain deserves credit as the one who brought the question of what segregation does to African-Americans into the mainstream. His 1968 paper on the spatial mismatch hypothesis argued that barriers to black mobility led to a spatial mismatch between where blacks lived and the location of jobs which hurt black wages and black employment. Over the past 40 years, the spatial mismatch hypothesis has received a great deal of attention.

My own view of this is that Kain (1968a,b) was right in emphasizing that segregation might impact black outcomes, but that his proposed mechanism is surely not the important channel. To begin with, at the time Kain was writing, blacks actually lived closer on average to jobs than whites did. However, Kain presciently pointed out that the suburbanization of employment would change that somewhat. Ellwood (1986) compares two black ghettos in Chicago, one of which was close to employment centers (the West Side) and one of which was not (the South Side). He finds no significant differences favoring the West Side. The literature has understandably moved to different explanations of why ghettos might matter, like neighborhood effects on the human capital of children, which I think are still within the spirit of the spatial mismatch hypothesis while not conforming to its exact letter. One interpretation of Kain's hypothesis is that he chose to emphasize such a tangible direct channel because more sociological explanations would have had no credibility in the restricted world of 1968 economists.

The empirical work on ghettos and neighborhood effects can be divided into two categories. First, there are papers that look at people who choose to live in different areas and compare the outcomes for these groups. Second, there are papers that use social experiments that actually have some form of exogenous variation where some relatively random group of the population is moved from one type of neighborhood to another. The first literature appears to find large neighborhood effects; the second literature finds effects that are much weaker.

Much of the discussion of social interactions belongs in the next section, so here I will restrict myself to the work specifically on segregation of African-Americans. These non-experimental papers compare African-Americans living in more segregated areas with African-Americans living in less segregated areas. These types of comparisons have been done both within and across cities.

The within-city literature begins with Kain (1968a,b), and has included a large number of papers looking at African-Americans living in more and less segregated neighborhoods within urban areas. The great problem with this work is that the centerpiece of urban economics is the assumption that people choose their locations. If African-Americans are living in both segregated and integrated neighborhoods, then they clearly had some choice about location. Their choices are unlikely to be random. Since African-Americans who are living in areas with more blacks are in general likely to be poorer, be less educated and perhaps have different tastes, there are many reasons to expect their outcomes to be different. In other words, outcomes may determine location choices, rather than the reverse. Moreover, the spatial equilibrium assumption requires us to think through why people would be moving to neighborhoods that do bad things to them. Its logic implies that if neighborhoods are doing something bad to their residents, then they must be getting something good back in return, like low housing costs.

The best papers in this literature focus on children, who presumably have little individual choice about their neighborhood (O'Regan and Quigley, 1998). The underlying model is presumably one in which parents trade the outcomes of their children against low prices and perhaps the comfort of being around friendlier neighbors. This literature generally finds worse outcomes for African-American children brought up in more segregated areas.

Cutler and Glaeser (1997) avoid within-city comparisons and instead look across metropolitan areas. Our approach is to look at whether the outcomes for young blacks become worse relative to young whites in more segregated metropolitan areas. There are two potential endogeneity issues to reckon with in this case. First, segregation may be higher in places where African-Americans do worse relative to whites. We try to solve that problem using the number of governments in the area and the Hoxby (2000) rivers instrument. Second, people sort across metropolitan areas, and less successful African-Americans may sort into more segregated metropolitan areas. We address this by looking at migration patterns.

We find that young African-Americans who grow up in more segregated metropolitan areas have much worse economic and academic outcomes than African-Americans who grow up in less segregated areas. This fact remains true when we control for the outcomes of whites in those metropolitan areas. African-Americans do worse in more segregated areas both in absolute terms and relative to the whites in those areas. The instrumental variables results are comfortingly close to the ordinary least squares results. Migration patterns seem to suggest that this is not the result of sorting across metropolitan areas. While no regressions of this form can ever be entirely convincing, it does still seem that African-American youths in more segregated areas have worse outcomes.

This non-experimental work contrasts strongly with the work of Katz, Kling, and Liebman (2001), who use the Moving to Opportunity (MTO) experiment. This experiment uses a Housing and Urban Development program that randomly allocated vouchers across recipients. Some of these vouchers required the recipients to move to low poverty neighborhoods. The families that received the vouchers and used them generally moved to better neighborhoods. The impact on the children was generally not huge and tended to be limited to girls (Katz, Kling and Liebman, 2007).

The MTO results certainly suggest that large scale social programs that resettle minorities may not be all that helpful. They also cast doubt on the previous results on segregation. It is still possible to defend the view that neighborhood effects are important, because the MTO experiment was limited in size and involved a particularly troubled subset of the population. Perhaps, the children moved by MTO had already been exposed to the worst effects of concentrated poverty. However, even people who believe in neighborhood effects, like myself, must also accept the fact that the MTO results have made us much more suspicious about the older cross-sectional findings on the effects of segregation.

Neighborhood effects, social interactions, crime and riots

In this section, I turn to the theory that underlies the neighborhood effects discussed earlier. These effects usually reflect a belief in some form of externality where the behavior of one person impacts the behavior of his neighbor. Generally speaking, we are interested in cases where there are positive complementarities, so that if a first person undertakes an action, his neighbor becomes more likely to also undertake that action. These theories are attractive because they offer the promise of explaining why some central cities have become centers of crime and social distress.

They are also a natural counterpart to the theories discussed in Chapter 4, where good ideas spread more easily in cities.

I will begin by discussing basic models of social interactions, and then I will turn to the empirical evidence on those social interactions. After that, I will specifically turn to crime and riots in urban areas.

All social interaction models share the common feature that each person's action is influenced by his or her neighbors. The influence might come from learning how to do something well or learning that it is socially acceptable to do something. The interaction might come from a real externality. In the section on riots that follows, the social interactions come from the fact that if the police are busy arresting one person, they can't as easily arrest someone else.

Glaeser, Sacerdote and Scheinkman (1996) presents a simple social interaction model that borrows from the so-called voter models of the physical sciences. In these models, people are organized along a line or a graph, and their probability of choosing a discrete outcome increases with the share of their neighbors that are also choosing that discrete outcome. In the simplest version of this model, people are organized along a line and social influence runs in only one direction, so that people only care about the person in front of them. The core equations of this model and the notation are given in Table 5.5.

We assume that people are split so that if there was no social influence, a proportion p of the population would want to undertake the action. We also assume that the population is split so that a proportion π of the population has weak social preferences and follows their natural impulses. The remainder of the population has stronger social preferences and chooses the action of their predecessor, no matter what its own innate preferences might have been. The parameter π captures the power of social interactions in this population. Essentially, social interactions turn a line that would have consisted of people randomly choosing their actions into a string of sequences. In each sequence, everyone follows the person with relatively independent preferences who came first in their sequence.

Table 5.5. Model for simple local social interactions

Actors	Individuals
They maximize	Utility
They choose	Whether or not to perform an action (discrete choice)
Notation	p: proportion of total population that wants to perform the action, independent of social interactions π: proportion of total population with choice unaffected by social interactions

This model predicts a much higher variance in outcomes across aggregates than a model with independent choices. If there were no social interactions, then the variance of an average of size N equals the variance of the individual actions (which would be $p(1-p)$ in this case) divided by N. However, in this model the variance gets multiplied by $(2-\pi)/\pi$ as N gets large. The term $(2-\pi)/\pi$ falls to one when the entire population makes its decisions independently and rises to infinity when everyone's choice depends on his or her neighbors. When there is a more complicated spatial structure, the variance scales up by a more complicated formula, but the basic result remains. Social interactions cause the variance of group level averages to rise.

Glaeser, Sacerdote and Scheinkman (1996) presents a local interactions model where individual choices depend on one's nearest neighbors. Global interactions models are at least as common. In local models, individuals are separated into distinct groups that might be a neighborhood or a class. In global models, everyone is equally influenced by everyone else in their group and not influenced at all by anyone outside of their group.

I will write down a benchmark global interactions model assuming that the outcome variable is continuous rather than discrete. The core equations of this model and the notation are given in Table 5.6. To follow standard practices, I start with an individual optimization problem where individual i receives private benefits from an activity, X_i, of $A_i X_i$ where A_i differs across individuals. We may think of A_i as equaling $\gamma Z_i + \varepsilon_i$, where Z_i is an individual specific parameter, γ is a parameter and ε_i is an individual-specific error term.

To capture the social interactions, we assume that benefits increase by β times the average choice of X in the individual's group, which is denoted $\hat{X}$. We also assume that individuals pay costs of $.5X^2$. Individuals then choose X to maximize $(A_i + \beta\hat{X})X_i - .5X_i^2$, which implies that $X_i = A_i + \beta\hat{X} = \gamma Z_i + \beta\hat{X} + \varepsilon_i$. This equation with no further modification provides the basis for the most common empirical approach to social interactions: regressing an individual outcome on a group average outcome. As I will discuss later, such regressions are fraught with peril, but so are all approaches to measuring social interactions.

It is worth noting that I am assuming a Nash equilibrium here where everyone is choosing X simultaneously and knowing what everyone else's choice of X is going to be. It is also worth noting that the individual maximization component of this model has been rigged to generate a simple linear function and that many models of this type just start with that linear function. My own preference is always to start with some sort of maximization, even if it is perfunctory as in this case.

Table 5.6. Model for global social interactions

Actors	Individuals
They maximize	$(A_i + \beta\hat{X})X_i - .5X_i^2$
They choose	X_i
Key equations	From the individual maximization: $$X_i = A_i + \beta\hat{X} = \gamma Z_i + \beta\hat{X} + \varepsilon_i$$ Aggregating this: $X_i = A_i + \beta\hat{A}/(1-\beta)$ Under the alternative specification: $$X_i = \frac{\alpha + (N-(N-1)\beta)\mu_i/N + \beta(\hat{\mu} - \mu_i/N)}{1-\beta}$$ For determining the regression coefficient: $$X_i = \gamma Z_i + \frac{\beta(\gamma\hat{Z} + \hat{\varepsilon})}{1-\beta} + \varepsilon_i$$
Notation	X_i: how much of the action X individual i chooses to perform A_i: coefficient on benefits from X, differs across individuals $\gamma Z_i + \varepsilon_i$: equals A_i γ : parameter Z_i : individual-specific parameter ε_i : individual-specific error term β : parameter $\hat{X}$: average choice of X in the community $\hat{A}$: average value of A in the community σ_A^2 : variance of A across people α : community-level variable μ_i : individual-specific variable, independent of α $\lambda\sigma_A^2$: variance of α $(1-\lambda)\sigma_A^2$: variance of μ_i $\hat{\mu}$: average value of μ_i in the community $\hat{\varepsilon}$: average value of ε_i in the community $\hat{Z}$: average value of Z in the community

To solve the model, we need to aggregate the equation $X_i = A_i + \beta\hat{X}$, which implies that $\hat{X} = \hat{A}/(1-\beta)$, where $\hat{A}$ is the average value of A in the community. This also then implies that $X_i = A_i + \beta\hat{A}/(1-\beta)$. This model predicts the same connection between social interactions and group level variances that we saw in the local interactions model. If the variance of A across people is σ_A^2 and those people are randomly sorted across groups, then the variance of $\hat{A}$ is σ_A^2/N. The individual level variance (i.e. the variance of X_i) is

$$\sigma_A^2\left(1 + \frac{\beta(2-\beta)}{N(1-\beta)^2}\right),$$

which will be close to σ_A^2 when N is large. The group level variance (i.e. the variance of $\hat{X}$) is $\sigma_A^2/N(1-\beta)^2$. The ratio of group level variance to individual level variance therefore equals $1/[(N-1)(1-\beta)^2+1]$.

As the importance of social interactions increases, we should expect to see the ratio of the variance of aggregates to the variance of individual outcomes get larger and larger. As in the case of local interactions, the ratio of individual to aggregate variances gives us an estimate of the power of social interactions. However, there are reasons why this procedure may not be so easy to implement in practice. Most naturally, the A parameters may not be randomly allocated across groups. This non-randomness might reflect sorting on observables or it might reflect community-level variables that increase or decrease the returns from activity X.

To see the problems that unobservable group characteristics would cause for a variance-based measure of social interactions, assume that $A_i = \alpha + \mu_i$ where α is a community level variable and μ_i is individual-specific and independent of α. I assume further that the variance of α is $\lambda\sigma_A^2$ and the variance of μ_i is $(1-\lambda)\sigma_A^2$. The aggregate outcome can then be written $\hat{X} = (\alpha + \hat{\mu})/(1-\beta)$ where $\hat{\mu}$ is the average value of μ_i. The variance of the aggregate is $\sigma_A^2\,(1+(N-1)\lambda)\,/N(1-\beta)^2$, which may be considerably higher than in the independent case because of the correlated shocks to A.

The individual outcome can be written

$$X_i = \frac{\alpha + (N-(N-1)\beta)\mu_i/N + \beta(\hat{\mu} - \mu_i/N)}{1-\beta}$$

or equivalently,

$$X_i = \frac{\alpha + \beta\hat{\mu}}{1-\beta} + \mu_i)$$

and the variance of this is

$$\sigma_A^2\left(1 + \frac{\beta(2-\beta)(1+(N-1)\lambda)}{N(1-\beta)^2}\right).$$

The ratio of group to individual variance then equals

$$\frac{1+(N-1)\lambda}{(N-(1-\lambda))(1-\beta)^2 + 1 - \lambda + \beta(2-\beta)\lambda N}.$$

With no social interactions and no common error term, this ratio would equal $1/N$. There are essentially two reasons why the variance of aggregates can be high relative to this term: (1) social interactions; and (2) common noise terms. The difficulty of handling the common noise is one reason why empirical work in this area is so difficult.

Social interactions predict large amounts of variation in aggregates over space and they also predict social multipliers. Social multipliers occur when the relationship between an exogenous variable and an endogenous variable is stronger at higher levels of aggregation. These social multipliers both suggest that empirical work will be sensitive to the level of aggregation at which it is performed and that differences in estimated parameters at different levels of aggregation give us clues about the extent of social interactions.

To see this, start with the equation $X_i = \gamma Z_i + \beta \hat{X} + \varepsilon_i$, which then implies that

$$\hat{X} = \frac{\gamma \hat{Z} + \hat{\varepsilon}}{1-\beta} \quad \text{and} \quad X_i = \gamma Z_i + \frac{\beta \left(\gamma \hat{Z} + \hat{\varepsilon}\right)}{1-\beta} + \varepsilon_i.$$

The across-group derivative of X (i.e. the derivative of $\hat{X}$) with respect to Z is $\gamma/(1-\beta)$; the with-group derivative of X (i.e. the derivative of X_i) with respect to Z is γ. The ratio $1/(1-\beta)$ is the social multiplier, which provides us with a measure of the extent of social interactions. The stronger are the level of social interactions, the bigger the social multiplier will be (Glaeser, Sacerdote and Scheinkman, 2003). Sometimes we consider the relationship between the aggregate coefficient and the individual regression coefficient that is not within group. Since the individual regression coefficient, regressing X_i on Z_i, is

$$\gamma + \frac{\beta\gamma}{1-\beta}\frac{\mathrm{Cov}(Z_i, \hat{Z})}{\mathrm{Var}(Z_i)},$$

this will not be too different from the within-group individual level coefficient if sorting on the basis of Z is modest.

Empirical approaches to social interactions

The most common empirical approach to social interactions has been to regress outcomes on the outcomes of the neighborhood, essentially estimating $X_i = A_i + \beta \hat{X}$ where the average $\hat{X}$ is now calculated omitting the contribution of the individual in question, i.e. for each i:

$$\hat{X} = \frac{1}{N-1}\sum_{j \neq i} X_j.$$

There are several problems with this approach, which were emphasized by Manski (1993). First, even if the model is literally correct and there is no correlation between values of A across individuals in the group, the estimated coefficient from a linear regression of this form will not be β, but rather $\beta(2(N-1)-\beta(N-2))/(N+\beta^2-1)$. The essence of the social interaction model is that an individual's outcome impacts his neighbors, and this means that the covariance between an individual outcome and a group outcome will be higher than β.

If this were the only problem inherent in social interaction regressions, then it could be solved by reinterpreting the regression coefficient. Unfortunately, there are other possible issues that are potentially even more severe. Most problematic is the fact that there is likely to be correlation in the A_i terms across members of the same group. Rarely are groups random, and there is every reason to expect sorting on unobserved variables, which would create a spurious social interaction. Omitted cost and benefit variables will likewise create a high correlation between individual and group that has little to do with true social interactions. This problem bedeviled the variance approach to measuring social interactions, and it remains in the regression approach.

There are essentially two empirical approaches to this problem. One approach looks only at settings where group formation is known to be random. For example, Sacerdote (2001) looks at the correlations across outcomes for roommates in an Ivy League school. Since roommates are randomly allocated within a matching algorithm, the correlation between unobserved error terms is thought to be zero. One problem with this approach is that it still requires there to be no exogenous variables that differ at the group level. Sacerdote is able to make a plausible case that this holds in his setting by controlling for the houses, and even entryways, in which roommates reside.

Unfortunately, this approach requires the existence of random social relationships, which are often hard to find. An alternative approach follows Case and Katz (1991) and uses predetermined individual characteristics (the Z variables) as instruments. This approach avoids some of the worst problems of social interaction regressions, but still faces its own difficulties. One of the potential problems of this instrumental variables approach is that the observed variables of one's peers must be uncorrelated with unobserved factors that would impact the outcome. For example, if we regress an individual's drug use on his neighbor's drug use using the education of the neighbor's parents as an instrument, we would have to believe that having highly educated neighbors is not correlated with any omitted variables that might reduce drug use on their own. In many cases, this may not be plausible.

A second problem, emphasized by Manski (1993), is that the Z variables of one's neighbors must not have a direct impact on an individual's outcomes. I am less troubled by this problem because I am comfortable thinking of a social interaction coefficient as combining the social interactions that come through the outcome and the social interactions that come through the exogenous variables. Still, for many public policy interventions, distinguishing between the two reasons for correlation with neighbors' exogenous characteristics will be quite important, and we have little chance of doing that.

I have already commented that similar problems plague attempts to use variances to estimate social interactions. The best that can be done in that case is to try to control for the amount of common variation in the A terms. Glaeser, Sacerdote and Scheinkman (1996) do this by controlling for observables and then trying to make reasonable assumptions about the shared variation in unobservables. It is not obvious that this is convincing. We also look at changes over time and control for area fixed effects.

The problems with social multiplier estimations are closer to the problems created by using exogenous characteristics as instruments. The social multiplier will be incorrectly estimated if the exogenous variables are correlated with omitted characteristics of the group, just as the instrumental variables estimates will be wrong when there is a correlation between neighbors' exogenous characteristics and unobserved individual characteristics. The social multiplier will also be incorrectly estimated if neighbors' exogenous characteristics have an independent impact on the outcome.

I have tried to be upfront about the problems facing estimating social interactions. My own sense is that the non-experimental literature still has value, despite its many problems, and it suggests that social interactions are important. However, the way forward is surely with more experimental evidence, where we can be surer that individual relationships are random.

Cities, crime and riots

Crime and violence are continuing problems for many big cities. Crime rates are generally much higher in big cities than they are in less dense areas. For example, in 1989 your probability of being victimized over a six month period was over 20 percent if you lived in a city with more than one million people, and less than 10 percent if you lived in a place with fewer than one hundred thousand residents (Glaeser and Sacerdote, 1999). Although the connection between cities and crime has declined significantly since the 1990s, there is still a tendency for cities to be associated with crime and other forms of social disorder. In this section, I discuss the basic economic model of crime that follows from

Table 5.7. Model for crime

Actors	Individuals
They maximize	Expected Utility = E [Benefits − Non-arrest costs − Arrest-related costs] $= B - \theta_i - PC$
They choose	Whether or not to become a criminal (discrete choice)
Key conditions	Condition for choosing to be a criminal: $B > \theta_i + PC$
	The elasticity: $-\varepsilon = -\dfrac{PCg(B - \hat{\theta} - PC)}{G(B - \hat{\theta} - PC)}$
Notation	B: benefits from choosing to be a criminal
	θ_i : non-arrest related costs, differs across people
	P: probability of a criminal being caught
	C: cost paid by a criminal who is caught
	$\hat{\theta}$: location-specific mean of the distribution of θ_i
	η_i: idiosyncratic component of θ_i
	$G(\eta_i)$: CDF of η_i
	$g(\eta_i)$: PDF of η_i
	$-\varepsilon$: the elasticity of crime with respect to P or C

Becker (1968) and then discuss riots and the reasons for an empirical link between crime and urban areas.

As a starting point, I assume that individuals make a discrete choice about whether or not to be a criminal. The core equations of this model and the notation are given in Table 5.7. Being a criminal delivers benefits of B to each potential criminal. Individuals also pay costs for their crime. Non-arrest related costs, denoted θ_i, differ across people and are meant to reflect the opportunity cost of crime and perhaps conscience. Also criminals must pay costs associated with the probability of arrest, denoted P, and the penalty if caught, denoted C. Our rational criminal then engages in crime if and only if $B > \theta_i + PC$. Note that this assumes that the criminal enjoys the fruits of his crime even if he is caught, which may or may not be correct depending on the setting.[10]

Becker (1968) used this inequality to predict a surprising range of things about criminal behavior and optimal punishment. For example, the rational crime framework makes the high recidivism rates that we observe in the real world seem natural, and the hopeful thought that criminals, once punished, would become law abiding seem a little silly. If $B > \theta_i + PC$ and the benefits of crime exceed its cost for a criminal before he served time, then why shouldn't the inequality continue to hold afterwards? After all, B has probably risen through the acquisition of human capital in the slammer. The costs of future punishment may be

[10] If the criminal only gets the benefits if uncaught, then he commits a crime if and only if $(1 - P)B > \theta_i + PC$.

higher because of repeat offender rules, but other costs may have fallen because the stigma associated with arrest may have declined.

To solve for the overall amount of crime, I assume that the distribution of θ_i is characterized by a location specific mean, denoted $\hat{\theta}$, and an idiosyncratic component, η_i, with cumulative distribution function $G(\eta_i)$ and density $g(\eta_i)$. This assumption, together with our inequality determining who will choose to be a criminal, tells us that the total number of criminals will equal $G(B - \hat{\theta} - PC)$. This then predicts that the total amount of crime will be increasing with B, the returns to crime, and decreasing with P and C, the twin determinants of arrest-related crime costs. The elasticity of crime with respect to P or C equals $-PCg(B - \hat{\theta} - PC)/G(B - \hat{\theta} - PC)$, which I denote $-\varepsilon$. Crime will also fall with $\hat{\theta}$, the mean level of individual costs in the community. It is this equation that has driven economists' tendency to believe in the importance of strong penalties facing criminals. A belief in the power of incentives leads naturally to the view that penalties will reduce crime.

Becker (1968) looked at the fact that the elasticity of crime with respect to P and C was identical and suggested that in many cases raising C can be cheap while raising P is expensive because raising the probability of arrest always requires some kind of added expenditure on policing. If fines are available as a penalty, then raising C involves little social cost and simply represents a transfer between the criminal and the state. In this case, it surely makes sense to make C extremely high and make P small; the same functional deterrence is achieved with less cost. This line of reasoning actually makes any form of moderate penalties a puzzle. Why don't we boil people in oil for double parking? Several explanations for this have appeared, including the possibility that the punishment is occasionally erroneous and such high penalties would be unfair. An alternative explanation is that high penalties create enormous potential for abuse by policemen and courts. George Stigler (1970) emphasized the role of marginal deterrence. If someone is already facing death for robbing a convenience store, what's to stop him from shooting the owner while he's at it? The marginal deterrence principle pushes towards lower penalties for smaller crimes.

An alternative approach is to assume that P is fixed and then ask about the optimal C. The core equations of this model and the notation are given in Table 5.8. To do this calculation, we need to assume that the social cost for each crime is K and that the cost of imposing C on society is rC. I am now blurring the line between the amount of crime and the number of criminals. This makes the most sense in the case of murders, where people tend to commit only one crime. It makes little sense in crimes like auto theft, where criminals are professionals who commit

Table 5.8. Model for optimal punishments

Actors	The state
They maximize	– Cost of criminal activity, so they minimize $(K + rPC)G(B - \hat{\theta} - PC)$
They choose	C: The punishment for arrested criminals
Key equations	FOC for optimal punishment: $rG(B - \hat{\theta} - PC) = (K + rPC)g(B - \hat{\theta} - PC)$
Notation	rC: cost of imposing punishment C K: social cost of a crime B: benefits from choosing to be a criminal θ_i: non-arrest related costs, differs across people P: probability of a criminal being caught $\hat{\theta}$: location-specific mean of the distribution of θ_i η_i : idiosyncratic component of θ_i $G(\eta_i)$: CDF of η_i $g(\eta_i)$: PDF of η_i $-\varepsilon$: the elasticity of crime with respect to P or C

large numbers of crimes. The optimal punishment will minimize the total cost of criminal behavior or $(K + rPC)G(B - \hat{\theta} - PC)$.

The first order condition for this problem is $rG(B - \hat{\theta} - PC) = (K + rPC)g(B - \hat{\theta} - PC)$, or $\log(C) = \log(K) - \log(P) - \log(r) + \log\left(\frac{\varepsilon}{1-\varepsilon}\right)$ which provides us with a basic guide for punishment across crimes. Punishment should be higher when the crime is socially more costly, and it should be lower when the probability of arrest is higher and when the cost of imposing punishment is higher. The punishment should also be higher when the elasticity of response to the punishment is higher.

Glaeser and Sacerdote (2003) examine the implications of this equation across types of murders. Across types of murders, we find a strong negative connection between the probability of arrest and the length of sentence that looks almost like the elasticity of minus one predicted by the equation. We also find a strong connection between the characteristics of the person killed and the length of sentence. Most notably, people who kill women get substantially longer sentences and people who kill African-Americans get substantially shorter sentences. These facts hold within the class of vehicular homicides, where the identity of the victim is likely to be more random. While the fact that people who kill African-Americans get shorter sentences seems in line with a general pattern of discrimination across society, the fact that people who kill women get longer sentences is more of a puzzle. I suspect that this probably has something to do with the emotional factors involved in sentencing and vengeance.

If we want to make sense of the connection between crime and cities, it makes sense to return to the basic supply of crime function, which is $G(B - \hat{\theta} - PC)$. Consider the impact of any exogenous variable Z

on the level of crime, where that variable can potentially impact the returns to crime, the probability of arrest, sentence length, or non-arrest related factors that make crime more costly. The connection between Z and the variable may either be causal (urban density makes it easier to steal) or correlational (crime-prone people may be attracted to cities for reasons unrelated to crime) reasons. If we let N denote city size, and if we assume that C is fixed by statute and independent of city size, then differentiating the supply of crime with respect to city size yields:

$$\frac{\partial \log(\text{Crime})}{\partial \log(\text{City/size})} = \varepsilon \frac{B}{PC}\frac{N}{B}\frac{\partial B}{\partial N} - \varepsilon \frac{N}{P}\frac{\partial P}{\partial N} - \frac{N\varepsilon}{PC}\frac{\partial \hat{\theta}}{\partial N}. \tag{5.6}$$

The relationship between city size and crime includes three terms: (1) the connection between city size and the returns to crime, (2) the connection between city size and the probability of arrest, and (3) the tendency of cities to attract particularly crime-prone individuals.

There are good theoretical reasons to think that all three forces might matter. In Chapter 4, I discussed the many reasons why we think that urban density increases the productivity of lots of activities. The productivity of criminals should also increase as the distance to potential victims shrinks in big, dense cities. Street crime is almost impossible in car-based exurbs, as it is extremely difficult without pedestrian traffic. Glaeser and Sacerdote (1999) estimate an elasticity of returns to crime with respect to city size of about .11.

Urban density might also make it harder to catch criminals. One typical method of solving crimes is to run down a list of suspects. The number of potential suspects increases with the size of the community, and as the number of potential suspects increases, so does the difficulty of solving many crimes. Glaeser and Sacerdote estimate an elasticity of probability of arrest with respect to city size of about −.08, so that as city size doubles, the probability of arrest declines by .08 log points, or about eight percent. Over the past 15 years, many big city police departments have managed to become much more effective, in part by exploiting new technologies that may have scale economies. These scale economies may have started to reverse the general tendency of policing to be less effective in urban areas that are crowded with suspects.

Cities also tend to be populated with lower income people from less intact families. Both poverty and single-parent families are strong correlates of crime, and controlling for these variables explains about one-half of the connection between city size and crime. Using various estimates for the elasticity of crime with respect to deterrence from Levitt (1996), we calculate that the lower probability of arrest in cities can explain about eight percent of the connection between crime and city size. The higher returns to crime in urban areas can explain about 13 percent of the connection between crime and city size.

This exercise of trying to explain the connection between crime and city size is an example of the decompositional approach to explaining empirical puzzles. The more general form of this approach is to take a starting relationship between some outcome Y and some variable Z. From economic theory, we know there are several variables X that impact Y, so we know that Y can be written $Y(X_1(Z), X_2(Z), \ldots, X_J(Z))$; hence, the overall relationship between Y and Z can be written:

$$\frac{Z}{Y}\frac{\partial Y}{\partial Z} = \sum_j \frac{Z}{X_j}\frac{\partial X_j}{\partial Z} \times \frac{X_j}{Y}\frac{\partial Y}{\partial X_j}.$$

The objective then is to identify the set of elasticities that make up this decomposition.

Riots

Riots essentially combine social interactions with crime. To think about riots, it makes sense to start with the function $G(B - \hat{\theta} - PC)$, which can be interpreted as the supply of rioters at any given time, which can be denoted R and which I assume varies from zero to one. I also assume that the $G(.)$ function is continuous. To address riots, we need to also assume that P is a weakly declining function of the number of rioters, $P(R)$. With this assumption, the equilibrium number of rioters solves: $R = G(B - \hat{\theta} - P(R)C)$. Both sides of this equation are increasing in R, which makes it possible to have multiple equilibria. The core equations of this model and the notation are given in Table 5.9.

Table 5.9. Model for riots

Actors	Individuals
They maximize	Utility = Benefits from rioting − costs from rioting
They choose	Whether to riot or not
Key equations	Equilibrium number of rioters: $R = G(B - \hat{\theta} - P(R)C)$
Notation	R: number of rioters B: benefits from choosing to riot θ_i : non-arrest related costs of rioting, differs across people $P(R)$: probability of a rioter being caught, weakly decreasing $\hat{\theta}$: location-specific mean of the distribution of θ_i η_i : idiosyncratic component of θ_i $G(\eta_i)$: CDF of η_i, continuous

If $0 = G(B - \hat{\theta} - P(\iota)C)$ for sufficiently small ι, and if $1 > G(B - \hat{\theta} - P(1)C)$, and if there exists some value of R at which $G(B - \hat{\theta} - P(R)C) - R > 0$, then there must exist at least three equilibria in the model. Equilibria are points where the function $G(B - \hat{\theta} - P(R)C) - R$ equals zero. This term will equal zero when $R = 0$, since no one wants to riot when the probability of arrest is high. For values of R around that point, there still will be no riots because $0 = G(B - \hat{\theta} - P(\iota)C)$. This assumption essentially means that an unburdened police is able to arrest the first rioter and, given that the first rioter knows he is going to be arrested, he won't riot.

Since $G(B - \hat{\theta} - P(R)C) - R$ equals zero when R equals zero and $G(B - \hat{\theta} - P(R)C) - R$ rises above zero for some R, then by continuity there must be a point R^* where $G(B - \hat{\theta} - P(R^*)C) - R^*$ equals zero and $-P'(R^*)Cg(B - \hat{\theta} - P(R^*)C) > 1$, since the function must be upward sloping at that point if it is going to reach a positive value. That crossing point is a second equilibrium, but it is unstable in the sense that an increase in the number of rioters further increases the number of rioters. To see the instability, we can assume ad hoc dynamics where the probability of arrest in period t is a function of the number of rioters in period $t - 1$ so that $R_t = G(B - \hat{\theta} - P(R_{t-1})C)$. In that case, $\partial R_t/\partial R_{t-1} = -P'(R_{t-1})Cg(B - \hat{\theta} - P(R_{t-1})C)$ and standard notions of stability require that this be less than one, or that $-P'(R_{t-1})Cg(B - \hat{\theta} - P(R_{t-1})C) < 1$.

Since $G(B - \hat{\theta} - P(R)C) - R$ is below zero when R equals one, there must also be a second point R^{**} where the function equals zero. At that point, it must be that $-P'(R^{**})Cg(B - \hat{\theta} - P(R^{**})C) < 1$ so that the function ends up being negative at $R = 1$. This third equilibrium is therefore a stable point where there is plenty of rioting.

The three equilibria shown in Figure 5.2 all help us to understand riots. The first equilibrium with no rioting represents most of the time when a riot is not in full fire. The third equilibrium with plenty of rioting represents a stable rioting equilibrium. The middle equilibrium is a tipping point. Once the number of rioters gets beyond that point, a full blown riot will result. If the initial number of rioters is below that point, then the riot will disappear. The model suggests that a riot requires some degree of coordination so that the number of rioters overwhelms the police force.

Historically, there have been three main ways in which this coordination occurs. First, it may be that the riot is centrally planned. Labor leaders, for example, planned the massive marches that lead to the New York City 1863 draft riot that was the deadliest riot in American history. Second, a well-known event, such as the acquittal at the Rodney King trial in Los Angeles, may serve as a focal point for coordinating rioting. Third, the riot may come out of an existing crowd that overwhelms policing, such as the crowds at soccer matches. The 1965 Watts Riot started with

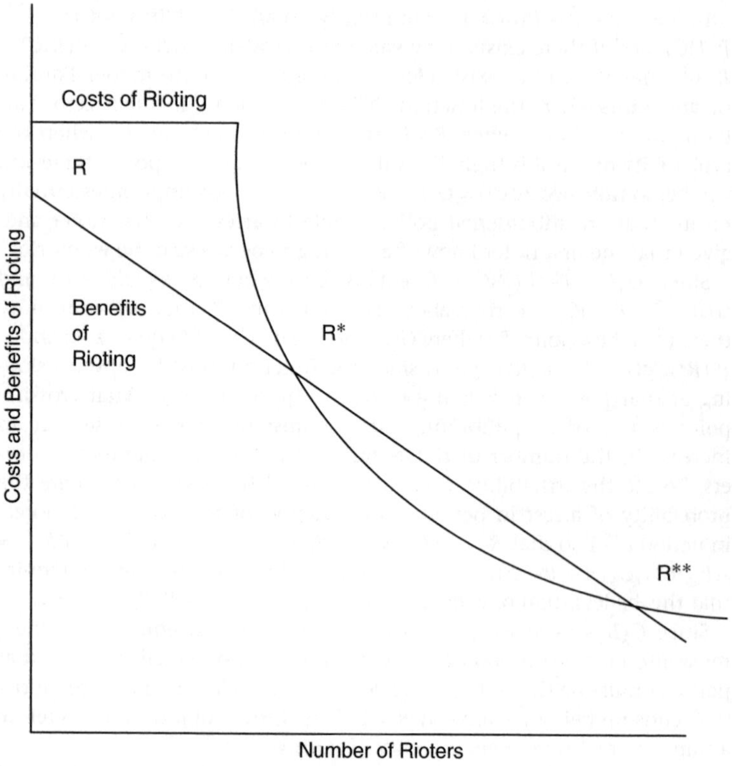

Figure 5.2. The costs and benefits of rioting

a bottle being thrown at a policeman arresting a youth in the Watts neighborhood. A crowd had formed and its size gave anonymity to the bottle-thrower and to the rioters who followed him or her.

It is hard to actually predict riots all that well. DiPasquale and Glaeser (1998) update an older sociological literature on the correlates of rioting and find that the race riots in the 1960s were not correlated with either absolute or relative poverty, but they were correlated with large numbers of unemployed African-American youths. Larger police forces were better able to cope with riots and the impact of rioting declines in cities with more police per capita. Across countries, urbanization and ethnic heterogeneity are the big determinants of rioting. The two variables interact strongly, which means that the countries with the most riots are those with ethnically diverse people living cheek-by-jowl in urban areas. Dictatorships seem to have fewer riots, which suggests that repression can be effective at blocking unrest.

The role of ethnic or religious diversity is a major part of understanding rioting. The US riots in the twentieth century were primarily race riots, which were generally initiated by whites in the first half of the twentieth century and then more commonly initiated by African-Americans during and after the 1960s. India has the most riots, and they are primarily Hindu versus Muslim. Even the 1863 draft riot had an element of ethnic conflict, with recent immigrants squaring off against longer term Americans. Why does ethnic strife seem to underpin urban unrest?

My own belief is that ethnicity doesn't lead automatically to conflict, but instead allows political entrepreneurs to build hatred (Glaeser, 2005). Social cleavages make it possible to blame outside groups for all sorts of trouble, and political entrepreneurs make the case that the outside group represents a threat. Riots then ensue as rioters think that they are harming a group that has done harm to them in the past and will do harm to them again in the future. I will discuss these issues further as I now turn to politics and local public finance.

6

Cities and public policy

Cities are formed by at least three different forces: human interactions, transportation and construction technologies, and government policy. Much of the last two chapters has focused on the good and the bad sides of human interactions. Transportation and construction technologies have played more of a supporting role, but they are often the exogenous forces that shift urban form, as demonstrated by the effect of the car on American cities over the past 50 years.

But government—both local and national—has regularly played a large role in shaping our cities. Many of the oldest of today's large cities grew great as political capitals, formed around imperial courts. Large scale national investments in infrastructure, particularly transportation infrastructure, continue to shape urban development, and local decisions also matter. Bad local government can drive away a mobile population.

Economics approaches the public sector in two different ways. The positive economics of government attempts to explain why governments look the way that they do. The normative economics of government attempts to tell governments what they should do. This section begins with a more positive look at the big issues in urban government. I start with a discussion of the famous Tiebout (1956) model of sorting and then discuss the pitfalls of local redistribution. After that, I turn to political favoritism and primate capital cities.

In the second section of this chapter, I specifically discuss four major public policy areas. I begin this section with the overall approach to place-based policies. I then turn to local tax policy and the Henry George theorem. I end by discussing land use controls.

Urban political economy

Charles Tiebout's 1956 *Journal of Political Economy* article is the starting point for all of modern local public finance. Tiebout was responding to

Samuelson's even more famous public goods article, which made it clear that private provision of goods like defense, which are non-rival and non-excludable, would be highly inefficient. Tiebout responded that if these goods were provided at the local level, a sort of market for governments would result where people could choose the services that fit their needs. As a result, something like efficiency would arise as people sorted into different localities based on the type of services that they provided. Tiebout also writes, although only in a footnote, that the threat of emigration might discipline local governments.

Tiebout's article is certainly brilliant and has had enduring impact through its emphasis on people sorting across communities to get different public services. However, he did not exactly prove that social efficiency would follow from local public governments. Bewley (1981) took up the challenge and wrote a superb article on the conditions under which local provision of government services can lead to something like a social optimum.

Bewley begins with the key equilibrium conditions for a Tiebout equilibrium, which are really the conditions for any spatial equilibrium. The primary requirement is the absence of spatial arbitrage: people can't improve their condition by moving. An added condition that becomes relevant now that governments have been added into the model is that people assume that government services and taxes are independent of their own location decisions. The second requirement for a Tiebout equilibrium is that government decisions satisfy some reasonable criterion like maximizing the welfare of their median voter. A general requirement is that everyone pays the same taxes and receives the same level of government services within a jurisdiction.

Bewley shows that there are really two key conditions for a Tiebout equilibrium to be optimal. First, there must be as many governments as there are types of people so that everyone in each area is homogenous. Second, public goods must be "public services" in Bewley's words, not "public goods," which means that the cost of these services is proportional to the number of people benefitting from these services. In the public goods scenario, there are scale economies that create an incentive for everyone to move into the same area, which then means that if there are many different governments that satisfy different tastes, we will lose the gains from scale in public goods.

When these two conditions break down, there are many different ways in which a Tiebout equilibrium can fail to be Pareto optimal. The core equations of this model and the notation are given in Table 6.1. I'll start with the assumption that everyone has a utility function of the form $av(g) + y - t$ where g is government output, y is pre-tax income, t represents taxes, and a is an individual parameter that may differ across

Table 6.1. Model with homogeneous consumers and public goods

Actors	Local governments.
They maximize	$\max_t \alpha v(g) + y - t$ Example functional form: $g = tn^{\gamma}$
They choose	The local government chooses taxes (t) to maximize consumers' utility, which is of the form $\alpha v(g) + y - t$. When utility is maximized, consumers will have no incentive to move out of their community.
First order condition	When $\alpha = 1$ and $g = tn$: $0.5v'(g) = 1$
Notation	g := government output, which depends on t y := pre-tax income t := taxes α := a parameter that may differ across people γ := an exponent that captures the scale economies in the provision of the local public good that runs from zero (for a pure public service) to one (for a pure public good)

people. When g is a public service, then output equals expenditures per capita, which will also equal t. When g is a public good, then output equals t times the number of people in the municipality or n. A more general formulation might be that $g = tn^{\gamma}$ where γ is an exponent that captures the scale economies in the provision of the local public good that runs from zero (pure public service) to one (pure public good).

In all of the examples that follow, I assume that there is a continuum of consumers of measure one. The consumers are deciding between two polities and I closely follow the examples in Bewley. Even with homogenous consumers, scale economies can lead to suboptimal equilibria. If we assume that $g = tn$ and $\alpha = 1$, then an equilibrium certainly exists where one-half of the population lives in each one of the communities. As long as tax policies are the same between the two communities, no one will have any incentive to migrate, as long as they follow the usual equilibrium assumptions that their moving won't change government taxes and services. Since everyone in each community is identical, the natural assumption would be that each government chooses g to maximize the welfare of their identical consumers so that $0.5v'(g) = 1$.

While this may be an equilibrium, it surely isn't optimal. The citizenry would be much better if they all lived in the same locality to exploit the scale economies that have been assumed in public goods. Of course, it might be reasonable to argue that this equilibrium is knife-edge in the sense that if either community gains a slight increase in population then everyone will crowd into that community. In his paper, Bewley

Table 6.2. Model with heterogeneous consumers and public goods

Actors	Local governments
They maximize	$\max_t \alpha v(g_i) + (1 - \mu)v(g_{i+1}) + y - t$ for $i \in \{1, 2, 3.4\}$
They choose	There are two communities, four different public goods, and four different consumers. The local government chooses taxes (t) to maximize consumers' utility, which is of the form $v(g_i) + (1 - \mu)v(g_{i+1}) + y - t$ for a type i consumer.
Equilibrium condition	When utility is maximized, consumers will have no incentive to move out of their community. No equilibrium conditions were explicitly given, but an example of an equilibrium was given: Type 1 and 3 people live together Type 2 and 4 people live together
Notation	i := type of consumer or public good $\in \{1, 2, 3, 4\}$ g := government output $\in \{0, 1\}$ y := pre-tax income t := taxes α := an individual parameter that may differ across people $1-\mu$:= a constant reflecting the extent to which type $i + 1$ public goods affects the utility of type i consumers *Note:* For type 4 individuals, the type $i + 1$ good is the type 1 good.

introduces entrepreneurial communities who can compete to attract residents. Such entrepreneurial communities would upset this inefficient equilibrium and end up in the more efficient equilibrium where everyone lives in the same place.

While inefficiently small communities may be an unstable equilibrium when consumers are homogeneous, this is not the case when consumers are heterogeneous. The core equations of this model and the notation are given in Table 6.2. Consider a simple case where α equals one for one-half of the population and a constant $\underline{\alpha}$ for the other half. In this case, there is an equilibrium where the half of the population that likes public goods lives in a community that sets $0.5v'(g) = 1$, and the other half lives in a population that sets $0.5\underline{\alpha}v'(g) = 1$. In this case, each group strictly prefers his own community to the other so there is nothing unstable about the equilibrium at all.

Moreover, as long as $\underline{\alpha}$ is sufficiently low, a one-community answer is not feasible when communities are entrepreneurial. Consider a potential equilibrium where the entire population lived in a single place that chose its public good provision to maximize the sum of total welfare in the community so that $0.5(1 + \underline{\alpha})v'(g) = 1$. A second community could then try to attract the entire half of the population with low levels of α that satisfy $0.5\underline{\alpha}v'(g) = 1$. Since a person with a value of α that equals zero will strictly prefer this new city, by continuity it must also be true that people with sufficiently low values of $\underline{\alpha}$ also strictly prefer the new community.

There is no integrated equilibrium, and the equilibrium with the population split between the two communities is quite stable. Yet this outcome fails to take advantage of the scale economies in providing the public good. A better outcome could occur if we allow differential taxes for the different groups, but there is no obvious means by which this could work since there are no observable differences between the two groups. Local governments don't achieve the first best case when scale economies are combined with heterogeneity.

I am not quite sure how important this challenge to the Tiebout viewpoint is in reality. Most things that local governments provide, such as schools, safety, and roads, don't feel like classic public goods to me. Schools and roads at least are both non-rival and non-excludable. The court system may be a classic public good, but policing certainly isn't. In many cases, my guess would be that public services suffer from diminishing returns more than increasing returns.

However, even when public goods are public services, a Pareto optimum doesn't result if there are more types of people than communities. Consider the case where α takes on three values, and imagine that there are two communities, each of which chooses the ideal α for one of the groups. In this case, two of the groups get exactly the value of spending and taxes that they want, but the third group does not. Moreover, if we actually allowed side payments between the groups, we could certainly make that group better off without harming either of the other two groups. The lack of group specific taxes essentially makes such side payments impossible.

Bewley gives us a particularly pretty example where too few communities leads to misallocation of people across areas. Consider a version of the model where there are four different public services ($i = 1, 2, 3, 4$) and four different types of people (again labeled 1, 2, 3, 4). Each person strongly prefers their own good and has a weak preference for the next good. To be more precise, assume that the welfare for person of type i is $v(g_i) + (1 - \mu)v(g_{i+1}) + y - t$. For type four individuals, the type $i + 1$ good is the type 1 good.

Assume further that g is not continuously supplied, but rather can only equal one or zero. In this case, it can be an equilibrium for type one and type three people to live together and for type two and type four people to live together, which is certainly suboptimal since those types have no common interests. In the political equilibrium the first community supplies exactly one unit of the type one good and one unit of the type three good while the second community supplies exactly one unit of the type two good and one unit of the type four good.

The tax rates will be the same, and no one will switch communities because they will lose $\mu v(1)$ by doing so. While this equilibrium is perfectly stable, a sufficiently entrepreneurial new community could break the equilibrium by offering a more sensible combination of public goods. I think that the key lesson here is that when people differ on lots of dimensions there is plenty of potential for people to be inefficiently sorted across communities.

I do tend to think that misallocation can be a big deal. For example, high income parents leave central cities to get better public schools for their children. This often means that they have longer commutes in order to get the public good that they want, but it isn't obvious that leafy suburbs have any innate advantages in providing schooling. If there were more school districts within urban areas, you could imagine the conditions of the Tiebout equilibrium being met and richer parents who want to live in a big city having access to better education.

While Bewley's paper helps us to understand the settings when decentralized governments will actually achieve a first best case, the more important public policy question is whether decentralized provision is good or bad. Tiebout is often cited as one of the patron saints of decentralization, although Thomas Jefferson and other states' rights advocates also deserve some credit. On the opposite side there is a healthy tradition, probably correctly traced to Alexander Hamilton and the Federalist Papers, of advocating government at a larger scale.

Certainly economics does not give a clear statement that centralization is good or bad. Tiebout emphasizes two benefits of decentralization: variety and incentives created by mobility. Variety could also be provided by a national government that allowed robust heterogeneity across localities, but for many reasons that might be difficult.

One of the most natural explanations of why you need decentralized authority to get real heterogeneity follows from the ability of national governments to redistribute across place, which I will address later. Residents of particular areas fear that redistribution with good reason. This fear tends to create enormous pressure to make sure that new forms of government largesse are spread equally across states even when this spending makes little sense. Each senator looks after his own area's interests not only in terms of overall budgeting, but also for each line item. This certainly deters heterogeneity. With local control, there is a clear sense that differences in budgets across areas don't represent spatial redistribution.

On a basic level, decentralization seems to replace government monopoly with competition across governments. Given how beneficial most economists think competition is in most private sector areas, it is hard not to think that the world is better off with competition across governments as well. Stronger incentives and more innovation (e.g. Wisconsin as the "Laboratory of Democracy") are thought to accompany the move to competition across governmental units.

Other advocates of decentralization have also argued that smaller governments empower their citizens and that decentralized governments support freedom by giving people an easy exit from excess tyranny. This last point is related to Tiebout's argument that the exit option creates good incentives for localities. Some say that more local governments will have better information about the needs of their citizens.

On the reverse side, the fans of centralization argue that there are national public goods, like security, that will be inefficiently provided at the local level. This is surely correct. More generally, there are probably many governmental activities where there are returns to scale, especially in the hiring of smart leadership. Scale economies push towards centralization. There are also many things, from environmental policy to transportation infrastructure, that create externalities across jurisdictions. The American states under the Articles of Confederation created barriers to interstate commerce. These externalities create a justification for government on a larger geographic scale, just as they created the justification for the American constitution.

The right answer on the level of decentralization surely differs across policy area. Defense is certainly best done at the national level. Transportation infrastructure requires regional planning. Many of the most important governmental services, like policing and schools, are done locally. My fondness for liberty certainly makes me much happier with the idea of local regulations on behavior than I am with nationwide bans. But one area where localities perform terribly is redistribution, and whenever government services, including schooling, have a major redistributive component, there are reasons to question local provision.

Localities and redistribution

To examine the interplay between decentralized government and redistribution, we turn to a slightly different model. The core equations of this model and the notation are given in Table 6.3. Here we assume that there are rich people and poor people, and the overall share of the population that is poor is denoted p. There is again measure one of total population in the country as a whole. The only thing that government does is to redistribute money from rich to poor. We assume that all rich people pay a common tax t and that money is then given to the poor in the form of redistribution, denoted r. If redistribution is done at the national level then the government budget constraint requires that $pr = (1 - p)t$.

Table 6.3. Simplest model of local redistribution

Actors	Voters in the population (namely, the median voter)
They maximize	$\max_r\{\log(y - pr/(1-p)) + a_{\text{Med}}\, p \log(\underline{y} + r)\}$ s.t. $pr = (1-p)t$
They choose	The level of redistribution (r) is chosen to maximize the utility of the median voter subject to the government's budget constraint (namely, $pr = (1-p)t$).
Key equation	$a_{\text{Med}} = \dfrac{\Delta p}{2(1-p)} + \hat{a}$
First order condition	$r = \dfrac{(\hat{a}(1-p) + .5\Delta p)y - \underline{y}}{1 + \dfrac{\Delta p^2}{2(1-p)} + \hat{a}p}$
Notation	p := proportion of the population that is poor t := tax that rich people pay r := redistribution to the poor a := a parameter that differs between rich people a is distributed uniformly among the rich on the interval $[\hat{a} - .5\Delta, \hat{a} + .5\Delta]$ for some $\hat{a}$, Δ a_{Med} := the a value for the median voters y := income of the rich $\underline{y}$:= income of the poor *Notes:* • There is measure 1 of the total population in the country • We assume $\underline{y} > \hat{a}y$ so that a community made out of rich people would not want to subsidize their poorer neighbors.

We assume that the utility of the poor is just the logarithm of their income, denoted $\underline{y}$, plus the redistribution. The utility of the rich is equal to $\log(y - t) + \sum_{\text{Poor}} a \log(\underline{y} + r)$ where a is a parameter that differs between rich people and y represents the income of the rich. If redistribution is done at the national level, and I use the governmental budget constraint, then the rich person's utility can be written: $\log(y - pr/(1-p)) + ap\log(\underline{y} + r)$. The rich individual on his own would choose

$$r = \frac{a(1-p)y - \underline{y}}{1 + ap}$$

and the derivative of this with respect to a is

$$\frac{\partial r}{\partial a} = \frac{(1-p)y + p\underline{y}}{(1 + ap)^2} > 0.$$

We will assume that the level of redistribution is chosen to satisfy the median voter, and we will assume that a is distributed uniformly among the rich on the interval $[\hat{a} - .5\Delta, \hat{a} + .5\Delta]$ for some $\hat{a}$, Δ. Since the poor always prefer more redistribution, then the median voter, denoted a_{Med}, satisfies $.5 = p + (1 - p)(\hat{a} + .5\Delta - a_{\text{Med}})/\Delta$ or $a_{\text{Med}} = \frac{\Delta p}{2(1-p)} + \hat{a}$, and the level of redistribution equals

$$r = \frac{(\hat{a}(1-p) + .5\Delta p)y - \underline{y}}{1 + \frac{\Delta p^2}{2(1-p)} + \hat{a}p}.$$

We can now compare this to a situation in which all redistribution is handled locally. We will assume that people only vote taxes to give to their own poor, but we can then check to make sure that, in equilibrium, redistribution to the poor of the other community is unattractive to the median voter. In particular, we assume that $\underline{y} > \hat{a}y$ so that a community made out of representative rich people would not want to subsidize their poorer neighbors. Since poor people in one community will not want to reduce their own redistribution by redistributing to their neighbors, then this condition ensures that more communities will concern themselves entirely with local redistribution. The exception would be a community that is filled with disproportionately rich people.

A Tiebout equilibrium requires there to be both a spatial equilibrium where rich and poor are indifferent across space and a political equilibrium where the preferences of the median voter determine the tax rate. I first consider the simplest version of this model where housing is free and only taxes and redistribution determine the choice of location. For i equal to one or two, I will let p_i, for $i = 1, 2$, denote the proportion of poor in the two communities respectively.

If there is no housing sector, there are essentially two types of pure strategy equilibria in this model. One case is that the two communities have the same proportion of poor and the same distribution of altruism among their wealthier inhabitants. In this case, the level of redistribution is the same as in the one city model.

In a second equilibrium, all of the rich live in one community and have no redistribution and all of the poor live in the second community and have high taxes, but no redistribution. For this to be an equilibrium, the median rich person must prefer to vote for no redistribution, i.e. $\underline{y} > \hat{a}y$, which we have assumed. Since poor people do not gain from being around the rich, there are no benefits to them from migrating. Since each rich person has measure zero, his migration won't help the poor, but will just raise his taxes, and so he won't move either. The result is a complete breakdown where redistribution has just led to total segregation.

Which of these two equilibria are stable? The concept of stability is hard to capture in this model since rich and poor will all move en masse if there is any difference in taxes or redistribution between the two communities. However, we can still talk generally about the

Table 6.4. Perturbed model of local redistribution

Actors	Voters in the population (namely, the median voter)
They maximize	$\max_{r_t}\{\log(y - p_{t-1}r_t/(1 - p_{t-1})) + a_{\text{Med}}\, p_{t-1} \log\left(\underline{y} + r_t\right)\}$ s.t. $p_{t-1}r_t = (1 - p_{t-1})t_t$
They choose	The level of redistribution in period $t(r_t)$ is chosen to maximize the utility of the median voter subject to the government's budget constraint (namely, $p_{t-1}r_t = (1 - p_{t-1})t_t$).
Key equation	$a_{\text{Med}} = \dfrac{\Delta p}{2(1 - p)} + \hat{a}$
First order condition	$r_t = \dfrac{(\hat{a}(1 - p_{t-1}) + .5\Delta p_{t-1})y - \underline{y}}{1 + \frac{\Delta p_{t-1}^2}{2(1-p_{t-1})} + \hat{a}p_{t-1}}$
Notation	p_{t-1} := proportion of the population that is poor in period t–1 t_t := tax that rich people pay in period t r_t := redistribution to the poor in period t a := a parameter that differs between rich people a is distributed uniformly among the rich on the interval $[\hat{a} - .5\Delta, \hat{a} + .5\Delta]$ for some $\hat{a}$, Δ a_{Med} := the a value for the median voters y := income of the rich $\underline{y}$:= income of the poor *Note:* This model differs from the previous one in that a group of poor people is now moved from one community to the other.

impact that small perturbations of poor or rich people will have on taxes and redistribution and whether this would seriously upset the equilibrium.

As long as $\underline{y} > \hat{a}y$ then a small perturbation which moved rich people into the poor area or vice versa would have little effect on the segregated equilibrium. The poor in the rich area wouldn't gain anything from moving and they might stay in the rich area, but they wouldn't induce any increase in redistribution as long as they constituted a sufficiently small group not to change the decision not to redistribute. The rich people in the poor area would be taxed highly and would choose to leave as soon as possible.

Is the equilibrium where the populations are evenly split stable? Consider a perturbation where a group of poor people was moved from one community to the other. The core equations of this model and the notation are given in Table 6.4. The new level of redistribution will satisfy

$$r_t = \frac{(\hat{a}(1 - p_{t-1}) + .5\Delta p_{t-1})y - \underline{y}}{1 + \frac{\Delta p_{t-1}^2}{2(1-p_{t-1})} + \hat{a}p_{t-1}}$$

and the new tax rate will equal

$$t_t = \frac{(\hat{a}(1 - p_{t-1}) + .5\Delta p_{t-1})y - \underline{y}}{1 + \frac{\Delta p_{t-1}^2}{2(1-p_{t-1})} + \hat{a}p_{t-1}} \cdot \frac{p_{t-1}}{1 - p_{t-1}}.$$

The derivative of the tax rate with respect to p_{t-1} equals

$$\frac{\partial t_t}{\partial p_{t-1}} = \frac{4\hat{a}(1 - p_{t-1})^2 y - 4(1 + \hat{a}p_{t-1}^2)\underline{U}_i + 2p_{t-1}((2 - p_{t-1})y + p_{t-1}\underline{y})\Delta}{(-2 + p_{t-1}(2 - 2\hat{a}(1 - p_{t-1}) - \Delta p_{t-1}))^2}.$$

The denominator is always positive, so this derivative is positive whenever $\hat{a}(1 - 2p_{t-1}) + p_{t-1}\Delta > 1$ holds. If we further assume that $p_{t-1} < 0.5$ (i.e. the poor are less than half the population in the community) then it suffices to require $p_{t-1}\Delta > 1$.

When these conditions hold, this higher tax rate will cause all of the rich to flee to the other town, but it may also cause all of the poor to flee as well. If

$$\frac{\partial r_t}{\partial p_{t-1}} = \frac{-4\hat{a}(1 - p_{t-1})^2 \left((1+\hat{a})y - \underline{y}\right) + 2\left((1 - p_{t-1})(1 - (1 + 2\hat{a})p_{t-1})y + (2 - p_{t-1})p_{t-1}\underline{y}\right)\Delta - p_{t-1}^2\Delta^2 y}{(-2 + p_{t-1}(2 - 2\hat{a}(1 - p_{t-1}) - \Delta p_{t-1}))^2} < 0,$$

then redistribution will fall as the number of poor increase and everyone will flee the community which received extra poor people. However, they will all flee to the second integrated community, so there is a sense in which integration is stable. If that condition fails to hold, which will occur if the least altruistic rich person doesn't care much about the poor, then the poor will follow the first group of poor and total segregation ensues.

Even this simple model suggests that one outcome from local redistribution is complete segregation of rich and poor with no redistribution whatsoever. Not only does this lead to more segregation than anyone in the community desires but it also creates total separation of rich and poor, which may have other adverse consequences. This type of reasoning leads to the view that local redistribution can have profoundly problematic consequences since increases in taxes cause out-migration of the rich and perhaps even an eventual reduction in the amount of redistribution going to the poor.

One criticism of this model is that our electorate is completely myopic. It votes on its taxes based on its current desires and does not internalize the fact that by raising taxes it will scare off its tax base. If the poorer voters are sufficiently forward-looking then they will reduce their demands for fear of scaring off their richer neighbors.

Table 6.5. Model of the Curley effect

Actors	Leader of the local government
They maximize	$\max_t (st - 1)q(t)$
They choose	Leaders of the local government choose tax levels (t) to maximize their net support in their community.
First order condition	$1 = -(t - 1/s)q'(t)/q(t)$
Notation	t := tax that rich people pay s := support the leader of the local government gets from the poor community $q(t)$:= proportion of the population that is rich

For example, consider a city with a fixed population of measure one of poor people. Assume that control of the tax rate is held by a representative of the poor who cares entirely about their welfare and assume that the number of rich people (denoted q) is a declining function of the tax rate. A leader that is trying to maximize the tax revenues going to his poor constituents will maximize $q(t)t$ which will lead to the first order condition $-tq'(t)/q(t) = 1$. The rich will be taxed, but not enough to kill off the golden goose.

The counter-argument to this view is the Curley effect, which suggests that some leaders of the poor may be more likely to lose power as the number of rich people in the area increases. Leaders like Boston's James Michael Curley, who owe their support to their poorest constituents, may face total opposition from richer voters. As such, they will have an incentive to impoverish their city to make sure that they face fewer potential opponents (Glaeser and Shleifer, 2005).

To model this in a simple manner, I assume that the leader is trying to maximize his total net support in the community. This equals the net support he gets from the poor community minus the rich voters who all support his opponent. The core equations of this model and the notation are given in Table 6.5. I assume that the net support this leader gets from the poor community is equal to a constant, s, times the total amount of redistribution that he delivers. In this case, the leaders maximizes $(st - 1)q(t)$ which implies a first order condition of $1 = -(t - 1/s)q'(t)/q(t)$. This will mean an increase in the amount of redistribution because the leader is trying to keep out his wealthy opponents.

While America has had plenty of Curleys over the last two centuries, I think that the trend in city leadership has been away from redistribution and towards competence. At the beginning of the twentieth century, American big city politics was often dominated by fights between machines and reformers. The machines tended to represent poorer immigrant populations and the reformers tended to represent the middle classes. Urban corruption declined over the course of the twentieth century, but in the 1960s, ethnic redistribution was still a major force driving city politics. Leaders, both black and white, like Coleman Young, Marion Barry and John Lindsay, were ardent supporters of redistribution. Young and Barry, but not Lindsay, may have also been motivated partially by the benefits of inducing their white opponents to leave.

By the 1970s, the costs of these policies had become obvious to a wide range of urban voters. As transportation costs fell, businesses and the wealthy found it increasingly easy to flee (i.e. $-q'(t)$ had risen), which meant that high redistribution cities increasingly became enclaves for the poor. Many places responded by replacing more progressive mayors with leaders who emphasized managerial skill over redistribution. Ed Koch, Rudy Giuliani and Michael Bloomberg are all examples of the movement away from local redistribution in New York City. I now turn to redistribution across places at the national level.

National redistribution

Americans are used to seeing a relatively dispersed urban system filled with hundreds of moderately sized cities. New York is vast, but it certainly does not dominate the country. Los Angeles and Chicago are also extremely large. The fastest growing metropolitan areas are all far from New York in the hotter states of South and Southwest.

In many other countries, the largest city, which is almost always also the capital city, can be an urban giant that dwarfs any other metropolitan area. This is true in some smaller, richer countries. Copenhagen dominates Denmark, and Lisbon dominates Portugal. Ades and Glaeser (1995) show that the share of the urban population that lives in the largest city decreases with country size, perhaps unsurprisingly. If there is any kind of an appropriate scale for a large city, then this would ensure that this city will be a large share of a tiny country and a tiny share of large country.

Ades and Glaeser (1995) also find that there is a strong link between national political systems and the size of primate cities. Countries that are dictatorships have primate cities that are about 50 percent larger than countries that are democracies. This effect is particularly strong in highly unstable regimes, and falls in extremely stable dictatorships. Why is there such a strong tendency for dictatorial regimes to have massive primate cities?

Even the most casual comparison of the policies of stable democracies and dictatorships gives us a clue about why dictatorships have such large capitals. In stable democracies, the rule of law tends to limit the tendency to support one area over another. Sometimes there is a tendency to redistribute to poorer areas, which I will discuss later, but usually there is significant opposition if government policies disproportionately favor one particular location. Institutions often have been put in place with empowered regional representatives who ensure that their areas don't end up doing too badly in the distribution of national largesse.

By contrast, dictatorships often starve their hinterlands while lavishing spending on their capital cities. This spending can take the form of large-scale construction projects which sometimes act to glorify their dictatorial builders. At other times, dictatorships indulge in trade policies, like protectionism towards manufactured goods that are overwhelmingly produced in the large cities, that indirectly aid the capital. Quite often, social services are much better in relatively modern capital cities than in the backward hinterlands. Proximity to power is often quite important to businessmen who want to get anything done, and as a result, they locate in the capital.

Ades and Glaeser (1995) go through the history of a number of major cities—Rome, Tokyo, London, Buenos Aires and Mexico City—and argue that political favoritism towards the capital was important during the key growth period of each of these cities. For example, Rome grew most dramatically during the last years of the Republic, which was a period marked by tremendous military success abroad and continuing political instability at home. As a result, the grain production of conquered territories like Iberia and Egypt was being funneled to the streets of Rome and distributed to hundreds of thousands of citizens if they came to Rome. This space-based largesse can easily explain why so many chose to come to the Eternal City.

A simple model of political survey can explain this pattern. The core equations of this model and the notation are given in Table 6.6. I assume that there are two locations in this country: the capital city and everywhere else. The political leader has a fixed sum of tax revenues, denoted T, to be distributed across the entire country. The leader's sole objective is to stay in power which yields utility of one. If the leader is ousted, his utility is zero.

There are two ways that a leader can be ousted: election and revolution. In stable democracies, elections are the relevant threat. Dictators fear revolution more. In some cases, leaders face both threats. The critical assumption is that only the capital city can revolt, but both regions have equal ability to vote. There is a strong historical basis for this assumption. The majority of effective popular (as opposed to military) revolts have been in capital cities. Revolts that are far away tend to have little impact. Additionally, when people march to the capital they are easy to disperse with the standing army, as were the Bonus marchers who came to Washington, DC during the Great Depression.

Table 6.6. Model of national redistribution with exogenous city size

Actors	The national leader
They maximize	$\max_{t_C, t_H}\{1-(1-\delta)E(Nf(t_C)+(1-N)f(t_H))-\delta R(Ng(t_C))\}$ s.t. $T = Nt_C + (1-N)t_H$ which is the same maximization problem (see notation section for explanation) as: $\max_{\Delta}\left\{\begin{array}{l}1-(1-\delta)E\begin{pmatrix}Nf(T+(1-N)\Delta)\\+(1-N)f(T-N\Delta)\end{pmatrix}\\ \delta R(Ng(T+(1-N)\Delta))\end{array}\right\}$
They choose	The national leader chooses the level of transfers to make to the city and to the hinterlands to maximize his probability of survival subject to his budget constraint $T = Nt_C + (1-N)t_H$.
First order condition	$f'(T-N\Delta) = f'(T+(1-N)\Delta) + \frac{\delta}{1-\delta}\frac{R'(r)}{E'(e)}g'(T+(1-N)\Delta)$
Notation	$N :=$ proportion of the population living in the capital city $t_C :=$ leader's per capita transfers to the capital city (C) $t_H :=$ leader's per capita transfers to the hinterland (H) $f(t_i) :=$ proportion of the population opposing the leader in an election, $i \in \{C, H\}$ $\delta :=$ relative importance of dictatorship to democracy in the determination of the identity of the leader (so higher values of δ represent a situation where dictatorship is more important than elections) $e :=$ total number of people who will oppose the leader $= Nf(t_C) + (1-N)f(t_H)$ $(1-\delta)E(e) :=$ probability the leader will be ousted in an election $g(t_C) :=$ share of the population that opposes the leader in an urban revolt $g(t_C) :=$ share of the urban population that opposes the leader in an urban revolt $r :=$ total number of revolutionaries $= Ng(t_C)$ $\Delta :=$ leader's tendency to favor the city $= t_C - t_H$ *Notes:* We assume $f'(t_i) < 0$ and $g'(t_C) < 0$

I assume that the there is a continuum of individuals that is of measure one. I let N denote the share of the population that lives in the capital city. This proportion N will be determined endogenously, but I will first treat it as a parameter. I let t_C denote the leader's per capita transfers to the capital city and t_H denote the leader's per capita transfers to the hinterland.

I assume that the share of the population that opposes the leader in an election equals $f(t_i)$ where i can represent C or H. I assume that $f'(t_i) < 0$ to capture the idea that generosity generates support. The total number of people who will oppose the leader politically then equals $Nf(t_C) + (1-N)f(t_H)$ and I denote that e. The probability that the leader will be ousted in an election equals $(1-\delta)E(Nf(t_C) + (1-N)f(t_H))$, where

δ is meant to capture the relative importance of dictatorship to democracy in this country. Higher values of δ decrease the importance of elections and increase the importance of dictatorship.

The share of the population that opposes the leader in an urban revolt equals $g(t_C)$, which is also decreasing. I assume that revolution is only effective in the capital and only the residents of the capital will bother to revolt. I denote the total number of revolutionaries r. The probability that the leader loses power to a revolution equals $\delta R(Ng(t_C))$. The overall probability of survival is then $1 - (1 - \delta)E(Nf(t_C) + (1 - N)f(t_H)) - \delta R(Ng(t_C))$.

If the populations in the two areas are fixed, then the leader maximizes his survival probability subject to the budget constraint $T = Nt_C + (1 - N)t_H$. I will engage in a slight change of variables to make things slightly clearer and let $t_C = t_H + \Delta$ for some positive Δ, so $T - N\Delta = t_H$. Essentially, Δ denotes the tendency to favor the city. The overall probability of survival can then be written:

$$1-(1-\delta)E(Nf(T+(1-N)\Delta)+(1-N)f(T-N\Delta))-\delta R(Ng(T+(1-N)\Delta)). \tag{6.1}$$

The first order condition for this equation is

$$f'(T-N\Delta) = f'(T+(1-N)\Delta) + \frac{\delta}{1-\delta}\frac{R'(r)}{E'(e)}g'(T+(1-N)\Delta). \tag{6.2}$$

The equation weighs the benefits of buying support in the hinterland against the benefits of buying support in the capital city. In both areas there is an electoral benefit, but in the capital city there is also the benefit of reducing the probability of revolution. In a perfect democracy, the term with g' in this equation equals zero, and the leader equalizes relative payments between the country and the hinterland. As elections become more important, the tendency to favor the capital city grows.

So far the model can explain why a dictator would disproportionately favor the capital city, but not why capital cities are so bloated in dictatorial regimes. To address that issue, I must endogenize N. The core equations of this model and the notation are given in Table 6.7. Specifically, I follow a reduced form and assume that N is an increasing function of the tendency to favor the city $N(\Delta)$. I assume that the dictator recognizes that his policies may impact the size of the capital city and now maximizes:

$$\begin{aligned}1 &- (1-\delta)E(N(\Delta)f(T+(1-N(\Delta))\Delta)+(1-N(\Delta))f(T-N(\Delta)\Delta))\\ &- \delta R(N(\Delta)g(T+(1-N(\Delta))\Delta)).\end{aligned} \tag{6.1'}$$

Table 6.7. Model of national redistribution with endogenous city size

Actors	The national leader
They maximize	$\max_{\Delta}\left\{\begin{array}{l}1-(1-\delta)E\left(\begin{array}{l}N(\Delta)f(T+(1-N(\Delta))\Delta)\\+(1-N(\Delta))f(T-N(\Delta)\Delta)\end{array}\right)\\ \delta R(N(\Delta)g(T+(1-N(\Delta))\Delta))\end{array}\right\}$
They choose	The national leader chooses the level of transfers to make to the city and to the hinterlands to maximize his probability of survival.
First order condition	$\frac{N'(\Delta)}{N(1-N)}\left(f(T-N\Delta))-f(T+(1-N)\Delta)-\frac{\delta R'(r)}{(1-\delta)E'(e)}g(T+(1-N)\Delta)\right)$ $+\frac{N'(\Delta)\Delta}{N(1-N)}\left(\begin{array}{l}(1-N)f'(T-N\Delta)+Nf'(T+(1-N)\Delta)\\+\frac{\delta R'(r)}{(1-\delta)E'(e)}Ng'(T+(1-N)\Delta)\end{array}\right)$ $f'(T-N\Delta)=f'(T+(1-N)\Delta)+\frac{\delta R'(r)}{(1-\delta)E'(e)}g'(T+(1-N)\Delta)$
Notation	$N(\Delta)$:= proportion of the population living in the capital city t_C := leader's per capita transfers to the capital city (C) t_H := leader's per capita transfers to the hinterland (H) $f(t_i)$:= proportion of the population opposing the leader in an election, $i \in \{C, H\}$ δ := relative importance of dictatorship to democracy in the determination of the identity of the leader (so higher values of δ represent a situation where dictatorship is more important than elections) e := total number of people who will oppose the leader $= Nf(t_C)+(1-N)f(t_H)$ $(1-\delta)E(e)$:= probability the leader will be ousted in an election $g(t_C)$:= share of the urban population that opposes the leader in an urban revolt r := total number of revolutionaries $= Ng(t_C)$ $\delta R(Ng(t_C))$:= probability the leader will be ousted in a revolution Δ := leader's tendency to favor the city $= t_C - t_H$ *Note:* This model differs from the previous in that now the size of the capital city (i.e. the proportion of the population that lives in the city) is determined endogenously.

The new first order condition is

$$\frac{N'(\Delta)}{N(1-N)}\left(f(T-N\Delta)-f(T+(1-N)\Delta)-\frac{\delta R'(r)}{(1-\delta)E'(e)}g(T+(1-N)\Delta)\right)$$

$$+\frac{N'(\Delta)\Delta}{N(1-N)}\left(\begin{array}{l}(1-N)f'(T-N\Delta)+Nf'(T+(1-N)\Delta)+\\ \frac{\delta R'(r)}{(1-\delta)E'(e)}Ng'(T+(1-N)\Delta)\end{array}\right)+f'(T-N\Delta)$$

$$=f'(T+(1-N)\Delta)+\frac{\delta R'(r)}{(1-\delta)E'(e)}g'(T+(1-N)\Delta). \qquad (6.2')$$

Equation (6.2′) includes two new terms that were not part of equation (6.2). The first term reflects the incentive that the leader has to move people out of the city into the hinterland to reduce the probability of uprising. If revolution is more likely to come from the city, then this creates an incentive to make the city smaller. In fact, there are several examples of dictatorial regimes that have either capped the size of the city (like Communist China) or moved the capital away from a population center (like Peter the Great's Russia), which acts to limit the size of the uprising.

The second term reflects the financial incentive to reduce the size of the city. Since the ruler spends more in that area, he has an incentive to reduce the size of that area. The remaining terms are the same as before. Also as before, when there is a perfect democracy the leader will allocate funds equally across the areas.

However, in this case the incentives to favor the capital city are less extreme because of the tendency of the population to respond to those incentives. In fact, it is even possible (when the probability of revolution is high, but the marginal effect of largesse on revolution is small) that dictators will actually tax the central city.

One question is whether, from a benchmark of zero spatial redistribution, a leader would have an incentive to increase redistribution to the capital city. This question requires looking at the derivative of the survival probability (6.1′) at the point where $\Delta = 0$, which equals $-\delta R'(Ng(T))\,(N'(0)g(T) + g'(T)N(1 - N))$, and this is always positive if and only if $-g'(T)/g(T) > N'(0)/N(1 - N)$. This condition means that the elasticity of unrest with respect to the level of transfers must be greater than $1/(1 - N)$ times the elasticity of city size with respect to the level of extra benefits given in the city.

If the leader's maximization problem is globally concave, then this condition determines whether the central city will be disproportionately subsidized or taxed. If we think that migration is likely to be sluggish, then we would expect the condition for subsidizing the capital to hold. Alternatively, if the population is extremely mobile, then the dictator might want to use his spending to disperse his citizens. The fact that dictators do seem to favor the capital city can be seen as evidence for the view that $-g'(T)/g(T) > N'(0)/N(1 - N)$ in fact holds. I now turn to optimal urban policies.

Optimal place-based policies

At this point, I turn from attempts to explain policy to prescriptions about policy. I discuss general attempts to subsidize and tax different

Table 6.8. Simplest model for place based national policies

Actors	The government
They maximize	$\max_N NV(N) + (1 - N)U$
They choose	The government needs to decide whether to increase or decrease city size (N) in order to maximize total welfare.
First order condition	$U + NV'(N) = 0$
Notation	U := welfare level in the hinterland, which is independent of how many people live in the hinterland $V(N)$:= welfare level in the city N := proportion of the population living in the capital city N^* := spatial or free market equilibrium city size, i.e. the value that satisfies the equation $V(N) = U$. N^{**} := optimal city size, i.e. the value that maximizes total welfare. *Discussion of dynamic migration:* $N_t - N_{t-1} = g(V(N_{t-1}) - U)$ is the dynamic migration equation N_t := proportion of the population living in the city in time t t := time period *Notes:* $g(0) = 0$, $g' > 0$

areas, local tax policy and land use controls. My primary focus is on the contribution that the spatial equilibrium approach adds to policy-making. The mobility of factors influences all of these topics and the goal of this section is to discuss that influence.

I begin my discussion by discussing top-down regional policies and their connection to localities. In general, regional policy is robust in Europe and quite weak in the US. The more centralized continental regimes have been more comfortable taking from wealthy areas and spending in distressed ones. American politicians, by contrast, have not found that strategy terribly attractive.

I begin with the simple normative economics of subsidizing city growth in a world where cities are created through externalities. This discussion follows Tolley (1974). As in the previous section, I assume a population of measure one that can either locate in a city or in the hinterland. The welfare level in the hinterland equals U, no matter how many people choose to live there. The welfare level in the city equals $V(N)$ where $V(.)$ is a function of the size of the city. Chapter 4 emphasized that city size impacts the economic productivity of a particular place; this assumption follows the claims of that chapter. The core equations of this model and the notation are given in Table 6.8.

I also assume that the city has some positive level of population and that we are observing an equilibrium where utility in the city is equal to utility in the hinterland, or $V(N) = U$. I let N^* denote the city size that satisfies this equation. Is the city too small or too large? Should government policy try to increase or decrease the city size?

Consider a welfare criterion of maximizing the total sum of well-being across people, which can be justified if costless transfers are available. In that case, the optimal city size maximizes $NV(N) + (1 - N)U$, which produces a first order condition of $V(N) - U + NV'(N) = 0$. I let N^{**} denote the city size that satisfies this equation. The second order condition for the social maximization problem is that $2V'(N) + NV''(N) < 0$ and I assume that this holds globally.

This social first order condition is certainly different from the private free market equilibrium condition, and it predicts that city size will be too small if and only if $V'(N^*) > 0$. If $V'(N^*) > 0$ then $V(N) - U + NV'(N)$ is strictly positive at N^* so utility can certainly be gained by pushing more people into the city. If $V'(N^*) < 0$ then $V(N) - U + NV'(N)$ is negative at N^*, so good urban policy would push people out of the city. As such, the decision about whether to subsidize or tax the city depends on whether $V'(N)$ is positive or negative at the free market equilibrium.

There is nothing remotely contradictory about assuming that $V'(N)$ is positive for most of the values of N but also believing that it is likely to be negative at the equilibrium city size. If I assume a dynamic migration equation where $N_t - N_{t-1} = g(V(N_{t-1}) - U)$ where $g(0) = 0$ and $g(.)$ is strictly increasing, so that positive returns to the city relative to the hinterland generates population inflows in the next period and negative relative returns generates population outflows, then it follows that $\partial N_t/\partial N_{t-1} = 1 + g'(V(N_{t-1}) - U)V'(N_{t-1})$ which is greater than one if and only if $V'(N)$ is negative at the free market equilibrium. If I assume that the world is characterized by a stable equilibrium where $\partial N_t/\partial N_{t-1} < 1$ then it must follow that $V'(N^*) < 0$ and free market cities are too big.

An alternative model might assume that there are two cities, with population N_1 living in the first city and population $1 - N_1$ living in the second city. The core equations of this model and the notation are given in Table 6.9. In this case, I let $V_1(N_1)$ denote the welfare in the first city and $V_2(1 - N_1)$ denote the welfare in the second city in the free market equilibrium $V_1(N_1) = V_2(1 - N_1)$. The social welfare maximizing distribution of populations maximizes $N_1 V_1(N_1) + (1 - N_1)V_2(1 - N_1)$ which yields the first order condition $V_1(N_1) + N_1 V_1'(N_1) - V_2(1 - N_1) = (1 - N_1)V_2'(1 - N_1)$. In this case, the size of the first city is too big if and only if $(1 - N_1)V_2'(1 - N_1) > N_1 V_1'(N_1)$ or $(1/N_1)\, V_2'(1 - N_1) > V_1'(N_1) + V_2'(1 - N_1)$. In this case, the optimal social intervention depends on where the externalities are stronger.

To consider stability, I now assume that $N_{1,t} - N_{1,t-1} = g(V_1(N_{1,t-1}) - V_2(1 - N_{1,t-1}))$ where $g(0) = 0$ and $g(.)$ is strictly increasing. It then

Table 6.9. Model for place based national policies with two cities

Actors	The government
They maximize	$\max_{N_1}\{N_1 V_1(N_1) + (1 - N_1)V_2(1 - N_1)\}$
They choose	The government needs to decide whether to increase or decrease the size of city 1 (N_1) in order to maximize total welfare.
First order condition	$V_1(N_1) + N_1 V_1'(N_1) - V_2(1 - N_1) = (1 - N_1)V_2'(1 - N_1)$
Notation	N_1 := proportion of the population living in the first city $1 - N_1$:= proportion of the population living in the second city $V_1(N_1)$:= welfare in the first city $V_2(1 - N_1)$:= welfare in the second city *Discussion of dynamic migration:* $N_{1,t} - N_{1,t-1} = g(V_1(N_{1,t-1}) - V_2(1 - N_{1,t-1}))$ is the dynamic migration equation $N_{1,t}$:= proportion of the population living in city 1 at time t t := time period *Notes:* $g(0) = 0$, $g' > 0$

follows that

$$\frac{\partial N_{1,t}}{\partial N_{1,t-1}} = 1 + g'(V_1(N_{1,t-1}) - V_2(1 - N_{1,t-1})\left(V_1'(N_{1,t-1}) + V_2'(1 - N_{1,t-1})\right),$$

which is less than one if and only if $0 > V_1'(N_{1,t-1}) + V_2'(1 - N_{1,t-1})$. Since this condition is not the same as $(1/N_1)\, V_2'(1 - N_1) > V_1'(N_1) + V_2'(1 - N_1)$ it is quite possible for the first city to be either too big or too small in a stable equilibrium.

The point of this exercise is that the presence of local agglomeration economies gives us little guide to whether government policy should be to subsidize or tax big cities. I think that this degree of ignorance suggests that attempts to pick urban winners are foolish. Government is unlikely to be particularly good at judging which cities should be subsidized and which should be taxed, and is quite likely to make its decisions on the basis of political factors that are unrelated to economic benefits. A wiser policy is surely for the national government to be neutral across cities, just as it should be neutral across firms. This same implication would seem to hold for government policies aimed at fighting urban decline.

Help poor people, not poor places

The slogan that is the title of this section is something of a mantra for many urban and regional economists. There are three primary arguments against place-based aid. First, the aid is inefficient because it increases the amount of economic activity in less productive places and decreases the amount of economic activity in more productive places. Second, the aid is not particularly equitable because the beneficiaries of the aid are the property owners in the impacted area, not the poorer people living in that area. Third, if there are negative spillovers associated with concentrated poverty, then place-based aid that bribes the poor to be in poor places may be particularly harmful.

To show these issues formally, I will discuss two different models. In both models, there are two areas and one is more productive than the other. In both models, there will be a spatial equilibrium that makes people indifferent between the two areas. In the first model, there is only one type of worker. In the second model, there are high and low human capital workers. The first model demonstrates misallocation across space due to place based policies and the fact that the benefits of these policies are reaped by landlords. The second model is used to show that poor people can actually be made worse off from place-based policies.

In the first model, the core equations and notation of which are given in Table 6.10, I assume that labor demand is defined by free entry of firms that have access to Cobb–Douglas production function $A_i K^{\alpha} L^{\beta} \bar{Z}_i^{1-\alpha-\beta}$, where (as in Chapter 3), K is mobile capital, L is labor, $\bar{Z}_i$ is location-specific fixed capital and A_i reflects a location-specific productivity parameter for $i = 1, 2$. Goods are sold at a price of one on the global market. The price of mobile capital is fixed at R. With these assumptions, the labor demand curve in each region is $L = \theta^{1/\eta} A_i^{1/\eta} \bar{Z}_i W^{(\alpha-1)/\eta}$ or $W = \theta^{1/(1-\alpha)} A_i^{1/(1-\alpha)} \bar{Z}_i^{\eta/(1-\alpha)} L^{-\eta/(1-\alpha)}$ where $\eta = 1 - \alpha - \beta$, W represents the wage, and $\theta = \alpha^{\alpha} \beta^{(1-\alpha)} R^{-\alpha}$.

Individuals consume exactly one unit of housing and this is rented from the housing sector. At time zero, developers built H_i units of housing in each region. I will not explicitly address the maximization equation

Table 6.10. Model for place-based aid firms

Actors	Firms
They maximize	Profit = $A_i K^{\alpha} L^{\beta} \bar{Z}_i^{1-\alpha-\beta} - RK - WL$
They choose	K: mobile capital L: labor
Key equations	From the profit max: $W = \theta^{1/(1-\alpha)} A_i^{1/(1-\alpha)} \bar{Z}_i^{\eta/(1-\alpha)} L^{-\eta/(1-\alpha)}$
Notation	W: wage (determined endogenously) R: rental price of mobile capital (fixed exogenously) A_i : location-specific productivity parameter $\bar{Z}_i$: location-specific fixed capital $\eta = 1 - \alpha - \beta$ $\theta = \alpha^{\alpha} \beta^{(1-\alpha)} R^{-\alpha}$

that led to this quantity of housing being developed as it is immaterial to this example. As of time one, there was a shock to the productivity of the two regions that increases the productivity of region two relative to region one.

At time one, I assume that population has risen, but that at equilibrium housing rents, new construction in region one cannot cover construction costs so that area one's population is determined by the housing built in period zero, or H_1. There is new construction in the second region to accommodate the total population of the nation, which equals one, so that the total number of homes and people in the second region equals $1 - H_1$. I further assume that there is free entry in the second region's construction sector and that developers require a rent of R_C to cover construction costs. This construction cost rent determines housing prices in the second region. Rent in the first region is denoted R_1 and is determined endogenously. I will drop that assumption shortly. The core equations of this model and the notation are given in Table 6.11.

Without any government intervention, the equilibrium conditions in this market are labor demand curves $\theta^{1/(1-a)} A_1^{1/(1-a)} \bar{Z}_1^{\eta/(1-a)} H_1^{-\eta/(1-a)} = W_1$, and $\theta^{1/(1-a)} A_2^{1/(1-a)} \bar{Z}_2^{\eta/(1-a)} (1 - H_1)^{-\eta/(1-a)} = W_2$ and the spatial indifference condition $W_1 - R_1 = W_2 - R_C$. My interest is in the impact of a place-based policy that subsidizes employers to hire workers in region 1. This subsidy will be paid for with taxes on employers that hire workers in region 2. There are, of course, many forms that region specific subsidies can take. The subsidy could target output or capital use. Such subsidies would be less effective at improving worker welfare than a direct subsidy for employment. As such, I focus on an employment subsidy.

Table 6.11. Model for place-based aid individuals

Actors	Individuals
They maximize	Utility = Wages − Housing costs
They choose	Location: region one or region two. People face a tradeoff between housing prices and wages.
Key conditions	Spatial equilibrium requires $W_1 - R_1 = W_2 - R_C$ Adding a subsidy we get new FOC $\theta^{1/(1-a)} A_2^{1/(1-a)} \bar{Z}_2^{\eta/(1-a)} (1 - H_1)^{-\eta/(1-a)} - \frac{H_1}{1 - H_1} s = W_2$
Notation	H_1: fixed units of housing in region 1 $1 - H_1$: homes in region 2 R_C: cost of new construction in region 2 R_1: cost of housing in region 1, determined endogenously s: Subsidy for employing workers in region one

To keep a balanced budget, the tax on region two workers must equal $H_1/(1-H_1)$ times the subsidy paid for employing region one workers, which is denoted s. I also assume that the tax and subsidy do not impact rental payments in the second region which remain fixed at R_C by construction costs. The new first order condition for region 1 labor is

$$\theta^{1/(1-\alpha)} A_1^{1/(1-\alpha)} \bar{Z}_1^{\eta/(1-\alpha)} H_1^{-\eta/(1-\alpha)} + s = W_1$$

and the new first order condition for region 2's labor demand is

$$\theta^{1/(1-\alpha)} A_2^{1/(1-\alpha)} \bar{Z}_2^{\eta/(1-\alpha)} (1-H_1)^{-\eta/(1-\alpha)} - \frac{H_1}{1-H_1} s = W_2.$$

Because the subsidy is perfectly targeted towards employment and because employment is rigidly determined by housing supply, nominal wages go up by exactly the amount of the subsidy. The fixed nature of housing supply makes labor into a fixed factor, and it actually reaps the full benefits of the employment subsidy. Of course, wages in the second sector are correspondingly reduced. The net impact on nominal wages across all workers is exactly zero.

However, this rise in wages is perfectly offset by an increase in housing costs in the first region, which must continue to satisfy $W_1 - R_1 = W_2 - R_C$. As such, R_1 increases by $s/(1-H_1)$. With this fact, the model now describes the winners and losers from the place-based intervention. I split the population into owners and renters in region one and region two.

Both owners and renters in region two are made worse off from this intervention. Wages decline and there is no change in housing rents or values. Renters in the first region see their wages rise by s but their housing costs increase by $s/(1-H_1)$. Overall, they are worse off after this intervention because the increase in rents more than offsets the increase in wages. The big winners are the owners in the first region who reap the full benefits from the wage increase.

In this example, the regional subsidy caused no distortions. The labor supply was fixed by a durable housing stock. The intervention did cause wages to rise in the distressed area, but housing costs rose by more than wages. As a result, the owners and landlords in the distressed region gained while the renters were actually hurt.

I now turn to a model where the subsidy will actually distort the location decision. To allow the subsidy to distort the location decision, it is enough to assume that it causes housing rents in the first region to rise enough to justify new construction. For the sake of symmetry, I assume that construction costs in the first region also imply a rental payment of R_C. I assume that there is still construction in the second region, so the impact of the subsidy is to make sure that there is growth in both regions.

Table 6.12. Model for place-based aid housing

Actors	Individuals
They maximize	Utility = Wages – Housing costs
They choose	Location: region one or region two. People face a tradeoff between wages and housing prices.
Key conditions	New equilibrium condition is: $\theta^{1/(1-\alpha)} A_1^{1/(1-\alpha)} \bar{Z}_1^{\eta/(1-\alpha)} h^{-\eta/(1-\alpha)} + s = \theta^{1/(1-\alpha)} A_2^{1/(1-\alpha)} \bar{Z}_2^{\eta/(1-\alpha)} (1-h)^{-\eta/(1-\alpha)} - \frac{hs}{1-h}$
Notation	H_1: housing in region 1, absent any subsidy h: housing in region 1 R_C: cost of new construction s: subsidy for employing workers in region one

Regional growth is, after all, the objective of many such regional policies. I let h denote the amount of housing in the first region after the subsidy and continue to use H_1 to denote the amount of housing that would have been in the first region absent any subsidy. The core equations of this model and the notation are given in Table 6.12.

In this case, rents are determined by the construction sector and if rents are equal across regions then wages are equal as well. This means that the equilibrium is characterized by the equation $\theta^{1/(1-\alpha)} A_1^{1/(1-\alpha)} \bar{Z}_1^{\eta/(1-\alpha)} h^{-\eta/(1-\alpha)} + s = \theta^{1/(1-\alpha)} A_2^{1/(1-\alpha)} \bar{Z}_2^{\eta/(1-\alpha)} (1-h)^{-\eta/(1-\alpha)} - hs/(1-h)$. This equation generates the share of housing in the first region as a function of the subsidy. As the subsidy rises, a greater share of housing and the labor force will be in the first region.

The subsidy has no impact on housing costs in the second region and increases housing costs by $\theta^{1/(1-\alpha)}(A_2^{1/(1-\alpha)} \bar{Z}_2^{\eta/(1-\alpha)} (1-H_1)^{-\eta/(1-\alpha)} - A_1^{1/(1-\alpha)} \bar{Z}_1^{\eta/(1-\alpha)} H_1^{-\eta/(1-\alpha)})$ in the first region. Nominal wages in the second region have declined by

$$\frac{hs}{1-h} + \theta^{1/(1-\alpha)} A_2^{1/(1-\alpha)} \bar{Z}_2^{\eta/(1-\alpha)} \left((1-H_1)^{-\eta/(1-\alpha)} - (1-h)^{-\eta/(1-\alpha)}\right).$$

Nominal wages in the first region have risen by

$$s - \theta^{1/(1-\alpha)} A_1^{1/(1-\alpha)} \bar{Z}_1^{\eta/(1-\alpha)} \left(H_1^{-\eta/(1-\alpha)} - h^{-\eta/(1-\alpha)}\right).$$

Since labor will move across areas in response to the subsidy, the wage increases in the first region are less than they would have been with fixed labor. The wage decreases in the second region are also smaller in magnitude than they would have been with fixed labor.

Renters and owners in the second region are made unequivocally worse off because of the subsidy. In the first region, wages minus housing costs decline by exactly as much as wages decline in the second region.

The total decrease in wages minus housing costs in the first region is the same as the decrease in wages in the second region:

$$\frac{hs}{1-h} + \theta^{1/(1-\alpha)} A_2^{1/(1-\alpha)} \bar{Z}_2^{\eta/(1-\alpha)} \left((1-H_1)^{-\eta/(1-\alpha)} - (1-h)^{-\eta/(1-\alpha)} \right).$$

The spatial equilibrium means that taxing renting workers in the second region to fund people in the first region is unlikely to increase welfare for either group. The total loss combines a loss due to the redistribution towards landlords and a loss due to the misallocation of labor across space. Owners still benefit in the first region.

Overall, the total output of the two regions together equals

$$\beta^{-1} \theta^{1/(1-\alpha)} \left(A_1^{1/(1-\alpha)} \bar{Z}_1^{\eta/(1-\alpha)} h^{\beta/(1-\alpha)} + A_2^{1/(1-\alpha)} \bar{Z}_2^{\eta/(1-\alpha)} (1-h)^{\beta/(1-\alpha)} \right).$$

This is less than it would have been without the subsidy. By inducing people to live in the innately less productive region, the overall output of the country falls.

I now turn to a slightly different model that again contains two areas, but that allows for human capital externalities as in Benabou (1993). The core equations of this model and the notation are given in Table 6.13. I assume that one-half of the population has high human capital of level $E > 1$, and one-half of the population has low human capital which I normalize to level 1. Output in each area is A_i times their human capital. There is a fixed stock of H_1 units of housing in the first region and housing in the second region has a fixed price of R_C which is meant to cover construction costs. I assume that .5 is greater than H_1.

As an added twist, I assume that each individual produces a high human capital child with probability $P(Q_i)$ where Q_i reflects the share of the population in your region that has a high level of human capital. Both high and low human capital parents place value V on having a high human capital child. There are two possible scenarios in this model depending on whether housing in the first region sells for a positive price. In the first scenario, housing in the first region sells for a positive price, and in that case,

$$A_2 - R_C + VP\left(\frac{1}{2(1-H_1)}\right) = A_1 - R_1 + VP(0).$$

In the second scenario, housing in the first region is free, and if I let h denote the total share of the population in the first region, which is less

Table 6.13. Model for place-based aid with human capital externalities

Actors	Individuals
They maximize	Utility = Output − Housing costs + Value of children
They choose	Location: region one or region two. People must tradeoff income, housing costs, and a better probability of having a high human capital child.
Key conditions	When housing in region 1 sells for a positive price: $A_2 - R_C + VP\left(\frac{1}{2(1-H_1)}\right) = A_1 - R_1 + VP(0)$ When housing in region is free: $A_2 - R_C + VP\left(\frac{1}{2(1-h)}\right) = A_1 + VP(0)$ When a subsidy is added to the second case: $A_2 - R_C + VP\left(\frac{1}{2(1-h)}\right) - \frac{hs}{1-h} = A_1 + VP(0) + s$
Notation	E: human capital of high-capital types A_i: region-specific productivity parameter – individual output equals human capital times this H_1: fixed stock of housing in region one R_C: cost of new construction in region 2 R_1: price of housing in region one (determined endogenously) Q_i: share of population in region i that is high human capital $P(Q_i)$: probability of an individual producing a high human capital child V: value to parents of a high human capital child h: share of the population living in region one s: subsidy for living in region one

than H_1, then the equilibrium condition is

$$A_2 - R_C + VP\left(\frac{1}{2(1-h)}\right) = A_1 + VP\,(0)\,.$$

The value of h rises to the point where the low human capital individuals are on the margin between staying in region one, which is free, or paying R_C to live in the second region.

In the first scenario, where the rents still have positive value, a tax subsidy to people living in the first region will have no impact on population levels. It will increase the rents paid in the first region by an amount that exactly offsets the subsidy. As in the previous case, renters in region one will be hurt and owners will benefit. Since the subsidy doesn't change the population, it will have no impact on the human capital of the next generation. This is the less interesting case.

In the second scenario, a subsidy of s to anyone who lives in the first region paid for by a tax of $hs/(1-h)$ on the residents of the second region will lead to a new equilibrium condition of

$$A_2 - R_C + VP\left(\frac{1}{2(1-h)}\right) - \frac{hs}{1-h} = A_1 + VP(0) + s.$$

The subsidy will increase the share of the population living in the first region. The subsidy is actually welfare enhancing for the population as a whole because it crowds the low human capital people into the first region, which causes average utility to rise by

$$\frac{h'(s)}{1-h}\left(\frac{1}{2}VP'\left(\frac{1}{2(1-h)}\right) - s\right) - h.$$

There is an externality when low human capital people move into region two that they create by lowering the probability that the next generation in that area will be high human capital, which the subsidy addresses. This result is not general, and would be offset if there was an externality associated with increasing the number of low human capital people in region one. In this model, the externality is a function of the share of low human capital in the region, and this remains one hundred percent in region one regardless of the subsidy.

The unfortunate effect of the subsidy is that the proportion of the low human capital parents' children that are high human capital will decrease whenever

$$P\left(\frac{1}{2(1-h)}\right) > P(0) + \frac{(.5-h)}{2(1-h)^2}P'\left(\frac{1}{2(1-h)}\right).$$

The subsidy to the poor region has the effect of making sure that poor people stay in a region that is filled with other poor people. This benefits the high human capital people since they get the benefits of a region that has fewer low human capital people. However, the children of the low human capital people will generally become less skilled if $P'(.)$ isn't too large because their parents are being bribed to live in a disproportionately low human capital area.

Overall, it is hard to be too sympathetic towards place based aid. Without externalities, that aid generally benefits landlords and does nothing for renters. It distorts the migration decision which leads to a misallocation of labor across space. Moreover, if human capital in the next generation is a function of the human capital in the area where children grow up, then bribing poor people to live in poor areas makes it likely that their children will be less skilled.

Table 6.14. Model for transfer payments fixed populations

Actors	The government
They maximize	Total utility of all people = $NV(t_1/P_1)+(1-N)V(t_2/P_2)$ subject to $T \geq Nt_1+(1-N)t_2$
They choose	t_1 and t_2: location specific transfers
Key equations	The FOC is: $\frac{P_1}{P_2}=\frac{V'(t_1/P_1)}{V'(t_2/P_2)}$ With CRRA: $\left(\frac{P_1}{P_2}\right)^{(1-a)/a}=\frac{t_2}{t_1}$
Notation	T: total government transfers to distribute N: size of population in region 1 $1-N$: size of population in region 2 P_1: price level in region 1 P_2: price level in region 2 V(real income): utility from transfers

Indexing transfer payments to local price levels

As a final topic in national policy at the regional level, I turn to the question of indexing transfer payments to local price levels (Kaplow, 1996; Glaeser, 1998). A large number of national governments have some form of transfer payments which are paid nation-wide. In most cases, economists think that it makes sense to index those payments to national price levels. After all, changing national price levels can be thought of as relabeling the units of exchange, and certainly it makes sense to use indexing to make real payments independent of arbitrary relabeling.

This logic has led many observers to think that transfer payments should be indexed to local price levels as well, but the analogy is far from perfect. To see this, we start with a government that has a fixed quantity of money, denoted T, to distribute to a population of size 1 that is split between two locations. The population of the first location is denoted N. The price level in the first location is P_1 and the price level in the second location is P_2. The core equations of this model and the notation are given in Table 6.14.

Urban economics insists that populations are mobile and that higher prices in one location offset the prices in another location. These claims will impact the optimal degree of indexing, but before I consider them I will start by looking at the situation where the population is not mobile. Furthermore, I will assume that the government is interested in maximizing the sum of V(Real Income) across all of the welfare recipients. The function $V(.)$ might be thought of as the utility level of the recipients so that the government is purely utilitarian. Alternatively, $V(.)$ might be any concave function imposed by the government which allows us to consider the possibility that the government puts much more weight on helping people who are poor.

Given these assumptions, the government's problem is to choose location specific transfer payments t_1 and t_2 to maximize $NV(t_1/P_1) + (1 - N)V(t_2/P_2)$ subject to the constraint that $T \geq Nt_1 + (1 - N)t_2$. This problem yields first order condition:

$$\frac{P_1}{P_2} = \frac{V'(t_1/P_1)}{V'(t_2/P_2)},$$

which means that the ratio of the marginal utilities equals the ratio of the price levels. If the price level is higher in place one than in place two, then real payments should be lower in place one than in place two. In other words, transfer payments should not fully compensate for higher prices because those higher prices make it more expensive to deliver the same level of real income (Kaplow, 1996).

This is one way in which interregional price levels differ from intertemporal price levels. If the price level rises between time t and $t + 1$ and this is foreseen, then the government will earn higher returns by investing between time t and $t + 1$ so that the cost of redistributing at that future date is not higher. Inflation does not make it more expensive for the government to deliver the same real transfer over time. However, across space it is unambiguously more expensive to deliver the same real income in a place with higher price levels.

The first order condition just tells us that real transfer payments will be lower in the high price area, but it doesn't tell us if nominal transfer payments will be higher or lower in the high price area. The concavity of $V(.)$ pushes us to make real transfer payments more equal, which pushes towards higher nominal payments in high price areas. The price effect pushes us to reduce payments in places with higher prices. As such, the question of whether nominal payments should be higher in high price areas will be dependent on functional form.

If the welfare function has the standard Constant Relative Risk Aversion form so that $V(t_1/P_1) = (t_1/P_1)^{1-\alpha}$, then the first order condition implies that $(P_1/P_2)^{(1-\alpha)/\alpha} = t_2/t_1$ and if $P_1 > P_2$ then $t_1 > t_2$ if and only if $\alpha > 1$. When the function is extremely concave, the government should provide higher nominal transfers in high price areas. When the function is reasonably linear, as it is when the coefficient of relative risk aversion is less than one, then the government should pay lower nominal transfers in high price areas. If $V(t_1/P_1) = \log(t_1/P_1)$, which corresponds to the $\alpha = 1/2$ case, then nominal payments are independent of the price level.

These simple calculations ignore the entire spatial equilibrium assumption that is at the heart of this book. To bring spatial equilibrium into the

Table 6.15. Model for transfer payments mobile populations

Actors	The government
They maximize	Total utility of all people = $NV\left(U^1(t_1/P_1(N), A_1)\right) + (1-N)V\left(U^2(t_2, A_2)\right)$ subject to $T \geq Nt_1 + (1-N)t_2$
They choose	t_1 and t_2: location specific transfers
Key equations	The spatial equilibrium condition: $U^1(t_1/P_1(N), A_1) = U^2(t_2, A_2)$ The government's FOC: $N'(t_1)\left(V\left(U^1\right) - V\left(U^2\right)\right) + NV'\left(U^1\right)\left(U_1^1\left(\frac{1}{P_1(N)} - \frac{t_1 P_1'(N)N'(t_1)}{P_1(N)^2}\right)\right) + V'(U^2)U_1^2\left(-N + \frac{N'(t_1)(T-t_1)}{1-N}\right) = 0$
Notation	T: total government transfers to distribute N: size of population in region 1 $1-N$: size of population in region 2 $P_1(N)$: price level in region 1, increasing function of N (normalized to one in region 2) $U^i(t_i/P_i, A_i)$: utility of a person in region i A_i: location-specific amenity parameter U_j^i: derivative of utility in region i with respect to its jth argument

model, I need to introduce three elements. First, I will assume that individual utility levels are a function of real income and a location-specific amenity, denoted A_i. The overall utility function is written $U^i(t_i/P_i, A_i)$. I assume that P_2 equals one, which might reflect an elastic supply of housing in that region, and I let P_1 be an increasing function $P_1(N)$ that rises with population size to capture the fact that housing supply slopes upward. The core equations of this model and the notation are given in Table 6.15.

The spatial equilibrium condition is then $U^1(t_1/P_1(N), A_1) = U^2(t_2, A_2)$ where U^i denotes the level of utility in region i. The government now maximizes the sum $NV\left(U^1(t_1/P_1(N), A_1)\right) + (1-N)V\left(U^2(t_2, A_2)\right)$ subject to the budget constraint $T \geq Nt_1 + (1-N)t_2$ and the spatial equilibrium condition. The spatial equilibrium defines a function $N(t_1)$ that maps the transfer level into the size of the population living in the first community through the equation: $U^1(t_1/P_1(N(t_1)), A_1) = U^2((T - N(t_1)t_1)/(1 - N(t_1)), A_2)$. Differentiating this equation yields:

$$N'(t_1) = \frac{P_1(N)(1-N)^2U_1^1 + P_1(N)^2N(1-N)U_1^2}{t_1(1-N)^2P_1'(N)U_1^1 + (T-t_1)P_1(N)^2U_1^2} > 0$$

where U_j^i denotes the derivative of utility in region i with respect to its jth argument.

The new first order condition for the government is

$$N'(t_1)(V(U^1) - V(U^2)) + NV'(U^1)\left(U_1^1\left(\frac{1}{P_1(N)} - \frac{t_1 P_1'(N)N'(t_1)}{P_1(N)^2}\right)\right)$$
$$+ V'(U^2)U_1^2\left(-N + \frac{N'(t_1)(T - t_1)}{1 - N}\right) = 0. \qquad (6.3)$$

Since the spatial equilibrium assumption requires that $U^1 = U^2$, equation (6.1) can be reduced to

$$\frac{U_1^1}{P_1(N)} + \frac{t_1 N'(t_1)}{N}\left(\frac{(T - t_1)}{(1 - N)t_1}U_1^2 - \frac{P_1'(N)}{P_1(N)^2}U_1^1\right) = U_1^2. \qquad (6.3')$$

This new first order condition suggests that including the spatial equilibrium condition into the optimization brings two new terms in the first order condition for optimal local price indexing. Both of these terms reflect the fact that population will move in response to the transfer payment. When population is not mobile, $t_1 N'(t_1)/N = 0$ and we are left with the old first order condition $U_1^1/P_1(N) = U_1^2$.

The first new term $\frac{t_1 N'(t_1)}{N}\frac{(T-t_1)}{(1-N)t_1}U_1^2$ reflects the fiscal advantages of moving populations from one place to another. When $T > t_1$ so that transfers are higher in the second area than in the first, then this term is positive and it acts to reduce the incentives to transfer more to the second region. When $T < t_1$, then this term acts to increase the incentives to transfer more to the second region where transfers are lower.

The second term, $-\frac{t_1 N'(t_1)}{N}\frac{NP_1'(N)}{P_1(N)^2}U_1^1$, reflects the gains of reducing prices that come from moving people out of the first region. In this model, this force always acts to reduce the transfers to the first region, but this is the result of the asymmetry that I assumed in housing prices. If more population raised housing prices in both regions, then the impact of rising housing prices on transfers across regions would be ambiguous.

Finally, it is worthwhile returning to the basic equality $U_1^1/P_1(N) = U_1^2$ which would hold if the population was immobile. This equality is, of course, the same as in the simpler example, but the intuition surrounding this equality is somewhat different because of the presence of amenities differences. If amenities are higher in the first region, then $P_1(N) > 1$ if the nominal transfer levels were the same. Those higher amenities could make U_1^1 higher or lower than U_1^2 depending on whether amenities and income are complements or substitutes.

If amenities and income are complements then this makes it more attractive to transfer money to the high amenity, high price areas. If they are substitutes then this makes it more attractive to transfer to the low amenity, low price area. Glaeser (1998) estimates a slightly different version of this equation and presents some empirical work suggesting complementarity between amenities and income, which suggests somewhat higher transfers to high price areas.

Without specifying functional forms and parameter values, this model generates no clear results about the degree to which transfer payments should be indexed to local price levels. It does, however, suggest that the naïve thought that transfer payments should be adjusted one-for-one to local price levels is wrong. The spatial equilibrium approach to economic policy suggests that this is unlikely to be either equitable or efficient. The right public policy needs to recognize that high prices make transfers to high cost areas more expensive and that those high prices are already compensating for something else. The right policy should also respect the fact that the population will respond to high transfers with migration.

Local tax policy

I now turn to the decision made by localities about their level of taxes. Consider a two region model with measure one of individuals each of whom earns income of Y. The core equations of this model and the notation are given in Table 6.16. The first region has n people and the second $1-n$ people. Each region is endowed with one-half of a unit of land. Each region also must raise T_i units of revenue. I will consider two possible scenarios. First, I consider a lump-sum tax where each region charges each one of their residents t_i. This tax could equivalently be

Table 6.16. Model for local tax policy

Actors	The government
They maximize	Total utility of all people = $Y - T_1 - T_2 + nV(.5/n) + (1-n)V(.5/(1-n))$
They choose	t_1 and t_2: Location specific taxes
Key equations	The FOC:
	$(1-n)(nV(.5/n) - .5V'(.5/n)) = n((1-n)V(.5/(1-n)) - .5V'(.5/(1-n)))$
	The spatial equilibrium condition:
	$Y - t_1 - P_1 L_1^* + V(L_1^*) = Y - t_2 - P_2 L_2^* + V(L_2^*)$
Notation	Y: exogenous income of individuals n: number of people in region 1 $1-n$: number of people in region 2 T_i: revenue that region i must raise t_i: lump-sum tax on residents in region i $Y - t_i - P_i L + V(L)$: individual utility L: land consumption of an individual P_i: endogenously determined price of land in region i $V(.)$: concave function L_i^*: individually optimal land consumption in region i

an income tax since income is exogenous in this model. In the second scenario, I will consider a tax on land.

Individuals have utility functions of $Y - t_i - P_i L + V(L)$ where L refers to land consumption, P_i is the endogenously determined price of land in region i and $V(.)$ is a concave function. The first order condition for land consumption is $V'(L_i^*) = P_i$, where L_i^* denotes the individually optimal land consumption in region i. The optimal allocation of people in this model maximizes $Y - T_1 - T_2 + nV(.5/n) + (1-n)V(.5/(1-n))$ which yields first order condition $(1-n)(nV(.5/n) - .5V'(.5/n)) = n((1-n)V(.5/(1-n)) - .5V'(.5/(1-n)))$ which is satisfied at $n = .5$. This could certainly be achieved by a central authority that taxes everyone with lump sum taxes. In that case, there would be no governmental reason to live in one place or another, land costs would be the same in both regions, and land consumption would be the same in both regions. I now consider the extent to which different tax regimes mimic this first best.

The spatial equilibrium assumption requires that $Y - t_1 - P_1 L_1^* + V(L_1^*) = Y - t_2 - P_2 L_2^* + V(L_2^*)$. I let n denote the population in region one, so that the balanced budget constraints are $nt_1 = T_1$ and $(1-n)t_2 = T_2$. Finally, the market for land must clear, which means that $nL_1^* = (1-n)L_2^* = .5$, so $V'(.5/n) = P_1$ and $V'(.5/(1-n)) = P_2$. These conditions can be combined into a single equilibrium condition:

$$n(1-n)V\left(\frac{1}{2n}\right) - \frac{1-n}{2}V'\left(\frac{1}{2n}\right) - n(1-n)V\left(\frac{1}{2(1-n)}\right) + \frac{n}{2}V'\left(\frac{1}{2(1-n)}\right) = (1-n)T_1 - nT_2. \tag{6.4}$$

As long as $T_1 \neq T_2$, this will not produce the first best result. Whenever $T_1 \neq T_2$, I can assume that the first region has the higher tax base. Differentiating equation (6.4) and using the implicit function theorem yields:

$$n'(T_1) = \frac{4(1-n)}{4(T_1+T_2) + \dfrac{n}{(1-n)^2}V''(0.5/(1-n)) + \dfrac{1-n}{n^2}V''(0.5/n)} < 0$$

which is negative if

$$n\left(t_1 + \frac{1}{(2(1-n))^2}V''\left(\frac{1}{2(1-n)}\right)\right) + (1-n)\left(t_2 + \frac{1}{(2n)^2}V''\left(\frac{1}{2n}\right)\right) < 0.$$

Whenever this condition holds, city size is declining in the size of the tax level, which means that the first region will always have too few people in it relative to the first best.

While lump sum taxes will not achieve the first best, a tax per unit of land of $2T_1$ in the first region and $2T_2$ in the second region will. In that case, the equilibrium condition becomes $Y-(P_1+2T_1)L_1^*+V(L_1^*)=Y-(P_2+2T_2)L_2^*+V(L_2^*)$ and the pricing condition $V'(L_i^*)=(P_i+2T_i)$ The first order condition can be written $-V'(L_1^*)L_1^*+V(L_1^*)=-V'(L_2^*)L_2^*+V(L_2^*)$ which is obviously satisfied when people consume the same land area in each region.

By imposing a tax on the immobile factor of land, this policy avoids distortions that occur from lump sum or income taxes. This simple model provides an example of the more general Henry George theorem (Arnott and Stiglitz, 1979). This theorem shows that financing public goods with a single tax on land, as Henry George famously argued, is efficient because it doesn't distort decisions to move to avoid high taxes. This result does not imply that a tax on property values is necessarily efficient if those values also include the value of structures put on the land. In that case, the tax will create a distortion that should produce too little construction.

Land use controls

In many countries, municipalities maintain an extraordinary amount of control over the development that is permitted within their borders. Within the US, the authority is often delegated to a zoning board which then adjudicates between developers, who want to build, and their neighborhood opponents. Local zoning boards are never the last word, however. Both the developer and the opponents of growth have the option of using the court system as well.

Perhaps the single most striking fact about land use restrictions in the US is the astonishing array of ways in which localities have made it difficult to build. Glaeser and Ward (2006) detail the different environmental, septic, and subdivision rules in greater Boston. There has been a steady increase in the number of local rules that go beyond the state's already significant regulations on new development. Glaeser and Ward (2006) follow Katz and Rosen (1987) and provide evidence suggesting that these rules do indeed reduce the amount of development and increase prices.

While it is certainly unsurprising that limits on development do indeed limit development and increase prices, the more important question is whether these regulations are welfare-enhancing or not. After all, there are real externalities associated with development that range from loss of sunlight on roads to the inconvenience of being around a construction site. Perhaps these regulations are an efficient means of countering these externalities.

To consider the welfare impact of zoning, I consider a two region model with a population of measure one. The core equations of this model and the notation are given in Table 6.17. At first, I will treat the second locale

Table 6.17. Model for the welfare impact of zoning

Actors	Society
They maximize	Total utility of all people = $N(V(N) - C) + (1 - N)\underline{U}$
They choose	N: The share of population in region 1
Key equations	The FOC is: $NV'(N) + V(N) - C - \underline{U} = 0$
Notation	$\underline{U}$: utility in the location 2 N: share of population in location 1 $V(N)$: utility from living in location 1, decreasing function of N C: cost of construction in region 1

as a reservation locale with no limits on new construction where people receive utility net of housing costs of $\underline{U}$. I will initially focus on the impact of limits on development in the first community. I let N denote the share of the population and housing that is located in the first community. To capture the presence of externalities, I assume that the flow of utility in the first community is $V(N)$ where $V'(N) < 0$.

Without any zoning, the cost of construction in the first community is C. In the absence of any land use restrictions, construction would continue in the first community until the point where $V(N) - C = \underline{U}$. The social optimum maximizes $N(V(N) - C) + (1 - N)\underline{U}$, which produces first order condition $NV'(N) + V(N) - C - \underline{U} = 0$, Since $V'(N) < 0$, the free development equilibrium has too much housing relative to the Pareto optimum. This creates a rationale for land use regulation.

Land use regulations can either be seen as a quantity restriction—reducing the number of units that can be built—or a tax on development. Treating land use regulations as a quantity restriction is surely closer to the letter of the laws. For example, minimum lot sizes do seem to directly reduce the total number of units that can be built. But treating land use regulation as a tax is in many cases closer to the reality of land use regulation. In the more expensive, generally coastal regions of the United States, almost any project needs to go through a costly approval process that can take years. In other areas, an expensive legal campaign can deliver a zoning variance for the developer. To me, that feels more like a tax than a quantity restriction.

I will first treat land use regulations as a quantity restriction, as in Glaeser, Gyourko and Saks (2005). The core equations of this model and the notation are given in Table 6.18. I assume that community one begins with N_0 homes. Through a political process, the community decides on the total number of added units that are going to be built, and that quantity is denoted Δ. The political process weighs the interests of current residents and the interests of the empty lot owners. Specifically,

Table 6.18. Model for land use regulations quantity restrictions

Actors	Town government
They maximize	Weighted sum of utilities: $\lambda N_0 V(N_0+\Delta)+(1-\lambda)\Delta\,(V(N_0+\Delta)-C-\underline{U})$
They choose	Δ: the number of new homes to be built
Key equations	The town's FOC: $\left(\frac{\lambda}{1-\lambda}N_0+\Delta\right)V'(N_0+\Delta)+V(N_0+\Delta)-C=\underline{U}$
Notation	$\underline{U}$ N_0: initial number of homes in community one Δ: number of new homes in community one to be built λ: weight on current resident's interests parameter C: cost of constructing a new region 1 home $V(N_0+\Delta)$: utility of a current resident $V(N_0+\Delta)-\underline{U}-C$: profits per new home

the quantity of new units is chosen to maximize λ times the utility of current residents plus $1-\lambda$ times the utility of empty lot owners.

I assume that current residents are living in their homes forever, so for them maximization involves maximizing their welfare, which is $V(N_0+\Delta)$. This is equivalent to maximizing their home values. The welfare of the owners of empty lots is the total revenues they receive from selling new homes. Each of these new homes will be sold for $V(N_0+\Delta)-\underline{U}$ and cost C to produce, so profits per home are $V(N_0+\Delta)-\underline{U}-C$. The total welfare of the owners of empty lots is just profits per home times the number of new homes built.

The town then chooses number of extra lots that can (and will) be developed to maximize $\lambda N_0 V(N_0+\Delta)+(1-\lambda)\Delta\,(V(N_0+\Delta)-C-\underline{U})$ which yields a first order condition of

$$\left(\frac{\lambda}{1-\lambda}N_0+\Delta\right)V'(N_0+\Delta)+V(N_0+\Delta)-C=\underline{U}. \tag{6.5}$$

If $\lambda=.5$ or $N_0=0$, the town's development decision will indeed yield the first best: $NV'(N)+V(N)-C=\underline{U}$. If the town starts empty, then it makes the right decisions because it is essentially just maximizing land value. One of the more general results in urban economics is that if cities are constructed by entrepreneurial developers, then those developers will internalize the externalities between neighbors in their development.

If $\lambda<.5$ and $N_0>0$, then there will be too many units, because the owners of empty lots ignore the interests of existing landowners. But there are good reasons to think that in communities that have a reasonable amount of development, $\lambda>.5$ is the case. Democratic processes empower voters more than owners of empty lots. In that case, there is too little development because the political process puts too much weight on the current owners relative to the interests of owners of vacant land.

If the vacant land was given to the homeowners, then the political process would again yield the efficient result. As such, another way to understand the reasons for too little development is that the developers of empty land are not fully compensating existing homeowners for the costs of their development. This can be understood as a breakdown in Coasian bargaining.

The model can also give us an empirical guide to figuring out whether the amount of land use regulation in an area is too high or too low. The socially optimal condition is: $NV'(N) + V(N) - C = \underline{U}$, which can be written:

$$\frac{\text{Price} - \text{Construction Cost}}{\text{Price}} = -\frac{\text{Density}}{\text{Price}}\frac{\partial\text{Price}}{\partial\text{Density}},$$

or the share of price that is markup over construction cost should be equal to the elasticity of price with respect to density. If the share of price markup over construction costs is higher than this elasticity, then there is too little home production relative to the social optimal. If share of price markup over construction cost is lower than this elasticity, then there is too little home production relative to the social optimum. Glaeser and Ward (2006) use this condition to suggest that land use regulations in Greater Boston have led to suboptimal levels of development.

I now slightly change the model and assume that the welfare flow in the first city is denoted $V_1(N)$ and the welfare flow in the second city is denoted $V_2(1 - N)$. The core equations of this model and the notation are given in Table 6.19. Construction costs are C in either city, so the social welfare maximizing level of development maximizes $NV_1(N) + (1 - N)V_2(1 - N)$ which yields a first order condition of $V_1(N) + NV'_1(N) = V_2(1 - N) + (1 - N)V'_2(1 - N)$.

The competitive equilibrium without any intervention sets $V_1(N) = V_2(1 - N)$, which is, of course, not necessarily Pareto optimal. If $V_i(\text{Size}) = V_0^i\text{Size}^{-\delta}$ where size equals N in area one and $1 - N$ in area two, then the competitive equilibrium is a Pareto optimum despite the presence of the externalities. If $V_i(\text{Size}) = V_0^i - V_1^i\text{Size}$, then in the Pareto optimum,

$$N = \frac{.5(V_0^1 - V_0^2) + V_1^2}{V_1^1 + V_1^2}.$$

Table 6.19. Model for land use regulations taxes

Actors	Benevolent government
They maximize	Sum of utilities: $NV_1(N) + (1 - N)V_2(1 - N)$
They choose	Taxes
Key equations	The government's original FOC: $V_1(N) + NV_1'(N) = V_2(1 - N) + (1 - N)V_2'(1 - N)$ The competitive equilibrium: $V_1(N) = V_2(1 - N)$
Notation	$V_1(N)$: welfare in the first city $V_2(1 - N)$: welfare in the city C: construction cost in both cities $V_i(\text{Size}) = V_0^i \text{Size}^{-\delta}$: one functional form for V $V_i(\text{Size}) = V_0^i - V_1^i \text{Size}$: a second functional form for V $V_i(\text{Size}) = V_0^i - \upsilon\text{Size}$: final functional form for V

In the competitive equilibrium,

$$N = \frac{V_0^1 - V_0^2 + V_1^2}{V_1^1 + V_1^2}.$$

The externalities lead to overbuilding in region one if and only if $V_0^1 > V_0^2$. The presence of externalities or even externalities that differ between regions is not enough to imply that the competitive equilibrium is inefficient. A distortion occurs if externalities are combined with differences in the intercept of demand.

What policies can deliver the Pareto optimum? Any tax policies that impose an incremental cost of $NV_1^1 - (1 - N)V_1^2$ for living in the first area will lead to the first best outcome. This can be done if each jurisdiction charges a tax of V_1^i times its population on every new development. A Pareto optimum can also come about if the first region imposes a tax (or subsidy) of $NV_1^1 - (1 - N)V_1^2$ on each new development and the second region does nothing.

Of course, a Pareto optimum does not come about if the second region does nothing and the first region imposes a tax of NV_1^1. A unilateral tax equal to the full extent of the externality does not work if the other district is not imposing a tax of its own. Moreover, we cannot judge whether a community is imposing the right tax by looking solely at the social costs of building in that community. The right tax can only be judged by comparing the tax on and social costs of development in a community with the tax on and social costs of development in the other communities that will absorb the blocked development.

The economic approach to urban development insists that turning off construction in one place means that more construction will appear someplace else. For that reason, the "think globally, act locally" slogan looks particularly foolish. If the opponents of growth consider only the adverse effects on their own community, then it is quite possible that imposing limits on development may actually make things worse.

To see this, I will assume that $V_i(\text{Size}) = V_0^i - v\text{Size}$ where v is the common extent to which more population causes a depreciation in quality of life. My goal is to compare the social surplus when there are no land use controls with the case where the first community imposes the full Pigouvian tax of vN and the second community does nothing. In the competitive equilibrium without any regulation, consumer surplus (i.e. the utility of an individual consumer) is $\frac{1}{2}(V_0^1 + V_0^2 - v)$. Note that this value is the same in both regions, as the spatial equilibrium condition requires.

If a full Pigouvian tax is imposed only in the first community then

$$N = 1/3 + \frac{V_0^1 - V_0^2}{3v}.$$

If the tax is not returned then individual welfare (i.e. utility) in either community would be $\frac{1}{3}(V_0^1 + 2V_0^2 - 2v)$. Total tax revenues are $\left(V_0^1 - V_0^2 + v\right)^2/9v$, which are then returned on a per capita basis, so total social welfare (i.e. the utility of a consumer in either region) is then

$$\frac{5V_0^1 + 4V_0^2 - 5v}{9} + \frac{(V_0^1 - V_0^2)^2}{9v}.$$

This quantity is higher than the social surplus in the unregulated case if and only if $2\left(V_0^1 - V_0^2\right)^2 > v\left(V_0^2 - V_0^1 + v\right)$. When the difference between the two intercepts is large, then this unilateral tax policy can improve matters. If on the other hand, the difference is small, then the unilateral tax will do more harm than good. Higher values of v, which mean stronger externalities, actually make the tax less likely to be helpful.

It is fitting that I end the book with this example because it helps to illustrate the power of the spatial equilibrium approach to urban policy. If an analyst just tried to use standard, non-spatial approaches to the externalities of development, that analyst might be tempted to suggest imposing a tax equal to the externality on the community created by the development. However, that non-spatial approach ignores the fact that there is a spatial linkage where stopping development in one place increases development somewhere else.

The mobility of people across space means that a seemingly sensible policy of imposing a tax on development equal to its external effects can reduce welfare by moving development somewhere else. Good policy needs to pay attention to all of the spatial connections and take them into account. We must both think and act globally. The spatial equilibrium approach gives us both insights into explaining the world and a guide towards government policy.

Appendix: Proofs of propositions

Proof of Proposition 1: If $\alpha \geq 0$, then the lowest amenity lot that is developed at time zero has a location specific amenity value of $a = m + \rho C - \theta(0)$ and the lowest amenity lot developed at time t has a location specific amenity value of $a = m + \rho C - \theta(t) = m + \rho C - \theta(0) - \alpha t$. Using Approximation 1, this implies that the growth rate of the city equals $f_{\min} \alpha t$.

If $\alpha < 0$, then no new lots will be developed. The least attractive lot, characterized by $a = \underline{a}$ that has been developed satisfies $\rho(\lambda - \rho C) = -\alpha\left(1 - e^{\rho\lambda/\alpha}\right)$ or $\rho(\theta(0) + \underline{a} - m - \rho C) = -\alpha\left(1 - e^{\rho(\theta(0+\underline{a}-m))/\alpha}\right)$. As long as $\underline{a} + \theta(t) > m$ or or $\lambda(\alpha) + \alpha t > 0$, the lot will remain occupied. Let $\tilde{\alpha}$ solve $\lambda(\tilde{\alpha}) + \tilde{\alpha} t = 0$, which has the unique solution

$$\tilde{\alpha} = \frac{-\rho^2 C}{\rho t + e^{-\rho t} - 1} < 0.$$

As the derivative of $\lambda(\alpha) + \alpha t > 0$ with respect to α equals

$$t + \frac{\lambda\left(e^{\rho\lambda/\alpha} - 1\right) + \rho C}{\rho\left(\lambda - \rho C\right)}$$

(which is always positive), for all cities with values of α above $\tilde{\alpha}$, $\lambda(\alpha) + \alpha t > 0$ and no units will be left unoccupied.

For all cities with values of α below $\tilde{\alpha}$, $\lambda(\alpha) + \alpha t < 0$ and $\underline{a} + \theta(0) + \alpha t < m$, so some lots will be left unoccupied. The number of lots left unoccupied will equal $N(F(m - \theta(0) - \alpha t) - F(\underline{a}))$ or $N(F(\underline{a} + \lambda - \alpha t) - F(\underline{a}))$, and using Approximation 1, this implies that the rate of decline will be $f_{\min}(\alpha t + \lambda)$.

Proof of Proposition 2: (a) We let $\alpha = \hat{\alpha} + \varepsilon$ and use $g(\varepsilon)$ to reflect the density of ε, which is mean zero and symmetrically distributed. The median growth rate will equal $f_{\min} \hat{\alpha} t$. The mean growth rate averaging over cities equals:

$$f_{\min}\left(\hat{\alpha} t - \int_{\varepsilon = -\hat{\alpha}(-\rho^2 C)/(\rho t + e^{-\rho t} - 1)}^{-\hat{\alpha}} (\hat{\alpha} + \varepsilon) t g(\varepsilon)\, d\varepsilon + \int_{\varepsilon = -\infty}^{-\hat{\alpha}(-\rho^2 C)/(\rho t + e^{-\rho t} - 1)} \lambda g(\varepsilon)\, d\varepsilon\right), \tag{A1}$$

which is obviously less than $f_{\min}\, \hat{\alpha} dt$. The difference between the mean and the median equals

$$f_{\min} \times \left(- \int_{\varepsilon = -\hat{\alpha}(-\rho^2 C)/(\rho t + e^{-\rho t} - 1)}^{-\hat{\alpha}} (\hat{\alpha} + \varepsilon) t g(\varepsilon)\, d\varepsilon + \int_{\varepsilon = -\infty}^{-\hat{\alpha}(-\rho^2 C)/(\rho t + e^{-\rho t} - 1)} \lambda g(\varepsilon)\, d\varepsilon\right)$$

and the derivative of this with respect to $\hat{a} = -\left(\int_{\varepsilon=-\hat{a}(-\rho^2C)/(\rho t+e^{-\rho t}-1)}^{-\hat{a}} tg(\varepsilon)d\varepsilon\right)$, which is negative.

(b) The expected growth rate for a city with characteristic z is:

$$f_{\min}\left((a_0+\beta z)t - \int_{\varepsilon=-a_0-\beta z-(-\rho^2C)/(\rho t+e^{-\rho t}-1)}^{-a_0-\beta z}(a_0+\beta z+\varepsilon)tg(\varepsilon)\,d\varepsilon + \int_{\varepsilon=-\infty}^{-a_0-\beta z-(-\rho^2C)/(\rho t+e^{-\rho t}-1)}\lambda g(\varepsilon)\,d\varepsilon\right). \tag{A1'}$$

The derivative of this growth rate with respect to z is

$$f_{\min}\beta t\left(1-\int_{\varepsilon=-a_0-\beta z-(\rho^2C)/(\rho t+e^{-\rho t}-1)}^{-a_0-\beta z} g(\varepsilon)\,d\varepsilon\right).$$

The difference in this derivative between when $a_0+\beta z=k$ and when $a_0+\beta z=-k$ if $k>0$ equals

$$f_{\min}\beta dt\left(\int_{\varepsilon=k-\rho^2C/(\rho dt+e^{-\rho dt}-1)}^{k} g(\varepsilon)\,d\varepsilon - \int_{\varepsilon=-k-\rho^2C/(\rho dt+e^{-\rho dt}-1)}^{-k} g(\varepsilon)\,d\varepsilon\right),$$

which by the symmetry of ε equals

$$f_{\min}\beta dt\left(\int_{\varepsilon=k-\rho^2C/(\rho dt+e^{-\rho dt}-1)}^{k} g(\varepsilon)\,d\varepsilon - \int_{\varepsilon=+k}^{k+\rho^2C/(\rho dt+e^{-\rho dt}-1)} g(\varepsilon)\,d\varepsilon\right).$$

This term is strictly positive by the fact that g(.) is single peaked.

Proof of Proposition 3: If the city is growing, then the growth rate for any time period of length τ equals $f_{\min}\tau$. If the city has lost population between time zero and time τ, the overall growth during that period must equal $f_{\min}(\lambda+a_\tau)$. Once a city begins to lose population, the future decline rate will be $f_{\min}a_\tau$, so that future decline will equal $a_\tau/(\lambda+a_\tau)$ times past decline.

Proof of Proposition 4(*a*): All cities for which is positive will have a value of S equal to zero. Thus, if $S=0$, the expected growth rate equals $f_{\min}tE(a\,|\,a>0)$, where $E(a\,|\,a>0)$ denotes the expectation of a conditional upon a being positive.

When S is greater than zero but less than $f_{\min}\tau\rho^2C/(\rho t+e^{-\rho t}-1)$, S will equal $-a_\tau$ and there will be no population change between time τ and time t. As $E(a\,|\,a>0)$ is a positive number, there must be a jump down in the expected growth rate as S rises above zero. There will be no relationship between S and later decline during this range.

When S is greater than $f_{\min}\tau\rho^2C/(\rho t+e^{-\rho t}-1)$, but less than $f_{\min}\tau\rho^2C/(\rho\tau+e^{-\rho\tau}-1)$, then the expected growth rate equals $-S(t-t^*)/\tau$. Differenting finds that

$$\frac{\partial \text{Growth}}{\partial S} = -\frac{t - t^*}{\tau} + \frac{S}{\tau}\frac{\partial t^*}{\partial S},$$

where t^* is defined by

$$\frac{\rho C}{\alpha} = \frac{1 - e^{-\rho t^*}}{\rho} - t^*,$$

which implies

$$\frac{\partial t^*}{\partial \alpha} = \frac{\rho C\left(1 - e^{-\rho t^*}\right)}{\alpha^2} \quad \text{or} \quad \frac{\partial t^*}{\partial S} = -\frac{\rho C\left(1 - e^{-\rho t^*}\right)}{\alpha^2 \tau f_{\min}}.$$

Thus,

$$\frac{\partial \text{Growth}}{\partial S} = -\frac{t - t^*}{\tau} - \frac{\left(1 - e^{-\rho t^*}\right)}{\tau}\left(\frac{\rho C}{-\alpha}\right),$$

which is negative.

When S is greater than $f_{\min}\tau\rho^2 C/(\rho\tau + e^{-\rho\tau} - 1)$, the expected growth rate equals $f_{\min}\alpha t$ so the impact of S on growth will equals $f_{\min}t\partial\alpha/\partial S$. The value of S equals $f_{\min}\lambda\left(\alpha\left(S\right)\right)$, so

$$f_{\min}\frac{\partial \alpha}{\partial S} = \frac{1}{\frac{\partial \lambda}{\partial \alpha}} \quad \text{or} \quad \frac{\alpha\left(1 - e^{\rho\lambda/\alpha}\right)}{\lambda - \rho C + \lambda e^{\rho\lambda/\alpha}},$$

which is always negative.

Proof of Proposition 4(*b*): The value of S equals $f_{\min}\max\left(\bar{\theta}(\tau) - \theta(\tau), \lambda\right)$. Using the notation that $\bar{\theta}(t)$ is the highest value that θ has reached as of time t, we know that if both $\bar{\theta}(t) - \theta(t) > \lambda$ and $\bar{\theta}(\tau) - \theta(\tau) > \lambda$, the growth rate between time zero and time t equals $f_{\min}\left(\theta(t) - \theta(\tau)\right)$. Alternatively, if $\bar{\theta}(t) - \theta(t) < \lambda$ and $\bar{\theta}(\tau) - \theta(\tau) < \lambda$, then urban development is determined by $f_{\min}\left(\bar{\theta}(t) - \bar{\theta}(\tau)\right)$. In the case where $\bar{\theta}(\tau) - \theta(\tau) > \lambda$ and $\bar{\theta}(t) - \theta(t) < \lambda$ (which requires $\theta(t) > \theta(\tau)$), then the level of growth equals $f_{\min}\left(\bar{\theta}(t) - \lambda - \theta(\tau)\right)$. Finally, when $\bar{\theta}(t) - \theta(t) > \lambda$ and $\bar{\theta}(\tau) - \theta(\tau) < \lambda$, the level of growth equals $f_{\min}\left(\theta(t) + \lambda - \bar{\theta}(\tau)\right)$.

We now define a new variable $\tilde{\theta}(t)$, which equals the maximal value that $\theta(t)$ takes on between time τ and time t. The distribution of $\tilde{\theta}(t)$ and $\theta(t)$ depend only on $\theta(\tau)$, not on $\bar{\theta}(\tau)$. The density of $\theta(t)$ conditional upon $\theta(\tau)$ is

$$\frac{1}{\sigma\sqrt{2\pi}}e^{-(\theta(t)-\theta(\tau))^2/2\sigma^2(t-\tau)}.$$

The density of $\tilde{\theta}(t)$ conditional on both $\theta(\tau)$ and $\theta(t)$ is

$$\frac{(4\tilde{\theta}(t) - 2\theta(t) - 2\theta(\tau))}{\sigma^2(t-\tau)}e^{-2\left(\tilde{\theta}(t)-\theta(\tau)\right)\left(\tilde{\theta}(t)-\theta(t)\right)/\sigma^2(t-\tau)},$$

and the cumulative distribution is $1 - e^{-2(\bar{\theta}(t)-\theta(\tau))(\bar{\theta}(t)-\theta(t))/\sigma^2(t-\tau)}$ (following Harrison, 1988, p. 8). Then $\bar{\theta}(t) = \max\left(\bar{\theta}(\tau), \tilde{\theta}(t)\right)$.

If $\bar{\theta}(\tau) - \theta(\tau) < \lambda$, then using the fact that $\bar{\theta}(\tau) = \theta(\tau) + S/f_{\min}$, the expected growth rate of the city equals $f_{\min}$ times

$$\int_{\theta(t)=\theta(\tau)+(S/f_{\min})-\lambda}^{\infty} \begin{pmatrix} (\theta(t)+\lambda-\theta(\tau)-S/f_{\min})\, e^{-2\lambda(\theta(t)+\lambda-\theta(\tau))/\sigma^2(t-\tau)} \\ + \displaystyle\int_{\tilde{\theta}(t)=\max(\theta(\tau)+S/f_{\min},\theta(t))}^{\theta(t)+\lambda} \left(\tilde{\theta}(t)-\bar{\theta}(\tau)\right) \frac{\left(4\tilde{\theta}(t)-2\theta(t)-2\theta(\tau)\right)}{\sigma^2(t-\tau)} e^{-2\left(\tilde{\theta}(t)-\theta(t)\right)\left(\tilde{\theta}(t)-\theta(\tau)\right)/\sigma^2(t-\tau)} d\tilde{\theta}(t) \end{pmatrix}$$
$$\times \frac{e^{-(\theta(t)-\theta(\tau))^2/2\sigma^2(t-\tau)}}{\sigma\sqrt{2\pi}} d\theta(t) + \int_{\theta(t)=-\infty}^{\theta(\tau)+(S/f_{\min})-\lambda} (\theta(t)+\lambda-\theta(\tau)-S/f_{\min}) \frac{e^{-(\theta(t)-\theta(\tau))^2/2\sigma^2(t-\tau)}}{\sigma\sqrt{2\pi}} d\theta(t).$$

The derivative of this with respect to S equals

$$-\int_{\theta(t)=\theta(\tau)+(S/f_{\min})-\lambda}^{\infty} \begin{pmatrix} e^{-2\lambda(\theta(t)+\lambda-\theta(\tau))/\sigma^2(t-\tau)} + \displaystyle\int_{\tilde{\theta}(t)=\max(\theta(\tau)+S/f_{\min},\theta(t))}^{\theta(t)+\lambda} \frac{\left(4\tilde{\theta}(t)-2\theta(t)-2\theta(\tau)\right)}{\sigma^2(t-\tau)} \\ \times e^{-2\left(\tilde{\theta}(t)-\theta(t)\right)\left(\tilde{\theta}(t)-\theta(\tau)\right)/\sigma^2(t-\tau)} d\tilde{\theta}(t) \end{pmatrix}$$
$$\times \frac{e^{-(\theta(t)-\theta(\tau))^2/2\sigma^2(t-\tau)}}{\sigma\sqrt{2\pi}} d\theta(t) - \int_{\theta(t)=-\infty}^{\theta(\tau)+(S/f_{\min})-\lambda} \frac{e^{-(\theta(t)-\theta(\tau))^2/2\sigma^2(t-\tau)}}{\sigma\sqrt{2\pi}} d\theta(t).$$

This is always negative. However, if $\bar{\theta}(\tau) - \theta(\tau) > \lambda$, then the expected growth rate of the city equals $f_{\min}$ times

$$\int_{\theta(t)=\bar{\theta}(\tau)}^{\infty} \begin{pmatrix} (\theta(t)-\theta(\tau))\, e^{-2\lambda(\lambda+\theta(t)-\theta(\tau))/\sigma^2(t-\tau)} \\ \displaystyle\int_{\tilde{\theta}(t)=\theta(t)}^{\theta(t)+\lambda} \left(\tilde{\theta}(t)-\theta(\tau)-\lambda\right) \frac{\left(4\tilde{\theta}(t)-2\theta(t)-2\theta(\tau)\right)}{\sigma^2(t-\tau)} e^{-2\left(\tilde{\theta}(t)-\theta(t)\right)\left(\tilde{\theta}(t)-\theta(\tau)\right)/\sigma^2(t-\tau)} d\tilde{\theta}(t) \end{pmatrix}$$
$$\times \frac{e^{-(\theta(t)-\theta(\tau))^2/2\sigma^2(t-\tau)}}{\sigma\sqrt{2\pi}} + \int_{\theta(t)=\bar{\theta}(\tau)-\lambda}^{\bar{\theta}(\tau)} \int_{\tilde{\theta}(t)=\theta(t)}^{\theta(t)+\lambda} \begin{pmatrix} \left(\min\left(\theta(t), \max\left(\tilde{\theta}(t), \bar{\theta}(\tau)\right)-\lambda\right)\right) \\ \times \dfrac{\left(4\tilde{\theta}(t)-2\theta(t)-2\theta(\tau)\right)}{\sigma^2(t-\tau)} \end{pmatrix} e^{-2\left(\tilde{\theta}(t)-\theta(t)\right)\left(\tilde{\theta}(t)-\theta(\tau)\right)/\sigma^2(t-\tau)}$$
$$\times \frac{e^{-(\theta(t)-\theta(\tau))^2/2\sigma^2(t-\tau)}}{\sigma\sqrt{2\pi}} d\tilde{\theta}(t)\, d\theta(t) + \int_{\theta(t)=-\infty}^{\bar{\theta}(\tau)-\lambda} (\theta(t)-\theta(\tau)) \frac{e^{-(\theta(t)-\theta(\tau))^2/2\sigma^2(t-\tau)}}{\sigma\sqrt{2\pi}} d\theta(t).$$

The derivative of this with respect to $\bar{\theta}(\tau)$ equals

$$\left(\bar{\theta}(\tau)-\lambda-\theta(\tau)\right) \int_{\tilde{\theta}(t)=\bar{\theta}(\tau)-\lambda}^{\infty} \left(\frac{\left(4\tilde{\theta}(t)-2\left(\bar{\theta}(\tau)-\lambda\right)-2\theta(\tau)\right)}{\sigma^2(t-\tau)}\right) e^{-2\left(\tilde{\theta}(t)-\left(\bar{\theta}(\tau)-\lambda\right)\right)\left(\tilde{\theta}(t)-\theta(\tau)\right)/\sigma^2(t-\tau)} d\tilde{\theta}(t)$$
$$\times \frac{e^{-\left(\bar{\theta}(\tau)-\lambda-\theta(\tau)\right)^2/2\sigma^2(t-\tau)}}{\sigma\sqrt{2\pi}} + \int_{\theta(t)=\bar{\theta}(\tau)-\lambda}^{\bar{\theta}(\tau)} \int_{\tilde{\theta}(t)=\theta(t)}^{\bar{\theta}(\tau)} \frac{\left(4\tilde{\theta}(t)-2\theta(t)-2\theta(\tau)\right)}{\sigma^2(t-\tau)} e^{-2\left(\tilde{\theta}(t)-\theta(t)\right)\left(\tilde{\theta}(t)-\theta(\tau)\right)/\sigma^2(t-\tau)}$$
$$\times \frac{e^{-(\theta(t)-\theta(\tau))^2/2\sigma^2(t-\tau)}}{\sigma\sqrt{2\pi}} d\tilde{\theta}(t)\, d\theta(t) + \left(\bar{\theta}(\tau)-\lambda-\theta(\tau)\right) \frac{e^{-(\theta(t)-\lambda-\theta(\tau))^2/2\sigma^2(t-\tau)}}{\sigma\sqrt{2\pi}}$$

which is positive. Thus, the expected growth rate rises with $\bar{\theta}(\tau)$ when $S = f_{\min}\lambda$, so that the expected growth rate jumps discontinuously from the point where S rises from less than $f_{\min}\lambda$ to the point where $S = f_{\min}\lambda$.

Proof of Proposition 5: (A) The expected growth in mean rents for a city with exogenous characteristic z equals $\alpha t(1 - f(a^*)/2f(a_{\text{med}}))$ when $\alpha > 0$, αt when $0 > \alpha > -\rho^2 C/(\rho t + e^{-\rho t} - 1)$, and

$$\alpha t\left(1 - \frac{f(a^*)}{2f(a_{\text{med}})}\right) - \lambda\frac{f(a^*)}{2f(a_{med})} \qquad \text{when} \qquad \frac{-\rho^2 C}{\rho t + e^{-\rho t} - 1} > \alpha.$$

Thus, if $\alpha = \alpha_0 + \beta z + \varepsilon$, then the expected change in rents for a city with characteristic z equals:

$$(\alpha_0 + \beta z)\, t\left(1 - \frac{f(a^*)}{2f(a_{\text{med}})}\right) - \frac{\lambda f(a^*)}{2\rho f(a_{\text{med}})} G\left(-\alpha_0 - \beta z - \frac{\rho^2 C}{\rho t + e^{-\rho t} - 1}\right)$$
$$+ \int_{\varepsilon = -\alpha_0 - \beta z - \rho^2 C/\rho t + e^{-dt} - 1}^{-\alpha_0 - \beta z} (\alpha_0 + \beta z + \varepsilon)\frac{f(a^*)}{2f(a_{\text{med}})} g(\varepsilon)\, d\varepsilon,$$

and the derivative of this with respect to z equals:

$$\beta t\left(1 - \frac{f(a^*)}{2f(a_{\text{med}})}\left(1 - G(-\alpha_0 - \beta z) + G\left(-\alpha_0 - \beta z - \frac{\rho^2 C}{\rho t + e^{-\rho t} - 1}\right)\right)\right).$$

The difference in this component if $\alpha_0 + \beta z = k$ and when $\alpha_0 + \beta z = -k$, if $k > 0$, using the symmetry of ε equals

$$\frac{\beta t}{\rho}\frac{f(a^*)}{2f(a_{\text{med}})}\left(\left(G\left(k + \frac{\rho^2 C}{\rho t + e^{-\rho t} - 1}\right) - G(k)\right) - \left(G(k) - G\left(k - \frac{\rho^2 C}{\rho t + e^{-\rho t} - 1}\right)\right)\right),$$

which is always negative since $G(.)$ is single peaked.

(B) If $\alpha = \alpha_0 + \beta z + \varepsilon$, the derivative of the growth rate of housing prices with respect to z equals

$$\frac{\beta t}{\rho}\left(1 - \frac{f(a^*)}{2f(a^{\text{med}})}\right)$$

when $\alpha > 0$. The growth in housing prices equals

$$\frac{\alpha}{\rho}\left(t - \frac{e^{\frac{\rho}{\alpha}(\theta + a_{\text{med}}(0) - m)}(e^{\rho t} - 1)}{\rho}\right)$$

when $0 > \alpha > -\rho^2 C/(\rho t + e^{-\rho t} - 1)$, and if $\alpha = \alpha_0 + \beta z$, then the derivative of this expression with respect to z equals

$$\frac{\beta t}{\rho} - \frac{\beta(e^{\rho t} - 1)}{\rho^2}\left(e^{\frac{\rho}{\alpha}(\theta + a_{\text{med}}(0) - m)} - \frac{(\theta + a_{\text{med}}(0) - m)}{\alpha} e^{\frac{\rho}{\alpha}(\theta + a_{\text{med}}(0) - m)}\right).$$

As α approaches zero, $(\theta + a_{\text{med}}(0) - m)/\alpha$ approaches negative infinity and therefore the first term in parentheses goes to zero. The limit of the second term equals the limit as x goes to infinity of $xe^{-\rho x}$ which is also zero. Thus the limit of the change in prices as α approaches zero equals $\beta t/\rho$.

(C) If $\alpha = 0$, the city has no population or price change. For a growing city, the change in price equals

$$\frac{\alpha t}{\rho}\left(1 - \frac{f(a^*)}{2 f(a^{\text{med}})}\right)$$

and the change in population equals $f_{\min}\alpha t$, thus the change in price equals

$$\frac{1}{\rho f_{\min}}\left(1 - \frac{f(a^*)}{2 f(a^{\text{med}})}\right)$$

times the percentage growth of the cities, and the slope of any positive line will equal this quantity. For cities with values of α that are between zero and $-\rho^2 C/(\rho t + e^{-\rho t} - 1)$, the change in population will be zero and the change in price will be negative. For cities will levels of α below $-\rho^2 C/(\rho t + e^{-\rho t} - 1)$, the change in median housing prices between time zero and time t is

$$\frac{(\lambda + \alpha t)}{\rho}\left(1 - \frac{f(a^*)}{2 f(a_{\text{med}})}\right) - \frac{\lambda}{\rho} - \frac{\alpha}{\rho^2}\left(e^{\frac{\rho}{\alpha}(\theta + a_{\text{med}}(t) - m)} - e^{\frac{\rho}{\alpha}(\theta + a_{\text{med}}(0) - m)}\right)$$

and the change in population equals $(\lambda + \alpha t)\, f_{\min}$. Thus, we need to show that

$$\lambda > \frac{-\alpha}{\rho}\left(e^{\frac{\rho}{\alpha}(\theta + a_{\text{med}}(t) - m)} - e^{\frac{\rho}{\alpha}(\theta + a_{\text{med}}(0) - m)}\right).$$

Using the fact that

$$\lambda = \rho C - \frac{\alpha}{\rho}\left(1 - e^{\frac{\rho\lambda}{\alpha}}\right),$$

the inequality follows because $1 - e^{\rho\lambda/\alpha}$ is greater than $e^{\frac{\rho}{\alpha}(a_{\text{med}}(0) - a^*(0))}$ $\left(e^{\frac{\rho}{\alpha}(\lambda + a_{\text{med}}(t) - a_{\text{med}}(0))} - e^{\frac{\rho\lambda}{\alpha}}\right)$.

References

Acemoglu, Daron and Joshua Angrist (1999). "How Large are the Social Returns to Education? Evidence from Compulsory Attendance Laws," *NBER Working Paper #7444*.

Ades, Alberto and Edward Glaeser (1995). "Trade and Circuses: Explaining Urban Giants," *Quarterly Journal of Economics*, 110(1): 195–227.

Alonso, William (1964). *Location and Land Use*. Cambridge, MA: Harvard University Press.

Anas, Alex, Richard Arnott and Kenneth A. Small (1998). "Urban Spatial Structure," *Journal of Economic Literature*, 36(3): 1426–1464.

Arnott, Richard and Joseph E. Stiglitz (1979). "Aggregate Land Rents, Expenditure on Public Goods, and Optimal City Size," *Quarterly Journal of Economics*, 93(4): 471–500.

Audretsch, David B. and Maryann P. Feldman (1996). "R&D Spillovers and the Geography of Innovation and Production," *American Economic Review*, 86(3): 630–640.

Bacolod, Marigee, Bernardo Blum and William C. Strange (2007). "Skills and the City," working paper.

Barro, Robert J. (1991). "Economic Growth in a Cross Section of Countries," *Quarterly Journal of Economics*, 106(2): 407–443.

Baum-Snow, Nathaniel (2007). "Did Highways Cause Suburbanization?," *Quarterly Journal of Economics*, 122(2): 775–805.

Becker, Gary S. (1965). "A Theory of the Allocation of Time," *Economic Journal*, 75(299): 493–517

Becker, Gary S. (1968). "Crime and Punishment: An Economic Approach," *Journal of Political Economy*, 76(2): 169–217.

Becker, Gary S. (1957). *The Economics of Discrimination*. Chicago: University of Chicago Press.

Becker, Gary S. and Kevin M. Murphy (1992). "The Division of Labor, Coordination Costs, and Knowledge," *Quarterly Journal of Economics*, 107(4): 1137–1160.

Benabou, Roland (1993). "Workings of a City: Location, Education, and Production," *Quarterly Journal of Economics*, 108(3): 619–652.

Berry, Christopher and Edward Glaeser (2005). "The Divergence of Human Capital Levels Across Metropolitan Areas," *Papers in Regional Science*, 84(3): 407–444.

Bewley, Truman (1981). "A Critique of Tiebout's Theory of Local Public Expenditures," *Econometrica*, 49(3): 713–740.

References

Black, Sandra E. (1999). "Do Better Schools Matter? Parental Evaluation of Elementary Education," *Quarterly Journal of Economics*, 114: 577–599.

Bond, Eric and Edward Coulson (1989). "Externalities, Filtering, and Neighborhood Change," *Journal of Urban Economics*, 26(2): 231–249.

Brueckner, Jan (1987). "The Structure of Urban Equilibria: A Unified Treatment of the Muth-Mills Model," in Edwin W. Mills (ed.), *Handbook of Regional and Urban Economics, Volume II*, Amsterdam: Elsevier, 821–845.

Brueckner, Jan (2000). "Urban Growth Models with Durable Housing: An Overview," in Jean-Marie Huriot and Jacques-Francois Thisse (eds.), *Economics of Cities*, Cambridge: Cambridge University Press, 263–289.

Carlton, Dennis W. (1983). "The Location and Employment Choices of New Firms: An Econometric Model with Discrete and Continuous Endogenous Variables," *Review of Economics and Statistics*, 65(3): 440–449.

Case, Anne and Lawrence Katz (1991). "The Company You Keep: The Effect of Family and Neighborhood on Disadvantaged Youth," *NBER Working Paper #3705*.

Ciccone, Antonio and Robert E. Hall (1996). "Productivity and the Density of Economic Activity," *American Economic Review*, (86)1: 54–70.

Conrad, Alfred and John Meyer (1958). "The Economics of Slavery in the Ante-Bellum South," *Journal of Political Economy*, 66(1): 95–130.

Costa, Dora and Matthew Kahn (2000). "Power Couples: Changes in the Locational Choice of the College Educated: 1940–1990," *Quarterly Journal of Economics*, 115(4): 1287–1315.

Cutler, David and Edward Glaeser (1997). "Are Ghettos Good or Bad?," *Quarterly Journal of Economics*, 112(3): 827–872.

Cutler, David, Edward Glaeser and Jacob Vigdor (2008). "Is the Melting Pot Still Hot? Explaining the Resurgence of Immigrant Segregation," *Review of Economics and Statistics*, 90(2) (forthcoming).

Cutler, David, Edward Glaeser and Jacob Vigdor (1999). "The Rise and Decline of the American Ghetto," *Journal of Political Economy*, 107(3): 455–506.

Davis, Donald and David Weinstein (2002). "Bones, Bombs and Break Points: The Geography of Economic Activity," *American Economic Review*, 92(5): 1269–1289.

DiPasquale, Denise and Edward Glaeser (1998). "The L.A. Riot and the Economics of Urban Unrest," *Journal of Urban Economics*, 43(1): 52–78.

Dixit, Avinash and Robert Pindyck (1994). *Investment Under Uncertainty*. Princeton, NJ: Princeton University Press.

DuBois, W.E.B. (1899). *The Philadelphia Negro: A Social Study*. Philadelphia: University of Pennsylvania, 1996.

Dumais, Guy, Glenn Ellison and Edward Glaeser (1997). "Geographic Concentration as a Dynamic Process," *NBER Working Paper #6270*.

Duranton, Gilles and Diego Puga (2005). "From Sectoral to Functional Urban Specialization," *Journal of Urban Economics*, 57(2): 343–370.

Eaton, Jonathan and Zvi Eckstein (1997). "Cities and Growth: Theory and Evidence from France and Japan," *Regional Science and Urban Economics*, 27(4–5): 443–474.

Echenique, Federico and Roland G. Fryer Jr. (2007). "A Measure of Segregation Based on Social Interactions," *Quarterly Journal of Economics*, 122(2): 441–485.

Ellison, Glenn and Edward Glaeser (1997). "Geographic Concentration in US Manufacturing Industries: A Dartboard Approach," *Journal of Political Economy*, 105(5): 889–927.

Ellison, Glenn and Edward Glaeser (1999). "The Geographic Concentration of Industry: Does Natural Advantage Explain Agglomeration?," *American Economic Review*, 89(2): 311–316.

Ellison, Glenn, Edward Glaeser and William Kerr (2007). "What Causes Industry Agglomeration? Evidence from Coagglomeration Patterns," *NBER Working Paper #13068*.

Ellwood, David T. (1986). "The Spatial Mismatch Hypothesis: Are There Teenage Jobs Missing in the Ghetto?," in Richard B. Freeman and Harry Holzer (eds.), *The Black Youth Employment Crisis*, Chicago: University of Chicago Press, 147–185.

Farley, Reynolds and William H. Frey (1994). "Changes in the Segregation of Whites from Blacks During the 1980s: Small Steps Toward a Racially Integrated Society," *American Sociological Review*, 59(1): 23–45.

Forman, Chris, Avi Goldfarb and Shane Greenstein (2003). "How Did Location Affect Adoption of the Commercial Internet? Global Village, Urban Density, and Industry Composition," *NBER Working Paper #9979*.

Fuchs, Victor R. (1957). *The Economics of the Fur Industry*. New York: Columbia University Press.

Fujita, Masahisa, Paul Krugman and Anthony Venables (2001). *The Spatial Economy*. Cambridge: MIT Press.

Fujita, Masahisa and Hideaki Ogawa (1982). "Multiple Equilibria and Structural Transition of Non-Monocentric Urban Configurations," *Regional Science and Urban Economics*, 12(2): 161–196.

Fuchs, Victor R. (1957). *The Economics of the Fur Industry*. New York: Columbia University Press.

Gaspar, Jess and Edward Glaeser (1998). "Information Technology and the Future of Cities," *Journal of Urban Economics*, 43(1): 136–156.

Giuliano, Genevieve and Kenneth A. Small (1991). "Subcenters in the Los Angeles Region," *Regional Science and Urban Economics*, 21(2): 163–182.

Glaeser, Edward (1994). "Cities, Information and Economic Growth," *Cityscape*, 1(1): 9–47.

Glaeser, Edward (1999). "Learning in Cities," *Journal of Urban Economics*, 46(2): 254–277.

Glaeser, Edward (1998). "Should Transfer Payments be Indexed to Local Price Levels?," *Regional Science and Urban Economics*, 28(1): 1–20.

Glaeser, Edward (2005). "The Political Economy of Hatred," *Quarterly Journal of Economics*, 120(1): 45–86.

Glaeser, Edward and Joshua D. Gottlieb (2006). "Urban Resurgence and the Consumer City," *Urban Studies*, 43(8): 1275–1299.

Glaeser, Edward and Joseph Gyourko (2006). "Housing Dynamics," *NBER Working Paper #12787*.

Glaeser, Edward and Joseph Gyourko (2005). "Urban Decline and Durable Housing," *Journal of Political Economy*, 113(2): 345–375.

Glaeser, Edward, Joseph Gyourko and Raven Saks (2006). "Urban Growth and Housing Supply," *Journal of Economic Geography*, 6(1): 71–89.

Glaeser, Edward, Joseph Gyourko and Raven Saks (2005). "Why Have Housing Prices Gone Up?," *American Economic Review Papers and Proceedings*, 95(2): 329–333.

Glaeser, Edward, Joseph Gyourko and Raven Saks (2005). "Why is Manhattan So Expensive? Regulation and the Rise in House Prices," *Journal of Law and Economics*, 48(2): 3310370.

Glaeser, Edward and Matthew Kahn (2001). "Decentralized Employment and the Transformation of the American City," *Brookings-Wharton Papers on Urban Affairs 2*: 1–63.

Glaeser, Edward, Matthew Kahn and Jordan Rappaport (2008). "Why Do the Poor Live in Cities? The Role of Public Transportation," *Journal of Urban Economics*, 63(1): 1–24.

Glaeser, Edward, Hedi D. Kallal, Jose A. Scheinkman and Andrei Shleifer (1992). "Growth in Cities," *Journal of Political Economy* 100: 1126–1152.

Glaeser, Edward and Janet E. Kohlhase (2004). "Cities, Regions and the Decline of Transport Costs," *Papers in Regional Science*, 83(1): 197–228.

Glaeser, Edward, Jed Kolko and Albert Saiz (2001). "Consumer City," *Journal of Economic Geography* 1: 27–50.

Glaeser, Edward and David Mare (2001). "Cities and Skills," *Journal of Labor Economics*, 19(2): 316–342.

Glaeser, Edward and Giacomo Ponzetto (2007). "Did the Death of Distance Help New York and Hurt Detroit?," mimeographed.

Glaeser, Edward and Bruce Sacerdote (2003). "Sentencing in Homicide Cases and the Role of Vengeance," *Journal of Legal Studies*, 32: 363–382.

Glaeser, Edward and Bruce Sacerdote (1999). "Why is There More Crime In Cities?," *Journal of Political Economy*, 107(6, Part 2): S225–S258.

Glaeser, Edward, Bruce Sacerdote and Jose Scheinkman (1996). "Crime and Social Interactions," *Quarterly Journal of Economics*, 111(2): 507–548.

Glaeser, Edward, Bruce Sacerdote and Jose Scheinkman (2003). "The Social Multiplier," *Journal of the European Economic Association*, 1(2): 345–353.

Glaeser, Edward and Albert Saiz (2004). "The Rise of the Skilled City," *Brookings-Wharton Papers on Urban Affairs*, 5: 47–94.

Glaeser, Edward, Jose Scheinkman and Andrei Shleifer (1995). "Economic Growth in a Cross-Section of Cities," *Journal of Monetary Economics*, 36(1): 117–143.

Glaeser, Edward and Andrei Shleifer (2005). "The Curley Effect: The Economics of Shaping the Electorate," *Journal of Law, Economics and Organization*, 21(1): 1–19.

Glaeser, Edward and Jesse M. Shapiro (2003). "Urban Growth in the 1990s: Is City Living Back?" *Journal of Regional Science*, 43(1): 139–165.

Glaeser, Edward and Kristina Tobio (2008). "The Rise of the Sunbelt," *Southern Economic Journal*, 74(3): 610–643.

Glaeser, Edward and Jacob Vigdor (2001). "Racial Segregation in the 2000 Census: Promising News, *Brookings Institution Policy Brief*.

Glaeser, Edward and Bryce Ward (2006). "Myths and Realities of Political Geography," *Journal of Economic Perspectives*, 20(2): 119–144.

Glaeser, Edward and Bryce Ward (2006). "The Causes and Consequences of Land Use Regulation: Evidence from Greater Boston," *NBER Working Paper #12601*.

Graves, Philip (1980). "Migration and Climate," *Journal of Regional Science*, 20(2): 227–238.

Gyourko, Joseph and Joseph Tracy (1991). "The Structure of Local Public Finance and the Quality of Life," *Journal of Political Economy*, 99(4): 774–806.

Helsley, Robert W. and William C. Strange (1990). "Matching and Agglomeration Economics in a System of Cities," *Regional Science and Urban Economics*, 20(2): 189–212.

Henning, John and Ronald Ridker (1967). "The Determinants of Residential Property Values with Special Reference to Air Pollution," *Review of Economics and Statistics*, 49(2): 246–257.

Henderson, J. Vernon (2003). "Marshall's Scale Economies," *Journal of Urban Economics*, 53(1): 1–28.

Henderson, J. Vernon (1974). "The Sizes and Types of Cities," *American Economic Review*, 64(4): 640–656.

Henderson, J. Vernon (1985). "The Tiebout Model: Bring Back the Entrepreneurs," *Journal of Political Economy*, 93(2): 248–264.

Henderson, J. Vernon and A. Mitra (1996). "The New Urban Economic Landscape Developers and Edge Cities," *Regional Science and Urban Economics*, 26(6): 613–643.

Holmes, Thomas J. (1998). "The Effects of State Policies on the Location of Industry: Evidence from State Borders," *Journal of Political Economy*, 106(4): 667–705.

Hoxby, Caroline M. (2000). "Does Competition Among Public Schools Benefit Students and Taxpayers?," *American Economic Review*, 90(5): 1209–1238.

Jacobs, Jane (1969). *The Economy of Cities*. New York: Random House.

Jaffe, Adam B., Manuel Trajtenberg and Rebecca Henderson (1993). "Geographic Localization of Knowledge Spillovers as Evidenced by Patent Citations," *The Quarterly Journal of Economics*, 108(3): 577–598.

Kain, John F. (1968a). "Housing Segregation, Negro Employment, and Metropolitan Decentralization," *Quarterly Journal of Economics*, 88: 263–277.

Kain, John F. (1968b). "The Distribution and Movement of Jobs and Industry," in James Q. Wilson (ed.), *The Metropolitan Enigma*, Cambridge, MA: Harvard University Press.

Kain, John F., John R. Meyer and Martin Wohl (1965). *The Urban Transportation Problem*. Cambridge, MA: Harvard University Press.

Kain, John F. and Joseph J. Perksy (1969). "Alternatives to the Gilded Ghetto," *The Public Interest*, 14: 74–83.

Kain, John F. and John M. Quigley (1972). "Housing Market Discrimination, Homeownership, and Savings Behavior," *American Economic Review*, 62(3): 263–277.

Kaplow, Louis (1996). "Regional Cost-of-Living Adjustments in Tax-Transfer Schemes," *Tax Law Review*, 51: 175–198.

Katz, Lawrence, Jeffrey Kling and Jeffrey Liebman (2007). "Experimental Analysis of Neighborhood Effects," *Econometrica*, 75: 83–119.

Katz, Lawrence, Jeffrey Kling and Jefferey Liebman (2001). "Moving to Opportunity in Boston: Early Results of a Randomized Experiment," *Quarterly Journal of Economics*, 116(2): 607–654.

Katz, Lawrence F. and Kevin M. Murphy (1992). "Changes in Relative Wages, 1963–1987: Supply and Demand Factors," *Quarterly Journal of Economics*, 107(1): 35–78.

Katz, Lawrence and Kenneth T. Rosen (1987). "The Interjurisdictional Effects of Growth Controls on Housing Prices," *Journal of Law and Economics*, 30(1): 149–160.

Krugman, Paul (1991a). *Geography and Trade*. Cambridge, MA: MIT Press.

Krugman, Paul (1991b). "Increasing Returns and Economic Geography," *Journal of Political Economy*, 99(3): 483–499.

Kydland, Finn E. and Edward C. Prescott (1982). "Time to Build and Aggregate Fluctuation," *Econometrica*, 50(6): 1345–1370.

LeRoy, Stephen F. and Jon Sonstelie (1983). "Paradise Lost and Regained: Transportation Innovation, Income and Residential Location," *Journal of Urban Economics*, 13(1): 67–89.

Levitt, Steven (1996). "The Effect of Prison Population Size on Crime Rates: Evidence from Prison Overcrowding Litigation," *Quarterly Journal of Economics*, 111(2): 319–351.

Lucas, Robert Jr. (1988). "On the Mechanics of Economic Development," *Journal of Monetary Economics*, 22(1): 3–42.

Lucas, Robert Jr. and Esteban Rossi-Hansberg (2002). "On the Internal Structure of Cities," *Econometrica*, 70(4): 1445–1476.

Manski, Charles F. (1993). "Identification of Endogenous Social Effects: The Reflection Problem," *Review of Economic Studies*, 60(3): 531–542.

Marshall, Alfred (1890). *Principles of Economics*. London: Macmillian.

Massey, Douglas and Nancy Denton (1993). *American Apartheid: Segregation and the Making of the American Underclass*. Cambridge, MA: Harvard University Press.

Mieszkowski, Peter and Edwin Mills (1993). "The Causes of Metropolitan Suburbanization," *Journal of Economic Perspectives*, 7(3): 135–147.

Mills, Edwin S. (1967). "An Aggregative Model of Resource Allocation in a Metropolitan Area," *American Economic Review Papers and Proceedings of the Seventy-ninth Annual Meeting of the American Economic Association*, 57(2): 197–210.

Mills, Edwin S. (1972). *Studies in the Structure of the Urban Economy*. Baltimore: Johns Hopkins Press.

Moretti, Enrico (2004). "Estimating the Social Return to Higher Education: Evidence From Longitudinal and Repeated Cross-Sectional Data," *Journal of Econometrics*, 121(1–2): 175–212.

Muth, Richard (1969). *Cities and Housing*. Chicago: University of Chicago Press.

O'Regan, Katherine and John M. Quigley (1998). "Where Youth Live: Effects of Urban Space on Employment," *Urban Studies*, 35(7): 1187–1205.

Rauch, James E. (1993). "Productivity Gains from Geographic Concentration of Human Capital: Evidence from the Cities," *Journal of Urban Economics*, 34(3): 380–400.

Ridker, Ronald and John Henning (1967). "The Determinants of Residential Property Values with Special Reference to Air Pollution," *Review of Economics and Statistics*, 49(2): 246–257.

Roback, Jennifer (1982). "Wages, Rents, and the Quality of Life," *Journal of Political Economy*, 90(6): 1257–1278.

Rosen, Sherwin (1979). "Wage-Based Indexes of Urban Quality of Life," in Peter Miezkowski and M. Strazheim (eds.), *Current Issues in Urban Economics*, Baltimore: Johns Hopkins University Press, 74–104.

Rosenthal, Stuart S. and William C. Strange (2004). "Evidence on the Nature and Sources of Agglomeration Economies," in J.V. Henderson and J.-F. Thisse (eds.), *Handbook of Urban and Regional Economics, Volume IV*, Amsterdam: Elsevier, 2119–2172.

Rosenthal, Stuart S. and William C. Strange (2006). "The Attenuation of Human Capital Externalities," working paper.

Rosenthal, Stuart S. and William C. Strange (2005). "The Geography of Entrepreneurship in the New York Metropolitan Area," *Federal Reserve Bank of New York Economic Policy Review*, December: 29–53.

Sacerdote, Bruce (2001). "Peer Effects With Random Assignment: Result for Dartmouth Roommates," *Quarterly Journal of Economics*, 116(2): 681–704.

Schelling, Thomas C. (1971). "Dynamic Models of Segregation," *Journal of Mathematical Sociology*, 1:143–186.

Schelling, Thomas C. (1978). *Micromotives and Macrobehavior*. New York: W.W. Norton.

Scherer, Frederic M. (1984). "Using Linked Patent Data and R&D Data to Measure Technology Flows," in Zvi Griliches (ed.), *R&D, Patents and Productivity*, Chicago: University of Chicago Press, 417–464.

Sen, Amartya (1976). "Poverty: An Ordinal Approach to Measurement," *Econometrica*, 44(2): 219–231.

Shapiro, Jesse M. (2006). "Smart Cities: Quality of Life, Productivity, and the Growth Effects of Human Capital," *Review of Economics and Statistics*, 88(2): 324–335.

Simon, Curtis and Clark Nardinelli (2002). "Human Capital and the Rise of American Cities, 1900–1990," *Regional Science and Urban Economics*, 32(1): 59–96.

Sinai, Todd and Joel Waldfogel (2004). "Geography and the Internet: Is the Internet a Substitute or a Complement for Cities?," *Journal of Urban Economics*, 56(1): 1–24.

Smith, Adam (1776). *An Inquiry into the Nature and Causes of the Wealth of Nations*. Chicago: Chicago University of Chicago Press, 1976.

Solow, Robert M. (1973). "Congestion Costs and the Use of Land for Streets," *Bell Journal of Economics and Management Science*, 4(2): 602–618.

Solow, Robert and William Vickrey (1971). "Land Use in a Long Narrow City," *Journal of Economic Theory*, 3(4): 430–447.

Stiger, George J. (1970). "The Optimum Enforcement of Laws," *Journal of Political Economy*, 78(3): 526–536.

Taeuber, Alma and Karl Taeuber (1965). *Negroes in Cities: Residential Segregation and Neighborhood Change*. Chicago: Aldine.

Tiebout, Charles M. (1956). "A Pure Theory of Local Public Expenditures," *Journal of Political Economy*, 64(5): 416–424.

Tolley, G.S. (1974). "The Welfare Economics of City Bigness," *Journal of Urban Economics*, 1(3): 324–345.

Van Nieuwerburgh, Stijn and Pierre-Olivier Weill (2006). "Why Has House Price Dispersion Gone Up?," mimeograph.

References

Von Thunen, Johann (1826). *The Isolated State*. Carla M. Waternberg (trans.), Oxford: Pegamon Press, 1976.

Warner, Sam Bass (1962). *Streetcar Suburbs: The Process of Growth in Boston, 1870–1990*. Cambridge, MA: Cambridge University Press.

Wheaton, William C. (1977). "Income and Urban Residence: An Analysis of Consumer Demand for Location," *American Economic Review*, 67(4): 620–631.

Index